In Jane Glover's long and hugely successful career as a conductor, she has been Music Director of the Glyndebourne Touring Opera, Artistic Director of The London Mozart Players and, since 2002, is Music Director of Chicago's Music of the Baroque. She has conducted all the major symphony and chamber orchestras in Britain, as well as many in the United States of America and across the world. She appears regularly at the BBC Proms and is a regular broadcaster, with highlights including a television series on Mozart. She is the author of *Mozart's Women* and she lives in London.

'Glover's story sweeps us away with her practitioner's musical insights, her attention to historical detail, and her placing of Handel's work in social and political context, which few of his biographers have attempted before. *Handel in London* is an unputdownable read.'
Hugh Canning, *Opera*

'*Handel in London* is a delight to read. It benefits enormously from being written by an expert who knows and loves the repertoire; and there is an extensive reader-friendly index. The bibliography contains some fifty volumes by authors who deal with Handel's music, but not one of them treats exclusively the topic she has chosen – and few of them can match the panache of her prose.'
Richard Stokes, *Financial Times*

'Not so much a biography of the composer as an exploration of the ways in which he used English audiences as a sounding board for artistic experiment, teaching them, in the process, how to listen to his music . . . At a time when most perspectives on Handel tend to be historical or biographical, Glover turns our gaze towards the creative artist, resilient, original and inspired, and asks us to listen more attentively to his tuneful voice.'
Jonathan Keates, *Literary Review*

'Written in elegant prose that wears its author's scholarship lightly . . . splendidly detailed . . . Glover deftly weaves musical analysis into her biographical flow. Her greatest achievement, however, is to give life and music a political and social context – much needed for a composer who was so frequently required to supply anthems for coronations and royal funerals, Te Deums for military victories, and, of course, background music for royal fireworks and barge trips.'
Richard Morrison, *The Times*

HANDEL
IN
LONDON

The Making of a Genius

JANE GLOVER

PICADOR

First published 2018 by Macmillan

This paperback edition first published 2019 by Picador
an imprint of Pan Macmillan
20 New Wharf Road, London N1 9RR
Associated companies throughout the world
www.panmacmillan.com

ISBN 978-1-5098-8208-3

1 3 5 7 9 8 6 4 2

A CIP catalogue record for this book is available from the British Library.

Typeset by Palimpsest Book Production Limited, Falkirk, Stirlingshire
Printed and bound by CPI Group (UK) Ltd, Croydon, CR0 4YY

Contents

List of Illustrations

Foreword

In Lincoln Cathedral one Christmas, I heard my first *Messiah*. I was nine years old. It swept me away, and at that moment I knew not only that my life would be suffused with music, but that Handel, and *Messiah*, would represent recurring themes in it.

In adulthood, I have duly spent more than forty years as a professional musician, working in opera companies and with orchestras and concert organizations, and Handel has indeed occupied a sizeable portion of my activity and my repertoire. I have conducted his operas and oratorios all over the world, including, as it happens, over one hundred performances of *Messiah*. A considerable part of the job of performing these great works is the assembly and preparation of singers, and, especially if the presenting organization offers repeated opportunities to develop a company, in the creation of teams to operate to the best of individual and combined abilities. To a much lesser extent (for there are whole departments these days devoted entirely to this task), I have been involved too in the courting of financial support, and the building of audiences. There is a whole part of being a performer which has nothing at all to do with actual performance.

In the eighteenth century, Handel encountered exactly the same obligations. Working at the heart of London musical activity for several astonishing decades, he not only composed masterpiece after masterpiece, but he carefully selected individual singers and musicians to deliver them, and moulded these disparate talents into companies that would, with modifications and evolutions, serve him repeatedly for several projects and over several seasons. To a large extent he was self-taught. In his early years, before his arrival in London, he had been presented with preselected casts of singers. He had assessed them and prepared them, but he had learned from them too about their capabilities, their limitations and their temperaments, and their weaknesses had been as educational as had their strengths. Just as, in those formative years, he had absorbed every musical influence and learned to define excellence, so he had developed a truly impressive ability to understand the human voice.

By the time of Handel's arrival in London, still only in his mid-twenties, he was already a real connoisseur of singers, and knew how to bring out the best in them. Like Mozart, who claimed that an aria should fit a singer 'like a well-cut suit of clothes', Handel's musical tailoring, once he had heard and assessed a voice, was exemplary. Whether dealing with an established star or a young beginner of raw promise, he was ever alert to colour, texture, range and contour. With a star, the relationship could be tetchy or even exasperatingly explosive: he famously threatened to throw the highly gifted but tiresome Italian soprano Francesca Cuzzoni out of a window if she disobeyed him, and there were many complaining stories about his dictatorial way of maintaining the highest possible standards. Handel nevertheless wrote to the strengths of his stars and achieved exquisite results with them. Then as now, it was not actually necessary to like an artist in order to make great music together. But his relationships with singers at the start of their careers, whose artistry he truly enabled, developed and triumphantly displayed, no doubt gave him infinitely more satisfaction. He trained their technique and guided them in expressive style and interpretation, and he encouraged them to inhabit their roles rather than simply recite them. In effect, he taught his singers to act, and similarly he could teach actors to sing. Susanna Cibber, for example, was an actress who, especially in collaboration with the great David Garrick, had considerable success on the London stage, but who, finding herself in Dublin when Handel was there giving the first ever performances of *Messiah*, was coached by him to deliver a legendary and affecting performance of 'He was despised'. In all cases, it was a reciprocal process: the singer's art inspired Handel to write in the way he did, and his music allowed that artistry to grow and prosper. But if, as does happen, a singer was in vocal distress or even crisis, Handel was especially sympathetic to this predicament too. Despite his reputation for severity, he was, without fail, sensitive to the vulnerable, and when a singer was in trouble, he would coax, rewrite, adapt and help.

From his earliest years, Handel's own gifts had always attracted the attention and support of wealthy patrons willing to back him and his enterprises, and throughout his career he continued to cultivate and tend his royal and patrician subscribers, inspiring their loyalty and generosity. His own duty and obedience to his monarch runs as a strong thread through the long narrative of his London years, and, with certain members of the royal family, these were enhanced too by genuine friendship and therefore a personal commitment. A vibrant, extremely visible and well-connected member of London society, and one moreover who had a great flair for the making and handling of money, Handel understood (in a way that Mozart for example lamentably never did) the whole business side of artistic enterprise, and was able comfortably to interact with those who held the purse strings.

There were, to be sure, many rough passages and setbacks

during the course of Handel's lengthy and prolific career, but none would fell him for long. His resilience would steer him towards his next centre of activity, and his entrepreneurial skills would again and again create environments in which his projects could be realized. A man of fathomless invention, exquisite artistry, workaholic energy and an insatiable appetite – for artistic and social delight, but indeed for good food and wine too – he essentially travelled alone through life. Unlike Mozart, who wore his heart perpetually on his sleeve and wrote literally hundreds of letters which vividly, even startlingly, reveal his state of mind, Handel was intensely private, rarely confiding his true feelings in his own, much more restrained, letters. Insights beyond the public facade therefore have to be gleaned, at one stage removed, from the anecdotes of others, raising questions then of authenticity and reliability. So however much Handel was always surrounded by people, and some of his many colleagues and patrons did become his friends, there was a real sense in him of a solitary mission, of private goals. That he achieved so many of his goals and with such immortal consequences is a tribute not only to his incomparable compositional skills, but to every aspect of his musical professionalism.

For me this has been, as well as a detailed investigation into Handel's activities and the context in which they happened, something of a personal process, for so much of what I do now is so similar to what he did then. Observing the manner in which he dealt with each situation as it arose – effectively, seeing with his eyes, and hearing with his ears – is still enormously instructive. Across the generations, Handel the professional musician and craftsman continues to educate and inspire.

Author's Note

1. NAMES: Many of the people appearing in this book anglicized their names when they settled in London. For clarity, I refer to its main subject as 'George Frideric Handel' throughout. (Even after his British naturalization, his name continued to be spelled in a number of ways.) For others, including the Hanoverian royal family, I have retained their German names until the point at which they themselves either were compelled or chose to change them.

2. CALENDAR: During Handel's lifetime, the English calendar changed. Until 1752 the year began on 25th March (Lady Day), according to the Julian calendar. In 1751, Parliament passed An Act for Regulating the Commencement of the Year; and for Correcting the Calendar now in Use. On 1st January 1752, England switched to the Gregorian calendar, with the result that 1751 was a short year. (To add to the confusion, Scotland had changed to the Gregorian calendar back in 1600.) For ease of modern comprehension, all dates in their Julian old style have been corrected into Gregorian new style.

Preface

The turbulence of seventeenth-century England was to have widespread repercussions in the eighteenth century, and not least on the cultural life of its capital city. The activities of a young German musician settling in London in the first decades of the new century would be partly directed, shaped and even constrained by political sensibilities, and it is greatly to the credit of George Frideric Handel that he could ride any political tension and upheaval, and turn it to his advantage.

In the seventeenth century, England beheaded one king and deposed another: the unpopular Charles I was executed in 1649, and James II dispatched in 1688. Charles I's elder son came to the throne as Charles II with the restoration of the monarchy in 1660, and was succeeded in 1685 by his brother, James II. But James's Protestant subjects were alarmed, for he had married his second wife, Mary of Modena, and was now a Catholic; and although his daughters, Mary and Anne, continued to be raised as Protestants, a new son, born into the Catholic religion in 1688, was destined to succeed him. Mary and Anne too were dismayed by the birth of their half-brother. They swore allegiance to their Protestant religion and to each other, and later in 1688, in what became known as the Glorious Revolution, Mary and her Dutch husband, William of Orange, invaded England and deposed her father. They assumed the throne together as William and Mary, while James and his baby son fled to France. Mary died of smallpox in 1694, leaving her husband to reign alone as William III.

As William and Mary were childless, the heir to the English throne was now Anne, who was married to Prince George of Denmark. Their son, William, Duke of Gloucester, seemed to ensure the continuation of the Protestant line, but young William died in 1700, aged only eleven. Since there were no further heirs either to William III or to Princess Anne, the next in line had to be the deposed James II or his son. So, in 1701, Parliament passed the Act of Settlement, decreeing that, unless Anne or William (were he to remarry) had further issue, the line would transfer to the nearest Protestant descendant of James I: his granddaughter, Sophia, Electress of Hanover, and her children and grandchildren. (At a stroke, over fifty Catholics with superior hereditary claims were bypassed.)

The city of Hanover was the centre of one of Germany's most prosperous and peaceful states, Brunswick-Lüneburg. It had been admitted in 1699 as the ninth electorate of the Holy Roman Empire, and its ruler, who had absolute power (he oversaw every important decision, whether relating to home or foreign affairs, budgets, criminal proceedings, military or ministerial appointments), had been granted the title Elector. The court of Georg Ludwig, son of the Dowager Electress Sophia, revolved around the glorious Leineschloss, on the Rhine, in the centre of the city, and the country palace of Herrenhausen, some three miles away, where the Electress Sophia had created magnificent baroque gardens. Here the arts thrived, while men of learning and accomplishment (including the mathematician and philosopher Gottfried Leibnitz)

frequented its halls. But there was tension and dissent too within these civilized surroundings. The electoral family, with its convenient ties to other powerhouses in Europe, was of chequered dysfunctionality. Disagreement between the generations (a recurring theme in the Hanoverian gene pool) was rife, and there were incivilities and even cruelties in their behaviour towards one another. And, in the first decade of the new century, the succession of the house of Hanover to the throne of England consumed their thoughts above everything else.

Princess Anne duly became Queen of England on the death of William III in 1702. But the continual threat posed by the descendants and supporters of the exiled James II, together with Anne's own paroxysms of retrospective guilt for having had a part in her father's deposition, seemed suddenly to put the whole Hanoverian succession in jeopardy. The Elector felt an alarming insecurity about the position to which he was destined, and so too did his newly married son, Prince Georg Augustus, and his bride, Princess Caroline.

It was in such anxious turmoil that the young German composer George Frideric Handel, fresh from triumphs in Italy, found himself in the summer of 1710. While this intelligent, alert and dazzlingly gifted musician will instantly have grasped the complexities of the ties between Hanover and London (a city he had it in mind to visit anyway), it is unlikely that he could have had any notion that his new connection to the electoral court would have the most profound consequences. Within a few years, the house of Hanover had indeed assumed the English throne (Queen Anne died, and Elector Georg Ludwig became George I), and Handel, too, had moved experimentally to London. They stayed, and he stayed. The sympathetic liaison between them, and especially with the young Prince and Princess (later George II

PREFACE

and Queen Caroline), approximately his own age and extremely enthusiastic for the arts, lasted for the rest of their lives. The history of music in London, and far beyond, was changed forever.

1

EARLY YEARS

'An infant rais'd by thy command'

[Saul]

The charismatic twenty-five-year-old who strode into Princess Caroline's drawing room in the spring of 1710 had been born into a medical family in late February 1685. George Frideric Handel (Georg Friederich Händl) was the son of Georg Händl, a barber-surgeon based in Halle, physician to the courts of Weissenfels and Brandenburg. With his first wife, Anna Oettinger, widow of a fellow surgeon, Georg had produced six children, most of whom either became doctors or married them; after Anna died in 1682, he married Dorotea Tausch, daughter of a neighbouring pastor. Dorotea produced four more children, of whom only two survived into adulthood: Dorotea Sophia and George Frideric. Young George Frideric was baptized in Halle's Liebfrauenkirche on 24th February, a few weeks before the birth in Eisenach of his great contemporary, Johann Sebastian Bach.

Many of the stories of Handel's childhood that have travelled across the centuries stem from his first biographer, John Mainwaring. Mainwaring's *Memoirs of the Life of the Late George*

1

Frederic Handel were published in 1760, just a year after the death of the subject. They were partly based on Mainwaring's own acquaintance with Handel, but partly also on conversations with J. C. Smith, the young German-born but (like Handel) English-naturalized musician who became Handel's assistant in his latter years. While these memoirs are always riveting and deeply touching, they must to an extent be read with a raised eyebrow, especially with regard to Handel's early years. Generational hearsay dissolves fable into fact, and historians have learned to question the unreliability of Mainwaring's memory. We cannot know, for example, if Handel's father's disapproval of the boy's passion for music was really as stern as Mainwaring implied: 'From his very childhood Handel had discovered such a strong propensity to Music, that his father, who always intended him for the study of the Civil Law, had reason to be alarmed. Perceiving that this inclination still increased, he took every method to oppose it. He strictly forbad him to meddle with any musical instrument; nothing of that kind was suffered to remain in the house, nor was he ever permitted to go to any other, where such kind of furniture was in use.'[1]

Nor should the faintly preposterous story of young George having 'a little clavichord privately convey'd to a room at the top of the house',[2] upon which he practised through the night while the household slept, be taken too literally; he was not yet seven years old when this is supposed to have happened. What does ring true, for it was a pattern repeated throughout Handel's life, is Mainwaring's account of princely support. In 1691, Dr Händl travelled to Weissenfels to visit his son Karl, in valet service to the Duke of Saxe-Weissenfels. Young George was initially forbidden to go too, but through sheer determination (and not a little athleticism), he ran for some distance after the doctor's departed

2

coach and persuaded his father to allow him after all to visit his half-brother. In Weissenfels the boy discovered many keyboard instruments on which he might practise ('and his father was too much engaged to watch him so closely as he had done at home'[3]). One morning he was playing the organ in the church, and the Duke, on hearing from his valet that it was his brother, a mere child, who showed such skill, 'demanded to see him'.[4] With ducal charm and the greatest diplomacy, he then reasoned with Dr Händl, and persuaded him to let the gifted boy study music seriously. Furthermore the Duke then 'fill'd his [the boy's] pockets with money, and told him, with a smile, that if he minded his studies, no encouragements would be wanting'.[5]

So Handel came under the tutelage of the organist of the Marienkirche in Halle, Friedrich Wilhelm Zachow. A fine all-round musician who composed and performed with equal success, Zachow was clearly a formidable teacher too. His duties at the Marienkirche included directing an impressive cohort of musicians in extended concerts every third Sunday; it was indeed fortuitous that, from an early age, the young Handel experienced at close quarters such high-level music-making, and moreover observed the methods and practices that went into it. He remained close to Zachow even after he left Halle, visiting him whenever he returned to see his own family, until Zachow's death in 1712. And the admiration must have been mutual, for Handel was a prodigious child. As Zachow guided his progress through the fundamental composing skills of harmony, counterpoint and score analysis, other areas of his education were not neglected. At the *Stadtgymnasium* young George would have studied languages (classical and modern), poetry and literature, mathematics, geography, ethics. The breadth of his progress in these non-musical subjects can be measured in a poem that he wrote at the age of twelve, upon the death of his father, in February 1697. Seven four-lined stanzas of iambic pentameters reveal not just the sadness of a child's bereavement, but a dignity and certainly a competence too. And, as he signed his name at the end, he added determinedly, '*der freien Künste ergebener*' ('dedicated to the liberal arts').[6]

In 1702, as he turned seventeen, Handel enrolled at the University of Halle. At almost exactly the same time he was appointed organist at the Domkirche, receiving a small salary – fifty thalers per annum – and free accommodation, so he was now relatively independent. Soon his activities at the Domkirche began to attract attention. Among those who heard of his musical prowess and came to visit him was Georg Philipp Telemann, just four years older than Handel. Telemann was a reluctant law student in nearby Leipzig, but had his sights on the opera house where he would shortly become Musical Director. These two young men became firm friends. They were united by musical distinction and also by a certain rebellious determination. (Telemann was infuriating Johann Kuhnau, Bach's predecessor at the Thomaskirche in Leipzig, by setting up rival concerts.) They continued to correspond, exchanging gifts and musical ideas, for the rest of their lives.

The next significant step for Handel was his move away from Halle. Inspired perhaps by Telemann's operatic leanings, he too was drawn towards cities with opera houses. Mainwaring tells us that Handel ('impatient for another situation'[7]) had visited Berlin in 1698, although this journey almost certainly happened after 1702, for in 1698 Handel would have been only thirteen – hardly an age for job hunting. Two genial opera composers, Giovanni Maria Bononcini and Attilio Ariosti, showed him kindness and encouragement ('Many and great were the compliments and

4

civilities which he received'[8]). Handel soaked up their influence, and decided to shift his own focus. In 1703, he went to Hamburg, 'on his own bottom'[9] (at his own expense), as Mainwaring approvingly reported. By now the eighteen-year-old Handel was able not only to fend for himself by teaching and playing in churches, but also to send money back to his widowed mother, in Halle.

Hamburg was a sound choice of city. It boasted a magnificent opera house, the Theater am Gänsemarkt, then the largest theatre in northern Europe and under the expert direction of Reinhard Keiser. The extremely versatile Handel was initially taken on as a violinist, but, as he was an even better keyboard player, and clearly a very quick learner, he soon assumed the responsibilities of continuo playing and even musical direction. At the time, opera was not, in the modern sense, conducted: it was controlled and led by the main harpsichordist, situated at the centre of the orchestra and immediately supported by other continuo instruments (cellos, lutes) – the true engine-room of the performance. Keiser clearly recognized Handel's huge potential, and gave him ever greater opportunities as he trained him and promoted him through the ranks. He even encouraged him to try his hand at composing operas – all this before he was out of his teens. Handel's apprenticeship in Hamburg, under the watchful gaze of a distinguished boss, was crucial to his development. He had been in the right place at the right time.

Another friendship from these years, with fellow composer and similar all-round musician Johann Mattheson, lasted for the rest of Handel's life. They played the organ together, took trips together, including one to Lübeck to investigate the possibility of succeeding Buxtehude as organist there, and performed in the pit for each others' operas. Their friendship was certainly vibrant. On one occasion Mattheson's *Cleopatra* was being performed at the Gänsemarkt Theater; the composer himself was to sing the role of Antonius, and Handel would direct the performances from the harpsichord. But Mattheson proposed that, after the stage death of his character, he should hasten to the pit and replace Handel at the helm. Handel would have none of it. Tempers flared, and the two young men rushed outside to fight a duel. Ever after, Mattheson claimed that only a large button on Handel's coat saved him from the accuracy of his sword, and that his friend's genius was thus spared for posterity. Within days these two hotheads were reconciled and their friendship was stronger than ever. But this early account of Handel's short fuse is a precursor of similar (if less life-threatening) outbursts later in his career.

By 1706 Handel's feet were itching again, and once more his ability to attract the attention of powerful nobility proved helpful. During his time in Hamburg, he had met the visiting Prince Gian Gastone de' Medici, son of the Grand Duke of Tuscany, who extended an invitation to come to Florence. It is not certain if he offered financial help, but, in any case, the independent and financially astute Handel was again 'resolved to go . . . on his own bottom'.[10] The invitation alone was enough to lure him to Italy, the country which had invented opera, oratorio and the cantata, and was still the European leader in all instrumental music (concerto and sonata) too. Handel was to be there for the next four heady years, spending time in all its important musical centres (Florence, Rome, Naples, Venice), avidly absorbing its language and culture and more than holding his own among the most illustrious practitioners in the business – composers and performers alike.

Throughout Handel's Italian years he was supported by powerful patrons: the Medici family in Florence; Cardinals Ottoboni,

Pamphili and Colonna and the Marchese Francesco Maria Ruspoli in Rome; and by the prominent Grimani family in Venice. Through these patrons and their establishments, Handel made contact with influential musicians, including Corelli, Alessandro and Domenico Scarlatti, Stradella, Vivaldi and Albinoni; and, far from being daunted by these luminaries, the twenty-one-year-old was energized by them. He lifted his own game, and thrived.

In Rome there was a papal ban on theatrical activity. But, with typical Italian flair, composers had circumnavigated the Vatican's decree by adapting the sacred forms of oratorio and cantata into immensely dramatic works. Using biblical texts, and sometimes classical literature and epic poetry too, they succeeded in satisfying their theatrical leanings while presenting entertainment under the guise of edification. These were paths that Handel could pursue with relish. He wrote over a hundred cantatas, many psalms and motets (including the miraculous *Dixit Dominus*), and his first oratorio, *La Resurrezione*, in Rome. He was drawn into competition with both Alessandro and Domenico Scarlatti, and was generally considered to have been the victor. His greatest success however was not in Rome, but in Venice, where his opera *Agrippina* was premiered in 1709. Venetian audiences considered themselves to be the ultimate arbiters of operatic fashion, and they could not praise Handel or his opera enough. As *Agrippina* was repeated again and again, they cried out, '*Viva il caro sassone!*' ('Long live the beloved Saxon!' – although, in fact, Handel was not from Saxony at all). Altogether, there were twenty-seven performances – an astonishing figure for a single season.

Handel gleefully rode this wave of triumph, relishing the quality of his performers throughout Italy, learning especially about Italian singers, and continuing to construct his network of colleagues and supporters. He connected with the librettists Antonio

Salvi, Paolo Antonio Rolli and Nicola Haym, with the violinists Prospero and Pietro Castrucci, and with the singers Margherita Durastanti and Giuseppe Maria Boschi, all of whom would re-appear in Handel's London life within a few years. With Durastanti, who sang for him in both Rome and Venice, he spent a considerable amount of social time too, and maybe his private passion was aroused. Another singer, Vittoria Tarquini, also turned his head. Although she had a husband – the French violinist Jean-Baptiste Farinel – she was separated from him, and, with a vibrant reputation as a gambler and a flirt, she was known to be the mistress of, among others, Gian Gastone de' Medici himself (she 'had for some time been much in the good graces of his Serene Highness',[11] as Mainwaring delicately put it). Now her name began to be linked too with that of young Handel, fifteen years her junior, and gossip of their liaison travelled across Europe.

It was in Venice, around the excitement of *Agrippina*, that Handel met Prince Ernst August of Hanover, brother of the Elector Georg Ludwig, together with the Hanoverian ambassador to Venice, Baron Kielmannsegg. He was also introduced to another ambassador, the British envoy, Charles Montagu, Duke of Manchester. Both Baron Kielmannsegg and the Duke of Manchester courted Handel and his evident talents, and invited him respectively to Hanover and to London. Handel accepted both invitations, heading first to Hanover, but with the intention of trying his luck in England too. But his Italian years had been a real turning point, and can even be seen as a microcosm of the manner in which Handel operated later. With the help of enthusiastic patrons who provided opportunity as well as financial support, he made excellent contacts with influential practitioners. Honing his craft and developing the strictest of disciplines through phenomenal workaholic energies, he produced a monumental portfolio of compositions which not only served their immediate Italian purposes, but whose material he could redeploy for years afterwards. In Italy, just as Mozart was to do half a century later, Handel had grown up as a musician.

∽

Travelling from Italy via Innsbruck, where he turned down an offer of employment from the Governor of the Tyrol, Handel arrived in Hanover in the late spring of 1710. There Agostino Steffani, who combined the careers of musician, churchman and diplomat, had just returned to the court where he had been Kapellmeister in the 1690s. For the last decade Steffani had moved more in diplomatic affairs, and now he also held an important ecclesiastical position, that of Apostolic Vicar, in northern Germany. He had decided to come back to Hanover and use it as a base from which to exercise his widespread ministerial duties. So it was not just one diplomat, Baron Kielmannsegg, who took Handel under his wing on his arrival in Hanover; Steffani too welcomed him with enthusiasm. It was he who introduced Handel especially to the Dowager Electress and Prince Georg Augustus. While Handel was certainly also presented to the Elector himself, Steffani judged – or Handel remembered – that equally important players in this Hanover–London connection, and in Handel's relevance to it, were the Elector's mother and son.

As had been confirmed in the 1701 Act of Settlement, the Electress Sophia was heir to the English throne after Queen Anne. Sophia was thirty-five years older than Anne, and would have been aware that she herself would probably never become Queen of England; her son, Georg Ludwig, would in fact be the one to assume the English throne. She had sent him to England as a young man, but unlike his mother, who spoke fluent English and was proud of her British ancestry, he had not warmed to the country or its people. In 1682 Georg Ludwig had married, disastrously, his sixteen-year-old cousin, Princess Sophia Dorotea of Celle. She bore him two children, Georg Augustus (born 1683) and Sophia (born 1688), but Georg Ludwig also took mistresses, including Melusine von der Schulenberg, who would bear him three children. Sophia Dorotea then took her own lover, a Count von Königsmarck, in 1692. Despite his own infidelities, Georg Ludwig was furious, claiming that his wife had brought disgrace upon the electoral family. Two years later the Count was seized on his way to Sophia Dorotea's apartments in the Leineschloss, and never seen again, presumably murdered. The marriage between Georg Ludwig and Sophia Dorotea was dissolved. She was banished to Ahlden Castle and effectively imprisoned there, forbidden to remarry, forbidden even to see her children (now eleven and five), and ostracized too by her own father.

That eleven-year-old boy, Georg Augustus, never did see his mother again, and never forgave his father for it. In 1705 he married Caroline, daughter of the Margrave of Brandenburg. Caroline, at twenty-two just a few months older than Georg Augustus, had had an equally traumatic childhood, since both her parents and then her two step-parents had all died before she was thirteen. She had been brought up by her guardians, the Elector and Electress of Brandenburg, later King and Queen of Prussia, and since Georg Augustus's father and Caroline's guardian, Charlotte, Queen of Prussia, were brother and sister, it is probable that Georg Augustus and Caroline had known each other through their teenage years. Unlike most Hanoverian unions, theirs was to be a highly successful marriage lasting thirty-two years. To be sure, there were some startling incompatibilities (in the broadest terms, she was intellectual and artistic, he more inclined to the military), but overriding these there was the great strength of genuine respect and affection. By the time Handel met them all in the spring of 1710, Caroline had already produced two of their eight children: their eldest son, Frederick (soon to be a thorn in his father's side, just as Georg Augustus was to the Elector), and their eldest daughter, Anne. This complicated family was to become central and constant in Handel's life.

Handel instantly made a dazzling impression in Hanover. The Dowager Electress Sophia referred to him in the most glowing terms, partly for his striking physique and intriguing Italian liaisons ('He is a good-looking man and the gossip is that he was the lover of Victoria' – this will have especially intrigued her, as Vittoria Tarquini's estranged violinist husband had once been Konzertmeister in Hanover), but mainly as 'a Saxon who surpasses everyone who has ever been heard in harpsichord-playing and composition'.[12] She noted that 'the Electoral prince and princess take a great deal of pleasure'[13] in his playing. Elector Georg Ludwig offered Handel the post of Kapellmeister, with a salary of 1,000 thaler. (Just eight years earlier, Handel's annual salary as organist at Halle's Domkirche had been fifty thaler.) But despite this large inducement, Handel was not yet ready to settle down, for, as Mainwaring put it, he 'loved liberty too well'.[14] He still had his invitation to London from the Duke of Manchester; the Elector Palatine in Düsseldorf, too, had expressed an interest in meeting the musician who was causing such a stir; and there were many other cities with thriving musical activity – Vienna, Dresden, Prague, Paris maybe – where Handel might try his luck. But the Hanoverians were determined to keep him. With the diplomat Kielmannsegg (and perhaps Steffani, too, in the background) doing the negotiations, it was decided to offer Handel an immediate leave of absence 'for a twelve-month or more, if he chose it'.[15] Not surprisingly, Handel accepted these extremely generous terms.

With high hopes and a full purse, he left Hanover in the early autumn of 1710. First, he travelled east, to Halle, to visit his mother – who, according to Mainwaring, was 'in extreme old age'[16] (she was fifty-nine) – and also his former teacher, Zachow. From there, he went back to Düsseldorf, where the Elector Palatine was disappointed to learn that Handel was no longer available, but gave him a set of silver dessert plates anyway. Handel continued his journey through Holland and crossed the North Sea, arriving in London a month before Christmas. As he sailed up the Thames, past the Tower of London, a spectacular building would have filled his eager gaze. St Paul's Cathedral had recently been completed at last, after thirty-five years of meticulous construction. If Sir Christopher Wren's magnificent achievement was a symbol of new beginning for the city, London was a new beginning for Handel.

2

LONDON, 1710

'Populous cities please me then'

[L'Allegro]

St Paul's Cathedral was not the only symbol of architectural regeneration in 1710; London was to be transformed in the first half of the eighteenth century. From a series of communities along the banks of the Thames, each within easy reach of open fields, it became an urban sprawl stretching into Middlesex and Surrey, with a new bridge, new roads and paving, new street lighting. Its great bisecting thoroughfare, the River Thames, connected its three clear divisions. As any eighteenth–century map of London shows, St Paul's was the central point. Near it lay the business district of Cheapside and the Royal Exchange, the Guildhall, the Customs House, the Lord Mayor's Mansion House (to be rebuilt in the 1730s) and the halls of many livery companies. Here emerged the new middle class, making its fortunes in insurance, trading and merchant banking. But its guilds and charitable institutions paid attention too to what lay beyond. London's East End (Wapping, Shadwell, Stepney) consisted of huddled communities in appalling living conditions and a polluted environment, finding work on the smog-choked quays and wharves of the river, or in the manufacturing, textile, distilling and brewing industries. Then to the west of St Paul's were great boulevards (Fleet Street, the Strand, Pall Mall) leading to the palaces of St James's and Kensington, where the court resided, and to the parliamentary buildings at Westminster. This fashionable West End was to be developed most spectacularly during Handel's lifetime, and he himself would become embedded in it.

During the early decades of the previous century, the Duke of Bedford had hired Inigo Jones to transform his property, the old Convent Garden, which had formerly supplied vegetables to Westminster Abbey, into an elegant piazza with fashionable residences. The trend that this started was interrupted by the Commonwealth, and later by the parallel disasters of London's Great Fire and then the plague, in 1666. But gradually similar schemes were instigated: Red Lion Square, Golden Square, Soho Square, Leicester Square. And, just after Handel's arrival, two events released funds which would engender a veritable spate of elegant development. First, anticipating the rapid growth of London's conurbation, in 1711 Parliament passed the Commission for Building Fifty New Churches, to be funded by the coal tax. Although the target of fifty was never achieved, the many churches that proliferated in the early decades of the eighteenth century were designed by the greatest contemporary architects, including Nicholas Hawksmoor (Christ Church, Spitalfields, St George's, Bloomsbury – with its bizarre steeple surmounted by a statue of George I), James Gibbs (St Martin-in-the-Fields), Thomas Archer (St John's, Smith Square – known as 'Queen Anne's Footstool' because, it is said, the monarch herself pointed out its resemblance to her own upturned furniture), and John

James (St George's, Hanover Square – where Handel himself would eventually worship). The second rush of money, released by the end of Marlborough's campaigns against the French, in 1713, was used to create the great squares laid out adjacent to those churches.

Hanover Square, next to St George's Church, was one of the first to be developed, in 1717, followed by St James's, Grosvenor, Cavendish and Berkeley Squares. Each area was laid out as a complete unit: elegant terraces of houses in the square itself, secondary streets with less expensive houses radiating away from it. (Off Hanover Square, Brook Street was finished in 1719; in due course, Handel would lease one of its new houses.) Beyond these secondary streets were further sets of backstreets, where servants and traders lived; each area included too a market place, and a graveyard attached to its church. Again, London's most gifted architects were deployed. They incorporated all manner of styles – Dutch, Italian, French, Palladian. (Many architects and land-owners had been on a grand tour.) Such was the rapid and impressive transformation of the city that Daniel Defoe wrote in his *A Tour Through the Whole Island of Great Britain* (1724–6), 'New squares, and new streets rising up every day to such a prodigy of buildings, that nothing in the world does, or ever did, equal it.'[1]

During his weeks in Hanover, Handel probably heard much about the lonely forty-five-year-old woman who reluctantly sat on the English throne. As the second daughter of the second son of Charles I, Queen Anne cannot in her childhood have had any thought that one day the mighty responsibility of ultimate office would be hers. But a whole series of traumatic events seemed to have thrust her into it. When her sister Mary died at the age of thirty-two, Anne had given cautious allegiance to the now sole regent, Mary's widower, William III, better known as William of Orange, for she was perforce his heir. Her happy marriage to Prince George of Denmark had produced no fewer than seventeen children, but all of them had died, most in infancy, and her heir, Prince William, who had suffered from encephalitis since birth, died heartbreakingly at eleven. The subsequent succession crisis had picked over the debris of her ignominious childbearing history in its public parliamentary way, and her distant cousins in Germany, with whom she felt no connection at all, had been lined up to take over from her. The death of her father James II in his French exile in 1702 had refuelled her well of guilt for having betrayed him, especially as, within a year, her brother-in-law William III died too (suddenly and unexpectedly, as a result of a fall from his horse, which stumbled on a molehill at Hampton Court), and she was indeed now upon her father's throne. Her subjects had little affection for her. She was shy, short-sighted and stout, and felt patronized and humiliated. Even her coronation (23rd April 1703) – which should have been the best day of her life – was ruined by agonizing gout: she had to be carried into Westminster Abbey, where she endured a ceremony lasting five and a half hours. She was, on that coronation day, still only thirty-seven years old.

One of the maids of honour to Anne's stepmother, Maria of Modena, was Sarah Jennings. Five years older than Anne, she became the trusted companion of the young princess, advising her on dress, demeanour and official responsibility, and she remained her favourite for twenty-seven years. Their friendship was intensely passionate and for Anne probably the most important relationship of her life, despite her successful marriage. Sarah married the soldier John Churchill, and, during the Glorious Revolution, it was the Churchills who persuaded Anne to escape from Whitehall down the back stairs, to the relative safety of Nottingham and, later, Oxford. After Churchill's distinguished military victories (he never lost a battle), the new monarchs, William and Mary, made him the 1st Duke of Marlborough. But they were still endangered by Jacobites, the followers of the exiled James II and his son (another James), and three years later Marlborough was dismissed on grounds of infidelity and suspicion of Jacobite sympathies. His wife Sarah was also removed from the royal household, and the resulting froideur between the royal sisters was never to thaw. Anne, more loyal to her long-term friend than to Mary ('I would rather live in a cottage with you than reign empress of the world without you',[2] she wrote to Sarah), took herself into exile too. Anne and her husband, together with the Churchills, moved into Syon House in Brentford, and it was only in 1695 that William III eventually restored them all to court.

When Anne became Queen in 1703, she appointed her husband Prince George as head of the navy, Marlborough as Captain General in charge of the army, and – still in thrall to her strong-willed and manipulative companion – Sarah to the three highest posts in her household: Mistress of the Robes, Groom of the Stole and Keeper of the Privy Purse. The circle was very tight.

❧

Anne's diffidence as a monarch, and the chaos of the previous half-century since the Restoration, saw a new era of parliamentary government, and the beginning of a rudimentary two-party system. The Whigs and Tories (both names derived, as it happens, from Scottish terms of abuse: *whiggamore*, meaning 'cattle driver', and *torai*, 'robber') had been gradually establishing themselves as opposing sides. While these were not political parties as we would recognize today, they were loose associations of men holding the same sets of views and principles, but not necessarily observing loyalty to any particular leader. In the broadest terms, the Tories represented the rights of the monarchy, the constitution, the Church of England and the gentry, as established by law and custom. The Whigs, on the other hand, were interested in the greater rights of Parliament, the mercantile classes and various nonconformist factions (religious or otherwise). Both William III and then Queen Anne tried to balance both parties in Parliament, though they themselves were mainly Tory sympathizers.

In 1700 the Hapsburg King of Spain died, after naming as his heir Philip of Anjou, grandson of Louis XIV of France. A year later England joined sides with the Netherlands and the Holy Roman Empire to oppose this French claim to the throne, and was thus drawn into the War of the Spanish Succession. So too was Hanover, as part of the Holy Roman Empire. When in 1704 Marlborough won his greatest victory, the Battle of Blenheim, in Bavaria, Prince Georg Augustus was fighting beside him, while his own father, Georg Ludwig, was commanding the Empire's army along the Rhine. Despite Marlborough's distinctions, the relationship between him and Anne began to decline as the Queen grew in confidence as a monarch, and she gradually distanced herself from Sarah's fierce and daily influence too. When Anne's husband Prince George died in 1708, the Whigs seized on her grief and consequent weakness as a decision-maker as an opportunity to disregard her wishes and form their own government. But the war continued to be expensive and unpopular, and Robert Harley succeeded in motivating the electorate back towards the

Tories. In 1710, just before Handel arrived in London, a general election returned a Tory majority, and Harley, leading the new ministry, began to seek a peace which might pull England out of the war altogether. Handel, coming from Hanover, must have been intrigued to register the ebb and flow of British support for this costly and casualty-ridden conflict.

Throughout these troubled years of the first decade of the eighteenth century, as Londoners adapted to a new monarch, a new government, new wars, and the constant jockeying for position in both court and Parliament that is ever the stuff of chatter in alehouses and in print, there was still time for recreation and culture. Much of it took place in the open air. There were crowd-pulling activities at the stocks, at Bedlam, where its inmates were on display for taunting, and, most gruesome, at the gallows. Fascination for the bizarre and freakish extended to parades of exotic animals, and all manner of weird stalls at Bartholomew Fair (in August) or May Fair (in May). There was sport in the streets and common grounds – bowls, football and a ball game (now played by children, but then by adults) called Prisoner's Base, supposedly derived from the days of border warfare. And on a more formalized and class-crossing level there were the gardens in St James's Park and Hyde Park, where all could come to relax and stroll in elegant surroundings, and where the court and aristocracy could be seen taking the air. Then, moving indoors, there were plays and concerts. Music thrived beyond the confines of court and church, and the eighteenth century saw a gradual increase in purpose-built halls for performance, the first among these being that in York Buildings, owned by the musical Clayton family. Another, more unusual, venue was the room above the Clerkenwell coal store owned by Thomas Britton, described as being very long and narrow, and with a very low ceiling. But despite these literal shortcomings, Britton's concerts were well supported, and soon after his arrival in London, Handel himself is said to have played the harpsichord for them.

But above all, and most prestigiously, it was at the theatre that Londoners took their recreation. At the beginning of the eighteenth century there were two main theatres in the capital, in Drury Lane and in Lincoln's Inn Fields, and in 1705 a third was added, in the Haymarket. Although this street was the depot for the distribution of hay to the vast equine population, and therefore one of the filthiest in London, its central position made it a promising site. The originally named Queen's Theatre (later the King's Theatre, and, nowadays, since the accession of Queen Victoria in 1837, Her Majesty's Theatre) was designed in 1704 by the soldier and playwright Sir John Vanbrugh, who was just beginning his new career as an architect (he would shortly embark on the Marlboroughs' great palace at Woodstock, named after the Duke's victory at Blenheim). His new theatre was largely financed by subscriptions from Whig aristocrats. Its interior was magnificent, but its acoustic was disastrous, rendering spoken text virtually inaudible. The solution to this problem was to abandon spoken drama altogether, and turn instead to the mounting of opera.

London had long had a complex relationship with opera. Born as '*dramma in musica*' in Italy at the turn of the seventeenth century, opera had discovered a seamless combination of drama and music through the invention of a reciting style ('*stile recitativo*', or 'recitative'), where unmeasured but fluent music enhanced the natural inflections of speech rhythm. Once this device was adopted as a carrier of dramatic narrative between more formalized songs (arias), choruses and dances, and presented amidst visual splendour, opera had spread rapidly throughout Italy and then to France, where it had been earnestly adapted to the French language. Germany, too, had experimented with opera in the vernacular, but had also become a purveyor of Italian opera per se. (Handel's very early training in Italian opera had, after all, been with Keiser in Hamburg.) But this enthusiasm for Italianate, through-composed musical drama was slow to find favour on the other side of the English Channel. England had its own rich theatrical traditions. Quite apart from the glories of Shakespeare and his fellow Elizabethan dramatists, Charles I – with the imaginative help of Inigo Jones – had developed the courtly entertainment of the masque, which involved music, dancing and lavish visual effects with ingenious machinery and lighting. Although Cromwell's Puritans had banned all theatre during the interregnum, the masque had returned during the reign of Charles II. The Restoration dramatists had tried hard to incorporate music into their dramas after the operatic manner, but had succeeded merely in creating a hybrid form in which music and drama were not so much combined as juxtaposed. The main drama was punctuated by long sections of musical entertainment, often with no relevance at all to the plot, resulting in a two-tier entertainment of frustrating incontinuity. The most distinguished examples of this ungainly art form came, inevitably, from Purcell, whose *King Arthur* (1691) and *Fairy Queen* (1692) contained ravishing music and ingenious construction. (His true operatic masterpiece, *Dido and Aeneas*, perfect in form, content, characterization and word-setting, was performed at a girls' school in the 1680s, rather than for a court or public theatre, and was therefore a miraculous, one-off irrelevance.) But inevitably audiences were

21

mystified by the semi-operas. Early in the eighteenth century, the English lawyer and musical enthusiast Roger North wrote of the 'fatall objection to all these ambigue enterteinements: they break unity, and distract the audience. Some come for the play and hate the musick, others come onely for the musick, and the drama is a penance for them, and scarce any are well reconciled to both . . . At last these were forc't to yield and give place to their betters the compleat operas.'[3]

The plunge into the deep waters of 'compleat' operas in the English language was taken by an interesting group of multi-national enthusiasts. Many English patricians, who had experienced opera in Europe on their grand tours, encouraged the practitioners in their employ to go abroad too, to acquire new skills and perspectives. Thus, Thomas Clayton (of York Buildings), a violinist in the King's Band during the reign of William III, went to Italy to study composition in 1704. Back home a year later, he joined forces with an Italian of German patronage, Nicola Francesco Haym, an all-rounder who was a highly proficient cellist, a writer and librettist, and also a passionate numismatist. Clayton duly wrote an opera in English, but 'after the Italian Manner: All Sung', *Arsinoe, Queen of Cyprus*, which was performed at the Drury Lane theatre in 1705 (the Haymarket theatre was not yet ready). Haym played principal cello.

Arsinoe did well enough to encourage more of the same, and in the following year Haym adapted and translated the Italian text of Bononcini's *Camilla*, which had just had a huge success in Naples. It too was popular in Drury Lane, and in 1707 Clayton teamed up with Joseph Addison, writer and politician (Lord Godolphin had recently commissioned his poem 'The Campaign', celebrating Marlborough's Blenheim victory). Together they produced Clayton's second opera, *Rosamund*. This however was a disaster: it lasted for only three performances (*Camilla*, in the previous season, had enjoyed over sixty), and Addison was put off opera forever. But as Vanbrugh's theatre opened, and more foreign performers were drawn to London, opera did seem to be catching on. And yet the very multi-nationality of the performers was often as confusing to the audience as the previous century's 'ambigue enterteinements' had been, for, after some half-hearted attempts to master English, many foreigners preferred to sing in their own languages. As Roger North reported, 'Some Scenes were sung in English and others in Italian or Dutch . . . which made a crowd of Absurdities as was not to be borne'.[4] Gradually, the Italian incomers won the day, and by the time of Handel's arrival in London, in 1710, opera was once more the exclusive preserve of its native country. It was performed in Italian throughout, with explanatory word-books in two languages offered to the audience – the eighteenth-century precursors of operatic surtitles.

Vanbrugh had lost money on his first operatic ventures in the Haymarket, so in 1708 he hired Owen Swiney to run his theatre. But Swiney did not last long. In 1710, he was ousted by the twenty-five-year-old Aaron Hill, playwright, critic, poet and adventurer, who had been managing the Drury Lane theatre. And it was Hill, in the Haymarket, who was now determined to make opera work properly in his dazzlingly beautiful theatre. Realizing that the visual component of a production was just as important as the music, he resolved to raise the quality all round:

The Deficiencies I found, or thought I found, in such ITALIAN OPERA'S as have hitherto been introduc'd among us, were, *First*, That they had been compos'd for Tastes and Voices, different from those who were to sing and hear them on the

English Stage: And *Secondly*, That wanting the Machines and Decorations, which bestow so great a Beauty on their Appearance, they have been heard and seen to very considerable Disadvantage.[5]

Seeing beyond Roger North's defeatism, therefore, Hill drafted a libretto which would 'form some Drama that, by different Incidents and Passions, might afford the Musick scope to vary and display its Excellence, and fill the Eye with more delightful Prospects, so at once to give two senses equal Pleasure.'[6]

The opera that Hill devised, in those first weeks in his new job, was called *Rinaldo*. He approached the Italian, Giacomo Rossi, and asked him to write the libretto. As Hill cast his eye around for the right composer to supply the 'Excellence' he sought from the music, Handel stepped off his boat from Europe, preceded by his reputation. With truly impressive instinct and decisiveness, Hill hired him.

3

~~~~~

THE FINAL STUART YEARS

'Cease, ruler of the day, to rise'
[Hercules]

It was a smart move to employ a newly arrived foreigner to compose what was in fact London's first specially written opera in
Italian. As Aaron Hill had so adroitly perceived, by 1710 the
macaronic fumblings of the local composers had led the whole
art form up a hopeless cul-de-sac. Opera needed a new blast of
energy, originality and, most especially, quality, and Handel's appearance must have seemed a godsend. Although he was only
twenty-five, his reputation was already stellar. The Italian poet
Giacomo Rossi, who immediately became his collaborator on *Rinaldo*, described him as 'the Orfeo of our century'.[1] Within weeks
of Handel being signed up by Hill for the Haymarket, he was
being presented to Queen Anne.

Handel could not have hoped for a more auspicious introduction, and he immediately got down to work on *Rinaldo* with
his customary propulsive energy. His colleagues – if necessary,
staying up all night to keep abreast of his pace – were swept along
in the wake of his creative flow. Rossi could not disguise his

25

amazement: 'to my great wonder I saw an entire Opera put to music by that surprising genius, with the greatest degree of perfection, in just two weeks'.[2]

The type of Italian opera that Handel had initially encountered in Hamburg, had developed in Italy and was now to present in London, was that which in due course would become known as *opera seria* (serious opera), to distinguish it from *opera buffa* (comic opera) – though in the early eighteenth century neither appellation was yet coined. The librettos of these operas were generally adapted from classical sources, and the plots were heroic, but included the important ingredient of love interest. Structurally, they were built on successions of arias in what was becoming the eighteenth-century stalwart, the da capo form: there would be three sections to each aria, the second one offering a contrast to the first, and the third being a repetition of the first, but, emotionally transformed as it has been by the impact and content of the middle section, now musically transformed too by vocal embellishment and ornamentation. The development of this da capo aria was fundamentally connected to the rise of the solo singer, both prima donna women (up to now, a relative rarity on the musical stage), and especially castrato men, who had been castrated at puberty if they had shown exceptional musical talent as boy singers, and had therefore retained their high voices. They became enormously popular, the best of them achieving what would today be considered pop-star status. But this parallel development of singer and da capo aria, while strongly propelling opera seria through the entire eighteenth century, was ironically also something of a stultifying force, for as ornamental repetition became ever more important, and aria structure literally turned back on itself, so too was a brake imposed on the unfolding of dramatic narrative. It was in those continuo–accompanied recitatives linking the arias that the story lurched forward; but the best composers of opera seria (Handel included) became skilled at investing these too with dramatic tension and musical affect, in scenes often of great power. Handel in particular had a flawless theatrical instinct, and, recognizing that contrast is the essence of drama, was ingenious at using his voices and the different instruments in his accompanying orchestras to maintain aural engagement. And nowhere did he demonstrate this instinct more powerfully than in the opera that was to be his London debut, *Rinaldo*.

Aaron Hill's chosen subject of *Rinaldo* was taken from Tasso's *Gerusalemme liberata*, and initially worked by him into a scenario, laying out the plot and the characters. This was then handed, more or less simultaneously, to Rossi for versification and to Handel for composition. Pursuing his own conviction of the necessity for stage spectacle as well as musical distinction, Hill made sure that there was ample opportunity in *Rinaldo* for both magic and military effects, and he made the opera more palatable to opera audiences by adding new threads of fictional love interest. But the old story of Rinaldo and the siege of Jerusalem was picked and then embellished by Hill with an expedient ear, too, to its political resonances: for noble Christian crusaders, read Marlborough and his mighty victories; for their Saracen opponents, read French Catholics. In dedicating his libretto to his monarch, Hill offered Queen Anne a delicate dose of wishful thinking, as she helplessly surveyed the toll being taken on her country's coffers by the War of the Spanish Succession.

With Handel snapping at his heels, Rossi worked day and night to turn Hill's scenario into a versified text. The relationship here between librettist and composer cannot have been altogether easy. With such a short amount of time available, Handel knew he could not compose a complete opera from scratch, but that he could pull one together using a great deal of material from his existing Italian operas and cantatas. Rossi's task was to fit new lyrics to old tunes, with by no means a free hand. Handel however had a very clear view: his priority was to demonstrate the breadth of his armoury. Although *Rinaldo* has only ten newly composed numbers, the assembly of these with thirty of his best earlier pieces produces a score which, on purely musical terms, is constantly breathtaking.

Handel was able to be expansive, even extravagant, in his choices because Hill had presented him with impressive forces. He had a roster of singers at the Haymarket which was as formidable as any in Europe, and, as it happened, Handel already knew some of them. The jewel in the crown was the Italian castrato Nicolini. Now thirty-eight (rather elderly for a singer, at that time), Nicolini had stayed in London after his debut performances in *Camilla* in 1708, and was evidently at the top of his game. Exotic as he was as a singer, and a castrato was still something of a rare bird for London audiences, it was for his dramatic skills that he was admired. The eighteenth-century English music historian Dr Charles Burney later recalled him as being 'a great singer, and still greater actor'.[3] In hiring him for the 1710–11 season, which now included the title role in *Rinaldo*, Hill paid him the princely sum of £860, more than a quarter of his entire singer budget. But the benefits were mutual: Hill and Handel got the most popular and talented artist to lead their cast, and Nicolini got not just a generous wage, but the best role he ever had.

The second-highest-paid singer (for the good, but lesser fee of £537) was another castrato, Valentino Urbani, known as Valentini. After him, Hill had hired (for £700 between them) the husband-and-wife team of the baritone Giuseppe Maria Boschi and the mezzo-soprano Francesca Vanini-Boschi. Both had been with Handel in Venice for his triumphant *Agrippina*, in 1709. And one of the two female sopranos Hill hired for the season would also have been known to Handel. Elisabeth Pilotti-Schiavonetti came from Hanover, along with her cellist husband, Giovanni Schiavonetti. Her vivid theatrical presence, as well as her vocal expertise, made her perfect for the wild sorceress, Armida, in *Rinaldo*, a role with which she became completely identified. (Her rival, Isabelle Girardeau, was given the altogether more bland role of the innocent Almirena, and a much lower fee – £300 as opposed to Pilotti-Schiavonetti's £500.) So an existing working relationship with at least three of his cast was a helpful starting point for Handel as he began to compile arias, old and new, for *Rinaldo*.

Instrumentally too there seemed no limit. Aaron Hill was determined to fulfil his own instruction 'to give two senses equal Pleasure'; as he took pains with the stage machinery for the creation of his magic and military effects, so he encouraged Handel, no expense spared, to be equally imaginative and inventive. (Handel thrived on this sort of freedom.) The scoring for *Rinaldo* was based on the normal forces of strings, oboes, bassoons and continuo; but, in the course of the opera, Handel included, sparingly, and always for special effect, four trumpets and timpani, and a small group of recorders. The variety and contrast of all these colours and textures also brought into play that most vital ingredient of Handel's compositional skills: his instinct for theatrical pace. Hemmed in as he was by the conventions of opera seria, he nevertheless found ample opportunity to create and release tension, to deliver all manner of musical pyrotechnics, and then to arrest any sense of time or motion with heartbreaking languid lyricism. His creative energies and ambitions were enabled by the encouragement of his employer and the familiarity of his colleagues.

Handel followed Hill's elaborate stage directions and in all cases provided complementary musical effect. The curtain opens onto the Christian camp outside the besieged city of Jerusalem, and within minutes comes Hill's first coup de théâtre: the King, Argante, bursts onto the scene, as the English version of the libretto tells us, 'drawn through the Gate in a Triumphal Chariot, the Horses white and led in by arm'd Blackamoors, He comes forward attended by a great number of Horse and Foot Guards'. Handel matches Hill's spectacle and gives his singer (Boschi) one of his best ever entrance arias, 'Sibillar gli angui d'Aletto', complete with trumpets and timpani in bellicose fanfares. Hill's second stage effect is to have the Amazon sorceress, Armida, sung in that first production by the charismatic singer Pilotti-Schiavonetti, appear 'in the Air, in a Chariot drawn by two huge Dragons, out of whose Mouths issue Fire and Smoke'. Handel enhances this visual impact with a ferocious summons of the Furies, 'Furie terribili', characterized by rushing strings and biting rhythms. As Armida outlines her strategy of devious enchantment (this section of recitative is given a sudden brief crown of string accompaniment to denote the magic), her second aria, 'Molto voglio, molto spero', is in complete musical contrast: a duet between her voice and a solo oboe. This is followed by Hill's scene-change to a 'delightful Grove in which the Birds are heard to sing, and seen flying up and down in the Trees', where Almirena (Girardeau) and Rinaldo (Nicolini) have a tender love scene. Ever the professional craftsman, Handel not only supplies a long instrumental introduction to the next aria in order to accommodate the scene-change, but scores Almirena's celebration of birds and nature, 'Augelletti', for the completely new colour of three recorders with strings. The sopranino recorder has elaborate virtuosic variations, and Handel was to repeat this successful idea many times in the course of his career when imitating birdsong. 'Augelletti' was one of the new numbers that he composed especially for *Rinaldo*, as he realized that nothing in his portfolio so far met either the musical or the scenographic demands of this particular moment.

No sooner is the audience lulled into these pastoral and amorous delights than there is yet another stage effect, as Armida bursts in to seize Almirena: 'a black Cloud descends, all fill'd with dreadful Monsters spitting Fire and Smoke on every side. The Cloud covers Almirena and Armida, and carries 'em up swiftly into the Air, leaving in their Place, two frightful Furies, who having grinn'd and mock'd Rinaldo, sink down, and disappear'. From here to the end of the act, the visual explosions cease, but Handel supplies spectacular aural diversities in the ensuing arias. Rinaldo's 'Cara sposa' is a bewildered slow lament (no trickery here, just glorious melody and accompaniment) for the disappearance of his sweetheart, with its contrasted middle section of rage towards her captors. He closes the act with a dazzling invocation of winds and tempests ('Venti turbini', aided by a solo violin and a solo bassoon) to help Rinaldo avenge his fury, and, equally important, to give Nicolini his great opportunity for applause.

The second act, the shortest of the three, begins beside 'a Calm and Sunshiny Sea', with mermaids 'dancing up and down in the Water' and a 'lovely Woman' (actually a decoy Siren) sitting in a boat. The other-worldliness of the Sirens is conveyed by Handel giving their literally arresting and alluring number 'Il vostro maggio' disconcerting phrase-lengths (five or seven bars) over harmonic stasis. Sure enough, Rinaldo is taken by the 'lovely Woman' in the boat. The scene changes to the garden of Armida's enchanted palace, where the captured Almirena is resisting the advances of Argante. As Handel set their dialogue in recitative, he added the instruction '*piange*' ('she weeps') at the end of Almirena's first line, thus setting up her great aria, 'Lascia ch'io pianga' ('Let me weep'), another slow and utterly affecting account of misery and loneliness. There is no showy ornamentation here at all, but the simplest of vocal lines, fragmented to represent literally the weeping of Almirena's text, and the orchestra shadows her with resolving dissonances and sympathetic support. This aria is a fine example of Handel knowing precisely how to use the constraints of the da capo form, for the suspension of dramatic impetus at such a moment of despair, into which Almirena is locked through hesitations and repetitions, is completely valid.

Handel gives sorceress and hero an angry duet, 'Fermati!/No, crudel', with fractured writing for the strings and a turbulent bass line: this is no polite exchange. Armida uses her supernatural powers – and more stage trickery – to transform herself into the seductive form of Almirena, to the utter confusion of Rinaldo. When he finally realizes it is all deception, he leaves Armida alone for her celebrated soliloquy, 'Ah! crudel', in which Handel added the plangent colours of solo oboe and bassoon. And the act ends in a scene which brilliantly propels the drama forward and even adds comedy. Argante, too, is confused by Armida's disguise, and makes advances to her. When he realizes his mistake he crossly tells her that he does not need her magic help any longer. Armida is beside herself with rage, ingeniously expressed by Handel in the aria 'Vò far guerra', where he adds yet another musical novelty – a monumental obbligato part for virtuoso harpsichord, which, of course, he would play himself. This dramatic close to the act, unprecedented in Italian opera in London or anywhere else, was a demonstration to his new audience of the breadth and depth of his own sensational musical gifts, and again guaranteed the greatest applause for both his prima donna and himself.

For the opening of the third act, Hill devised another impressive visual picture: 'A dreadful Prospect of a Mountain, horribly steep, and rising from the Front of the Stage, to the utmost Height of the most backward Part of the Theatre; Rocks, and Caves, and Waterfalls, are seen upon the Ascent, and on the Top appear the blazing Battlements of the Enchanted Palace, Guarded by a great Number of Spirits, of various Forms and Aspects'. In his next coup de théâtre, this mountain splits apart (a dramatic sinfonia by Handel accompanies this big scenic moment). Sensibly, all the fast-moving action which follows is set in recitative, neither Hill nor Handel having the slightest desire to suspend the narrative at this point. But musical devices are brought in again to propel the drama towards its final outcome. The duet 'Al trionfo del nostro furore' ratchets up the pace by bringing in solo oboe and bassoon, in a vigorous number of anticipated victory and love. And Almirena sings one of the most puzzling, and therefore memorable, arias in the opera, the oddly metered (between 3/8 and 2/4) 'Bel piacer', taken from *Agrippina*. It is almost as if Handel is checking that his audience is still alert at this stage of the opera, teasing them with rhythmic eccentricity. The final climactic scene ties together all the military, political and amorous threads. With electrifying effect (if people were not alert before this moment, they certainly would be now), Handel brings in four trumpets and timpani ('*tutti gli stromenti militari*') for the 'March of the Christian Crusaders' – significantly, much more impressive than an earlier, rather tame march of the parading Saracens. In the same vein, Rinaldo rallies his troops with the thrilling 'Or la tromba', where Handel continues the massive military accompaniment, and, after the ensuing Battaglia, still characterized by the magnificent trumpets, it is all but over.

Whatever shortcomings there are in Rossi's libretto, Aaron Hill cannot but have rejoiced at Handel's ceaselessly inventive musical realization of his elaborate scenario. All the stage effects had been accommodated, enhanced and embellished by the music; each of the three acts began strongly and ended spectacularly; and the general energy of the narrative drove dynamically through to the climax, despite the necessity to pause for statutory arias for all participants. Even the music for the secondary characters – for instance, Rinaldo's fellow Christian supporter, Eustazio, sung by Valentino Urbani – is excellent, with arias of quality and variety that transcend their insipid texts. Handel had seized his opportunity with vigorous glee, and poured all he had into it.

During the frantic run-up to *Rinaldo*'s opening, Handel had to fulfil another obligation and perform for Queen Anne on her birthday. His cantata 'Echeggiate, festeggiate' was played on 6th February 1711 before the monarch herself, and for the occasion Handel took with him his colleagues from the opera. It was a truly spectacular affair:

. . . being the Queen's Birth-day, the same was observed with great Solemnity: the Court was extream numerous and magnifi- cent; the Officers of state, Foreign Ministers, Nobility, and Gentry, and particularly the Ladies, vying with each other, who should almost grace the Festival. Between One and Two in the Afternoon, was perform'd a fine Consort, being a Dialogue in Italian, in Her Majesty's Praise, set to excellent Musick by the famous Mr. Hendel, a Retainer to the Court of Hanover, in the Quality of Director of his Electoral Highhness's Chapple, and sung by Cavaliero Nicolini Grimaldi, and the other Celebrated Voices of the Italian Opera: with which Her Majesty was extreamly well pleas'd.[4]

This performance of the birthday music was the first of Handel's own London appearances as a practitioner, coming as it did three weeks before the opening of his opera. It was an auspicious debut, and by the end of that day, the fact that Her Majesty 'was extreamly well pleas'd' with Handel's music would have been noted and shared by the most influential people in the capital.

The first press announcement of *Rinaldo* appeared in the *Daily Courant* on 13th February 1711, gloriously misprinting its title as '*Binaldo*' and, in further indication of current linguistic confusions in the opera world, naming its composer as 'Giorgio Frederico Hendel'.[5] The opera opened at the Queen's Theatre in the Haymarket on 24th February, and there were altogether fifteen performances in a run which closed on 2nd June. It was to be revived annually for the next three years, and again in 1717; and two decades later, in 1731, Handel would make a complete revision of it and present it to London all over again. In total, *Rinaldo* had more performances in his lifetime than any other of Handel's operas. He certainly got returns from those two weeks' frantic labour.

For immediate purposes, audience comprehension was assisted by the bilingual word-books. The entire text, together with the stage directions, was printed in parallel translation, and the light in the auditorium was evidently sufficient to give those with genuine curiosity and enthusiasm the opportunity to follow the story closely. And London's theatregoers were enraptured by

Rinaldo, not just for its visual audacity, but for the unprecedented quality of the musical performance. Handel's own artistry at the harpsichord, given prominence especially in 'Vò far guerra', did not go unnoticed, as Mainwaring subsequently remembered: 'His Playing was thought as extraordinary as his Music'.[6]

But needless to say there were detractors, and they certainly had their platform from which to voice their antipathy. The *Spectator*, a brand-new publication in 1711, was edited by its founders Joseph Addison and Richard Steele, friends from their clever schooldays at Charterhouse. Like its predecessor, the recently closed *Tatler*, it appeared six days a week for the price of a penny per issue, and consisted of a single essay, plus a selection of (real or fictional) letters. Addison, still smarting from his own failure as an opera librettist, was the first to leap into print with an ungenerous response to *Rinaldo*'s success. In the edition dated 6th March 1711, he mocked Hill's extravagant designs by referring to 'Nicolini exposed to a Tempest in Robes of Ermin, and sailing in an open Boat upon a Sea of Paste-Board', and hurled disdain at Rossi by deliberately misquoting his diffident preface. Addison's main target was the use of live birds for Almirena's aria, 'Augelletti', in her 'delightful Grove', which he mercilessly worked into a sneering anecdote:

As I was walking in the Streets about a Fortnight ago, I saw an ordinary Fellow carrying a Cage full of little Birds upon his Shoulder; and, as I was wondering with my self what Use he could put them to, he was met very luckily by an Acquaintance, who had the same Curiosity. Upon his asking him what he had upon his Shoulder, he told him, that he had been buying Sparrows for the Opera. Sparrows for the Opera, says his Friend, licking his Lips, what? are they to be roasted? No, no, says the other, they are to enter towards the end of the first Act, and to fly about the Stage.

This strange Dialogue awakened my Curiosity so far, that I immediately bought [the word-book of] the Opera, by which means I perceived that the Sparrows were to act the part of Singing Birds in a delightful Grove: though upon a nearer Enquiry I found ... though they flew in Sight, the Musick proceeded from a Consort of Flageletts and Birdcalls which was planted behind the Scenes.

. . .

But to return to the Sparrows; there have been so many Flights of them let loose in this Opera, that it is feared the House will never get rid of them; and that in other Plays they may make their Entrance in very wrong and improper Scenes ... besides the Inconveniences which the Heads of the Audience may sometimes suffer from them.[7]

No sooner had Addison's opprobrium appeared in print than Steele joined in. His remarks in the *Spectator* of 16th March indicate that not all the stage effects had gone entirely to plan on the opening night. There were after all no real horses, for example, on stage for Argante's first-act entrance ('The King of Jerusalem is obliged to come from the City on foot, instead of being drawn in a triumphant Chariot by white Horses, as my Opera-Book had promised me'), and some of the scene changes had been quite crudely delivered and executed ('we were presented with a Prospect of the Ocean in the midst of a delightful Grove', and so on). Buried beneath the bitter hilarity of their criticism, however, is the real source of Addison's and Steele's disquiet: *Rinaldo* was sung in Italian. Steele confessed to preferring the rival entertainment at Covent Garden, *Whittington and his Cat*, 'because it is in our own Language',[8] while Addison, in summarizing the recent craze for bilingual opera in London before 1710, concluded, 'at length the Audience grew tir'd of understanding Half the Opera, and therefore to ease themselves entirely of the Fatigue of Thinking have so order'd it at Present that the whole Opera is perform'd in an unknown Tongue.'[9]

This sardonic ribaldry was chauvinistic, but its basic premise – that opera in a foreign language was incomprehensible to most of the audience – was not inappropriate, and the argument would continue for years – indeed, for centuries.

During the course of *Rinaldo*'s initial run, the music began to appear in print. The English publisher John Walsh, based just off the Strand, had recently detected a need for the distribution of the sort of music amateur musicians heard at parties or in the theatre, and he was circulating all manner of pieces to be played at every level of society, from young ladies in their drawing rooms to fiddlers in the street. In April 1711 he brought out 'All the Songs set to Musick in the last new Opera call'd, Rinaldo'. The arias were reduced to the vocal line and a bass line (so the delights of Handel's orchestration were not apparent), and some of them were transposed to keys within the easier reach of amateur enthusiasts. This was the first music that Handel published under his own name, and the first in a long series of collaborations with Walsh, whose family firm continued to be his publisher for the rest of his life. So popular were these volumes, Walsh had to reissue them twice before the end of *Rinaldo*'s run, and these reprints had Handel's identity elaborated to 'Signor Hendel Maestro di Capella di Sua Altezza Elettorale d'Hannover', in clear acknowledgement of his salaried obligations to the court which all Londoners knew was to be their own future. And, sure enough, once *Rinaldo* was over, as Mainwaring put it, 'it was time for him to think of returning to Hanover'.[10]

But *Rinaldo* had opened doors, and Handel was now accepted in drawing rooms all over the capital. Friendships with people of all ages were established in these first London months, from the highest echelons of the aristocracy to the ten-year-old Mary Granville, who in adult life would become one of Handel's closest friends and supporters; during that first winter, he played to her in the drawing room of her uncle's house. (Afterwards, her uncle, Sir John Stanley, a commissioner of customs, asked her if she thought she could ever play as well as Handel himself. She recalled, years later, that her reply was forthright: 'If I did not think I should, I would burn my instrument!'[11])

Before he left England, Handel went to take his leave of the Queen. She had not attended any performance of *Rinaldo*, for all its dedication to her and its having taken place in the theatre that bore her name. But she was clearly aware of the opera's success and the impact the young composer had already had on London society, and, like her distant cousins in Hanover, she was not immune to his charm. Mindful perhaps of that very connection, as Mainwaring reported, 'her Majesty was pleased to . . . intimate her desire of seeing him again. Not a little flattered with such marks of approbation from so illustrious a personage, he promised to return, the moment he could obtain permission from the Prince, in whose service he was retained.'[12]

༄

Handel's return journey to Hanover was not exactly direct. He travelled via Düsseldorf, where he spent a few days being entertained by the Elector Palatine Johann Wilhelm. His host, nervous perhaps that wrath was being incurred on his behalf in Hanover, wrote a careful letter for Handel to deliver to the Elector Georg Ludwig, and another to his mother, the Dowager Electress Sophia:

> The bearer of this note, Herr Händel, Kapellmeister to your most beloved son, His Highness, Elector of Brunswick, will kindly communicate to you that I have kept him here with me for a few days, in order to show him several *instruments* and to learn his opinion of them. Now I place in Your Highness perfect confidence, as would a friend and a son, and herewith earnestly entreat you, at the same time, that you may deign to show me an acceptable favour, to my highest and everlasting *obligation*: straightway by your noble intercession, supreme above any other, persuade your son to this end, that he shall not interpret amiss the delay of the above-mentioned Händel, occurring against his will, and that consequently this man may yet again be established and *retained* in the grace and protection of his Prince Elector.[13]

Between Düsseldorf and Hanover, Handel spent time too in Halle, with his family, who were coping with the recent tragic death of his two-year-old niece, daughter of his pregnant sister, Dorotea Sophia. But once back in Hanover, he energetically renewed his obligations to the Elector, and his friendship with his son and daughter-in-law. In addition to composing a 'variety . . . of things for voices and instruments',[14] as Mainwaring rather unhelpfully reported, he also wrote twelve chamber duets, to words by Ortensio Mauro, for Princess Caroline herself. It was, Mainwaring confirmed, 'a species of composition of which the Princess and court were particularly fond'.[15]

Handel was based in Hanover for just a year. He had easy access to Halle, so he could continue to visit his mother and family, as he certainly did for the happier event of the christening of Dorotea Sophia's new daughter, in November 1711. The baby was named Johanna Friederike, after Handel, who as her godfather would remain closely committed to her for the rest of his long life. Handel could also maintain contact with his old teacher Zachow, up until his death at the age of forty-eight in the summer of 1712. But for all his German roots and obligations, Handel's thoughts were never far from England. He corresponded with Andreas Roner, a fellow German musician who had settled in London, asking for English texts from the violinist and poet John Hughes, and declaring firmly that he had been working hard at learning English ('*j'ai fait, depuis que je suis parti de vous, quelque progres dans cette lange*'[16]). He had every intention of returning.

In April 1711 the Habsburg Emperor Joseph I died of smallpox. His younger brother Charles, the alternative claimant to the Spanish throne, inherited Austria, Hungary and the Holy Roman Empire, and it was no longer in Britain's interests for him to have Spain too. So the compromise that Harley had long advocated was proposed in Utrecht later that year: Philip of Anjou, the other claimant to the Spanish throne, should continue to rule Spain, but should relinquish his right to the French succession. Although the Treaty of Utrecht was indeed eventually adopted, its passage through all the interested countries was painfully slow, not least in Britain. The Tories, with their big majority, carried it easily through the House of Commons, but the more Whig-based House of Lords was hostile. Queen Anne was compelled to create twelve new peers in a single day (more than Queen Elizabeth had created in her entire fifty-five-year reign) in order to force the treaty through. London was tense. Harley survived two assassination attempts (the second of which – an eighteenth-century precursor of the parcel bomb, consisting of pistols in a hatbox – was foiled by none other than Jonathan Swift, who disarmed the device). The Queen was so relieved at his narrow escape that she created him Baron Harley, Earl of Oxford and Earl Mortimer, Lord Treasurer and Knight of the Garter. She herself was desperate to see the end of the war, and she was distancing herself increasingly from the bombastic Marlboroughs. Despite the military brilliance of the Duke of Marlborough, Queen Anne no longer relied upon his counsel, nor even on that of his wife, Sarah, whose behaviour towards her sovereign had by now become unbearably imperious and disdainful. At the end of 1711 the Marlboroughs were both dismissed, and the Queen transferred her affections, and the role of Keeper of the Privy Purse, to Sarah's cousin, Abigail Masham, a member of her household since 1704. Abigail was also a cousin of Harley, and her husband was one of the Queen's twelve new peers. London lapped up these dramatic internecine comings and goings with passionate interest.

On 26th December 1711, a formidable letter appeared in the *Spectator*, signed by three people who had all been in at the start of bringing opera to London: Thomas Clayton, Nicola Haym and Charles Dieupart. They were attacking the trend of offering entertainment in a foreign language. Their aim, they stated, was to make 'all Foreigners who pretend to succeed in *England*

to learn the Language of it as we ourselves have done, and not to be so insolent as to expect a whole Nation, a refined and learned Nation, should submit to learn them'.[17]

And they certainly had a point. Even with their bilingual word-books, most of the audiences at the opera would have failed to follow more than its basic narrative thread. Nevertheless, *Rinaldo*, still in Italian throughout, was revived in the Haymarket for nine performances. Nicolini and Pilotti-Schiavonetti repeated their magnificent roles of Rinaldo and Armida (though the rest of the cast was changed), and firm instructions were issued to the audience that 'by Her Majesty's Command no Persons are to be admitted behind the Scenes'.[18] (Clearly, all precautions were being taken not to disrupt the all-important set changes, after their unfortunate malfunctions of the previous season.) And there were moves afoot to bring back the chief perpetrator of this theatrical phenomenon.

By the end of the summer of 1712, Handel had got permission from the Elector of Hanover to go back to England 'on condition that he engaged to return within a reasonable time',[19] as Mainwaring again rather vaguely reported. Whether the interpretation of that 'reasonable time' was ever made specific by Elector Georg is not known; certainly Handel showed no sign of adhering to any agreed schedule. What is clear is that the Elector had no objection to releasing him. With the situation in Europe now at last settling after years of war, and the Hanoverians keenly aware of their future as rulers in Britain, the sanctioning of Handel's return to Anne's court could even have been a move of the subtlest political expediency.

෴

By the autumn of 1712, Handel was once more in London, and he immediately embarked on another winter of ferocious activity.

43

For the Queen's Theatre he wrote not one but two operas: first, *Il Pastor fido*, performed six times between 22nd November and 21st February, and then *Teseo*, performed thirteen times between 10th January and 16th May. Rossi was again his librettist for *Il Pastor fido*, but, most interestingly, for *Teseo* it was Nicola Haym, who had advocated against opera in Italian so recently and so vehemently, but who now changed sides and entered into a long collaboration with the returning giant.

But this season was to be somewhat different. During *Rinaldo*, Aaron Hill had been removed from the Queen's Theatre because he had overspent so lavishly in order to create his sensations. Sets and costumes were seized, and instructions were issued that they were to be imaginatively reused rather than replaced, and Owen Swiney had been brought back from Drury Lane to take Hill's place. Handel may well have expected continuity, and the sort of visual extravagance that Hill had so enthusiastically provided; if so, he was surely disappointed by the new restraints. He will have missed too the sterling gifts of his star singer Nicolini, who had returned to Italy. But other singers were familiar to Handel: his own Armida and Eustazio, Pilotti-Schiavonetti and Valentini, were back; Valeriano Pellegrini, who was brought in to replace Nicolini, had sung Nerone in Handel's *Agrippina* in Venice, in 1709; and the rest of the company were all decent singers who had been in the revival of *Rinaldo*. It was not, on the face of it, unpromising.

In the event, the winter season turned out to be an anticlimax. *Il Pastor fido* was a lightweight story, based on Guarini's famous *tragicommedia pastorale*. Rossi reduced Guarini's five acts to three, and his eighteen characters to six, and Handel himself removed much of the recitative in his process of composition, so the narrative, sung as ever in its Italian language, was even more mystifying than usual. The music was again largely drawn from pre-existing arias, though Handel added a fine overture and seven new numbers. *Il Pastor fido* was performed in tandem with another pastoral piece, *Dorinda*, a compilation (pasticcio) by several composers; the two works shared casts and the hand-me-down sets and costumes). But the need to serve these two new wines in the old bottles from the Haymarket's scenic stores disappointed audiences. An 'Opera Register', begun that year by Francis Colman, recording the titles, dates and cast lists of all operas performed in London, noted succinctly of *Il Pastor fido*, 'Ye Habits were old, and Ye Opera short'.[20]

Teseo, which followed *Il Pastor fido* into the Queen's Theatre, was an altogether more substantial work. The literary turncoat, Haym, took a libretto written in French, in 1675, by Quinault, for Lully, and reworked it, in Italian, for his English audience. Interestingly, he retained Quinault's five-act structure – the only one in Handel's entire operatic output – but adapted the aria texts so as to be suitable for the Italian da capo form. The storyline was altogether more inspiring to Handel, who wrote twenty-four new numbers, assembled with sixteen borrowings, all of striking quality. Especially fine is the music for Medea, yet another sorceress, whose character develops magnificently throughout her many solos, towards total disintegration in defeat. Again, Handel had the weaponry for his villainous female, from throbbing strings, an oboe solo and an exquisite vocal line in 'Dolce riposo' (Medea is of course anything but tranquil), with its disquieting interruptions and imitations, to a wild incantation scene in the central act, to her final incoherent collapse in the fifth act ('Morirò ma vendicata'). Whatever the fate of *Teseo* as a whole, the role of Medea remains one of Handel's most powerful creations. Together with her great predecessor, Armida, in *Rinaldo*, she established a trend for the composer, who throughout his career would continue to excel in music for similarly unpredictable occultists.

Unlike *Il Pastor fido*, *Teseo* was allowed some new sets and costumes; the new theatre manager, Owen Swiney, doubtless agreed with Aaron Hill's passionate belief that visual presentation was as important to audiences as were musical content and execution. So here, as Colman's 'Opera Register' reported, 'all Ye Habits [were] new and richer than ye former with 4 New Scenes, and other Decorations and Machines'.[21] But these had to be paid for, and Swiney, finding himself after the second performance still with huge bills which he could not meet, snatched the takings from the box office and disappeared into the night. 'Mr Swiny Brakes & runs away & leaves ye Singers unpaid ye Scenes & Habits also unpaid for', as Colman cheerfully continued. At this point, the singers, and presumably Handel too, took matters into their own hands: 'The Singers were in Some confusion but at last concluded to go on with ye operas on their own accounts, & divide ye Gain among them.'[22] By the end of *Teseo*'s thirteen performances, audiences were thin. Handel cannot have felt anything like the buzz of triumph that had been his after *Rinaldo*. He had however made important partnerships with two people who would be crucial to him in future years: first with Haym as a librettist, and then with the man who had to assume management of the Queen's Theatre after Swiney's abrupt flit, John Jacob Heidegger, son of a Professor of Theology in Zurich and generally known as 'the Swiss Count'.

The lukewarm reception of his operas might have persuaded Handel to return to Hanover. But he had other commissions in England. In the wake of the peace agreements being sealed in Utrecht (the famous treaty was eventually signed on 13th March

1713), there were preparations for its formal celebration in London. Handel was asked to write settings of the Te Deum and Jubilate, two canticles from the service of Morning Prayer adopted by the English reformers from the Roman Catholic office of Matins. England had made a habit of marking ceremonial occasions and military victories with these canticles, since Purcell's *Ode to St Cecilia* of 1694. Handel completed his 'Utrecht' Te Deum, the first of five settings that he would produce over the years, on 14th January 1713, just after the opening of *Teseo* on the 10th January, and the Jubilate too was finished between those turbulent performances. Although these formal works, very much after the manner of their distinguished Purcellian forebears, were previewed in the Banqueting House, Whitehall, in March, around the time of the actual signing of the treaty, they were not officially performed until 7th July, in St Paul's Cathedral. And by then Handel had also written his great ode, *Eternal Source of Light Divine*, for Queen Anne's forty-eighth birthday, on 6th February.

This extended ode was another turning point for Handel in London. He had, to be sure, performed for Her Majesty on her birthday two years earlier, with Nicolini and other colleagues from *Rinaldo*. But now he wrote for the musicians of the Chapel Royal, and, aware as he always was of the strengths and weaknesses of his performers, he recognized quality when he experienced it. The choir of the Chapel Royal was directed by William Croft – a skilful musician, whose supremacy in English church music was in danger of being usurped by Handel – and it boasted among its generally well-disciplined and accomplished group one extraordinary talent, the alto Richard Elford, as well as others who might be given eloquent solo lines. The text of the ode was by Ambrose Philips, and its repeated refrain, 'The day that gave great Anna birth, / Who fix'd a lasting peace on earth', was a topical reference to the Queen's role in the peace negotiations. For the opening of the ode, describing a gentle sunrise, Handel wrote an astounding arioso passage for Elford's solo alto, with sustained strings and a single trumpet – a masterstroke which added calm majesty to a passage of natural reverence. Each appearance of the refrain was punctuated by a solo movement, and the final section, 'United nations shall combine', was for double choir. The cumulative as well as allegorical effect of this structure – which lasts over forty minutes – is awe-inspiring, and Handel would draw upon the ingredients of its success in later ceremonial pieces. At the Chapel Royal he also met the bass Bernard Gates, who sang the solo verse, 'Let envy there conceal her head'. Roughly his own age, Gates was pursuing a distinguished career which would interlace for decades with that of Handel, and eventually brought him to the exalted position of Master of the Choristers at Westminster Abbey. And the verse 'Kind health descends on downy wings' was a lovely duet for one of Handel's theatre singers, Jane Berbier (who had sung Eustazio in the 1712 revival of *Rinaldo*, and was now Dorinda in *Il Pastor fido* and Arcane in *Teseo*), and a young pupil of William Croft, Anastasia Robinson, who would soon become an important member of Handel's theatrical circle. In the event, the 'Birthday Ode' was not performed on its intended day, as the Queen was suffering severely from her perpetual gout, and made only a brief appearance in public (to play cards). But although the anthem was possibly not even performed for a whole year, it did strengthen Handel's foothold at court, as he progressed from passing visitor to repeated and welcome participant.

On the title page of the word-book to *Teseo*, Handel had been described as '*Maestro di Capella di S.A.E. di Hannover*', in full acknowledgement of his German loyalties. But in that summer of 1713 his salary in Hanover was not renewed. There was nothing sinister in this: he simply was not in attendance to earn it, and the Elector was anyway making some cuts in his household expenses in the wake of the high cost of his own commitment to the war. But within a few months, in what could almost be seen as a recip-rocal gesture, Queen Anne herself, who had always been rather taken by Handel, granted him an enormous pension for life, of £200 per annum, 'unto our Trusty and well-beloved George Frederick Handel Esq',[23] as the citation said – a form of words which continues to this day. Communications between London and the Elector Georg were maintained by the Hanoverian diplo-mat Thomas Grote, who sent back reports of London's formal celebrations of the Treaty of Utrecht and of Handel's part in them. Mainwaring's memoirs of 1760 completely misconstrued the situation in 1713: 'The time had again elapsed to which the leave he had obtained, could in reason be extended. But whether he was afraid of repassing the sea, or whether he had contracted an affection for the diet of the land he was in; so it was, that the promise he had given at his coming away, had somehow slipt out of his memory.'[24]

The implication was that Handel had blotted his copybook by not returning to Hanover. But at no stage was alarm registered, either in Hanover itself or through its London envoy. And so he carried on building his London network, reviving *Rinaldo* again in May 1713, and embarking on yet another opera.

Silla is one of Handel's operatic enigmas. There is no record of its ever having been performed, certainly not at the Queen's Theatre in the Haymarket; and if, as is perhaps more likely, it received a private performance, this too has remained undocumented. The quality of both its libretto, by Rossi, and indeed of Handel's treatment of it, is frankly disappointing, and suggests haste in preparation. If Rossi's somewhat careless adaptation of an old story seems clumsy and formulaic (the worst possible combination), so too does Handel's setting. Despite some impressive individual arias, which would find happier homes in future operas, Handel missed opportunities he would normally have relished (triumphal marches, storms at sea, ghostly dances) and failed to imbue any of his characters with any depth or colour.

These anomalies can perhaps be explained by the probability of a single private performance somewhere, and a vital clue is in the dedication of the libretto to the Duc D'Aumont, the recently arrived French ambassador in London. In the wake of the peace settlement, Britain and France, former bitter antagonists, were making earnest efforts to bury hatchets. Louis XIV sent D'Aumont to London to show the English some effusive generosity, which manifested itself in magnificent masked balls and entertainments. Perhaps it was at one of these that *Silla*, hastily cobbled together for exactly the voice types of the company for whom Handel had been writing all season in the Haymarket, received a performance. And the subject matter, of a badly behaving and cruel military dictator, could also have had satirical meaning, for D'Aumont had repeatedly charged Marlborough, Britain's chief of armed forces, with deliberately prolonging the war. Both the Marlboroughs had recently crashed out of favour at court after their years of intense domination, and this operatic humiliation could therefore be seen as an occasion of spectacular Schadenfreude. Certainly London audiences would not have missed its resonances, and Handel too, now thinking like a true Londoner, would have understood them perfectly.

∾

Since his first arrival in London in 1711, Handel's social contacts had revolved around the Queen's Theatre in the Haymarket, for which he had by now written three operas. The architect of that theatre, and now too of Blenheim Palace, the Marlboroughs' great house near Oxford, was Sir John Vanbrugh. He was also a member of the Kit-Cat Club, a literary and political gathering begun around the time of the Glorious Revolution of 1688, when it would meet in a pie house owned by Christopher (Kit) Catling. It was founded by the publisher Jacob Tonson, whose original idea was to treat promising young writers to dinner, with fine pies and fine wines, in exchange for first refusal of their best works. It was therefore a good networking opportunity for young literary lions, and popular too with well-heeled noblemen with strong political allegiances, for, in addition to its relevance in the book world, it became a forum for the fierce exchange of political views. The Kit-Cat Club generally espoused the Whig cause in supporting the Protestant succession; by the second decade of the eighteenth century, its members included the formidable political and literary figures of Lords Halifax (the principal architect of constitutional stability, limiting the power of the monarch), Carlisle and Burlington, the writers and *Spectator* editors Addison and Steele, and the portraitist Sir Geoffrey Kneller, who indeed painted all his fellow members. (These portraits now hang in the National Portrait Gallery.) Still the club's prime moving spirit, Jacob Tonson bought a house in Barn-Elms (Barnes), just outside London, had it restored by Vanbrugh for free board and lodging, and set it up as an alternative meeting house for the Kit-Cats. Close to this house in Barn-Elms was a mansion owned by a Mr Henry Andrews, and, according to Hawkins' *General History of the Science and Practice of Music* of 1776, it was this Mr Andrews who was Handel's landlord, if not his host: 'Being now determined to make England the country of his residence, Handel began to yield to the invitations of such persons of rank and fortune as were desirous of his acquaintance, and accepted an invitation from one Mr Andrews, of Barn-Elms in Surry, but who also had a town residence, to apartments in his house.'[25]

It is unclear whether Handel's tenancy (or acceptance of hospitality) was actually in Barn-Elms or in Mr Andrews' London residence. In 1799, William Coxe, stepson of Handel's pupil and copyist, J. C. Smith, wrote in a book of Handelian anecdotes that, a year later, it was in fact both:

'In the course of the summer, Handel passed several months at Barn Elms in Surrey, with Mr Andrews; and in the winter, at that gentleman's house in town.'[26]

Handel's other generous host in these early London years was the young Richard Boyle, 3rd Earl of Burlington. Only nineteen in 1713, he was already (since the age of ten, in fact) the owner of many titles and many properties, including Burlington House in Piccadilly, a country seat in Chiswick, and huge estates in Yorkshire and Ireland. *Il Pastor fido* and *Teseo* had both been dedicated to him, and many later writers, including both Hawkins and Coxe, state that Handel actually lived at Burlington House for three years. Here, as in the Kit-Cat context in Barn-Elms, Handel met other artistic and literary luminaries, including Alexander Pope, John Gay, and the Queen's personal physician and amateur musician, Dr John Arbuthnot, whom he would already have encountered at court. Coxe described their Piccadilly relationships:

'Pope not only had no knowledge of the science of music, but received no gratification from "the concord of sweet sounds". Gay was pleased with music without understanding it, but forgot the performance when the music ceased to vibrate. Arbuthnot, on the contrary, who was a judge of music, and a composer, felt the merits of Handel, and conceived an esteem for him'.[27]

Pope, Gay and Arbuthnot had founded the Scriblerus Club, a rival group to the Kit-Cat Club (of which they were not members, any more than Handel was). Significantly, Handel was able to move freely, confidently, gregariously, but carefully between all these literary milieux, and make his own significant contribution. As Gay was to report, in his poem, *Trivia*, of the activities at Burlington House (giving a perfectly credible impression of appreciating what he heard there, for all Coxe's dismissal of his musical sensibilities):

> There Hendel strikes the Strings, the melting Strain
> Transports the Soul, and thrills through ev'ry Vein;
> There oft I enter (but in cleaner Shoes)
> For Burlington's belov'd by every Muse.[28]

Indeed, the combination of Vanbrugh and the Kit-Cat Club, Burlington and the Scriblerus Club, a vibrant social network of artistic and political movers and shakers, and an intense commitment to the Protestant (that is, Hanoverian) succession, had monumental significance for Handel. He never declared allegiance to one political faction or another, any more than he opened up his own heart to a permanent romantic attachment. He was a perpetual outsider. But his progress through London society, and his interpretation of political and amatory events in his music, show his canny and instinctive understanding of both.

And here Handel was quietly securing his own position in advance of the big political shake-up that was sure to come.

Queen Anne's gout, which had so ruined her coronation for her, had continued to trouble her with increasing frequency, and she suffered too from porphyria. She was known to have a fondness for alcohol (a recent statue of her, erected outside St Paul's Cathedral, amused her subjects, who noted that she faced not the cathedral itself but the wine shop opposite), which may have exacerbated her ailments. She still harboured crippling feelings of guilt as she contemplated the whole question of her succession, for it was she who had connived in the deposition of her father, James II, and her own inability to produce a surviving heir had resulted in the naming of the Electress Sophia of Hanover as her successor. Ideally she wanted her half-brother James Stuart, now twenty-five years old and agitating in his French exile, to change his religion, at which point she could have repealed the whole Act of Settlement and secured the Stuart line for the next generation. But, in March 1713, the Pretender unequivocally confirmed his refusal to renounce his Catholic faith, and Queen Anne was back where she started, gloomily facing the inevitability of handing her throne to people she had never met and instinctively disliked. By the autumn of 1713, when the new Hanoverian Resident, Georg von Schutz, arrived in London, rumours among Whig circles persuaded him that the Queen was, in fact, 'totally prejudiced' against the Hanoverians, and that she would 'endeavour to leave the crown to the greatest stranger rather than . . . the Electoral family'.[29] Whatever her true feelings, Queen Anne was undoubtedly dismayed by this tittle-tattle. In the spring of 1714, she sent Thomas Harley, cousin of her minister, on a special dip-lomatic mission to Hanover: he was to offer the Electress Sophia a pension from her own Queen's Civil List. Anne further vouch-safed to do anything in her power, 'consistent with her honour, her safety and the laws', to protect the succession, as Horace Walpole recalled in his memoirs, in 1798. And she restated her resolve at the opening session of Parliament, in March 1714, complaining that any contrary insinuations were 'the height of malice'.[30]

But there were rumblings too in Hanover. The Electoral family had been pressing for some presence in Britain, possibly in the form of Georg Augustus, son of the Elector. Queen Anne had vehemently resisted any such suggestion, fearing that a rival court might be set up in her kingdom, weakening her own author-ity. She had however, as a courtesy, in 1706 admitted the Electoral Prince to the Order of the Garter, and bestowed on him a liberal handful of titles: Duke of Cambridge, Earl of Milford Haven, Viscount Northallerton, Baron Tewkesbury. Now, in 1714, the Whigs were encouraging Georg von Schutz to petition for the Prince actually to take his seat in the House of Lords. Appalled though the Queen was by this, she was persuaded by Harley that, legally, she could not refuse. As rumours spread avidly through London (bells were rung and toasts were raised to the impending arrival of the Electoral Prince), Anne again succumbed to fever and incapacity. In May she recovered her strength, and indeed her resolve, and she wrote firmly to Hanover, fiercely denying their request after all. Curiously, this communication did in fact precipitate the end of the quarrel, for, within days of receiving the Queen's letter, the eighty-three-year-old Dowager Electress Sophia collapsed and died; and shortly after that Queen Anne herself again became ill and suffered a series of strokes. On 1st

August, she too died. Her physician, Dr Arbuthnot, reported to Alexander Pope that 'sleep was never more welcome to a weary traveller than death was to her'.[31] She was forty-nine years old.

Ensconced in Burlington House, receiving daily bulletins about Hanover, and, from Dr Arbuthnot, about Her Majesty's health, Handel awaited the now inevitable change. His old employers, and indeed friends, were about to assume the throne. But would the Pretender make a move to claim it for himself? Would there be civil war?

4

HANOVER IN LONDON

'From mighty kings he took the spoil'

[Judas Maccabaeus]

The solemn moment when the House of Stuart ceased to rule in Britain was marked with little sadness. Queen Anne's coffin, noted by her subjects as being 'even bigger than that of the Prince . . . who was known to be a very fat and bulky man',[1] lay in state at the Palace of Westminster for some days. On 24th August 1714, it was interred in the Henry VII Chapel at Westminster Abbey, beside that of her husband and adjacent to those of her children. Immediately after the Stuart Queen had died, the Hanoverian, Georg Ludwig, was proclaimed British George I, to minimal applause. England nervously awaited the predicted Jacobite uprising: ports were closed, defences were prepared. But nothing happened. In France, Louis XIV had officially recognized James Stuart as King of England since 1701, but now distanced himself from his cause, refusing him any financial backing – refusing him even an audience, when the Pretender travelled to Paris to consult him. James scuttled back to his retreat in the Duchy of Lorraine with no option but – for the time being – to remain patient.

Meanwhile the Duke and Duchess of Marlborough instantly returned from their own exile in Europe to London, where, with little sensitivity to the current mood, they staged a triumphal homecoming and awaited the arrival of the new regime. For nearly a month there was stasis. Lord Bolingbroke, one of the more troublesome personalities in Queen Anne's final administration, observed, 'Sure there never was yet so quiet a transition from one government to another'.[2]

In Hanover the long-anticipated moment had come, and the new British King, now styled George as he anglicized his name, issued detailed instructions for his family and his officials. He himself would travel to London with his son Georg Augustus, followed shortly by his daughter-in-law Caroline, and his three granddaughters, Anne (aged five), Amelia (three) and Caroline (one). His grandson Frederick, still only fourteen years old, would remain in Hanover as the family's representative, with his great-uncle, Ernst August (George's youngest brother) in loco parentis, instructing the boy in the business of government. George would take with him his closest advisers, Baron von Bernstorff, Baron von Bothmar, and Jean de Robethon, a French Huguenot refugee who had been secretary to William III before travelling to Hanover and becoming secretary to Bernstorff. Then there was Baron von Kielmannsegg, the Hanoverian diplomat who had first met Handel in Venice in 1709 and encouraged him to go to Hanover, there negotiating his generous terms of employment. He too would travel to London, together with his wife Sophia, whose own relationship to the new King was exceptionally close. An intelligent and witty woman, she was alleged by some to be the illegitimate daughter of George's father, and therefore his own half-sister. Whether or not this was true, she was definitely George's mistress, as was one of his mother's former ladies-in-waiting,

Ehrengard Melusine von der Schulenberg, who bore him three children. She too would accompany the new King to London. George's own wife, of course, to whom he remained maliciously cold and unforgiving, would remain imprisoned in Ahlden Castle.

The next two British monarchs, father and son, duly travelled together to their new kingdom through Holland, where eventually (delayed by contrary winds) they boarded a boat provided by the Royal Navy. They landed at Greenwich on 18th September, and were met with pomp at Greenwich Palace, with its recently completed new additions by Wren. From there they processed with equal ceremony into London. As that great English woman of letters, Lady Mary Wortley Montagu, wryly observed, the new King arrived surrounded 'by all his German ministers and play-fellows male and female'.[3] George established himself and his entourage in St James's Palace, with the apartments opposite made over to his son, whom he pronounced Prince of Wales. Grasping then some political nettles, he immediately dismissed Harley and Bolingbroke, whom he had never trusted. (Harley was to be imprisoned in the Tower of London for two years, while Bolingbroke fled to France and to the court of the Pretender, James Stuart). On the advice largely of Bothmar, who had by then been in England for some time, he appointed two Whigs who had supported the Hanoverian succession, James, Earl Stanhope and Charles, Viscount Townshend, to head his government. He also reinstated his old military ally, the Duke of Marlborough, as commander of the army. Princess Caroline arrived with her daughters in early October, and on 20th October, George I was crowned in Westminster Abbey, accompanied by what was to him another bewildering display of ceremonial paraphernalia. Gradually, London adjusted to this new identity. The Queen's Theatre in the

Haymarket was renamed the King's Theatre, and when it opened for its new season on 23rd October, just three days after the coronation, the Prince and Princess of Wales were in the audience.

Handel's unreliable biographer, Mainwaring, continuing his fanciful assumption that Handel had somehow forgotten to return to Hanover, now implied that the arrival in London of his German patrons caused the composer considerable embarrassment, and that 'conscious how ill he had deserved at the hands of his gracious patron . . . [he] did not dare to shew himself at court'.[4] In truth, Handel was by no means in any bad odour. His music was deployed immediately. On 26th September, just a week after the King took up residence, a Te Deum of Handel's (possibly the 'Utrecht' setting) was performed at the Chapel Royal, and then on 17th October, between the arrival of Princess Caroline and her daughters and the coronation itself, he produced another. Known ever since as the 'Caroline' Te Deum, this second setting had another fine solo for the alto Richard Elford, here in musical dialogue with a flute. After his unforgettable opening movement in the late Queen's 'Birthday Ode' the previous year, Elford could enjoy a neat moment of symmetry, as he now sang for a future Queen of England. Sadly he died just a few days later, aged only thirty-eight. But Handel's ties to his old employers were thoroughly re-established, and especially to the younger generation, roughly his own age (the Prince and Princess were both thirty-one, he was twenty-nine) and with whom he had been so close in Hanover. In addition, King George confirmed the continuation of Handel's generous royal pension, established by Queen Anne.

Rinaldo was revived for the third time in the newly renamed King's Theatre, and there was added excitement, early in 1715, when Nicolini returned to London and to his title role. Pilotti-Schiavonetti too was back for Armida. The Prince and Princess of

Wales attended a performance on 15th January, their presence no doubt contributing to a full house. Without the royals, *Rinaldo* fared less well (Colman reported 'a very thin house this night'[5] on 29th January), and the old arguments about opera in a foreign tongue resurfaced. For an English nation with a German king and a practice of using French as the language of international communication, Italian was surely the least appropriate language for its entertainment. At the Drury Lane theatre, in March 1715, two of London's theatrical luminaries collaborated on 'A New Musical Masque', *Venus and Adonis*, sung in English. The German-born composer, Johann Christoph Pepusch, had been in London as a viola player and harpsichordist since 1704, and Music Director at Drury Lane since 1714. Here he joined forces with the distinguished actor and playwright Colley Cibber. Singers were poached from the Haymarket, including Jane Berbier and Margerita l'Epine (who had sung for Handel in *Il Pastor fido*, *Teseo* and revivals of *Rinaldo*, and who would, in due course, marry Pepusch). But at the Haymarket Heidegger took this challenge in his stride. He was about to present a new opera, *Amadigi*, by Handel, confirming in the preface that Handel had written it in Burlington House. It was dedicated to Lord Burlington himself, and the libretto, adapted (probably by Haym) from de la Motte's *Amadis de Grèce*, was printed by the Kit-Cat founder, Jacob Tonson.

Amadigi was a happy return for Handel to a medium in which he excelled: the magic opera. With Nicolini back for another title role, Pilotti–Schiavonetti on hand for her third great sorceress, and a libretto rich in scenic as well as emotional potential, he must have felt on surer territory after the aberration of *Silla*. Its scale is smaller than that of *Rinaldo* or *Teseo*: there are only four main characters (the other two being taken by Anastasia Robinson, in her first new creation, and Diana Vico, another veteran from *Rinaldo* revivals), plus a tiny appearance at the end for a subsidiary magician. But *Amadigi*'s content is of real distinction. As Burney concluded, 'There is more invention, variety and good composition than in any of the music dramas of Handel which I have yet carefully and critically examined'.[6]

Amadigi again called for spectacle and visual trickery accompanied by appropriate music: 'The Enchanted Porch splits asunder & falls at the Sound of a loud boisterous Symphony'; 'Monsters ascend from the bowels of the Earth; and Thunder is heard in the Air'; 'The Cave changes into a beautiful Palace; and after a short but pleasant Simphony, a Chariot descends covered with Clouds'. Such was the importance of all these scenic effects that, again, the public was urged not to try to gain access to the stage area, lest they disturb vital machinery. As the *Daily Courant* published, on 25th May, 'And whereas there is a great many Scenes and Machines to be mov'd in this Opera, which cannot be done if Persons should stand upon the Stage (where they could not be without Danger), it is therefore hop'd no Body, even the Subscribers, will take it Ill that they must be deny'd Entrance on the Stage.'[7] Handel rose to all this, and to the strengths of his star performers, for whom he produced some of his most imaginative music. Several numbers were, as usual, reworkings of existing arias, including nine from *Silla*, so if that work had indeed had a private performance in the previous year, its audience must have been sufficiently select for Handel to entertain no anxiety at all about reusing its content so soon. But there were new numbers too, including, for Nicolini, 'Sento la gioia', with a rousing trumpet solo, 'Pena, tiranna', with solo oboe and bassoon, and a glorious siciliano, 'Gioie, venite in sen'. Handel's best music is that for his wild sorceress, who runs the full gamut of extreme emotion, and is perhaps even more humanly and subtly drawn than her prede-cessors. She ends her life in a tragic sarabande ('Io già sento'), with fragmented, incoherent and finally truncated utterances of suicide.

Amadigi ran in conjunction with performances of *Rinaldo* (so Pilotti-Schiavonetti and Nicolini really earned their fees that summer), and on two occasions the King himself attended. There was no performance in late May: 'Satt. King George's Birth day ye 28th. *No Opera.*'[8] In late June there was an excessive heatwave in London and the theatre had to remain closed. And the most troubling disruption came towards the end of the season. Colman recorded, 'No opera performed since ye 23 July, ye Rebellion of ye Tories and Paptists being ye cause – ye King and Court not liking to go into such Crowds these troublesome times.'[9] The Pretender was finally pulling together considerable support for his claim to the English throne and threatening to restore the House of Stuart. The theatres closed, and Handel went quietly to ground in Burlington House.

The Jacobite Rebellion of 1715, known ever afterwards as 'the Fifteen', was of little lasting impact, but at the time caused ex-treme tension in the capital and beyond. There was still vociferous Tory support for the Jacobite cause, and armed rebellions against the new government were threatened. In Scotland, the Earl of Mar rallied great support for James Stuart, proclaiming him their lawful sovereign, and there were satellite uprisings in Wales, Devon and Cornwall, with the promise of more recruits from other parts of the British Isles. In due course Lord Mar's campaign, defeated as much by its own incompetence and disorganization as by any opposition, was put down by the Duke of Argyll; and the late arrival of James Stuart himself, by sea to Scotland and in a depressed and feverish state, provided none of the expected momentum. Eventually he retreated to France early in February 1716, and thence ever further away to Italy, his entire campaign in ruins. For Tory Jacobite sympathizers this was disastrous, as Stanhope and Townshend could now persuade the King that the opposition party was not to be trusted at all. Like Queen Anne before him, King George had hoped to form a mixed government of both parties, but now all the Tories were replaced at court, in the ministry and in local government. The Whigs would continue to dominate governments for the next half-century.

The King called upon Marlborough to command the army from London (little knowing that the wily Duke had hedged his bets on his return from exile and sent the huge sum of £4,000 to the Pretender, in support of his cause too). Successful though the outcome was, it would be Marlborough's final command, for in May 1716, he suffered the first of a series of debilitating strokes. The Prince of Wales, a passionate soldier, desperately wanted to be involved in all these military excitements, especially as he sought to carve out some role for himself in his strange new city, but he was forbidden to take part because of the potential danger to the heir to the throne. He and his father disagreed, and the antagonism between them – deep-seated for years, since the King's brutal treatment of the Prince's mother, back in Hanover – increased.

After the Pretender's ignominious departure, London's cultural activity gradually came back to life and the King's Theatre reopened. *Amadigi* was revived. But there seemed to be much less energy and purse now for Italian opera in London. Had the craze in fact blown itself out? Handel was certainly looking beyond the

Haymarket for his creative sustenance, but not beyond England. He travelled to Germany that summer (as did his monarch, in fact) to visit family and friends in Halle, but he clearly had no intention of doing anything other than returning to London. And when he did so, he brought with him an old friend from his days at the university in Halle: Johann Christoph Schmidt. According to the memoir of William Coxe (son-in-law to Schmidt's own son), Handel's persuasive charisma ('that great master's powers') tore Schmidt from the woollen trade 'in which he might have acquired a large fortune had he not been seduced by his passion for music'.[10] Like Handel, Schmidt was to remain in London for the rest of his life, initially earning his living as a viola player, but becoming integral, too, to Handel's activities. At first, he was his 'treasurer', taking care of some of the business side of Handel's operation. But at the same time he was acquiring the skill of music copying, and within a few months he had become principal copyist for Handel. He headed a team of other copyists, among whom were members of his own family, whom he brought over from Germany to join him. Eventually, like his boss, he anglicized his name, to John Christopher Smith.

King George tended to shy away from public occasions and ceremonial formalities, which he disliked, but the Prince of Wales thrived on them and on the public approbation that he reaped from them. His own happy domesticity with his wife and daughters in St James's Palace was a warm contrast to the King's stark solitude in the opposite apartments (despite the fawning courtiers and the mistresses – 'the Maypole and the Elephant', as Mesdames Kielmannsegg and Schulenberg were known). Their disagreements over recent military strategy, not least in the Prince of Wales's desire to be a part of it, were well known. And, although King George was encouraging his son to learn at his

side the whole mechanism of parliamentary government (so different from the absolute power he had wielded in Hanover), again
he drew lines beyond which it was inappropriate for the Prince to
tread. When the King told Parliament of his plan to be absent in
Germany that summer, his ministers advised against his going,
because of the vulnerability of the situation in Scotland. But they
could not stop him, for they themselves had, as a courtesy, repealed the requirement in the Act of Settlement that the monarch
should obtain leave of absence, as it was unbecoming to the
crown. So he went, and the Prince remained in London, spending a pleasant summer at Hampton Court, and increasing his
popularity as he continued to make contact with local people. But
his father had refused to let him act as official Regent, exerting
power, begrudgingly allowing him to be granted instead the title
of 'Guardian of the Realm'. Important decisions in the affairs of
state were all referred to the King in Hanover, and the Prince's
discontent enlarged again.

By late 1716, both Handel and the King were back in London.
It seems that Handel carried with him the text of a German-
language Passion oratorio by Barthold Heinrich Brockes: *Der für
die Sünde der Welt gemarterte und sterbende Jesus*; and, with no new
operas on his horizon, he turned his energies towards composing
his Passion. It is likely that his old Hamburg friend, Mattheson,
had been instrumental in commissioning it, and was involved too
in its performances, which he faithfully recorded, in various German cities, over the next few years. But in London Handel had no
use for it (if his audiences had problems with opera in Italian,
they would not be likely to welcome a Passion setting in German),
and in fact this foray into a German text was an isolated one:
Handel would write little more in his mother tongue. Unlike his
great contemporary, J. S. Bach, who spent most of his working

life in German ecclesiastical environments, constantly setting German texts for over 200 cantatas and soon indeed to excel in the composition of Passion settings, Handel's path had taken him away from his roots, for ever.

The London theatres reopened in December 1716, and the season closed in June 1717. There had been no new work by Handel or anyone else, and opera did finally seem to be on the wane. An altogether lighter entertainment, the masquerade – a masked ball with a little music – seemed to be the new craze. And, for the moment anyway, audiences were rather more engaged in, and indeed divided by, the spectator sport of observing the quarrels in their royal family. There had been an assassination attempt on the Prince of Wales. At the Drury Lane theatre a shot was fired, which went safely over his shoulder; but the incident only increased his newsworthiness, his perceived bravery and therefore his popularity. On 17th July, the King gave what was for him a rare and very ostentatious party. He and his entourage travelled by river from Whitehall to Chelsea, took supper ashore at Lord Ranelagh's villa, and returned the same way in the early hours of the morning. The *Daily Courant* excitedly listed various 'Dutchesses' and barons ('Persons of Quality')[11] on the guest list, but there were glaring absentees. A report of this spectacular event, told to Berlin by the Prussian ambassador, Friedrich Bonet, concluded with the telling remark, 'Neither the Prince nor the Princess took any part in this festivity'.[12] The wedge between father and son was now deeply driven.

What their Royal Highnesses will have been genuinely sad at missing on the night of this river party was the music, now known as the 'Water Music', composed especially for the occasion by Handel. The King had long enjoyed masquerades, and also, back in Hanover on the lake at his electoral palace Herrenhausen, water parties; and it was his own idea to have something of the sort on the Thames. He asked Baron Kielmannsegg to organize it, and Kielmannsegg sensibly approached Heidegger, who was in charge of these masquerades on the dry land of the King's Theatre. Heidegger declined, and Kielmannsegg found himself not only overseeing it himself, but also paying for it. He called in Handel, and the result was a triumph. As Bonet described, 'Next to the King's Barge was that of the musicians, about fifty in number, who played on all kinds of instruments, to wit trumpets, horns, hautboys, bassoons, German flutes, French flutes, violins and basses; but there were no singers. The music had been composed especially by the famous Handel, a native of Halle, and His Majesty's Principal Court Composer.'[13]

Those fifty musicians worked hard that evening. According to the *Daily Courant*, 'His Majesty liked [the music] so well, that he caus'd it to be plaid over three times in going and returning. At Eleven his Majesty went ashore at Chelsea, where a Supper was prepar'd, and there was another fine Consort of Musick, which lasted till 2; after which His Majesty came again into his Barge and return'd the Same Way, the Musick continuing to play till he landed.'[14] And the enjoyment of this music was by no means limited to the King and his 'Persons of Quality', for the whole river was crowded with boats of all sizes, which formed an orderly aquatic throng to accompany the monarch as he processed sedately up and down London's mighty artery.

Handel's music for this extraordinary event was his most substantial yet for instruments alone, with 'no singers', as Bonet had observed. But even though he was away from his theatrical or ceremonial heartlands, Handel more than met the bizarre challenge of producing music that would be both playable and audible on a moving barge in the open air; as so often, his guiding principles were texture and contrast. In addition to his normal orchestral basis of strings, oboes and bassoons, there were sets of trumpets, timpani, horns and flutes, with sopranino recorders, and altogether he produced twenty-two separate movements, which make up almost an hour's music. The addition of the strong brass instruments was a practical solution to alfresco performance, and the rousing movements involving these would have resounded thrillingly between the opposing river banks, and been enjoyed, too, by the pursuing flotilla of the King's subjects. The subtler-textured numbers involving flutes or recorders were probably intended for the 'fine Consort of Musick' which accompanied the supper at Lord Ranelagh's villa. The actual order in which these twenty-two movements were originally performed is not clear, but it is highly likely that the overseeing Handel based his decisions about what to play when on the appropriate acoustical circumstances. It was only when the music got into print much later, in 1788, that it was organized into groups connected by key and instrumentation (hence the notion that there are three separate suites). All the music is of the highest quality, and Handel combined his natural showmanship and exuberance with respect for his monarch and a completely professional awareness of the demands of the occasion. It is no wonder that the King was so delighted by the effect of it all that he ordered it to be repeated so often throughout the long night.

The absence of the Prince and Princess of Wales on that July evening could have been attributed (though it was not – filial antagonism was too obvious for excuses to be sought) to the state of Caroline's health, for she was pregnant with their fifth child, and the first to be born in Britain. In October she gave birth to their second son, consolidating the male line of heirs and the Hanoverian dynasty. And yet this unfortunate infant was to be the final catalyst in the breakdown of the relationship between King and Prince. First, there were disagreements about the child's name. Caroline wished to call her son William, but the King insisted on George. A tetchy compromise was reached, and the child was named George William. Next, there was a blazing row about one of the godparents. The Prince wanted to invite his uncle, Ernst August, who was supposedly supervising young Frederick's activities back in Hanover, though he had recently been appointed Bishop of Osnabrück. This wish too was countered: the King and his government dictated that this important role should be entrusted to the Lord Chamberlain, the recently appointed twenty-four-year-old Duke of Newcastle. Inevitably the Prince of Wales was overruled, but this rankled so much with him that, on the day of the baby's christening, 28th November, he had an angry exchange with poor Newcastle, accusing him of acting dishonourably and, according to some reports, challenging him to a duel. This was too much for the King, and he banished his son from St James's Palace. With some willingness the Prince did indeed storm out, naturally taking with him his wife – whom the King had naively assumed would remain in her royal apartments. The Prince and Princess settled in Leicester House, in what is now Leicester Square. But their three daughters astonishingly had to remain at court, for, as royal grandchildren, they were technically 'property of the crown'. The Prince was only too familiar with his father's stubborn cruelty towards members of his family. Ever since his childhood, he himself had been denied access to his incarcerated mother, and now he was being denied access to his own children. He made attempts through the law to assert his paternal rights, and even tried secretly to visit his daughters without permission, but failed in all these endeavours. He had certainly established his independence from his father, as he and Caroline set up almost a rival court in Leicester House, but the price he and his family paid was immense and painful. And a tragic corollary to this seismic series of events was that the baby George William, over whom all these public rows had been conducted, died, aged only three months.

The whole of London was gripped by royal trauma, and for those close to the King or his son, either as members of their households or simply part of their court circles, these crises were deeply unsettling. As sides were drawn, there was a disastrous consequence for opera in the Haymarket, for the rival courts effectively evaporated the patronage necessary to sustain a commercial company. There would be no further operatic activity for three years. Handel was one of many whose personal loyalties were seriously split between King and Prince of Wales, and his action at this difficult time was to distance himself – literally. Through his social milieu, based in Piccadilly, he came into contact with one of the most colourful and extrovert personalities of the early Georgian era, James Brydges, whose town residence was in Albemarle Street, close to Burlington House. And it was Brydges who offered Handel the opportunity to escape.

James Brydges, some ten years older than Handel, had completed his education at the University of Wolfenbüttel, where he had made helpful contacts with the court of Hanover. Back in London, at the beginning of the eighteenth century, he had been appointed Paymaster General of the forces for Marlborough's campaigns, and in this position had lined his own pockets through the short-term investment of the government monies entrusted to him. In a staggering feat of embezzlement, which at the time was not deemed at all illegal, he snaffled the high-interest returns from these investments for himself, and quickly amassed a fortune of £600,000. As he built his wealth, so he did his social status. Early in the reign of George I, Brydges had pulled his old Hanoverian strings and secured the earldom of Carnarvon; later, in April 1719, he would be further ennobled as the 1st Duke of Chandos, so there had clearly been no perception of disgrace for his financial dealings. In due course, through a number of other investments, including the South Sea Company, he endured a symmetrically steep series of losses, and by the time of his death, in 1744, he was virtually penniless. Jonathan Swift's comment, 'Since all he got by fraud he lost in stocks', was an apt epitaph for an ingenious swindler. But in his days of prosperity, Brydges made a significant contribution to the artistic development of individual architects, painters and musicians; and one of these was Handel.

From his late wife's estate, James Brydges bought Cannons, a large house near Edgware, and set about rebuilding it as a grand Palladian mansion. He hired James Gibbs to design the two main fronts, on its south and east sides, and to add a luxuriously finished chapel. Several painters, including Sir James Thornhill and Antonio Bellucci, were then employed for the internal decoration. Daniel Defoe, in his *A Tour Through the Whole Island of Great Britain*, in 1725, wrote, 'This palace is so Beautiful in its Situation, so Lofty, so Majestick the Appearance of it, that a Pen can but ill describe it.'[15] Within this magnificent edifice, Brydges then assembled a musical establishment, and between 1715, when he began his 'Cannons Concert', and 1721, when the crash of the South Sea Company dramatically propelled his financial ruin, he built a cohort of twenty-four singers and instrumentalists, and a fine collection of instruments too. Pepusch was one of those appointed, as

'Master of the Music', and he stayed in that undemanding position until as late as 1729. As Defoe continued, 'the Duke maintains there a full Choir, and has the Worship perform'd there with the best Musick, after the manner of the Chappel Royal, which is not done in any other Noble Man's Chappel in *Britain*; no not the Prince of *Wales's*, though Heir Apparent to the Crown.'[16]

For Handel, in mid-1717, this musical haven in the country-side must have seemed infinitely alluring, and for Brydges the acquisition of Handel to his private 'court' was a great feather in his cap. As Mainwaring later gushed, 'Whether HANDEL was *provided* as a mere implement of grandeur, or *chosen* from motives of a superior kind, it is not for us to determine. This one may venture to assert, that the having such a Composer, was an in-stance of *real* magnificence, such as no private person, or subject; nay, such as no prince or potentate on the earth could at the time pretend to.'[17]

Here at Cannons, from the late summer of 1717, Handel changed gear, temporarily abandoning the theatre and concen-trating instead on church music. James Brydges' new chapel was not yet completed, but he had had the nearby church of St Law-rence, Whitchurch redecorated in the Italian baroque style, and was using this for worship. For the Cannons musicians and the church's intimate but sumptuously theatrical space, Handel wrote his third Te Deum setting, perhaps to celebrate some Brydges family occasion, in late 1718, and eleven mighty, multi-partite anthems, now known as the Chandos or Cannons anthems. These were amassed in just over eighteen months, Handel throw-ing himself into this new challenge with his characteristic energy as soon as he arrived. By late September 1717, Brydges wrote to Dr Arbuthnot, 'Mr Handle has made me two new Anthems very noble ones & most think they far exceed the first two. He is at work on 2 more & some Overtures to be plaied before the lesson.'[18] Handel had written some psalm settings to Latin texts in his Roman years. Now he set English verses, with some texts drawn from more than one psalm, and with his usual recycling technique he reworked some of the music from the Italian psalms into the new pieces. The various scorings reflect the gradual re-inforcement of the Cannons musical establishment: six of the anthems are for just a three-part choir, while the others are for four- or five-part forces. The instrumental basis is small, with just two violins and continuo embellished by a single oboe, though two of the anthems also use recorders, and there is evidence, too, of a bassoon and double bass. There were no violas in any of this music for Cannons, so there were none yet on the payroll.

But perhaps the most interesting new development for Handel in his palatial, but essentially rural, retreat was his concentration on working with English texts, both within the chapel and beyond it. That still-raging debate about the relevance of opera in a language incomprehensible to most of its audience had not passed him by, and, cut off from the glare of London theatre and at the same time driven by his current experience of working with English psalm texts, he now experimented with dramatic music in English. One work which had its roots in this workshop period was *Esther*, a biblical story whose libretto, immediately inspired perhaps by the 1715 play by Thomas Brereton, *Esther; or Faith Triumphant*, had many distinguished hands in it, including those of Handel's Burlington friends, Pope, Gay and Arbuthnot. It is uncertain if *Esther* was ever actually performed at Cannons, but it would resurface in London twelve years later.

Handel's colleague Pepusch had recently had a success at the Drury Lane theatre with his masque *Venus and Adonis*, and now Handel too turned his attention to a pastoral subject in English,

Acis and Galatea. Here he produced a profound masterpiece whose lasting impact, like that of *Esther*, would be felt much later. In Italy, back in 1708, he had written a version of the same story, *Aci, Galatea e Polifemo*, and now he gave it a completely new treatment, for five singers plus a five-part chorus (probably, in fact, the same soloists in ensemble), which, after the manner of a Greek chorus, both takes part in the action and comments upon it. Again, luminaries from Handel's Burlington House acquaintance collaborated to adapt the Sicilian myth from Ovid's *Metamorphoses*: John Gay wrote the first version of the libretto, and Alexander Pope expanded it with its choral-commentary additions. Both libretto and score are masterful. In a sense, each could stand on its own without the other, but their combination, a total truly exceeding the sum of its parts, is a work which is just as intensely thrilling on an intimate scale as *Rinaldo* is on the large scale.

The story of this mini-opera is uncluttered by subplots. Acis, a shepherd, and Galatea, a sea nymph, are happily in love, but the monster, Polyphemus, is also smitten with love for Galatea. Jealous of Acis, he kills him. Galatea uses her divine powers to turn Acis into a fountain, in whose tragic waters she can bathe forever. Simple though this plot is, it gave Handel the opportunity to demonstrate all his theatrical and emotional powers and insights, as he delivered music that was variously amorous (Acis's 'Love in her eyes sits playing', and his duet with Galatea, 'Happy we'); or pastoral (Galatea's 'Hush ye pretty warbling choir', with another of Handel's birdlike recorders); or dramatically tense (Acis's friend, Damon, asks anxiously, 'Shepherd, what art thou pursuing?'); or frankly comic (Polyphemus's 'O ruddier than the cherry' – a grotesque expression of lust, with a low bass voice accompanied by a ridiculously piping sopranino recorder); or searingly tragic

(Acis's whole death scene, 'Help, Galatea', her own lament, 'Must I my Acis still bemoan', and many heartbreaking choruses, including 'Wretched lovers' and 'Mourn all ye Muses'). With or without a fully staged production – and there are elaborate descriptions in the libretto of potential visual treats, too – this masque was probably the most important step that Handel took at Cannons. His setting of the English language here above all shows that he is increasing his mastery of its foibles, and his sure-footed representation of so many human emotions tears directly at the heartstrings. Scored for Brydges' small cohort of strings (still without violas) and continuo, plus oboes doubling recorders, there is never any sense of anything missing. After performances of *Acis and Galatea* at Cannons, Handel put the score away for some years. But, as with all his best material, he would later find opportunities to pull it off the shelf. And meanwhile the leap he had taken in his surroundings of the grand and the pastoral had been immeasurable.

In the summer of 1718, Handel's younger sister, Dorotea Sophia, died in Halle. Her funeral oration, given by Johann Michal Heineck on 31st July, enumerated not only her own virtues, but also those of her family, and indicates how her brother's achievements on foreign soil were a source of considerable local pride: 'God had given her a devoted husband, a marriage fruitfully blessed, a goodly portion, many joys in her only brother, whose quite especially and exceptionally great Vertues even crowned heads and the greatest ones of the earth at the same time love and admire'.[19]

Handel, greatly distressed, was anxious to go home to mourn

with his mother, with his sister's widower, Michael Dietrich Michaelson, and with his seven-year-old god-daughter, Johanna Friederika. He wrote frequently to his brother-in-law, reiterating his own grief, his concern for his beloved family and his intention of seeing them all at the earliest opportunity. That opportunity, however, was being much delayed, as he explained in some anguish in a letter to Michaelson, in February 1719:

> Dearest Brother,
>
> I beg that you will not judge of my eagerness to see you by the lateness of my departure; it is greatly to my regret that I find myself kept here by affairs of the greatest moment, on which (I venture to say) all my fortunes depend; but they have continued much longer than I had anticipated. If you knew my distress at not having been able to perform what I so ardently desire, you would be indulgent towards me; but I am hoping to conclude it all within a month from now, and you can rest assured that I shall then make no delay but set out forthwith. Pray, dearest brother, assure Mama of this, as also of my duty; and inform me once again of the state of health of yourself, Mama and all your family, so as to relieve my present anxiety and impatience. You will realize, dearest brother, that I should be inconsolable, did I not expect very soon to make up for this delay by remaining all the longer with you.[20]

These 'affairs of the greatest moment, on which . . . all my fortunes depend' (despite his grief, Handel could not conceal his excitement) were indeed time-consuming and of major import. Handel was in intense discussions with a small group of influential men to formalize the production of Italian opera again in

London, by setting up a fully sustained company, based at the King's Theatre in the Haymarket. As Mainwaring described:

> During the last year of his residence at Cannons, a project was formed by the Nobility for erecting an academy in the Haymarket. The intention of this musical Society, was to secure to themselves a constant supply of Operas to be composed by Handel, and performed under his direction. For this end a subscription was set on foot: and as his late Majesty was pleased to let his name appear at the head of it, the Society was dignified with the title of the Royal Academy.[21]

The project was masterminded by two of Handel's closest associates, his patrons Lords Burlington and Chandos (as Brydges was about to become), together with the Duke of Newcastle (a future Prime Minister, albeit the unfortunate pawn in the recent final rift between the King and his son), who became the Royal Academy's first Governor. They formed a joint-stock company, and invited subscriptions of £200, to be collected in a series of five-per-cent 'calls', with the optimistic suggestion that there might be a profit of twenty-five per cent. The King himself contributed £1,000, as he granted his 'Letters Patent' for 'the Encouragement of Operas'. Burlington, Chandos and Newcastle all matched their monarch's donation with their own sums of £1,000; two other enthusiasts also risked more than the asking price (the Duke of Portland at £600, Viscount Castlemaine at £400). Fifty-eight other 'Persons of Honour' were quickly corralled, each for their £200, and £10,000 was raised. The Royal Academy would involve the professional talents of the theatre manager, Heidegger, working with Handel. They were in business. Together with dynamism and visionary ambition, these operatic founding fathers had huge confidence: their 'Letters Patent' were for a period of twenty-one years.

As early as February 1719, the *Original Weekly Journal* reported, rather prematurely, 'Mr Hendel, a famous master of Musick, is gone beyond Sea, by Order of his Majesty, to Collect a Company of the choicest Singers in Europe, for the Opera in the Hay-Market.'[22]

In fact Handel did not go 'beyond Sea' until three months later. On 14th May, Lord Newcastle issued him with a 'Warrant & Instructions' to 'repair to Italy Germany or such other Place or Places as you shall think proper, there to make Contracts with such Singer or Singers as you will judge fit to perform on the English Stage'.[23] A new chapter in the life of Handel, and in the operatic life of London, was about to begin.

5

THE LAUNCH OF THE
ROYAL ACADEMY

'Music, spread thy voice around'
[Solomon]

In that summer of 1719, not only Handel but his monarch too travelled 'beyond sea': King George went to Germany for his annual visit to his beloved Hanover. For two years now he and his son had been at loggerheads, with neither of them having gained anything at all from their feud. The Prince of Wales's independence in Leicester House had not reflected particularly well on him with the British public, any more than had the King's open intransigence with regard to his grandchildren. While London continued to be agog with excitement at every twist and turn of this saga, there was in truth little sympathy for either side: the court was demeaned and therefore weakened, and the government was increasingly dismayed. Various ministers made efforts to heal the rift, often working through one or other of the King's mistresses, Melusine von der Schulenberg, or Sophia von Kielmannsegg, both of whom were known to have persuasive power with the monarch; but to no avail. Outwardly at least George continued to reject his son, gradually emphasizing instead the closeness of his two female advisers. He repeatedly ennobled his 'Maypole' and 'Elephant' with British titles, Melusine as Duchess of Munster in 1716, and of Kendal in 1719, Sophia as Countess of Leinster in 1721, and of Darlington in 1722. (Baron Kielmannsegg, Sophia's husband and Handel's long-time supporter, had died in November 1717, shortly after organizing his triumphant river party with the 'Water Music'.) The King had no time for his daughter-in-law, the truly interesting, astute and cultivated Caroline, Princess of Wales, whom he described as '*cette diablesse Madame la Princesse*', mainly because she never failed to defeat him in conversational combat. But there were signs that his heart was softening towards the younger members of his family. Some courtiers' letters from the time suggest that in fact Caroline was allowed to slip into St James's Palace to see her children. And when the King set off for Hanover, in May 1719, he issued instructions that the Prince and Princess could have full access to their daughters. Perhaps some sort of reconciliation was at last on the cards.

Handel left London with his customary enthusiasm and energy. The main purpose of his trip was to secure the services of the brilliant Italian castrato Francesco Bernardi, from Siena, known everywhere therefore as Il Senesino. Senesino was currently under contract in Dresden, where the glittering court of the Saxon Elector Frederick Augustus I boasted one of Europe's most impressive musical establishments, with a roster of some exceptional musicians. Handel arrived in July, in time to witness its work at its finest, as Dresden magnificently celebrated a royal wedding with performances of no fewer than three operas. These were all composed and conducted by Antonio Lotti, whom Handel had first met in Venice. Among the excellent casts were two singers familiar to

Handel, and who were indeed also on his shopping list: his old friends, Margherita Durastanti and Giuseppe Maria Boschi. He had known them both in Florence before they sang for him in *Agrippina* in Venice, and then Boschi had been with him in London for the sensational first run of *Rinaldo*, in 1711. But even these experienced and much-travelled singers were eclipsed by the current operatic sensation, Senesino, whom Handel was instructed to engage 'as soon as possible . . . and for as long as possible'.

Born in 1686, just a year after Handel, Senesino had by 1717 had a considerable career in the great opera houses of Italy. He had arrived in Dresden with a huge salary in 1717, and there his association with Lotti, and especially with the opera *Teofane*, brought him yet greater acclaim. Despite being somewhat cantankerous to deal with, and also a little unprepossessing in appearance (the composer Quantz carefully described his looks as being 'more suited to the part of a hero than a lover'), he was a performer of truly outstanding gifts, with a flawless technique, a good ear, perfect diction and a considerable stage presence. On hearing him in *Teofane*, Quantz wrote, 'He had a powerful, clear, equal and sweet contralto voice, with a perfect intonation and an excellent shake [trill]. His manner of singing was masterly and his elocution unrivalled . . . His countenance was well adapted to the stage, and his action was natural and noble.'[1]

Handel was confident he could lure Senesino to London. His instructions were to entice him, and others, with considerable fees; and in a letter written soon after arriving in Dresden to Lord Burlington, who was on a similar shopping expedition in Italy, he effectively implied that the deal was done: 'I am waiting here for the engagements of Sinesino, Berselli and Guizzardi to be concluded and for these gentlemen (who are, I may say, favourably disposed) to sign contracts with me for Great Britain'.[2] In the event, none of these singers was immediately available, for they were locked into their Dresden contracts. But the important connection had been made, and the promise of financial reward even greater than that in Dresden (Handel was proposing a salary of £2,000 – over £300,000 in today's money) ensured that Senesino would indeed make his way to London 'as soon as possible'. Meanwhile, Handel collected his friend Margherita Durastanti, hiring her for the princely salary of £1,000 per season (though it was but half the sum being waved at Senesino), and rekindling a working relationship with her that would continue for another fifteen years. Boschi too would soon be tempted back to London.

Handel himself had made a strong impression in Dresden, playing before the Elector and his court, and attracting attention in a wide social circle. His energy and eccentricity, however, did not please everybody. In December 1719, he failed to respond to an invitation from the Field Marshall Count Jacob Heinrich Flemming, the Prime Minister of Saxony. Flemming wrote crossly to one of Handel's pupils in London, the eighteen-year-old Petronella Melusina Schulenberg (illegitimate daughter of the King and his 'Maypole'): 'I hoped to see Mr Hendel and intended to speak to him in laudatory terms of you, but there was no opportunity. I made use of your name to persuade him to call on me, but either he was not at his lodgings or else he was ill. It seems to me that he is a little mad; however he should not behave to me in that way.'[3] Perhaps the Count was attempting to issue a reprimand via this poor girl: 'I wished to tell you all this so that you in your turn may give your master a hint or two.'

Whether or not Handel got his fingers rapped on his return to London at the beginning of 1720, he was again energized to discover that much had taken place in his absence. Lord Newcastle had busily continued to assemble the Academy's subscribers and its creative team. From November 1719, he had called regular meetings of 'Patentees' at the Haymarket theatre, as he formalized structures and made crucial appointments. Sensibly realizing that it would be essential to have some genuine Italian blood in a venture devoted to Italian opera, he had engaged Lord Burlington's Italian teacher, the poet and librettist Paolo Antonio Rolli, as the Academy's Italian Secretary. Rolli would have the overall responsibility of preparing librettos for Handel (whom he had originally met in Rome) and other composers, and would coincidentally provide excellent contact with composers and singers in Italy. Rolli had been in London since the winter of 1715–16, teaching Italian language and literature to many aristocratic pupils with an eye on a grand tour, and insinuating himself into the circle of Caroline, Princess of Wales, at Leicester House, where he became a regular presence. He had already published some collections of poetry, and written an opera libretto in Rome. His credentials for the Royal Academy of Music were therefore wholly appropriate. But his involvement was by no means always benevolent. In his many surviving letters to various Italian friends, Rolli emerges as an individual of mischief and malice, gossiping wildly and often indiscreetly about his non–Italian colleagues, mocking them as they surged forward with their new venture, and regularly conveying the impression that they did not know what they were doing. As the news reached London that Handel, in Dresden, had secured the services of Durastanti, for instance, Rolli wrote to the Abbate Giuseppe Riva, the resident Modenese ambassador in London: 'It is said that Durastanti will be coming for the Operas: Oh! What a bad choice for England! I shall not enter into her singing merits but really she is an Elephant!'[4]

On 30th November 1719, it was minuted that 'Mr Hendell be Ma[ste]r of the Orchestra with Sallary'.[5] Heidegger's involvement too was recognized, and Lord Manchester was elected as Deputy Governor. Instructions were issued with regard to the hiring of available composers, for clearly Handel could not be the sole provider. In Italy, Lord Burlington had secured the services of Giovanni Bononcini, whose *Camilla* had been such a success back in 1706. A third composer, the Venetian Giovanni Porta, was invited to write an opera for the opening season. Dr Arbuthnot, who had lost his position as court physician after Queen Anne's death, but who still maintained a lucrative private practice, was another of the Academy's directors. His duties ranged from negotiating terms with singers to asking his friend Alexander Pope to 'propose a Seal with a Suitable Motto for it, for the Royal Academy of Musick'.[6] (Pope, apparently, declined.) Then an orchestra too began to be assembled. Twenty-five string players (seventeen violins, two violas, four cellos and two double basses) were supplemented by four oboes, three bassoons, a lute and a trumpet. Handel was to direct the performances from the harpsichord, and a second harpsichord could possibly be doubled by one of the cellists. The extraordinary cellist-librettist-numismatist, Nicola Haym, was there, as were two other musicians whom Handel had first encountered back in Rome: the violinist brothers, Pietro and Prospero Castrucci. Both pupils of Corelli, they had come to London in 1715 at the invitation of Lord Burlington, and so had been at Burlington House during Handel's time there. Pietro, the elder brother and more distinguished player, became the orchestra's leader. Another Roman import was signed up, the cellist and composer Filippo Amadei, as was the Flemish all-rounder John Loeillet (oboist, flautist, harpsichordist and composer). Despite being less visible and certainly less highly paid (though they did not do badly), these multitasking instrumentalists were every bit as impressive as the singers they were to accompany.

As Lord Newcastle continued to make calls on the Academy's 'Patentees' to deliver their monetary contributions and pay for all these hirings, another joint-stock company began to generate excitement. The South Sea Company had been founded in 1711, at Harley's instigation, to take over £9 million of the national debt in return for a monopoly of trade with Spanish South America. Although in effect it did very little trading, the Company had by 1720 become an established part of the country's credit system, and its directors now boldly proposed to take over the entire national debt, currently standing at over £50 million, on terms highly advantageous to the government. With the steady intervention of the Chancellor of the Exchequer, Robert Walpole, a more realistic compromise figure of £30 million was agreed; the South Sea Company was confident of paying off the debt quickly and making a handsome profit. Once the deal was carried through Parliament, there was intense clamouring for shares, and the price rocketed. The parallel excitements of financial and operatic fortunes were, predictably, drawn by Sir Richard Steele, now editing a satirical paper called the *Theatre*, in which he published acerbic comments about opera in Italian. In the issue dated 1st March 1720, appeared the lines, 'Yesterday South Sea was 174. Opera Company 83, and a Half. No Transfer'[7], followed a week later by a longer item involving a fictitious singer: 'At the rehearsal on Friday last, Signor NIHILINI BENEDITTI rose half a Note above his Pitch formerly known. Opera Stock from 83 and a half, when he began; at 90 when he ended.'[8]

If Steele considered both the South Sea Company and the Royal Academy of Music to be dubious investments, he was to be proved correct in only one instance. Handel had bought £500 of

South Sea stock, back in 1715, but had sold it on by the time everyone else was rushing for it. As he returned from Dresden, early in 1720, with his singers and his new responsibilities, he had other concerns, and deadlines to meet.

To open its first season at the King's Theatre in the Haymarket, the directors of the Royal Academy of Music programmed two operas: *Radamisto* by Handel, to a libretto by Haym, and *Numitore* by Porta, to a libretto by Rolli. *Radamisto*, with its heroic subject, pleasing designs and a rich orchestration, as Handel deftly deployed his distinguished instrumental forces, must have been intended for the grand opening. But in the event the opening was not grand, nor was it *Radamisto* that was performed. Throughout March and April 1720 there were delays and substitutions. The date originally chosen to launch the Academy, 10th March, came and went, as the Haymarket theatre was showing harlequinades performed by a visiting French company. It was only on 2nd April that the theatre again became a house for opera, but it was for *Numitore*, by the relative stranger (Porta), rather than *Radamisto*, by the starry resident at the heart of the Academy (Handel). *Numitore* was altogether a very low-key affair, barely reported in the press. But just over three weeks later, on 27th April, *Radamisto* did finally reach the stage, and it was the event that the Academy's directors had anticipated. As Mainwaring recalled: 'The crowds and tumults of the house at Venice were hardly equal to those in London. In so splendid and fashionable an assembly of ladies . . . there was no shadow of form, or ceremony, scarce indeed any appearance of order or regularity, politeness or decency. Many, who had forc'd their way into the house with an impetuosity but ill suited to their rank and sex, actually fainted through the excessive heat and closeness of it.'[9]

But it was not just the music that occasioned such hysteria, for it was a moment of profound political import too. The King and the Prince of Wales, together in public for the first time since 1717, attended that opening. And it is highly likely that the major shifts in the Academy's final weeks of preparation were in fact driven by this sensational royal reconciliation.

King George was the head of the Royal Academy of Music and had been involved in it since its birth. Opera was one of his enthusiasms, and his countryman, Handel, one of his close circle. Handel's dedication of *Radamisto* to his monarch in the preface (the only one he ever wrote himself) implied that in fact the King had already heard some of the opera, perhaps in rehearsal or in private preview: 'I have been still the more encouraged . . . by the particular Approbation Your Majesty has been pleased to give to the Musick of this *Drama*: Which, may I be permitted to say, I value not so much as it is the Judgment of a Great Monarch, as of One of a most Refined Taste in the Art.'[10] But even as Handel and his colleagues moved between St James's Palace and the Haymarket in the run-up to their opening night, there were some intense negotiations taking place in Leicester House. Caroline, Princess of Wales was close, both in friendship and in temperament, to Robert Walpole, a man on his own path to political eminence, currently First Lord of the Treasury and Chancellor of the Exchequer. It was Walpole who was determined to reunite the King and his son, and he worked on the Prince of Wales together with Caroline. He also operated in St James's Palace through the powerful 'Elephant', the recently ennobled Melusine, Duchess of Kendal. Then the Princess of Wales's eleven-year-old daughter Anne contracted smallpox, and Caroline was desperate to be with her. *Radamisto* was delayed; *Numitore* opened and played for its six unremarkable performances. On the day it closed, 23rd April, the Prince of Wales went to St James's Palace to meet his father in private, and knelt uncomfortably before him. If the King was still cool, ungracious and ultimately unforgiving, he did at least see the merit of unlocking their stalemate. The Prince and Princess were allowed to see Anne and their other children later that same afternoon, and on the following day, a Sunday, King and heir attended the Chapel Royal together. They agreed to maintain separate establishments – the Prince had no desire to return to St James's Palace any more than the King wanted him back there – but to demonstrate their reconciliation in public, as and when appropriate. Three days later, on 27th April 1720, their appearance together at the opening of *Radamisto* caused a sensation, and there was fainting in the aisles.

But according to Mainwaring, *Radamisto*, on that historic night, was by no means completely upstaged by the royal reconciliation: 'the applause it received was almost as extravagant as his AGRIPPINA had excited'.[11] For, yet again, Handel had excelled himself. The libretto, by his cellist colleague, Haym, on their third collaboration, was based on an actual historical event described by Tacitus, about internecine warfare between the two ruling families of Thrace and Armenia, in AD 51. After *Rinaldo*, *Teseo* and *Amadigi*, Handel's three magic operas, *Radamisto* feels completely new: this is an opera about heroism, strong emotion and forgiveness, without the need for sorceresses or supernatural effects. While the sets had to be large for the stage of the King's Theatre (Act II is described as 'A Plain, through which runs the River Araxes; on one side whereof ruins of ancient buildings, one of which is a subterranean Cave'), some of them were now of a simplicity hitherto unimaginable (Act I: 'A royal tent with a seat and a table'). There were still scene changes before the audience's eyes ('While the Symphony is playing, the Assault on the City is begun, at which time the Scene changes to a Court before Rada-mistus's Palace'), but concentration on music and characterization, rather than visual virtuosity, perhaps revealed a new confidence in the settled seriousness of opera, after its temporary absence from London, and confidence too in the standard of singers being hired, whether imported or home-grown.

Radamisto was certainly devised as a vehicle and heroic title-role for Senesino, with Margherita Durastanti cast as Radamis-to's wife, Zenobia. But when Handel learned that neither Senesino, nor indeed the bass, Boschi, was yet released from Dresden, he had to effect some quite radical readjustment. He moved Durastanti to the title role and gave Zenobia to the half-Italian Anastasia Robinson (his Oriana in *Amadigi*). The fact that Handel could exchange male and female singers for the same male role indicates just how fluid theatrical stereotypes had become, even with regard to gender. In Elizabethan plays, female roles had been taken by boys and young men. Now women were not only fully recognized as stage performers, but were deemed acceptable – and indeed credible – as interpreters of male roles. The gender-crossed casting that Handel applied, especially now as he solved the problem of his star singer's temporary absence, in fact accelerated a comfortable tradition. Throughout the eight-eenth century, and indeed beyond it (Cherubino in *Le nozze di Figaro*, Orlofsky in *Die Fledermaus*, Oktavian in *Der Rosenkava-lier*), it was unremarkable for young male roles to be sung by women.

As a result of the shifting of roles, two British singers found themselves thrust into the limelight. A Scottish tenor, Alexander Gordon, took the role of the villain, Tiridate; the hero's sister,

Polissena, was given to the soprano Ann Turner Robinson. Daughter of a composer (William Turner) and wife of an organist (John Robinson), Ann retained her maiden name in addition to her married one, presumably to avoid confusion with Anastasia Robinson. But if Handel had to wait until later that year for his ideal cast to arrive from Dresden, the music that he wrote for these local singers shows that they were perfectly accomplished technicians, with a more than adequate command of the Italian language; and, after he had trained and rehearsed them, they evidently delivered his opera with distinction on that heady opening night.

Throughout *Radamisto*, Handel's level of invention and audacity is consistently high, reflecting the gifts of his instrumentalists as well as of his singers. He added horns to the already generous orchestral allocation of strings, oboes doubling flutes, bassoons and trumpet, and wrote prominent obbligato parts for individual musicians. There are several oboe solos for Loeillet, a violin solo for Castrucci, a cello solo for Haym, and some spectacular trumpet flourishes. Singers too are rewarded with superb arias – as many as seven each for Durastanti and Anastasia Robinson, and five for Ann Turner Robinson. Confined as he was by the opera seria format of da capo arias interspersed with recitative, Handel still managed to create and release dramatic tension by his instinctive feel for contrast and pace. This is demonstrated at the very opening of the opera. The curtain rises on Polissena, who establishes a tragic mood in her appeal to the gods for protection ('Sommi Dei'), a hesitant, bleak and sparsely accompanied aria of great emotional conflict. After her friend Tigrane, a young prince played by another female soprano (Caterina Galerati), urges her to get away from her faithless husband, in 'Deh! Fuggi il traditore', with scampering runs in the strings and oboes, she rebukes him. Her pleading 'Tu vuoi ch'io parta' is as slow and affecting as is her first aria, but here Handel changes the colour (and Loeillet his instrument) by adding a flute to the strings. As her vile husband Tiridate enters, with his military belligerence and thirst for destruction, his 'Stragi, morti' is wildly agile, with mighty trumpet flourishes and agitated rhythms, only for this to be followed by Radamisto's 'Cara sposa', set to the most intimate accompaniment of them all, continuo harpsichord and cello (played at the King's Theatre by Handel himself and by his librettist, Haym).

And so it continues throughout the opera. Textures, dynamics, tempos, moods and colours are constantly varied, and the audience is swept along by the artistry of sophisticated musical narrative. For all the dazzling displays of vocal and instrumental virtuosity, it is as always the arias of grief and despair that are the most searing. Radamisto's 'Ombra cara', from the second act, when he believes his wife to have drowned, has to number among the greatest that Handel ever wrote. In an adagio (carefully modified 'ma non troppo') that somehow manages to accommodate both the impetus of restlessness and the stasis of wretchedness, a sublimely simple vocal line is suspended over just the string instruments, engaged in solemn contrapuntal exchange. Burney was to describe the aria as 'the language of philosophy and science' against which all else seemed 'the frivolous jargon of fops and triflers'.[12]

Whatever the pressures on Handel in the tense build-up to *Radamisto*'s opening, his creative flow was by no means impaired. Rather, it thrived. Beside his many-coloured arias, there were duets and dances, and a superb finale with the whole cast singing together, their collective outbursts interspersed with three internal duets as the couples paired off. (Handel's experience with the balance and variety of choral forces in his Cannons anthems was certainly paying dividends here.) And the heraldic sinfonias for brass instruments, which recur throughout the opera, are more than glorious indications of a composer confidently at the height of his energies and powers: they are somehow also symptomatic of a time when the King himself regularly attended the opera (which the failing Queen Anne had never done). Six years into Hanoverian rule, there was tremendous artistic originality and productivity in London. At the same time as Daniel Defoe was writing *Robinson Crusoe*, and Jonathan Swift *Gulliver's Travels*, the Royal Academy of Music was properly launched with *Radamisto*, and the King himself, both in name and in person, was its enthusiastic figurehead.

Radamisto enjoyed huge success throughout its ten performances. The King came to see it again on 1st May, this time bringing not only the Prince of Wales, but the Princess too; and, two weeks after that, Caroline herself returned for a second time, accompanied by her eldest daughter, Princess Anne, now happily recovered from her smallpox. This first experience of opera instilled in the young girl a lasting passion that matched that of both her parents. The Princess clearly loved the theatre, the singers and even Handel himself. Indeed, he soon became teacher to her and to her sisters, Amelia and Caroline. Anne was the most especially musical of the three, and Handel taught her singing, composition and figured-bass accompaniment. As she grew up and developed these skills under his tutelage, she continued to be an ardent supporter of all his operatic activities. Meanwhile her grandfather, the King, shortly before the close of *Radamisto*'s run, cemented further his approbation of his friend and countryman, granting Handel his 'First Privilege of Copyright', whereby Handel could enjoy the legal right to print his music without fear of piracy or abridgement. *Radamisto* was the first of his works to be published under this security, in July 1720. On the same day that George issued Handel his Privilege, he left London for his annual visit to Hanover.

But the King's return to the place he still considered to be home was to be dramatically truncated. In his absence, London suffered a terrible financial crisis. As the share price for stock in the South Sea Company had continued to rise all year, other smaller companies had been floated on the Stock Exchange. (The government had recently passed the Bubble Act, threatening legal action to any company operating without a proper charter.) The South Sea Company panicked slightly, and applied for writs against these smaller companies, hoping to demonstrate its own stability as opposed to the fragility and unreliability of the others. But this gesture served only to dent public confidence in all companies, including the South Sea Company itself. Throughout August and September, stock plummeted dramatically, from £1,000, where it had stood in June, to £150. Numerous shareholders, including Handel's recent patron, Lord Chandos, and several members of the government, were ruined. On 23rd September, Rolli wrote to Riva: 'My dear Riva, what ruination has the Southsea crash caused! The whole nobility is at its last gasp; only gloomy faces are to be seen. Great bankers are going bankrupt, great shareholders just disappear and there is not an acquaintance or friend who has escaped total ruin. These rogues of Company Directors have betrayed everybody and I assure you the tragic worst is feared.'[13] By mid-October, he was enraged: 'They ought to be gibbeted these South Sea Directors, who have ruined all my friends – and I very

95

much fear that they will in consequence have ruined the Academy. God damn'em . . .'[14]

But while Rolli's friends suffered at the bursting of the South Sea bubble, some canny financial operators had survived. Jonathan Swift wrote in his poem 'The South Sea Project':

> Ye wise Philosphers! Explain
> What Magick makes our Money rise,
> When dropt into the *Southern* Main;
> Or do these Jugglers cheat our Eyes?

and continued:

> The Nation then too late will find
> Computing all their Cost and Trouble,
> Directors Promises but Wind,
> South-sea at best a mighty Bubble.

Handel himself had greatly reduced his shares well before the crash. The ever more cantankerous Sarah, Duchess of Marlborough had also read the signs correctly ('This project must burst a little and come to nothing'[15]) and kept her money in the Bank of England. Thomas Guy, a bookseller and speculator, had sold his own stock, too, at exactly the right time, making a huge profit of £20,000 (over three and a half million today), with which he founded Guy's Hospital. And Robert Walpole, who had joined in the frenzied investment earlier in the year, sold out again before the summer and avoided personal ruin. He did however return to the capital from his home in Norfolk, to try to impose order on the chaos, and the calm sagacity with which he did so won him great respect and increased popularity. When Walpole informed the King in Hanover of the gravity of the crisis, George – still unwilling to trust the Prince of Wales with any authority – returned reluctantly to London. Any instability in his government threatened confidence in his own rule; and James Stuart was still agitating beyond the Alps.

It was into this seething cauldron of financial trauma that the Italian star singer and his three colleagues arrived from Dresden. Senesino, together with the soprano Maddalena Salvai, the tenor Matteo Berselli and the bass Giovanni Maria Boschi, were all in London by mid-September, and their compatriot, Rolli, while considering Senesino 'a noisy busybody and certainly not the soul of discretion',[16] was fussing over their domestic arrangements and finding them sumptuous lodgings in Leicester Street. A month later the composer Bononcini also arrived. The Royal Academy's second season, despite being planned and rehearsed among the embers of others' financial ruin, was to be even more spectacular than its first. The opening opera, by the newcomer Bononcini to a libretto by Rolli, would be *Astarto* (dedicated to Lord Burlington), in which Senesino would at last make his London debut. After its premiere on 19th November, Mrs Mary Pendarves – who, as the ten-year-old Mary Granville, had met Handel in 1710 and would soon become a close member of his circle – wrote to her sister: 'The stage was never so well served as it is now, there is not one indifferent voice, they are all Italians. There is one man called Serosini who is beyond Nicolini both in person and in voice.'[17]

Meanwhile Handel was restoring *Radamisto* to the vocal scoring he had originally envisaged. The title role was rewritten for Senesino's castrato, Durastanti was moved from Radamisto back to Zenobia (it was not inappropriate that she should now be playing the wife, rather than a male role, as she was pregnant at the time), and the other new singers were given greater prominence.

Altogether eight arias were removed and ten others exchanged for them, there was a new duet, a quartet and much revision of recitative. It was practically a new work. Handel's supreme professionalism is shown in the facility with which he adapted and revised the opera for the new singers. It was not merely a case of transposing Radamisto's music down from Durastanti's soprano register to Senesino's lower one; he accommodated too the specific glories of Senesino's technique (brilliant coloratura and phenomenal breath control) in the new music, all of which both strengthened the character of the title role and displayed the gifts of its interpreter. In the duet with Zenobia, 'Se teco vive', he simply switched the musical lines for the two singers. Thus Durastanti, now singing Zenobia, retained the music she had originally learned and sung as Radamisto, and Senesino sang in his own register. The roles of Polissena and Tiridate, now for Salvai and Boschi (a bass, as opposed to Alexander Gordon's tenor), were similarly strengthened both dramatically and musically, showing the newcomers' greater vocal prowess – Boschi's new arias, for example, incorporate rushing scales and wild leaps of register, making Tiridate even more aggressive. But, in the final scene, Boschi was given four extra lines of emollient recitative, as he apologized for his behaviour – a redeeming feature for a stage villain, perhaps, and welcome to a singer who was hoping again to please his London audiences.

After the opening, on 28th December 1720, some newspapers mistakenly referred to Senesino as Nicolini, who had long since left London, which cannot have given the vain Italian much regard for the British public. There is a sense too of there having been some tension between Senesino and Handel in the rehearsal room: the singer had some outburst, and Handel, whose fuse was never long, called him 'a damned fool'. But – as so often happens

– if their professional relationship was never to be easy, the quality of what they produced together in performance was clearly extraordinary. Early in 1721, Joseph Mitchell published his poem 'Ode on the Power of Musick', and it contained the ravishing and heart-warming lines:

> Who knows not this, when *Handell* plays
>   And *Senesino* sings?
> Our Souls learn Rapture from their Lays,
> While rival'd Angels show amaze
> And drop their Golden Wings.[18]

Margherita Durastanti, about whose arrival in London Rolli had been so negative, but who had already served Handel so well, sang the last performance in her new role as Zenobia on 25th February 1721. She was by then in the final stages of her pregnancy, for just two weeks later an announcement in the *Evening Post* confirmed not only the birth of her daughter, but the fact that the King himself, together with young Princess Anne, would stand as godparents for the infant. Durastanti would remain close to the royal family as she continued her career both in London and elsewhere, for even her frequent pregnancies never kept her from the stage for long. After the birth of this, her first child, she was back at the King's Theatre almost immediately, on 28th March, singing with Senesino, Anastasia Robinson, Salvai and Boschi in a benefit concert, and rehearsing hard for the Academy's imminent final offering of that winter season, *Muzio Scevola*. Caroline, Princess of Wales was also pregnant in that winter, and gave birth to her fifth surviving child in April, the first to be born after the death, in 1718, of her infant son, George William. Prince William, Duke of Cumberland (this time there was no problem with his name) would grow up to be the inheritor of the Hanoverian military mantle, sealing his unfortunate notoriety in conflict with Bonnie Prince Charlie, who as it happens had been born just a few months earlier, at the end of December.

The King received the news of the birth of his grandson during that premiere of *Muzio Scevola*: the performance was interrupted by loud applause greeting the announcement. It is unlikely that such an intrusion into the evening would in fact have damaged its flow, for it was already curiously incoherent. No fewer than three composers had been drafted in for this project. Perhaps the Academy's directors were trying to emphasize the harmony between their distinguished musicians, as Handel, Bononcini and the cellist-composer Amadei were each invited to contribute one act. Or perhaps, rather more cynically, the directors were beginning to detect distinct signs of rivalry between them, and threw the scheme at them as fuel for precisely that fire. For, truth to tell, factions were already forming. The newly arrived Italian singers, together with Bononcini, Rolli and the (significantly Catholic) half-Italian Anastasia Robinson, were a powerful and close-knit little group, all living near one another and quite possibly expressing their sympathy to the Jacobite cause. Handel on the other hand remained loyal to his Protestant roots and to his monarch, and his own supporters were staunch in their approval. *Muzio Scevola* was dedicated to the King – perhaps significantly, as the plot concerned reconciliation. All seven of the Academy's star singers (Senesino, Durastanti, Salvai, Robinson, Galerati, Berselli and Boschi) took part, and there were ten performances.

The fallout from the South Sea Company crisis was still reverberating. On 8th July, for example, the *London Gazette* carried the announcement:

> The Court of Directors of the Royal Academy of Musick finding several Subscribers in Arrear on the Calls made on them this year, do hereby desire them to pay in the same before Thursday the 20th Instant, otherwise they shall be obliged to return them as Defaulters, at a General Court to be held that Day, for their Instructions how to proceed: And it appearing to the said Court of Directors on examining the Accounts, that when the calls already made are fully answered, there will still remain such a Deficiency to render it absolutely necessary to make a further Call to clear this year's Expence.[19]

By the end of the summer, the directors were even threatening legal action: 'These are to give further Notice to every such Defaulter, That unless he pays the said Calls on or before the 22nd of November next, his Name shall be printed, and he shall be proceeded against with the utmost Rigour of the Law.'[20]

The Academy's turmoil reflected what was happening on a wider scale. In the aftermath of the South Sea crash, Walpole had to confront the common belief throughout the country that many government ministers, including the Hanoverian imports and even the King himself, had all been involved in the scheme entirely for their own gain, despite knowing that it was riddled with corruption. The King was in fact in the clear, as he had been in Hanover when the buying of stock had been at its most hysterical. But others in high places had to be seen to be punished. Walpole knew that any disgrace to senior Whig politicians would cause the government to fall, so his focus fell on the Hanoverians, Bothmar,

Bernstorff and de Robethon, who had accompanied the King on his accession. They had remained influential ever since, but henceforth their power was diluted. With many other Protestants also in this unfortunate spotlight, the Catholics – including the Italian opera stars – became more visible; and in its own way the next Academy season would be a symptom of precisely this shift. Of the five operas mounted in 1721–2, only one was by the Protestant Handel. Apart from the shared *Muzio Scevola*, the others were by the Catholics Amadei and Bononcini.

In May 1722 the once mighty Duke of Marlborough died, having lately been much enfeebled by a series of debilitating strokes. Bononcini, not Handel, was summoned by his widow to write the funeral anthem. With over 230 subscribers, Bononcini's recent publication of *Cantate e duetti*, dedicated to the King, was hugely popular, and for a while his profile was undoubtedly higher than that of his Protestant colleague. Handel, however, bided his time: his chief focus was still the Academy, but his interests extended way beyond it. He was enjoying the new organ in St Paul's Cathedral, and, in the Queen Anne Tavern opposite, the convivial company of its organist, Maurice Greene, and the lay clerks. Handel was Music Master to the Prince of Wales's daughters. And recognizing that, even in a year of fluctuating visibility, his whole operatic activity was becoming a thriving business, he expanded it. He established his friend Johann Christoph Schmidt, now John Christopher Smith, not merely as his chief copyist, but as the manager of his compositional workshop. He delegated to Smith and his growing team, which included Smith's own family, the copying of scores, the production of performing materials and the overseeing of all music for publication. The Smiths would remain loyal to Handel for the rest of his life.

Handel's single new contribution to the Academy in that

1721–2 season was *Floridante*, to a libretto by Rolli, dedicated to the Prince of Wales. The cast, led by Senesino, consisted of all the singers from the previous season, with the exception of an indisposed Durastanti, who was replaced by the ever-willing Anastasia Robinson. The libretto on which Rolli based his story was originally Scandinavian, but he tactfully set his version in more remote Persia, for the subject – the restoration of a rightful heir to the throne – was tricky at a time of Catholic confidence and Hanoverian discomfort.

Bristling though it may be with political innuendo, Rolli's libretto is sadly flawed in construction, and the poetry is undistinguished. In his need to give equal musical prominence to all his demanding Italian singers, he repeatedly interrupted the main action with arias for the secondary characters, greatly to the detriment of the theatrical flow that Handel so relished. But Handel still managed to circumvent the deficiencies and produce some remarkable numbers, both for his expensive and irascible Italian star and for his colleagues. Although the text failed to supply him with material on which to create his customarily superb and cohesive musical characterization, he could still provide individual delights. Two duets are the musical highlights, one for Senesino and Robinson ('Ah, mia cara' – a slow and utterly affecting shared lament in E minor, with simple string accompaniment), the other, for Salvai and Baldassare, as their supporters, perfectly contrasted with textural delights ('Fuor di periglio', with pairs of oboes, horns and bassoons). Most of Senesino's arias are slow and intensely lyrical, demonstrating again his supreme ability to shape and sustain long lines, and his technique in fast music too is allowed to shine in several arias. This was the first new role Handel wrote expressly for him, and Senesino cannot have been disappointed. But in balancing the needs of his colleagues,

Handel supplied them too with varied and enriching arias, which on purely musical if not dramatic terms would have more than satisfied both singers and audiences. *Floridante* had fifteen performances, spread over five months; Bononcini's new operas were even more popular; and for the first and only time the Academy declared a dividend that year of seven per cent.

But just as the 1721–2 season was drawing to a close, there was news of another Jacobite conspiracy and rumours of a plot to assassinate the King as he made his way to Hanover for his annual retreat. The King cancelled his visit, troops were amassed in London's Hyde Park, and Catholics were ordered out of the city. The main conspirator was thought to be the Bishop of Rochester, Francis Atterbury, a friend of Swift, Gay, Arbuthnot and Pope, but a high Tory and a well-known sympathizer of the Jacobite cause. Back in 1715, Atterbury had refused to sign the House of Lords document declaring allegiance to the Hanoverian (Protestant) succession, and, from 1717, he was known to be in regular correspondence with James Stuart. In May 1722 Walpole had Atterbury arrested for treason and imprisoned in the Tower. Although there was not enough evidence to convict him, Atterbury was banished, and Walpole's firmness of hand during the potential crisis was widely applauded. But the huddle of Catholic composers and singers in London was largely dispersed. Bononcini was not re-engaged; Rolli was replaced by Haym; and Handel returned to the fore in the Haymarket.

If the Academy directors were at all alarmed by the turn of these events, they were determined to hang on to Senesino at all costs. Furthermore, they were keen to reinforce quality again, and find another singer in Senesino's league. For some time, they had had their eyes on the twenty-four-year-old Italian soprano Francesca Cuzzoni, who had learned her craft in numerous opera houses all over Italy, before breaking into stardom in Venice, in the 1718–19 season. While keen to come to London, Cuzzoni was confident of her own worth and drove a hard bargain. Rolli had reported to Riva in 1720 that 'Cuzzona has been engaged for this year; as for next year she refuses to come for less money than at Siena'.[21] By the autumn of 1722 she had finally been reeled in, and, on 27th October, the *London Journal* announced: 'There is a new Opera now in rehearsal at the Theatre in the Hay-Market, a Part of which is reserv'd for one Mrs. *Cotsona*, an extraordinary Italian Lady, who is expected daily from Italy. It is said, she has a much finer Voice and more accurate Judgment, than any of her Country Women who have performed on the English Stage.'[22]

A new era for the Royal Academy of Music, and for Handel, was about to begin.

6

THE FORTUNES OF THE ROYAL ACADEMY

'Ah! think what ills the jealous prove'

[Hercules]

The woman who was to make the most profound impact on London operatic life in the 1720s did not in fact turn up until the end of 1722. Despite the lure of her astronomical salary, Francesca Cuzzoni delayed her arrival in order to marry the composer and harpsichordist Pier Giuseppe Sandoni, and this carefree disregard for agreed obligation was a taste, perhaps, of things to come. As the Royal Academy of Music, with increasing impatience, put on hold the opera planned for her London debut, they mounted revival after revival: the patchwork *Muzio Scevola*, Bononcini's *Ciro* and *Crispo*, and Handel's *Floridante* were all pulled off the shelf and hastily reconstituted for a few performances each. *Ottone* – so carefully selected – would have to wait.

Like Senesino, Cuzzoni had made her reputation in Italy. She had been appearing regularly in Venice since 1718, and often – as yet unproblematically – beside the soprano who was to become her notorious adversary, Faustina Bordoni. Also like Senesino,

Cuzzoni was clearly an extraordinary musician as well as a superb singer. She had a gloriously timbred voice, with a wide range, immaculate technique, perfect pitch and unparalleled artistry. Although she was not a beautiful woman, nor even a very good actress, she held her audiences by the sheer power of her musical distinction. Years later, Giovanni Battista Mancini could still recall her brilliance in the greatest detail:

> It was difficult for the hearer to determine whether she most excelled in slow or rapid airs. A native warble enabled her to execute divisions with such facility as to conceal every appearance of difficulty; and so grateful and touching was the natural tone of her voice that she rendered pathetic whatever she sung, in which she had leisure to unfold its whole volume. The art of conducting, sustaining, increasing, and diminishing her tones by minute degrees, acquired her, among professors, the title of complete mistress of her art.[1]

Mancini praised her cantabile line, her perfect trills, her shaping of phrases and the accuracy and sweetness (by no means a regular combination) of her high notes. Handel would have been relishing the prospect of working with a singer of such prowess and sovereignty.

The libretto that Handel and Haym selected for Cuzzoni's debut was adapted from Lotti's *Teofane*, recently seen by Handel in Dresden. There the cast had included Senesino, Durastanti and Boschi, who would reprise their roles in the new version of the story. In his rewriting of the text, Haym also retitled it *Ottone*, perhaps to massage the vanity of Senesino as he grimly contemplated a tide of attention for someone else, for his character now became the title role. The plot is not easy to follow, even in performance, involving many components instantly recognizable as the very stuff of opera seria: ambition for political power, two pairs of lovers, thwarted passion, disguise, rebellion, imprisonment, a storm, reconciliation and resolution. Senesino, as Ottone, would play opposite Cuzzoni, as Teofane; a second pair of lovers would be taken by Gaetano Berenstadt (a castrato who had once sung for Handel in a revival of *Rinaldo* in 1717, and now returned to London to join the Academy) and Anastasia Robinson; two political schemers were to be sung, as they had been for Lotti, in Dresden, by Durastanti and Boschi. The cast was of the highest and most even quality that Handel had ever assembled, and so too was the music that he wrote for them.

Careful to balance prominence for his two stars, both qualitatively and quantitatively, Handel was even-handed. Senesino and Cuzzoni each had seven arias, a shared duet and the final chorus. (Durastanti was given six arias in addition to the final chorus, Robinson five, Berenstadt four, and the ever-undemanding Boschi three.) Cuzzoni's lauded technical gifts were reflected in spectacular coloratura arias ('S'or mi dai pace', for instance) and also in slow lyricism ('Affanni del pensier' – a remarkable siciliano, with its gently lilting 12/8 rhythm, in the affecting key of F sharp minor). Her renowned musicianship was challenged in steep chromaticism and unexpected turns of phrase requiring sophisticated musical comprehension and precise tuning. Senesino's arias hit consistently equal heights, as had his music in *Floridante*: they serve all aspects of his technique and stage presence too; and the duet with Cuzzoni at the end of the opera must have been the greatest thrill for the audience. The quality continued throughout the music for the other singers, especially in the mellifluous duet between Robinson and Durastanti, 'Notte cara', at the end of the second act.

After Cuzzoni's belated arrival, *Ottone* was rushed into rehearsal. But almost immediately there was a problem: Cuzzoni did not like her quiet opening aria, 'Falsa imagine'. Perhaps she wanted something flashier with which to announce her presence in London. She had been used to getting her own way in Italian opera houses, but she met her match in Handel, who refused to pander to her. According to a famous anecdote related by Mainwaring:

> Having one day some words with CUZZONI on her refusing to sing *Falsa imagine* in OTTONE; Oh! Madame, (said he) je scais bien que Vous êtes une veritable Diablesse: mais je Vous serai scavoir, moi, que je suis Beelzebub le Chef des Diables. [I see you are a real devil: but I would have you know that I am Beelzebub, the Chief Devil] With this he took her up by the waist, and, if she made any more words, swore that he would fling her out of the window.[2]

It is highly unlikely that Handel was in any way serious in this threat. He certainly had a temper and a perfectionist's insistence on discipline. But in his description of himself as Beelzebub, there is an indication too of hilarity and self-mockery. In this, his first encounter with Cuzzoni, he rather cleverly deflated a potentially explosive situation by resorting to humorous banter, while simultaneously underlining the fact that he was in charge. Not only did Cuzzoni obediently sing 'Falsa imagine', but she continued to sing it in concerts for the next thirty years. It is in fact an exquisite aria, with a taut vocal line fractured by emotional rests, and the simplest accompaniment of just harpsichord and cello (played originally, of course, by Handel and Haym). For Handel, this type of continuo aria was always of supreme importance, and inevitably implied confidence in his singer, who had to convey raw emotion with minimal instrumental support. The aria suited Cuzzoni perfectly, and for the moment the beast was tamed.

In contrast to Cuzzoni's tantrums, the quieter discomforts of another singer were more troubling. For a number of reasons, Anastasia Robinson was in a highly emotional state in the autumn of 1722. She was engaged in a clandestine affair with, and was indeed secretly living with, the elderly and eccentric Charles Mordaunt, Earl of Peterborough. Although she had had a huge success in the previous season with Bononcini's *Griselda*, in which she had taken over the title role at short notice from an indisposed Durastanti, she must have felt threatened by Cuzzoni. Furthermore, and this would have made her feel even more vulnerable (as with all singers), she detected changes and insecurities in her voice. When she had first sung for Handel, back in 1713, in his 'Birthday Ode' for Queen Anne, she was a high soprano. But gradually she had lost the top of her range, and perhaps her fluency in coloratura too, and the roles written for her in *Radamisto* (Zenobia), *Muzio Scevola* (Irene) and *Floridante* (Elmira) had all reflected Handel's careful sensitivity to this: in general, they lie lower, and the arias are slower. Being of a naturally gentle disposition, Anastasia preferred not to play tough women. But now, with Matilda in *Ottone*, there were aspects of the character and her music that deeply upset her. Too nervous to confront Handel himself, Anastasia instead wrote an impassioned letter to her good friend, Giuseppe Riva, asking for his help in securing the further intervention of Lady Darlington, the King's 'Maypole'. Would she perhaps bend Handel's ear?

Now I want your advice for myself, you have hear'd my new Part, and the more I look at it, the more I find it impossible for me to sing it; I dare not ask Mr Hendell to change the Songs for fear he should suspect (as is very likely) every other reason but the true one. Do you believe if I was to wait on Lady Darlinton to beg her to use that power over him (which to be sure she must have) to get it done, that she would give herself that trouble [?]

Anastasia continued by spelling out some of her problems:

I am very sensible the Musick of my Part is exstreamly fine, but I am as sure the Caracter causes it to be of that kind, which no way suits my Capacity: those songs that require fury and passion to express them, can never be performed by me according to the intention of the Composer, and it is as true as strange, that I am a Woman and cannot scold. My request is, that if it be possible (as sure it is) the words of my second song *Pensa spietata Madre* should be changed, and instead of reviling Gismonda with her cruelty, to keep on the thought of the Recitativo and perswade her to beg her Sons life of Ottone . . . I have some difficultys also in the last I sing, but for fear that by asking too much I might be refus'd all, I dare not mention them.[3]

With or without the help of Lady Darlington, Anastasia got her way. 'Pensa, spietata madre' was indeed replaced by the heart-stopping tenderness of 'Ah! tu non sai', and the undemanding 'Nel tuo sangue' was added. Far from threatening to throw her out of the window for having made bullying demands, Handel recognized the genuine distress of an unconfident and gentle woman, and made the necessary changes.

Ottone opened at last on 12th January 1723. The King was in attendance that night, and other members of the royal family came ten days later. There would be fourteen magnificent performances, and Cuzzoni was a sensation. As Monsieur de Fabrice wrote again to Count Flemming, just after the premiere: 'In the end the famous Cozzuna not merely arrived but even sang in a new opera by Hendell, called Othon – the same subject as the one in Dresden – with enormous success; the house was full to overflowing. Today is the second performance and there is such a run on it that tickets are already being sold at 2 and 3 guineas which are ordinarily half a guinea, so that it is like another Mississippi or South Sea Bubble.'[4]

The *London Journal*, too, on 19th January, noted public admiration for Cuzzoni: 'His Majesty was at the Theatre in the Hay-Market, when Seigniora Cotzani performed, for the first Time, to the Surprize and Admiration of a numerous Audience, who are ever too fond of Foreign Performers. She is already jump'd into a handsome Chariot and an Equipage accordingly. The Gentry seem to have so high a Taste of her fine Parts, that she is likely to be a great Gainer by them.'[5]

But from those who still harboured disbelief in the whole notion of Italian opera for English audiences, there was incredulity. John Gay wrote bitterly to Swift:

As for the reigning amusements of the town, it is entirely music; real fiddles, base-viols, and hautboys, not poetical harps, lyres and reeds. There is nobody allowed to say, 'I sing', but an eunuch, or an Italian woman. Everybody is grown now as great a judge of music, as they were in your time of poetry, and folks, that could not distinguish one tune from another, now daily dispute about the different styles of Handel, Bononcini, and Attilio. People have now forgotten Homer, and Virgil, and Caesar, or at least, they have lost their ranks; for, in London and Westminster, in all polite conversations, Senesino is daily voted to be the greatest man that ever lived.[6]

While *Ottone*'s performances continued, Senesino, Cuzzoni and Durastanti performed also in Ariosti's *Coriolano* and Bononcini's *Erminia*. Without doubt they were highly paid, but they earned every penny of their salaries as they learned, rehearsed and performed up to three operas at the same time – a punishing discipline that would not be tolerated by most singers of later eras. *Ottone*'s final performance, on 26th March, was a benefit night for Cuzzoni. She sang three new arias, and was rewarded handsomely ('some of the Nobility gave her 50 Guinea's a ticket'[7]). Meanwhile Handel was writing the season's final offering, *Flavio*, to a libretto by Haym. Although it is set in a seat of political power (and indeed could be interpreted as a satirical attack on Walpole and his current policies), it is also a domestic comedy, and perhaps its lightness and brevity reflected fatigue at the end of six gruelling months. Nevertheless, *Flavio* was popular with the public, and there were eight well-supported performances.

It was however in that season that the first signs emerged of tensions within the Royal Academy of Music. Fabrice, in his letter to Count Flemming, had observed, '. . . there exist two factions, the one supporting Hendell, the other Bononcini, the one for Cenesino and the other for Cossuna. They are as much at loggerheads as the Whigs and Tories, and even on occasion sow dissension among the Directors.'[8]

Londoners had ever been accustomed to drawing sides, whether for the King against the Prince of Wales, for the Whigs against the Tories, for the Protestants against the Jacobite Catholics. Now, they were similarly lined up in support of either Handel or Bononcini.

The King's annual donation of £1,000 to the Royal Academy of Music was received in June, and the directors immediately chose to spend it on a substantial refurbishment 'by some of the best Masters'[9] of the King's Theatre in the Haymarket. Handel too, fortified by the healthy state of his own personal finances, turned his attention to builders and decorators. His royal pension, originally bestowed by Queen Anne, had recently been doubled. In February 1723 he had received the title of 'Composer of Musick for his Majesty's Chappel Royal', while his position as Music Master to the King's granddaughters was formalized, possibly in recognition of his loyal allegiance to the Hanoverian royal family in the midst of recent Catholic disarray. British composers may have felt some resentment at Handel's rise in court circles. The head of the musical establishment at the Chapel Royal and at Westminster Abbey was William Croft, whose own compositions had been regularly deployed at routine services in both venues, and for some special events too, not least the coronation of King George, in 1714. On the other side of town Maurice Greene had, in 1718, aged only twenty-two, become organist at St Paul's Cathedral, where he continued to welcome Handel to play its mighty organ (and indeed acted as his bellows blower). Both Croft and Greene could well have surmised that not only the throne, but now important musical positions, too, were becoming overrun by foreigners; and perhaps it was at about this time that Handel himself began tactfully and tactically to think about becoming a naturalized British subject. Certainly there was never a notion of returning permanently to his homeland. Rather, with the security of his royal stipends, of his Academy 'sallary' and the returns from his investments, he sought positively to put down roots.

In the summer of 1723, Handel moved into a newly built terraced house in Brook Street, Mayfair, part of a huge development on the Grosvenor Estate. This was a good address in a good part of London: by 1736, it was described as 'For the most part nobly built and inhabited by People of Quality'.[10] Number 25, of which Handel was the first occupant, was one of four adjoining houses, each on three floors with a basement and attic. Those three main floors, between the kitchens in the basement and the servants' quarters in the attic, all had a larger front room, a smaller back room, and a closet; and Handel not only lived here but based his entire working operation here too. On the ground floor, where he would have eaten all his meals, he may have initially set up Schmidt (or Smith, as he now was) to make scores and orchestral parts, before that operation became too large; later he sold his music, and tickets or subscriptions to his concerts, from there. On the first floor, he used the larger front room as a rehearsal space for coaching his singers, and the smaller back room as a study in which to compose. Both rooms had keyboard instruments (a harpsichord, a chamber organ or a clavichord) in them. Above this floor, there was the main bedroom at the front, and a dressing room, with its attached closet, at the back. Here Handel lived and worked, in genteel if unostentatious comfort, for the rest of his life.

Handel now began to enjoy his stability and independence. There were many positive elements in his life: financial and domestic freedom, court approbation, the Royal Academy of Music, the best singers and musicians in Europe, a supportive team in his workshop, and, for the most part, trusted and invigorating colleagues. Sharing much of his success was Nicola Haym, his collaborator now for a decade. The immensely gifted cellist-librettist had been literally at Handel's side in the conception, the composition, and most significantly the performance, of five operas thus far (*Teseo*, *Amadigi*, *Radamisto*, *Ottone* and *Flavio*). As they prepared together in Brook Street for the Academy's new season, their collaboration would reach astonishing new heights.

∽

The season opened on 27th November, with operas by all three of its composers, Bononcini (*Farnace*), Handel (a revival of *Ottone*) and Ariosti (*Vespasiano*). All the stars of the previous year were re-engaged, including Anastasia Robinson, whose vulnerability and vocal insecurity cannot have been eased by London society's growing disapproval of her relationship with Lord Peterborough, to whom she was now secretly married. They had spent the summer in Paris together (he was about to become British ambassador there), she giving concerts with Bononcini, who had rewarded their friendship by dedicating *Farnace* to Lord Peterborough. Back in London, there was a bizarre backstage incident at a performance of *Vespasiano*, when Senesino was provocatively over-amorous in his scenes with Anastasia, described by the disapproving Lady Mary Wortley Montagu as 'the too-near approach of Senesino in the opera'.[11] After the performance, Lord Peterborough physically attacked Senesino, in front of the whole cast. The public too was in uproar: the *Weekly Journal* reported 'a civic Broil . . . among the Subscribers . . . which turned all the Harmony into Discord';[12] and the pamphlet writers continued to make gleeful hay from this episode, fuelling the belief that the opera world was full of ill-mannered and selfish hotheads.

Though he cannot have been unaware of it, Handel remained blissfully aloof from this particular brouhaha. Aside from his royal obligations, his chief focus was on the Haymarket's next production, on which he had been working with Haym, in Brook

Street, for several months. He was normally a prodigiously fast worker, but on this occasion he took his time, rethinking, adjusting and improving. The end product of this unprecedented and painstaking activity was *Giulio Cesare*, arguably Handel's greatest opera, and indeed one of the greatest operas from the whole of the eighteenth century. Almost twice as long as its predecessor, *Flavio*, *Giulio Cesare* is in a class of its own. Every aspect of it – its musical range and invention, its dramatic credibility, its pace, its characterization, the very sweep of its theatrical narration – is consistently excellent. Yet again, Handel had raised the bar.

The complex plot begins at the point in history when Cesare (Julius Caesar), having defeated Pompeio (Pompey) in Greece, is now in Egypt, where Cleopatra and her deranged brother, Tolomeo (Ptolomy), are joint rulers. Cesare has negotiated a peaceful settlement with Pompeio's widow, Cornelia, and son, Sesto (Sextus); but Tolomeo delivers Pompeio's severed head to them, igniting outrage in Cesare, traumatized despair in Cornelia, and a passionate determination for revenge in Sesto. Cleopatra too is appalled by her brother's action and allies herself to Cesare, at the same time using her not inconsiderable wiles to enchant him. Tolomeo's general, Achilla, instructed to guard Cornelia, in fact falls for her and changes sides too. It is young Sesto who, joining with Cesare to lead a revolt, eventually kills Tolomeo. Cleopatra, with Cesare at her side, welcomes their former enemies, Cornelia and Sesto, and is proclaimed Queen of Egypt.

The action of *Giulio Cesare* is constant, varied, and spectacular. All six characters are strongly drawn and their motivations exceptionally clear. This is not at all the standard two-couples-plus-supporters structure, with pairs of lovers singing duets and a tidy resolution at the denouement. Here, plot strands are much more sophisticated and surprising, with gruesome shocks, alluring interludes, a duet rather between mother and son, and a triumphant outcome which nevertheless embraces both tragedy and nobility. The audacity of the libretto and its construction inspired the greatest invention from Handel too. The whole score is of a dazzling quality, from its recitatives driving the action, through its matchless sections of accompanied recitative (where the action is similarly propelled, but enhanced by greater musical succulence), to aria after aria for every possible affect, to duets and greater ensembles. The orchestra Handel deployed was richer by the addition of four horns, and arrestingly adorned by a stage band of exotic instruments for a scene in which Cleopatra lays on a vision of Mount Parnassus as part of her seduction of Cesare. Here nine musicians represent the Muses, playing a harp, viola da gamba and theorbo, plus the more standard string quartet, oboe and bassoon. One number includes another spectacular violin solo for the leader of the orchestra, Pietro Castrucci (Handel continued to reward his gifted colleagues in the pit with challenging moments of exposure), and in general the orchestral palette too is constantly varied as the numbers ensue.

After the cool reception afforded to both Bononcini's *Farnace* and Ariosti's *Vespasiano*, the Haymarket singers must have been thrilled with their new opera. They had considerably more to learn than for any other opera hitherto, but they cannot have failed to appreciate their collective progression out of forlorn mediocrity. Cuzzoni, as Cleopatra, had the lion's share: eight arias, two accompanied recitatives, a duet and the final chorus, while Senesino, as Cesare, had seven arias, two accompanied recitatives, that same duet and the final chorus. Anastasia Robinson and Margherita Durastanti, as Cornelia and Sesto, had respectively five and four arias, plus their mother–son duet and the final chorus; there were five arias also for Berenstadt as Tolomeo, and three for the redoubtable Boschi as Achilla. The role of Cleopatra was surely the greatest and most enduringly brilliant – relished by generations of sopranos ever since – that Handel wrote for Cuzzoni. Powerful, mercurial, selfish, manipulatively sexy, yet capable too of great tenderness, Cleopatra is as multifaceted as is her Shakespearian counterpart. She even disguises herself as a slave girl in order to gain anonymous access to Cesare. And Handel revelled in her every aspect. There are hugely challenging coloratura flourishes in the forthright 'Da tempesta', sensuously alluring lines in 'V'adoro, pupille' (on 'Mount Parnassus', with its little onstage orchestra of Muses), there is heart-rending despair in 'Piangerò la sorte mia', and genuine tenderness – even, at last, some selflessness – in the accompanied recitative in which she bids farewell to the weeping maidservants who are to be taken from her ('Voi, che mi fide ancelle'). Cleopatra remains one of the most challenging and most rewarding roles in the entire soprano repertoire.

In the title role, Senesino was likewise stretched to the full: his Cesare is both military commander and besotted lover. His aggression, shown in no fewer than four coloratura arias, calls on his famously brilliant technique; and his military cunning is also expressed in the extraordinary 'Va tacito e nascosto', in which he resolves to get the better of Tolomeo by acting like an astute huntsman. The music prowls threateningly, and Senesino's slow, quiet, intense vocal line is supported by one of Handel's four horns to complete the aural picture of a hunting scene. Balancing the heroic numbers are arias of gradual infatuation with Cleopatra: 'Non è si vago e bello', after he first sees her (a seemingly innocuous allegro, nonetheless redolent of aroused curiosity) and 'Se infiorito' (after the Mount Parnassus extravaganza), with Castrucci's solo violin and some inner textural richness from two bassoons, as well as oboes. And in the third act Cesare's soliloquy is a remarkable scena of accompanied recitative and slow aria, in which he expresses loss and despair. After all this, Cesare and Cleopatra come together for a final duet of almost shallow lightheartedness, in a brisk 12/8, a cynical indication perhaps that the partnership between them, like that of Senesino and Cuzzoni themselves, is ultimately a fragile union of political expediency.

While admirably serving his two stars, Handel reserved his deepest emotion for the secondary level of singer. Both Robinson and Durastanti, as Cornelia and Sesto, were given ravishing and truly heartfelt music, not least in the tragic duet between them ('Son nata/nato a sospirar'), which closes the first act. And Berenstadt, as the unhinged Tolomeo, had appropriately wild arias – violent, disjointed, illogical. The recitatives too are dramatic and vibrant, perfectly realized by Handel with his unerring instinct for natural dialogue supported and enhanced by the revelatory language of harmonic progression. The singers cannot have failed to be aware, as they studied, memorized and rehearsed *Giulio Cesare*, that they had moved up a level. And this marked leap in quality, even in the context of Handel's customary excellence, is a reflection too of the very distinction of those singers. Handel would not have written such music if his cast, whom he now knew so well, could not have delivered it. Difficult though some of them may have been, these gifted people enabled Handel to produce one of his very finest scores, which in itself is a tribute to them.

Giulio Cesare opened at the Haymarket Theatre on 24th February 1724. It had thirteen sold-out performances, by far the longest run of any opera that season. It was dedicated, by Haym, to Caroline, Princess of Wales. This was a pertinent reminder of

the close association between the German composer and the Hanoverians at court. Haym's customarily flowery prose proclaimed that
'if [Handel] has the fortune to meet Your Royal Highness's approval
he will have nothing else to wish for.' There were some opera-goers
who complained, possibly at *Giulio Cesare*'s length, including the
Lancaster poet, John Byrom, who wrote to his wife, 'I . . . went to
the opera of Julius Caesar . . . It was the first entertainment of this
nature that I ever saw, and will I hope be the last, for of all the diversions of the town I least of all enter into this.'[13] Nevertheless,
there was now no question that Handel was the brightest star in
London's social and artistic firmament.

By the end of the 1723–4 season, the members of the Haymarket company were physically exhausted, and some of them
decided that they had had enough. Margherita Durastanti
announced her retirement (prematurely, as it happened), and
enjoyed the lavish fruits of a benefit concert mounted to mark it.
A decidedly unchivalrous Mr Le Coq reported to Count Ernst
Christoph Manteuffel, also in Dresden:

Durastanti . . . retired on the day of her benefit with a cantata
in praise of the English nation. She said that she was making
way for younger enchantresses. That one day brought her more
than a thousand pounds sterling. Her benefit last year brought
in nearly as much, not to mention her salary of 1200 guineas a
year. Have you ever heard, Monseigneur, of prodigality and
favour to equal this towards a woman [already] old, whose voice
is both mediocre and worn out? That is what the English are
like.[14]

Anastasia Robinson too, after her two years of social and vocal
discomfort, retreated quietly into her private life with Lord

Peterborough; and the castrato secondo uomo, Gaetano Berenstadt, went back to Italy. Bononcini, whose operas had been upstaged by those of Handel at the Academy, was also on the verge of returning home to Italy, but was at the last minute snatched up by none other than Henrietta, the new Duchess of Marlborough (she had become a duchess in her own right after the death of her father). Like her mother Sarah, Henrietta was a notable eccentric, but she had kept in contact with Bononcini after his composition of the funeral music for the great Duke, in 1722, and now she offered him an irresistible annual stipend of £500 to direct private concerts at her residences in London and Blenheim. He would remain in this undemanding post for the next ten years.

Anastasia Robinson was replaced by an Italian mezzo-soprano, Anna Dotti, and Berenstadt by Andrea Pacini, known to Senesino from their time together in Venice some fifteen years previously. Most interestingly, the Academy also engaged a tenor, Francesco Borosini, and one moreover not in the first flush of youth – he was approaching forty, which at that time was elderly for a singer. Hitherto, tenors had not featured prominently in Handel's Haymarket company. Two obscure Italians, Baldassare Benedetti and Matteo Berselli, had taken small roles in 1720 and 1721, together with the unlikely Scot, Alexander Gordon, who had created Tiridate in *Radamisto* in 1720, but been replaced by the bass, Boschi, as soon as the Italians had arrived from Dresden. There was as yet no expectation at all of tenors assuming heroic or amorous leading roles. But the older Borosini arrived just as Handel was composing an opera with a crucial father–daughter relationship, and Borosini's experience and dramatic talents were welcome and useful. The cast structures of the new season would be subtly recalibrated.

While the Academy sought to refill its singer roster in the summer of 1724, it made no such effort with regard to its composers. Bononcini was not replaced; his workload was merely redistributed between Handel and Ariosti, who would each supply two new operas in the forthcoming season. Ariosti produced *Artaserse* and *Dario*, but Handel's contribution was by far the greater. He opened the season in October with *Tamerlano*, revived *Giulio Cesare* at the beginning of January, and followed these with *Rodelinda* in February. And, as if all this were not enough, for the final production, he arranged a pasticcio – a collection of arias from several other composers, linked by his own new recitatives – entitled *Elpidia*. There were to be sixty-two performances that season at the Haymarket theatre, and forty-six of them were Handel's. It was not however a mere numerical triumph. The confluence of *Giulio Cesare*, *Tamerlano* and *Rodelinda* in the same season was probably the peak of all Handel's achievements, in whatever discipline. Both the new works, *Tamerlano* and *Rodelinda*, were shorter than the mighty *Giulio Cesare* (around thirty numbers each, compared to *Cesare*'s forty-four), but their quality, invention, variety and narrative integrity were in the same vein as those of their illustrious predecessor. Yet again, the immensely hard-working singers, now more than ever deserving of their vast wages, were rewarded with unparalleled material.

The libretto of *Tamerlano* was reworked by Haym from a version written by Piovene for Gasparini, in Venice, in 1711, and Handel began drafting his score in July 1723. But when the new singers arrived, the tenor, Francesco Borosini, brought with him a later version of the opera, also by Gasparini, called *Il Bajazet*, in which Borosini himself had played the title role, and which had a magnificent finale incorporating a death scene. Borosini was no doubt keen that this scene should appear in the new London version. Sure enough, Handel, ever alert to arresting development, seized on the new material and considerably revised what he had already composed.

The plot concerns the Tartar Emperor, Tamerlano (Tamburlaine), his tyrannical treatment of his Turkish captives, the Emperor Bajazet and his daughter, Asteria, and Asteria's secret liaison with Tamerlano's ally, the Greek Prince Andronico. Although he is betrothed to Irene, Princess of Trebizond, Tamerlano also falls for Asteria and proposes to take her as his wife, freeing her father, if she accepts him, and passing Irene over to Andronico. He tells Andronico that Asteria has agreed to this plan; Andronico and Asteria quarrel. When Tamerlano invites Asteria to sit beside him on the throne, Bajazet throws himself on the floor, instructing his daughter to mount the throne only by walking, literally, over his prostrate body. Asteria produces a knife, with which she has intended all along to kill Tamerlano, who, enraged, threatens everyone with death. Bajazet is to be returned to his prison. Asteria, reduced to a slave, now tries to administer poison to Tamerlano, but Irene prevents Tamerlano from sipping it, at which point Bajazet surprises everyone by drinking it himself. Tamerlano, shocked and appeased, at last resolves to give Asteria to Andronico, and to marry Irene after all.

This intense story was a perfect foil for *Giulio Cesare*. It continued the theme of innocence and integrity clashing with a dangerous potentate; but, unlike *Giulio Cesare* with its Egyptian locations and seashores, *Tamerlano*'s action is all confined in enclosed spaces, the two most dramatic scenes happening in a throne room and a prison. Focusing as it does on bravery, self-sacrifice and an overwhelming sense of propriety in the face of bullying aggression, *Tamerlano* is the most human yet of all

Handel's operas, and once more his cast members were all provided with hugely fulfilling roles. Cuzzoni and Senesino (who
clearly never did villains) were Asteria and Andronico. Their
courage and love occupy the centre ground of the opera, and
again their music, including a magnificent duet, is its major part.
But dramatically both Tamerlano (Pacini) and especially Bajazet
(Borosini) are spectacular roles too. Tamerlano's music gives clear
evidence of Pacini's great coloratura technique, while Borosini's
Bajazet was stretched in many directions, not least in his requested final scene, where Handel was at his most brilliantly
inventive. Anna Dotti, the replacement for Anastasia Robinson,
sang Irene's five good arias, and the faithful Boschi, returning for
his eighth Handel role, was given his moments in the spotlight
with two decent arias. Handel reflected the internal, literally
chamber settings of the narrative with similar modesty of orchestration. There are no brass instruments at all (no outdoor fanfares
or hunting analogies), and the only variant on the basic instrumentation of strings, oboes, bassoons and continuo, is pairs of
recorders and flutes, possibly even some early clarinets, in the
most tender numbers.

Of Senesino's nine arias, the first, 'Bella Asteria', is an intimate
and heartfelt soliloquy, a solemn outpouring of love performed
by the opera's star and its creators (Handel on harpsichord,
Haym on cello). As with Cuzzoni's notorious 'Falsa imagine' in
Ottone, or Sesto's 'Cara speme' in *Giulio Cesare*, this continuo
aria persuaded the audience to listen in a different way to Andronico and his tender feelings. Again, Senesino's coloratura
('Più d'una tigre') and matchless ability to spin a musical line
('Cerco in vano') are well exploited, and he had many accompanied recitatives too. Cuzzoni similarly had opportunities to
emphasize her sublime lyricism ('Se non mi vuol amar', 'Se

1. Handel's birthplace, in Halle.

2. Handel's baptism certificate, in the Register
of the Marktkirche, 24th February 1685.

3. Queen Anne

4. George I

5. Aaron Hill, the prescient Londoner who first engaged Handel in 1710.

6. James Brydges, later 1st Duke of Chandos, who employed Handel at his palatial country home, Cannons.

7. Francesco Bernardi,
known as 'Senesino':
one of Handel's
greatest, and most
tiresome, singers.

8. The soprano
Francesca Cuzzoni,
whom Handel once
threatened with
defenestration.

9. Faustina Bordoni, always known as Faustina: her rivalry with Cuzzoni aroused passionate confrontations among their audiences.

10. The opera banner in Hogarth's print *The Bad Taste of the Town* shows Cuzzoni literally raking in piles of money at the opera house.

11. 25 Brook Street: Handel's home from the summer of 1723 until his death there in 1759.

12. Handel's right-hand man, J. C. Smith.

13. Handel's autograph score of his Coronation anthem 'Zadok the Priest', with its brilliantly controlled opening.

14. Scenography for the final scene of Handel's *Giulio Cesare*.

15. George II

16. Queen Caroline

potessi un dì placare'); and her slow aria after the suicide of her father ('Padre amato', in F sharp minor), with its contrasting section of coloratura rage towards Tamerlano, is one of the most extraordinary in the opera. There is an interesting duet for the two castratos, Senesino and Pacini, 'Coronata da gigli e di rose', at the very end, when, moved by Bajazet's death, the placated Tamerlano turns his corner and joins his Greek ally in magnanimity. And here the hyperactivity of the accompanying string writing suggests that this may have been another solo violin moment for Castrucci.

One of the chief features of *Tamerlano* is its increased dramatic energy. The two climactic scenes, in the throne room and in the prison, move with unprecedented musico-dramatic pace, because Handel breaks or discards all the rules. After Asteria's failed attempt to assassinate Tamerlano, she and her father are briefly reunited, in what would be an emotional duet, except that, across it, Tamerlano is raging furiously; this is therefore a highly sophisticated trio of two people versus one. When Tamerlano storms out, Asteria addresses the remaining characters in turn, asking them if she did the wrong thing. One by one they reply to her, each with an aria beginning with the word, 'No'. None of these 'No' arias is in the customary da capo form: here Handel gives Bajazet, Andronico and Irene single-section exit arias, brief but intense; and, as they leave her alone at last, she (Cuzzoni) reflects on what she has done, in what is probably her finest aria, 'Se potessi un dì placare'.

But even this tight sequence is as nothing compared to the drama of the music that unfolds in the final prison scene. Bajazet announces that he has taken poison as the only way to release himself from Tamerlano's tyranny. In a series of accompanied recitatives raging against his enemy, and mini-arioso arias in which he tenderly expresses his love for his daughter, interrupted by an outpouring of dismay from Asteria herself, Bajazet moves inexorably towards his onstage death. As the poison at last claims its victim, Bajazet's final words are agonizingly fractured, and dropped effortfully into unexpected parts of the rhythmic meter. The transition between these utterly contrasted musical gestures is as smooth and deft, and just as powerful, as anything written half a century later by Mozart. This sophisticated scena is not just a shocking conclusion to the action, brilliantly realized by Handel; it serves also to underline all the themes of the story: the ultimate defeat of tyrannical oppression, despite the futility of resistance; the triumph therefore of good over evil; and, as it happens, the bond too between parent and child. Here the father–daughter relationship to an extent develops the mother–son relationship of Cornelia and Sesto, in *Giulio Cesare*. After all these harrowing events, another convention, the final 'coro' in which all the characters unite for a moralistic conclusion, is different again. 'D'atra notte già mirasi a scorno' is solemn and pensive, and in a minor key. And it lacks not only a tenor line, for Bajazet lies dead on the stage, but a soprano line too, for the distraught Asteria is weeping over her father's corpse.

Handel's engagement with the extreme human predicament in *Tamerlano* is unprecedented. The immense trouble that he took, over the summer of 1724, just as he had with the writing of *Giulio Cesare*, making changes, moving arias, tightening recitatives, and totally rewriting his final scene as his singer arrived with irresistible new material, paid theatrical dividends. *Tamerlano* is one of Handel's darkest operas, and certainly one of his most brilliant. It opened on 31st October 1724. According to Lady Bristol, who wrote to her husband as soon as she got home, 'the Royal Family were all there, and a greater crowd than I ever saw'.[15] There were nine more performances through the month of November. But although the houses were full, reaction to *Tamerlano* was mixed. Audiences were perhaps perplexed by what they had seen: by an unconventional ending (not by any means a standard *lieto fine*, or happy ending), and perhaps, too, by the disjunct nature of what they had heard. Lady Bristol continued her letter by informing her husband that the opera had 'tired me to death, so that I am come home to go to bed as soon as I have finished this'; and the notoriously unmusical Lady Mary Wortley Montagu described the whole evening as 'execrable'.[16] The new contralto Anna Dotti, it seems, was by no means in Anastasia Robinson's league, and was cruelly mocked. After the sensational and universal acclaim of *Giulio Cesare*, *Tamerlano*'s less than ecstatic reaction restored London's opera audiences to their slightly fractious norm.

Not that Handel or any of his cast would have had much time to notice. The singers immediately went on to rehearse and perform Ariosti's *Artaserse*, and then to put together a revival of *Giulio Cesare*, no less. Anna Dotti now played Cornelia; Pacini moved from one crazed potentate to another, and sang Tolomeo; and, most extraordinarily, the elderly tenor, Borosini, was cast as the young boy, Sesto. Handel had to do some more rewriting to accommodate all these changes. There was a new aria for Pacini, and three for Borosini, which carefully showed the older Sesto as less of an excitable youth, more of a considered young man. But a real casualty of the recasting was the loss of the glorious Sesto–Cornelia duet, for it would no longer work with the octave displacement of a tenor Sesto. Handel shortened the recitatives throughout the opera, and cut completely two very small roles (Curio and Nireno) – though, towards the end of the ten-performance run, he reinstated Nireno as Nirena, with two new arias for a soprano, Benedetta Sorosina. (This was perhaps some sort of audition process, with Handel trying out a newcomer to the company; if so, Sorosina failed it, for she never reappeared.) The run of *Giulio Cesare* ended on 9th February, just four days before these indefatigable singers opened in their next new opera, *Rodelinda*, yet another masterpiece.

Handel and Haym had been working on *Rodelinda* for some weeks, exerting on it the same care that they had on its two predecessors. The story was taken ultimately from a *tragedie* by Corneille, but principally from a libretto by Salvi, which Haym skilfully adapted. (Handel would turn to Salvi librettos for six later operas.) Another plot with labyrinthine turns, this tells of the Kingdom of Lombardy, which has been usurped by Grimoaldo; the rightful King Bertarido, whose sister, Eduige, is betrothed to Grimoaldo, has fled, leaving behind his wife, Rodelinda, and their young son. Grimoaldo now desires Rodelinda for himself and rejects Eduige. Bertarido returns in disguise and, with the help of his sister and his councillor Unulfo, is briefly reunited with Rodelinda, but Grimoaldo seizes and imprisons him. Eduige throws a sword into Bertarido's cell, and with it Bertarido wounds Unulfo, whom he mistakes for the enemy executioner. Nevertheless they manage to escape through an underground passage. Rodelinda and her son find blood in the dungeon and now believe Bertarido to be dead. Grimoaldo becomes delirious with jealousy and uncertainty, and falls into a sleep. His ally Garibaldo turns traitor and attempts to kill him. It is Bertarido who intervenes, and kills Garibaldo. Grimoaldo recognizes Bertarido's noble act, renounces his own claim to the throne, and reunites Bertarido with his family. He will rule instead in Pavia, with Eduige as his wife.

For all its political and military context, *Rodelinda* is, like *Tamerlano*, essentially a domestic story about relationships, not warfare: married love is its strongest thread. Loyalty and courage, too, are important elements, and the use of disguise, the support of a second woman (here, the role of Eduige is similar to that of Irene), the rejection of unwanted suitors and a scene in a prison cell all continue themes from the previous opera. Again, characterization is exceptionally strong, especially in the case of the title role herself. Steadfast, defiant, yet tender and passionate, and with a darker vulnerability that allows her moments of suicidal despair, Rodelinda was, for Cuzzoni, yet another creation of many facets. Once more Handel responded with varied music which illuminated the supreme gifts of his star singer. On the one hand, she mourns Bertarido, whom she believes to be dead, in 'Ho perduto il mio caro sposo', or 'Ombre, piante', with its added flutes for pathos; on the other, she shows spirit and force (and Cuzzoni's coloratura) in rejecting Grimoaldo, in 'L'empio rigor', or 'Morrai, si'. Perhaps her greatest scene is that towards the end of the second act, when she is told that Bertarido is still alive, at which point she sings the siciliano, 'Ritorna o cara', radiant with tender and exquisite joy. But after the briefest of reunions with her husband – there is no duet yet, for they are interrupted – and some excellent dramatic recitative incorporating Bertarido's prison and death sentence, the duet that does ensue is one of shared grief: 'Io t'abbraccio', in Handel's key of anguish, F sharp minor. When, on the discovery of bloodstained clothes in the prison cell, Rodelinda again believes she has lost her husband, she sings yet another lament, 'Se mio duol non è si forte', with flutes again added for colour and pathos, and with divided bassoons at the heart of the texture. Altogether Cuzzoni sang nine arias or duets in addition to the final chorus. Absorbing and memorizing all these while performing Cleopatra in the revival of *Giulio Cesare* was a phenomenal feat of stamina, made all the more so by

131

the fact that she was pregnant at the time. However ungracious Horace Walpole was ('she was . . . not a good actress; dressed ill; and was silly and fantastical'[17]), Cuzzoni was truly a woman of remarkable talent and extraordinary fortitude.

Senesino too was widely stretched as he prepared Bertarido's seven arias at the same time as he was performing Cesare. He will have relished his first appearance, returning to his kingdom in disguise (as a Hungarian, apparently – '*vestito all'Ungara*') and entering the cemetery to read the funerary inscription on his own tomb. A tense accompanied recitative seamlessly becomes the E major lament, 'Dove sei?', one of Handel's best-loved arias. More accompanied recitative later in the act leads to a coloratura aria to end it, 'Confusa si miri', as he believes Rodelinda thinks him dead and has accepted another. Senesino's best music comes in the second act, with his trademark soliloquy set in a '*luogo delizio*', and a truly beguiling echo aria, 'Con rauco mormorio'. This siciliano portrait of nature is warmly scored for recorders and flutes as well as bassoons again in the middle of the orchestral palette, and the answering effects are by no means limited to one instrument: various combinations of winds and strings alternate unexpectedly in the truly unpredictable manner of a natural environment. This scena contains Senesino's most enchanting music, but his most powerful comes in the prison scene. Just as he had done in *Tamerlano*, Handel relishes a claustrophobic space and creates the tense aria, 'Chi di voi', with a slow pace and in the darkest key of B flat minor. Here too Handel breaks the rules: this is not a da capo aria turning back on itself, for it is interrupted by the arrival of Unulfo, with its disastrous consequences. Bertarido attacks his friend, whom he has failed to recognize in the dark. The loyal friendship between the two men is in itself another of the strengths of *Rodelinda*, and Bertarido's final aria, 'Se fiera belva', with its forthright coloratura in C major, is a confirmation of gratitude towards Unulfo.

Once again the brilliant Cuzzoni and Senesino carried the opera with their rich musical characterizations so deftly supplied by Handel's ever-fertile invention. But the other singers played their part too, especially the remarkable tenor, Borosini, as the multilayered Grimoaldo, a villain with redeeming features – not least a conscience. Continuing to exploit the intense dramatic focus that Borosini had shown in *Tamerlano* – especially in Bajazet's final scene – here too, in the third act, Handel gives Grimoaldo an extended solo scena, with several contrasting sections, at the end of which he falls into his delirious sleep. In the first part, an accompanied recitative of broken sentences punctuated by wildly scurrying strings, Grimoaldo is in imaginary dialogue with the Furies. Gradually his violent energy subsides into an exhausted larghetto in F sharp minor (that key of anguish again), deceptively seductive as it seems to promise a full aria of calm and returning sanity. But this cannot be sustained; the sensuously moving strings sink into static chords as Grimoaldo's energy ebbs away. The ensuing siciliano aria, 'Pastorello', is quietly implicit of an unhinged mind: there are tiny internal repetitions and a fragmented line in the opening ritornello, matched by vocal phrases of self-pity and defeat. Grimoaldo literally sings himself to sleep, as Handel made clear in his stage direction.

Even in rehearsal this new opera was generating excitement, as the Scottish tenor, Alexander Gordon, reported. Since his appearances in *Radamisto* and *Flavio*, Gordon had given up singing for a career as a scholar, author and publisher. He was nonetheless still in contact with Handel and his colleagues at the Haymarket company, and visited them all there, as he described in a letter to Sir John Clark on 12th February: 'Having the liberty of the house

I went to the opera house & heard Julius Caesar which pleasd me exceedingly but the new one to be acted for the first time next Saturday exceeds all I ever heard.'[18]

Gordon's judgement was not wrong. *Rodelinda* duly opened on the following day and was another instant success. Like *Giulio Cesare* and *Tamerlano*, it was immediately published by Walsh, and the impressive list of subscribers included Charles Jennens and Newburgh Hamilton, who would both become librettists for Handel in later decades. There were fourteen performances of *Rodelinda*, and there would have been a fifteenth had one not been cancelled through the illness of Senesino. The Royal Academy of Music was at the crest of a wave. And yet what followed, in the season's two remaining productions, was already the sound of a distant death-knell.

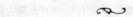

Four days after the last performance of *Rodelinda*, Ariosti's *Dario* opened. Ariosti was the oldest of the three composers who had been thrown into collegiality in the Haymarket, and the least combative. If there was a healthy rivalry, it was between Handel and the now-departed Bononcini. As the season drew to a close, in May 1725, John Byrom (who had been so bored by *Giulio Cesare*) penned his 'Epigram on the Feuds between Handel and Bononcini':

> Some say, compar'd to Bononcini
> That Mynheer Handel's but a Ninny;
> Others aver, that he to Handel
> Is scarcely fit to hold a Candle;
> Strange all this Difference should be
> 'Twixt Tweedle-dum and Tweedle-dee![19]

Byrom was very pleased with his witty sextet, which did the rounds: in Cambridge, for example, it 'made the whole Hall laugh at Trinity College'.[20] But although Ariosti did not have such a high profile as 'Tweedle-dum and Tweedle-dee', he was their highly respected colleague. Perhaps even as early as 1702 (when Ariosti and Bononcini were both working for King George's sister, the Electress of Brandenburg, and may or may not have been visited in Berlin by Handel), their paths had crossed, especially in London. They played in the orchestra for each other's operas, and shared the Academy's composing duties amicably enough. Ariosti had recently published a collection, dedicated to the King, of cantatas and pieces for his instrument, the viola d'amore, for which he claimed to have 764 subscribers. (Later that century, the historian Hawkins would challenge this astonishing statistic, suggesting rather that Ariosti had listed everybody he knew and had therefore solicited, rather than those who had actually paid.) Whether or not he had the backing of the entire House of Lords, Ariosti's star was in fact on the wane. *Dario* was to be his penultimate work for the Academy, and his last new opera, and its six performances were a puny total in comparison with the long runs of Handel's great trio that same season. From now on, Handel's works increasingly dominated the Academy's schedules.

Dario was a damp squib, but the Academy's final production for 1724–5 was something altogether novel, perplexing and, in retrospect, alarming. The directors of the Academy had been in contact again with the colourful Owen Swiney, who had fled so ignominiously from the London opera scene in 1712, with the takings from that night's performance of *Teseo*. Swiney was now living in Venice, from which distance he had apparently, through Nicola Haym, been advising the Academy on Italian singers and composers. Perhaps invited to suggest a work for the season's conclusion, Swiney sent them *L'Elpidia*, a setting by several composers of a libretto by Apostolo Zeno. With an ear to the vocal talents of the Academy's star singers, all of whom he knew well, Swiney had put together a selection of arias and supplied some recitatives as well. But once the score was in London, it was considerably altered. The singers themselves weighed in with suggestions of other arias which would better suit their gifts, and which moreover would already be mastered by them and would not therefore require yet more technical preparation and memorizing at the end of a long season. It was Handel who finally oversaw the complex process of combining all the ingredients into some sort of coherent whole, and who then directed the performances in the Haymarket. *L'Elpidia* was thus the Academy's first pasticcio opera. The emphasis was on music specifically chosen to demonstrate the vocal prowess of the operatic stars, rather than on dramatic continuity and credibility. Coming at the end of a glorious season, including the sophisticated *Giulio Cesare*, *Tamerlano* and *Rodelinda*, the triumph of *L'Elpidia* is chillingly ironic.

Owen Swiney was somewhat tetchy in his Venetian exile, and he begrudged the success that others were enjoying at the Haymarket theatre. Nevertheless, he played a crucial role in contracting for London the great Italian soprano, Faustina Bordoni. Always known simply as Faustina, she, like Cuzzoni, had had great success in her native Venice, where she had been brought up under the tutelage of Alessandro and Benedetto Marcello, and where she had made her debut in 1716, at the age of nineteen. She had recently spread her wings beyond Venice and then beyond Italy, and been contracted also for Munich and Vienna. Faustina and Cuzzoni were almost exactly the same age and voice type, and the Academy had for years wanted to present them both, together with Senesino, and to boast therefore that the three greatest singers of the age were assembled at the Haymarket. In April 1725, the Academy's directors had instructed Swiney to persuade Faustina to come, and by June he had made a special journey to Parma, where she was performing, and signed her, as was baldly announced by the *London Journal* on 4th September: 'Signiora *Faustina*, a famous Italian Lady, is coming over this Winter to rival Signiora *Cuzzoni*'.[21]

It was also reported that Faustina's salary would be £2,500. (In fact, she was to be paid exactly the same as Cuzzoni: £2,000.) Because of her contractual obligations to Vienna in the coming winter, she would not be available until the following spring. But this delay can only have enhanced her reputation in London, among both her future colleagues and, especially, her audiences, as they relished the prospect of more great singing and more fiery internecine warfare.

Although Cuzzoni must have known that she needed to keep her voice in particularly fine and competitive condition, she had other concerns in that summer of 1725. Mrs Pendarves wrote to her sister on 22nd August 1725: 'Mrs Sandoni (who was Cuzzoni) is brought to bed of a daughter: it is a mighty mortification it was not a son. Sons and heirs ought to be out of fashion when such scrubs shall pretend to be dissatisfied at having a daughter: 'tis pity indeed, that the noble name and family of Sandoni should be extinct. The minute she was brought to bed, she sang "La Speranza", a song in Otho.'[22]

Two members of the Haymarket company – the tenor Francesco Borosini, and the castrato Andrea Pacini – decided to head home to Italy. Their participation in Handel's three most recent operas had been the pinnacle of their musical experience: neither would ever again be part of music-making at such a stellar level.

Pacini retired within a few years and entered the priesthood. He was replaced at the Haymarket by another castrato, Antonio Baldi, and Borosini by the tenor Luigi Antinori. Recognizing that Faustina would not be arriving in time for the opening of the following season, the Academy also swiftly contracted another soprano, Livia Constantini. Handel braced himself for operas in which no fewer than three singers must now have equal exposure.

While his Italian colleagues departed for their homeland, and the King too visited Hanover after a two-year gap, Handel stayed in London for the summer, persuaded to do so by what he described, rather vaguely, as 'the state of my affairs'.[23] He wrote an affectionate letter to his brother-in-law, Michael Dietrich Michaelsen, who had recently remarried after the death of Handel's sister. Handel thanked Michaelsen for taking care of his elderly mother, apologized for his continued absence and for the infrequency of his letters, and sent special love to his 'beloved god-daughter', his niece, Johanna Friederika. Handel never sent any of his own news, let alone bragged about his recent successes. His ties to his family were now, in his fortieth year, very loose. For all the challenges, the Academy and Handel's obligations to the Hanoverians at court were rooting him firmly in London. Happily settled in his brand new home in Brook Street, Handel felt more English than German, and his thoughts were turning ever more towards making this a permanent and official arrangement.

The King was also thinking about the future. All too aware that his own accession to the British throne had come about through the deposition of the Stuart line, he was keen to maintain the dynastic health of his own. In cahoots with his daughter, Sophia Dorothea, now somewhat unhappily, albeit comfortably, married to Frederick Wilhelm I of Prussia, and mother of Wilhelmina and Frederick, King George entertained hopes of marrying his grandchildren to each other. Wilhelmina and Frederick would be perfect partners for Frederick and Anne, the two eldest children of the Prince of Wales and Princess Caroline. As Walpole was successfully negotiating a treaty with France and Prussia that summer, it was perhaps an appropriate moment to cement Anglo-Prussian friendship in the time-honoured manner of expedient political matrimony. But despite his regal power the King's machinations were stalled. He had not even consulted the Prince and Princess of Wales, who strongly resisted the proposal, even though they had not seen their eldest child since they had left Hanover in 1714. For once, Caroline found herself on the same side as the King's mistresses, for they too opposed the cousins' marriage. King George and his daughter planned to return to their schemings on his next visit to Hanover, in two years' time.

After the unlikely success of *L'Elpidia*, Swiney, in Venice, was convinced that London audiences needed more pasticcios, and began to bombard his Haymarket colleagues with librettos and scores, all carefully selected according to the vocal capacities of the principal singers. Haym was the chief recipient of Swiney's ideas – and, indeed, of his ire when the Academy refused to adopt all his suggestions – and it was he who set about constructing their second pasticcio, *Elisa*. Haym thus being fully occupied, the Academy approached the disgruntled librettist, Rolli, whom they had dismissed in the Catholic purge of 1722. He now returned to write two librettos for Handel in the coming season, *Scipione* and *Alessandro*, but he was still fundamentally hostile to his host country and to its operatic exploits. Rolli continued to write letters of malicious gossip to his regular correspondents.

One of these, Giuseppe Riva, further disseminated Rolli's edgy perspective in a letter of his own to the great scholar, Lodovico Antonio Muratori, in September 1725. It is a revealing document on many levels.

Riva begins, 'The operas performed in England, fine though they are as regards the music and the voices, are so much hackwork as regards the verses. Our friend Rolli, who was commissioned to compose when the Royal Academy was first formed, wrote really good operas, but having become embroiled with the Directors, the latter took into their services one Haym, a Roman and a violoncellist, who is a complete idiot as far as Letters are concerned.'[24] (That swipe at Haym must surely have originated with Rolli.) Riva goes on to dismiss the Academy's composers, 'with the exception of our compatriot Bononcino', and then to describe a formula, which he sneeringly claims to be that required by English audiences. He rattles off a wild list of arbitrary requirements: the subject matter should be 'straightforward, tender, heroic, Roman, Greek or even Persian, and never Gothic or Longobard'; there should be two equal female parts, for Faustina and Cuzzoni; Senesino's part 'must be heroic'; all the other parts should have three arias each; and there should be a duet at the end of Act II, between the two ladies. But although there were recognizable fragments of accuracy in the format that Riva outlined, it was a mockery of the sort of operas presented thus far by the Academy. As Handel in particular had assembled for a supportive theatre his perfect ingredients – classy singers, a good libretto from a practical colleague, his own instinctive dramatic gifts – he had actually smashed conventions and formulae in order to create powerful narratives endowed with the most inspired music. If there had been a formula, it was of one prima donna (Cuzzoni) and one primo uomo (Senesino), plus a second couple and two others duly ranked behind them. But, ironically, all that was about to change. London would very soon realize the mathematical impossibility of having two leading ladies. As Handel and his colleagues were to discover, in attempting to afford absolute parity to two or three vibrant egos, the very dramatic charge and theatrical energy of opera itself would be compromised and reduced.

∾

The 1725–6 Royal Academy season opened, rather ominously, with a revival of a pasticcio. *L'Elpidia* returned on 30th November for five performances, followed by eight more of *Rodelinda*, with the new singers necessitating some revisions to the musical material. The new pasticcio, *Elisa*, on which poor Haym had laboured so earnestly, opened in January 1726. It was a disaster; the Academy was forced to drop it after only six paltry performances. A revival of the ever-popular *Ottone* was mounted and ran for nine performances. This too required revisions for the new singers. (Cuzzoni still obediently and gratefully sang her 'Falsa imagine', however.) And then at last in March 1726 there was a new opera, albeit not the one originally planned. It had been expected that Faustina would have arrived by then, but she was further delayed – just as Cuzzoni had been before her first London appearance. *Alessandro*, which had been carefully prepared with an even-handed distribution of arias, was temporarily shelved. It was an emergency, and Handel and Rolli rushed to produce a swift substitute. They came up with *Scipione*, which was produced so quickly (in just a few weeks) that its creators did not even have time to think of a dedicatee.

Scipione is another heroic piece with backward glances to

past successes. There is a prison scene, much moral and heroic strength and magnanimity, and some glorious individual numbers, including the now statutory continuo aria ('Dolci auretti') for Cuzzoni. (Handel and Haym really had tamed her there: she completely recognized that intimate moments were just as effective as impressive displays of technical wizardry.) The opera opens with an instrumental march, originally intended for *Alessandro*, but borrowed here for Scipione's triumphal arrival; this has now become *Scipione*'s most celebrated number. But in general, no doubt due to the haste with which it was assembled and perhaps also to Rolli's lack of true dramatic instinct, it was on a decidedly lower level to that of its three great predecessors. As Burney cannily remarked, 'There seems to be less of Handel's accustomed fire, originality and contrivance in the airs . . . than in any of those that preceded this period.'[25] But the public must have liked it well enough, for it ran for thirteen successive performances; and by the time of its last, on 30th April, the great Faustina had arrived.

Just a year younger than Cuzzoni and altogether more striking (indeed she was very beautiful), the twenty-five-year-old Faustina was very assured technically, with exceptional breath control, excellent diction and astonishing agility. She was also a fine actress, with what was clearly total commitment to emotion and situation. As Quantz concluded, and Burney translated, 'in short, she was born for singing and for acting'.[26] But Cuzzoni was the more lyrical and expressive of the two. They should have complemented one another perfectly, especially as Handel was meticulous in giving them equal exposure. But even before they appeared in public, factions were drawn. Cuzzoni's loyal supporters included the King himself, Lady Pembroke, the Duke of Rutland and most of the resident Italian community, led by Rolli,

Riva and Bononcini. London's aristocratic gentlemen were drawn instead to the alluring newcomer, though their wives doggedly maintained their allegiance to Cuzzoni too. By the time *Alessandro* opened, on 5th May, with all the royal family present, there was not a ticket to be had. Within a month, there had been thirteen performances; a fourteenth had devastatingly to be cancelled, along with any possibility of continuing the run, owing to Senesino again falling ill. There was then no notion of the common practice of understudying; if any one of the opera's three stars was indisposed, the performance would be cancelled. It is tempting to wonder just how ill Senesino really was, as, for the second time in two years, he forced the closure of a production. Perhaps his incapacity was induced by his no longer being, literally, centre stage.

As King George attended the opening night, he would have recognized much in *Alessandro*'s plot, for Rolli had based his libretto on *La superbia d'Alessandro*, by Ortensio Mauro and Steffani, first performed in 1690, in Hanover. In that the story concerns Alexander the Great and his equal passion for two women – one a princess, the other a slave – it was a cleverly chosen vehicle for its assembled superstars. Alessandro believed himself to be the son of Jove, and therefore invincible, so the opera also pandered to the vanity of Senesino, even giving him a swashbuckling first entrance, as he literally scales a city wall and destroys it. (This action was perhaps more symbolic than the opera's creators realized.) With the by now familiar ingredients of assembling armies, prison scenes, accusations of treachery and demonstrations of loyalty, the opera moves somewhat predictably towards a double wedding at the end. The characterization is unsubtle (there is none of the brilliant complexity of Cleopatra or Bajazet or Grimoaldo), but the music that Handel supplied for this

unremarkable narrative is superb. All the individual arias for Senesino, Cuzzoni and Faustina reflect their special gifts. For Senesino,
there were fast ones for his famed coloratura ('Vano amore', 'Ri-
solvo abbandonar'), balanced by those of ingenuous simplicity ('Il
cor mio'). For Faustina, whom Handel knew only by report when
he wrote the opera, there were special challenges for her coloratura too ('Alla gabbia d'oro', 'Brilla nell'alma'). Handel of
course knew very well where Cuzzoni's strengths lay, and he gave
her a full palette of expressive eloquence, especially in her trademark siciliano ('Che tirannia d'amor'). The numerical balance of
arias for the three stars was scrupulously observed. Perhaps Handel's skill – and also his barely concealed sense of humour – is at
its most impressive in his construction of the first appearance
of the two women. After Alessandro has destroyed the city wall,
Lisaura (Cuzzoni) and Rossana (Faustina) step onto the stage
simultaneously to survey its ruins. In an accompanied recitative
(that most democratic of devices, for both singers can be included
and given affecting instrumental support, without one dominat-
ing the other), each asks a question: 'Che vidi?', 'Che mirai?'
('What have I seen?'). They then sing together for the final eleven
bars. Territory has been marked. This will not have been lost on
members of the audience, as they delightedly prepared for the
sport to come, and started counting.

But interestingly, in all the accounts of the success of *Alessandro*, there is no hint of any difficulty between Faustina and
Cuzzoni. It was only after its abrupt closure and the departure of
the allegedly ailing Senesino that rumours of friction began to
circulate; these would be eagerly stoked in the following season.
Cuzzoni might perhaps have been disgruntled at not being part-
nered with Senesino at the final outcome of *Alessandro*, but given
her musical prominence throughout the opera, and her constant

bevy of adoring fans, headed by the monarch himself, there is no evidence at all that she felt even slightly threatened by Faustina. Handel's care in crafting their partnership had worked brilliantly.

Handel and his team proposed to follow *Alessandro* with another story already familiar to King George. *L'Alceste*, based on the play by Euripides and with a score by Mattio Trento, had been performed, in 1679, in Hanover, where the then nineteen-year-old Electoral Prince Georg would have seen it. Cannily renaming it as *Admeto*, probably as another sop for Senesino who would again assume the now-title role, Handel and Haym reworked it for London, recognizing its neat balance of good roles for their stars (especially their numerate divas: Faustina could play Admeto's wife, Alceste, and Cuzzoni the Trojan princess, Antigone). There is comedy amongst the Greek tragedy, and real emotion amongst the supernatural elements, and Handel as ever wrote idiomatically for all situations and with his unique understanding of the vocal strengths of his singers. Together with *Admeto*, the Royal Academy proposed, for the 1726–7 season, an opera each by Ariosti and Bononcini. So the original trio of composers was to be reunited, as the Academy directors were happy to declare, as if there had never even been a split: 'after the Excellent Opera composed by Mr. Handel . . . Signior Attilio shall compose one; And Signior Bononcini is to compose the next after that. Thus, as this Theatre can boast of the three best Voices in Europe, and the best Instruments; so the Town will have the Pleasure of hearing these three different Stiles of composing.'[27]

Unfortunately, each of those 'three best Voices in Europe' was to let the Academy down. Senesino was first: his rapid departure to Italy after the closure of *Alessandro* extended to an absence of several months. He sent messages of continued indisposition through illness, although he had been spotted by Owen Swiney in Bologna in mid-August, evidently in perfect health. In fact Senesino had been buying land and property in and around Siena, and was spending much happy time and passion (and those lavish London fees) on remodelling his city palazzo. The exasperated Academy directors attempted to replace him in the autumn of 1726, but there was simply nobody of his stature available, and in desperation they decided to await his return, and meanwhile hired out the Haymarket theatre to a troupe of Italian comedians. The two sopranos, perhaps equally frustrated at having to wait idly for Senesino's return, began to get on each other's nerves, and by November rumours of friction were rife.

Over in the rival theatre in Lincoln's Inn Fields, the proprietor, John Rich, decided to revive Bononcini's *Camilla*, first seen twenty years earlier, in 1706 – and significantly in English. Not only was Rich relighting the fiery old topic of opera in the vernacular rather than in an incomprehensible foreign language, he was also exploiting the current tensions at the Haymarket. The spoken prologue at his opening performance, on 19th November, referred both to Senesino's continued truancy and to the increasingly bitter relationship between Faustina and Cuzzoni:

> . . . Ye British Fair, vouchsafe us your Applause,
> And smile, propitious, on our English Cause;
> While Senesino you expect in vain,
> And see your Favours treated with Disdain:
> While, 'twixt his Rival Queens, such mutual Hate
> Threats hourly Ruin to yon tuneful State.[28]

This might be dismissed as satirical mischief, had not the genial Mrs Pendarves, who was in the Cuzzoni camp and knew the singer well, confirmed that all was not well in a letter to her sister a week later: 'That morning I was entertained with Cuzzoni. Oh how charming! how I did wish for all I love and like to be with me at that instant of time! my senses were ravished with harmony. They say we shall have operas in a fortnight, but I think Madam Sandoni [Cuzzoni] and the Faustina are not perfectly agreed about their parts.'[29]

Two weeks after that, there was yet more, in a report in *Mist's Weekly Journal*, on 10th December: 'Our last Advices from the Haymarket take Notice of a second Reconcilement between the Rival Queens . . . an unhappy Breach being made betwixt them since their first Reconcilement, occasioned by one of them making Mouths at the other while she was singing. This Treaty has been three Months in negotiating, and could never have been brought about had it not been for the great Skill and Address of some of the ablest Ministers of the Royal Academy.'[30] Although this report too is based entirely on hearsay, the relationship between Faustina and Cuzzoni – whether they liked it or not – was unquestionably the hottest topic of London gossip.

At last Senesino returned, and the Royal Academy season opened on 7th January 1727 with Ariosti's *Lucio Vero*. It had just seven performances and was immediately followed and completely overshadowed by Handel's *Admeto*, which premiered on 5th February. All the royal family were present, and so too were swarms of the eager public. *Admeto* ran for seventeen performances, and, according to Colman's 'Opera Register', 'the House filled every night fuller than ever was known at any opera for so long together'.[31] But although *Admeto* has Handel's consistently distinguished music, it was no longer this quality that was causing such a rush for tickets. The Cuzzoni–Faustina supporting factions were now extremely antagonistic; by April, they were audibly barracking each other during the performances, and the singers themselves were becoming unsettled. According to the Countess of Pembroke, Cuzzoni was told that she would be hissed off the stage as soon as she set foot on it, whereupon, not surprisingly, she threatened not to perform at all. Lady Pembroke claimed that it was she herself who persuaded her to sing; but when Cuzzoni was indeed then vilely catcalled, her own supporters gave the same treatment to Faustina, whose voice could barely be heard through the public racket. And these unseemly events all took place before the bewildered eyes of the fifteen-year-old Princess Amelia, granddaughter of the King. Dismayed by such an embarrassment, Cuzzoni asked Lady Pembroke to send a grovelling apology to Amelia's mother, the Princess of Wales, and the Countess did so through a lady of the bedchamber, Mrs Charlotte Clayton. That performance of *Admeto*, on 4th April, turned out to have been the last, as the remaining two were cancelled. First, Faustina got measles, and then Cuzzoni also succumbed to illness – in her case, vocal exhaustion. Among much speculation as to whether or not both sopranos were genuinely ill, there is the possibility that the two divas together took matters into their own hands and agreed to claim indisposition. For them as performers, *Admeto* was permanently tainted.

What Handel, with his short temper and insistence on high standards, made of all this is not known. From his command position in the pit he would have witnessed every unsavoury development, and been able to do nothing about it. He too would have been sensitive to the presence of royalty (Princess Amelia was his pupil), not least because in recent months he had finally taken the monumental step of following his monarch in adopting England as his own nation. In February, he had formally applied for British naturalization, and it had been quickly passed through Parliament: the King himself had signed his assent to the Bill on 20th February. Georg Friederich Händl was now George Frideric Handel, a British subject, a property-leasing Londoner and an important cog in the wheel of formal court music, as well as that of all the theatrical shenanigans. As his sopranos cancelled their final performances of *Admeto*, he revived *Ottone* for two performances and then *Floridante* for two more, both operas requiring some modifications to accommodate new singers. And meanwhile the Royal Academy tried to turn the page on all the recent disturbances and move to their final new opera of the season, Bononcini's *Astianatte*.

Loyally dedicated by Bononcini to his colourful patron, the Duchess of Marlborough, *Astianatte* was a story taken by Haym, via Salvi, from Racine's *Andromaque*. Its first night had to be postponed as Cuzzoni was apparently not back to vocal health, and even after its eventual opening, on 6th May, she was still clearly in difficulties, for the directors of the Academy tried to release her from her obligations and find a replacement. But the King intervened, telling the directors that he would refuse ever to attend the opera again or continue his annual gift of £1,000 unless Cuzzoni was reinstated. So she stayed. But then, at *Astianatte*'s ninth performance, on 6th June, there was yet another 'Disturbance . . . occasioned by the Partisans of the Two Celebrated Rival Ladies',[32] and this one was even worse, for the Princess of Wales herself was in the audience. As the hissing and catcalling grew to unacceptable levels, whoever was directing in the pit took the sensible decision to cut the third act completely and wrap up the performance with the final chorus. But the damage was done. Cuzzoni and Faustina were blamed. For months now there had been satirical pamphlets circulated in their names: *An Epistle from Signor Senesino to Signora Faustina*, followed immediately by *Faustina's Answer to Senesino*, in March; *An*

149

Epistle from Signora Faustina to a Lady (possibly the Duchess of Marlborough), in early June. Now came *A Full and True Account of a most horrible and bloody Battle between Madam Faustina and Madam Cuzzoni*, in which the ladies were accused of having come to blows on stage. Lord Hervey wrote to Stephen Fox: 'In short, the whole world is gone mad upon this dispute. No Cuzzonist will go to a tavern with a Faustinian; and the ladies of one party have scratched those of the other out of their list of visits'.[33]

But in fact a week later, an event of true magnitude put all this unseemly hooliganism into perspective. King George had gone to Hanover, no doubt planning to pick up his attempts to arrange marriages for his grandchildren, and generally to get away from his British responsibilities and relax in the only place where he felt truly at home. He had not been completely well that year, suffering from what were described as fits, but had recovered sufficiently to embark on his long journey. After crossing the North Sea, the King and his entourage travelled steadily through Holland, spending the night of 9th June in Delden. On the following morning, an hour after setting off again, he fainted. He was revived, and insisted on continuing his journey towards his next planned stop – his brother's palace at Osnabrück. By the time he arrived, he was barely conscious. During the course of the ensuing night, the King died. As the English newspapers reported in the coming days:

Our most late Gracious Sovereign was seized with a sudden illness . . . as he was in the coach between Delden and Nordhorn on his way to Hanover: his majesty was presently let blood, and had such remedies as were judged proper administered to him; and travelled on to his Highness the Duke of York's at Osnabrück, where he arrived about ten that night. But notwithstanding all the physicians could do for his recovery, he departed this life on the 11th, about one in the morning, in the 68th year of his age and the 13th of his Reign; a Prince endowed with all the royal virtues.[34]

Britain was in mourning; walls were hung with purple and black drapes, and the London theatres closed. The unseemly rowdiness of the opera audiences evaporated completely as the nation assumed an air of obedient solemnity.

7

NEW BEGINNINGS

'Now a different measure try'

[Solomon]

Nobody in Britain much regretted the passing of George I. He had never mastered the English language, was wooden in public, loathing the stunning pageantry that so often accompanies monarchy, and was despised for his cruelty to his wife. His feud with the Prince and Princess of Wales had split the court, but there was no doubt that the King's subjects sided instinctively with the younger family, evicted so derisorily from the King's immediate environment, with damaging consequences to the children who had been used as pawns in an ugly power-game. King George's frugality had been shared by his plain but powerful mistresses, but not by his warm and intelligent daughter-in-law, the wronged Princess Caroline. It is hardly surprising that George had never been taken to the nation's heart.

Politically, George had been detached from the administrative process. Where Queen Anne had diligently attended council meetings and been involved in the making of decisions, George's discomfort with the English tongue and his failure to grasp the many complexities of the parliamentary system led him to withdraw increasingly from its centre. Ironically, this manifestation of negativity was to have a positive impact, for Parliament assumed democratic power. George's reign saw the emergence of strong individuals who absorbed and defined the role of Prime Minister: first, Robert Harley (later Lord Oxford), and then the towering figure of Robert Walpole. King George accepted the strictures of the Act of Settlement, and heeded the advice of his ministers. In his recognition that Harley and especially Walpole were the men he needed – which in itself allowed his country to prosper and progress – George actually made secure the precarious throne he had ascended. Personally, George loved music, theatre and the arts, and he had had a considerable hand in consolidating the presence of Italian opera in his capital, and most especially in the establishment there of Handel. Handel's naturalization – literally George's final royal assent before he left England for the last time – could even be regarded as the first Hanoverian King of Britain's most significant legacy, for its repercussions would change the course of music in England forever.

George Augustus, Prince of Wales, was not informed of his father's death until three days after the event. The bearer of the grave announcement was Walpole. He went to Richmond to demand an immediate audience on an extremely urgent matter, but was refused admittance. News of this almost comical turn of events, at a moment of profound constitutional crisis, was soon the subject of gossip. César de Saussure, writing the latest in a series of lengthy journalistic letters to his family in France, described the situation in such racy detail that it almost implied he himself had witnessed the whole encounter:

The Prince and Princess were having their midday rest, the weather being sultry. The lady-in-waiting refused to waken them, although Sir Robert declared he wished to inform them at once on a matter of the highest importance. The lady, after much hesitation, yielded. The Prince of Wales was greatly surprised at Sir Robert Walpole's desire to speak to him. Being very hasty, he sent back word to the effect that he considered the minister very bold and impertinent at daring to come into his house and disturb him, and that he might go away again, for he would not see him. Sir Robert continued pressing to be permitted a few minutes' interview, just sufficient to communicate very important news, and as the Prince's room was adjoining and the door a little ajar, the Prince heard this answer, which put him in such a state of fury that he was on the point of rising to throw Sir Robert out of the room, when the Princess, who possesses many qualities and amongst them prudence, quieted her husband by telling him that undoubtedly there must be news of importance, and with some difficulty she obtained the Prince's permission to join Sir Robert in the next room.

Sir Robert, addressing the Princess, said, 'Madam, I am in despair that His Royal Highness will not permit me to be the first of his subjects to do him homage. I have brought a letter, acquainting him with the death of his Majesty the King, his father.' The Prince, who was listening from his apartment as to what the message might be, heard, and entering the room with looks of fury demanded the letter. Sir Robert threw himself at the Prince's feet, and offering the letter made a touching little speech, and you must know that he is very eloquent, and one of the best talkers in the kingdom. The Prince and Princess retired into their apartments, and after consulting together for a few minutes they reappeared, their eyes wet with tears.[1]

The quiet authority of Caroline was notable. It was she who persuaded her husband that Walpole should remain in post, contrary to the expectations of both monarch and indeed Walpole himself, for their relationship hitherto had been stormy and fragile. But as César de Saussure confirmed,

> The Queen, who is a very capable woman and has much influence over the King, managed little by little to make him believe that he could not find a more capable man in the whole kingdom or one who knew more about finances and the affairs of the interior than Sir Robert Walpole (and she was right), that he could be counted on in any emergency, having great influence everywhere, and that he had been the factor in the late king's reign for bringing money into empty chests, and that no doubt he could do the same for the new king.[2]

Walpole cannily offered his new King a generous Civil List of £830,000 per annum, and George II was won over. Walpole resumed and increased his power, and England was freed from major political problems for many years. Any anxiety that the Pretender might again choose this brief fracture of royal continuity as a moment to lay claim to the throne was in the event unfounded. There was no stirring at all from James Stuart, and the accession was entirely peaceful.

George I was buried at Herrenhausen, close to the tomb of his mother, some three months after his actual death. None of his London family travelled to Germany for the funeral. His fondest relative, and the one who did attend, was his grandson Frederick, who in 1714 had been left in Hanover. The new King George brought out and displayed portraits of his own mother Sophia Dorotea, whom he had long intended to liberate from her castle and perhaps even bring to London, declaring her Queen Dowager. However, after thirty-three years of lonely Ahlden imprisonment, she had died just the year before. George II's three eldest daughters, who had come over with their parents from Hanover as very small children, were now in their teens. Eighteen-year-old Anne, sixteen-year-old Amelia and fourteen-year-old Caroline – all pupils of Handel – had survived their bizarre separation from their parents, with whom they were now permanently reunited, as they were with their younger siblings. William (six), Mary (four) and Louise (three) had all been born in London, after the death of the infant George William, in 1712. This considerably larger royal household therefore established itself in various royal palaces. And George II did continue at least one of his father's customs, for he too enjoyed the company of mistresses, especially that of Henrietta Howard, who with her husband Charles had been part of George and Caroline's household since their Hanover days. Henrietta remained in close proximity to the King, who saw her on a daily basis. Queen Caroline evidently knew all about the arrangement.

Unlike his father, the new King loved pomp and pageantry, and was determined that his coronation, to take place in Westminster Abbey on 11th October, would be more lavish and spectacular than the last. Caroline too would be crowned in the same ceremony. The Duke of Grafton, the Lord Chamberlain, was in overall charge of the proceedings, while the Archbishop of Canterbury, William Wake, drew up an appropriate order of service, based on formats used at previous coronations. The increase in scale, so desired by the new King, was reflected in both the ceremonial and the ecclesiastical arrangements.

In order that the public could properly see the procession of royalty and eminent guests, a raised walkway was constructed between Westminster Hall and the Abbey, and, beyond it, for yet better viewing, stands and boxes. Tickets were issued by the Earl Marshal's office, and were swiftly taken. For the service inside the Abbey, visual splendour was to be matched by aural splendour, and George II himself took a personal interest in these details. There would be impressive forces of assembled singers and musicians: the choirs of the Abbey and of the Chapel Royal were to be combined (as they still are, on important ceremonial occasions) and supported by many instrumentalists. There had however recently been a change of leadership at the Chapel Royal. In August 1727, just after the death of George I, the chapel's organist and composer, William Croft, had also died, and his successor, Maurice Greene, of St Paul's Cathedral, had been appointed on 4th September. Greene might naturally have assumed that his immediate task would be the composition of the special music for the coronation of his new King, but in fact George and Caroline personally overruled this, turning instead to their friend and compatriot, Handel. As the press announced on 9th September, 'Mr. Hendel, the famous Composer to the Opera, is appointed by the King to compose the Anthem at the Coronation which is to be sung in Westminster-Abbey at the Grand Ceremony.'[3] There was no greater endorsement of Handel's position at the heart of London's artistic life, nor in the affections of the royal family, than this personal command.

And so it was Handel who eagerly supplied four anthems to be deployed at significant junctures of the coronation service. There was considerable public enthusiasm for these, and on two occasions in the fortnight before the event, they were rehearsed in public, to great approbation. *Parker's Penny Post* reported, on 4th October, 'Mr Hendle has composed the Musick for the Abbey at the Coronation, and the Italian Voices, with above a Hundred of the best Musicians will perform; and the Whole is allowed by those Judges in Musick who have already heard it, to exceed any Thing heretofore of the same Kind.'[4] The report added the announcement that the following week's rehearsal would be 'kept private, lest the Crowd of People should be an Obstruction to the Performers'. But the rehearsal four days later seems not to have been private at all; rather, it was witnessed by 'the greatest Concourse of people that has been known'.[5]

On coronation day itself, the procession on the raised walkway was formidable, and so long that it lasted over two hours. Phalanxes of bishops and clergy, sheriffs and aldermen, judges, barons, knights, heralds, musicians and politicians (including Walpole – 'the only Knight of the Garter who is not noble',[6] as César de Saussure meticulously reported) all made their stately way into the Abbey. At times they were slowed to a halt as the file of walkers narrowed to enter the Great West Door. One of those thus held up was the redoubtable Sarah, Dowager Duchess of Marlborough, who, to the delight of the crowd, rested her legs by taking a drum from one of the soldiers and sitting on it. At last, towards the end of the procession, came the royal family itself. The King wore crimson velvet trimmed with ermine and gold lace, and his train was borne by four young noblemen and the Master of the Robes. The Queen's dress was adorned with literally millions of pounds' worth of precious stones, many of them hired or borrowed for the occasion. Although she also carried a sceptre and an ivory rod, she complained ever after that the weight of her dress was 'the worst thing I had to bear'.[7] She was attended by her daughters, Anne,

Caroline and Amelia, also magnificently attired. César de Saussure was overwhelmed: 'It is impossible for me to make you understand and imagine the pomp and magnificence of this solemn occasion ... Everything in it was grand and sumptuous. Persons of an advanced age, who have seen the coronations of King James II, of William III and Mary, of Queen Anne, and of King George I, are all agreed that the magnificence of the present coronation has far surpassed that of the preceding.'[8]

Once inside the Abbey, a certain amount of disorder ruffled the edges of the elaborately planned service. The Archbishop of Canterbury, presiding, made notes on his order of service, implying that not everything was going as it should and that it was partly the fault of the musicians ('the negligence of the Choir of Westminster'[9]). Clearly the numbers involved, and the inclusion of the musicians in the middle of a long procession, prevented the choir from being in the right place at the right time, ready to sing the introit, 'I was glad', as the royal party entered the Abbey. It was therefore omitted, and the knock-on effect of this, together with the fact that separate bodies of choirs were then positioned in opposing galleries, led to more confusion; at one point, two anthems were begun by different choirs at the same time. All this would have dismayed Handel as much as it did the Archbishop, who crossly scribbled on his order of service, 'All irregular in the music'.[10] But gradually the chaos subsided. The service settled into its planned splendour, and George and Caroline were duly crowned to the accompaniment of four personally commanded and brilliantly devised anthems.

Both collectively and individually, Handel's multipartite Coronation anthems show his genius for detailed structure, contrast, texture and colour. The first of them, 'Let Thy Hand be Strengthened', was sung at the 'Recognition', after the 'Entrance', and was lightly scored for strings and oboes, with five-part choral writing. This was balanced by the last of them, 'My heart is inditing', which accompanied 'The Queen's Coronation', towards the end of the service, and was identically scored, if with six-part choral writing. Between them, at 'The Anointing' and then 'The Putting on of the Crown', came the two mightiest, 'Zadok the Priest' and 'The King Shall Rejoice', which called for seven- or eight-part choral writing, and added trumpets and timpani. So Handel's sense of musical and dramatic symmetry is already telling, for the central addition of trumpets and the expanded choral texture added aural brilliance to the most significant parts of the ceremony. But his masterly control of text and forces is apparent too in each individual anthem. 'Let Thy Hand be Strengthened' is the most straightforward, with clear word-setting through calm counterpoint. With 'Zadok the Priest', Handel brought in yet another ingredient to his impressively assembled forces: the architecture of the Abbey itself. Never before or since has a piece of music so reflected that mighty building. Quiet opening string arpeggios rolled through the great transept, under its vaulted ceiling, approaching the very area of 'Anointing' through a controlled crescendo, and exploded into the rafters with the massive choral entry, supported by trumpets and timpani. The effect, one both ceremonial and reverential, was electrifying. It is not difficult to understand why this anthem was deployed then for the coronation of George II's eventual successor, and fellow Handel admirer, his (yet to be born) grandson, George III; and as a result it has been performed at every coronation since.

The brass and choral splendour of 'Zadok the Priest' was continued in 'The King Shall Rejoice', an anthem of exuberant vitality and genuine joy. And then it was Caroline's turn. As the new Queen, attended still by her daughters, received her own crown, the gentler intimacy of 'My heart is inditing' not only provided a virtual running commentary on what was actually happening ('Upon thy right hand did stand the Queen in vesture of gold'; 'Kings' daughters were among thy honourable women' – this was the perfect choice of text for such a moment), but also reflected the genuine affection and warmth felt by Handel towards the family to whom he had been allowed to become so attached. The young princesses in particular must have adored their own verse, which indeed seems an almost personal tribute to them from the teacher whom they so admired.

The coronation service lasted nearly four hours, and afterwards the long procession wound its way back to Westminster Hall. The King and Queen displayed their crowns to the people, and Walpole and two other knights threw special silver coins, stamped with effigies of the new King, into the crowd. Inside Westminster Hall, where Handel's colleague John Heidegger was in charge of the lighting, 1,800 candles were lit in just three minutes, causing some alarm to the Queen and her ladies, as flames darted along trains of flax. But there was no harm done, and a sumptuous banquet followed. And when at last the royal party retired ('very fatigued and weary', according to César de Saussure) to St James's Palace, and the other guests too were able to leave, the great doors were 'thrown open and the crowd allowed to enter and take possession of the remains of the feast'. It took just half an hour for everything, 'even the boards of which the tables and seats had been made', to disappear.[11]

∾

For George II, there was just one more family matter to settle: his son Frederick must be brought over from Hanover to assume the role of Prince of Wales. Frederick was now twenty-one, and perfectly content with the extravagant lifestyle he was enjoying in Hanover, where he presumed he would remain, and indeed rule, for his grandfather had proposed precisely this in his will. But George II ignored the wishes of George I. Aware of Frederick's constant pursuit of pleasure, he preferred to bring him to London where he could keep his behaviour under close surveillance. So early in 1728 Frederick was virtually seized during a ball in Hanover, and firmly escorted to England within twenty-four hours. He came with extreme bad grace and a staggering £100,000 of debt. George II refused his son the same allowance from the Civil List that he himself had enjoyed as Prince of Wales, and in fact reduced it from £100,000 to £24,000 – which in real terms was still an enormous sum. Frederick was furious at having been summoned and then humiliated, and another fierce intergenerational family feud was launched in St James's Palace. Neither George II nor, more surprisingly for such a warm and intelligent woman, Caroline ever trusted or even apparently liked their elder son, and this animosity was only to increase as the years unfolded. Frederick was never given any responsibility as Prince of Wales; when George II left the country his authority remained with the Queen. So Frederick pursued his own interests. He took his seat in the House of Lords, but beyond that had no connection with the political process. He built up his own household, pointedly offering many positions to old servants of his grandfather. And he devoted much time to music, a passion he shared with his sisters. He played the cello, he composed, and he became increasingly involved with the opera. He began to attend performances in the Haymarket; and, like his sisters, he developed a close relationship with Handel.

Since the coronation, opera production had resumed after the closure of theatres during the period of official mourning. Throughout that summer of impatient inactivity, the press had tried energetically to rekindle the feud between Cuzzoni and Faustina. Many satirical pamphlets had been produced, some in prose, some in verse, some indecent, all of them furious at the huge salaries the two divas were commanding. Chief among these had been *The Devil to Pay at St. James's: or, A full and true Account of a most horrid and bloody Battle between Madam Faustina and Madam Cuzzoni*, which accused them of calling each other names ('Bitch and Whore') and fighting 'like any Billingsgates'.[12] Similarly, a pamphlet purporting to be the script of a 'Small Farce', entitled *The Contre Temps; or, Rival Queans*, included among its 'Dramatis Personae' not only 'F-s-na' and 'C-z-ni', but also 'S-s-no', 'H-d-l', 'H-d-r' and many others.[13] Great fun though all this was, it quickly burnt itself out. And when, three weeks before the coronation, the new season opened in the Haymarket with a revival of *Admeto*, using the very same singers, there was absolutely no trouble at all, either on stage or amongst a subdued audience. Public attention had moved on from that particular feature of, truly, the silly season.

Handel's first new opera that autumn was *Riccardo Primo*, to a libretto by Rolli. This had actually been drafted earlier in the year, intended possibly to end the previous season in the spirit of patriotism that followed Handel's naturalization. But it was now the perfect opera with which to mark George II's coronation and entertain the many English and European dignitaries who had come to London to celebrate it. Handel and Rolli revised the earlier draft, partly out of necessity (one of their singers, Anna Dotti, had retired over the summer, so the part written for her was removed completely), and partly to emphasize the topical relevance. They strengthened the plot, and brought in patriotic references to the glory of the British monarchy. *Riccardo Primo* opened on 11th November, a month after the coronation, and continued for ten more performances, until just before Christmas. It was based on the third Crusade, and Rolli's poetic dedication to George II referred to Richard the Lionheart as his '*guerriero Predecessore*'. The story, of Richard the Lionheart and two women (Costanza and Pulcheria – Constancy and Beauty) who both claim his affections, was the perfect blueprint for the Academy's singers, for it neatly embraced also the remains of the prevailing operatic conflict. Senesino, always on for a noble and heroic title role, sang Riccardo, and as usual Handel wrote for him arias designed to demonstrate his coloratura technique, balanced with those which allowed him the greatest lyricism. Costanza and Pulcheria were Cuzzoni and Faustina, both of whom likewise had arias displaying their specific strengths. Most of Cuzzoni's nine arias are in minor keys and of an elegant, tragic nature, while Faustina's seven are more fiery and brilliant. The stalwart Boschi was given two sturdy arias. The opera was designed by Joseph Goupy, an old friend of Handel's from his days in Rome, and then his colleague at both Burlington House and Cannons, and he produced no fewer than ten different locations. There was musical munificence too, as befitted the general mood of celebration, for Handel included in his rich orchestration horns, trumpets, timpani, recorders and an exotic '*traversa bassa*', or alto flute. The orchestral writing is as accomplished as ever. There are extremely dramatic effects, beginning with busy scales and arpeggio figurations in the strings, and thunderous rolls on the timpani, depicting a sea storm (an opening to the opera fully reminiscent of Shakespeare's *Tempest*, and presaging Gluck's *Iphigénie en Tauride*). Later there are splendid military fanfares, introducing trumpets in a '*bellicosa Sinfonia*', or attached to a chorus, or simply free-standing as a march.

The magnificence of recent events in Westminster Abbey, and their association therefore with the power and majesty of a monarch, were easily recalled in *Riccardo Primo*. But so too, more subtly, was the establishment of peace between the allegedly warring divas. In Handel's autograph there is a stage direction, which appears in none of the printed editions, but which may nevertheless be seen as an important instruction from the composer himself: 'She [Pulcheria] takes Costanza by the hand and they go out'. Such a physical gesture of amity, occurring in the very first scene of the opera, was surely a firm directive also to the audience that hostilities were over and that they too should now behave with decorum.

And indeed this does seem to have been some sort of turning point. Far from being rivals, Cuzzoni and Faustina, with Senesino too, were demonstrably now a team. They all sang together at the Festival of St Cecilia, towards the end of their run of *Riccardo Primo* ('some of the best songs out of several operas',[14] wrote Mrs Pendarves). But with the rowdy ferocity of competition now dutifully suppressed, the sheer fun of attending opera performances dwindled, and so did the audiences. Londoners had certainly been excited by the coronation, by the popularity of the new King, his Queen and his large family, and by the promise therefore of a new era. But the stock market had wobbled throughout 1727, and some of the Academy's subscribers had withheld, or at least been late with their payments. Those large salaries for the star singers still had to be paid, even if Senesino's serial indispositions had significantly reduced the number of performances given. The Academy's directors had repeatedly appealed, with threat even of legal action, to their subscribers, and there were tensions between them. Handel himself seems to have stayed determinedly aloof from all this, continuing to work at his most ferocious pace, rewriting or revising old operas and planning two new ones. But his great friend Mrs Pendarves, passionately loyal though she was to the operatic cause, could not fail to recognize a change in the air. She wrote to her sister on 25th November 1727: 'I doubt operas will not survive longer than this winter, they are now at their last gasp; the subscription is expired and nobody will renew it. The directors are always squabbling, and they have so many divisions among themselves that I wonder they have not broke up before; Senesino goes away next winter, and I believe Faustina, so you see harmony is almost out of fashion.'[15]

For those who had continued for decades to proclaim the absurdity of opera being sung by overpaid foreigners in an incomprehensible language, this suggestion of a decline in operatic fortune was more than welcome. The opportunity was seized. John Rich, running the rival theatre at Lincoln's Inn Fields, revived Bononcini's old opera in English, *Camilla*, for the second time in two years. Then in January 1728, with brilliant provocative flair, Rich produced John Gay's *The Beggar's Opera*. This was a ballad opera in English, using popular tunes interspersed with Gay's dialogue, and it was a blistering satire not only on current politics, attacking Walpole's government and its perceived corruptions, but also on every aspect of Italian opera. Satire had been popular in London ever since the formation of the Scriblerus Club in 1714. Every weakness or misdemeanour of those with power or influence, whether royalty or in government, was soon turned to mischievous art. Shortcomings were exposed, hypocrisies chastised. In 1714, Pope's *Rape of the Lock* had highlighted the vanities and moral degradation of the upper classes. Now, at the end of the 1720s, Pope's great colleague Swift, having published *Gulliver's Travels* in 1726, was at work on his *A Modest*

Proposal, in which he ridiculed British colonialism with the suggestion that the impoverished Irish could solve their economic problems by selling their children for food. The first dated painting by the artist William Hogarth was indeed *The Beggar's Opera*, depicting a scene from Gay's play. After this auspicious debut, Hogarth never looked back, and he specialized in paintings and engravings of all aspects of London life. (One even featured Cuzzoni literally raking in piles of gold coins being poured out in front of her.) His popularity laid the ground also for the later, equally vibrant cartoonists Thomas Rowlandson and James Gillray, and his biting social commentary could even be said to have led to that of Dickens in the following century. So in a very real way, Handel's Italian operas in the Haymarket actually stoked the fires for London's satirical geniuses. And Gay's *Beggar's Opera* was at the heart of it all.

The story of *The Beggar's Opera* already mocked the format of current Italian opera. Polly Peachum, daughter of a gang leader, secretly marries Macheath, a highwayman. When Macheath visits a brothel, he is betrayed by an ex-lover and imprisoned. The gaoler's daughter, Lucy, frees him, but he is recaptured and sentenced to death. At the last moment, on the very scaffold, he receives a royal pardon. So there are clear operatic parallels here: two rival women (Polly and Lucy) and a colourful, charismatic man (Macheath) mock the eternal triangle of Cuzzoni, Faustina and Senesino. There is a quarrel between Polly and Lucy, which the Cuzzoni and Faustina factions would have found hilarious, and a dungeon scene that evokes the prisons of Handel's serious operas. The royal pardon too is surely a travesty of the last-minute manoeuvre and magnanimous forgiveness which enforced the operatic happy ending. Gay's lively spoken dialogue was interspersed with popular tunes, including 'Over the hills and far away', 'Lillibulero' and 'Greensleeves', which ridiculed the necessity for elaborate virtuosity in Handel's arias; and there were borrowings, too, from iconic 'serious' composers, including Purcell and indeed Handel himself, in the form of minuets from the 'Water Music' and a march from *Rinaldo*. But, devastatingly accurate though these attacks on opera were, the real targets were loftier. Peachum, a thief, womanizer and double-dealer, was a thinly disguised portrayal of Walpole. Macheath was a combination of two well-known contemporary criminals, Jack Sheppard and Jonathan Wild, whose own vibrant stories had recently enthralled Londoners; they had been hanged at Tyburn, respectively, in 1724 and 1725. For the eager audiences in Lincoln's Inn Fields, there were resonances and innuendos to be enjoyed on every level.

The Beggar's Opera was a phenomenon. It ran for no fewer than sixty-two performances (the Academy's operatic runs with difficulty made it into double figures), and, according to popular epigram, it 'made Gay rich and Rich gay'. Mrs Pendarves wrote sadly, 'The Beggar's Opera entirely triumphs over the Italian one';[16] and in later years Lord Hervey recalled in his memoirs that 'even those who were most glanced at in the satire had prudence enough to disguise their resentment by chiming in with the universal applause'.[17] Walpole indeed went to see it himself and inevitably hated it, and when a sequel, *Polly*, was proposed, he prevailed upon the Lord Chamberlain to ban it. But Rich and Gay had more than made their mark, and an insolent pull of focus away from Italian opera had been effected.

∽

Determinedly in his own furrow, Handel nevertheless ploughed on. While *Riccardo Primo* was in performance, he had been working on *Genserico*, but for some reason he abandoned this after a few numbers and turned instead to his old colleague, Haym, for a new libretto. Haym suggested adapting something by a young poet who, still in his twenties, was the rising star of opera in Italy, and would soon become the most distinguished librettist of the whole of eighteenth-century opera seria: Pietro Metastasio. They chose *Siroe*, which had excellent roles for Senesino, Faustina and Cuzzoni, some elaborate disguises and deceptions, and of course, defying the current mockery in *The Beggar's Opera*, a good prison scene.

But Haym's enthusiasm for Metastasio as a poet had to be tempered by the requirements of his colleagues. Metastasio's finely structured work was brutally filleted and sliced, as Haym expanded the roles for Cuzzoni, Faustina and Senesino, and therefore shrank those of everyone else. With dramatic impetus thus distorted, plot comprehension virtually collapsed, and, although rare in a Handel–Haym collaboration, no character emerged with any real sympathy. But Handel's individual musical numbers, incorporating five of the six from the abandoned *Genserico*, are of great quality, especially Senesino's prison lament in the third act. The arias for the big three were enough to bring the audiences back, and in total there were eighteen performances. The opening night was attended by George II and Queen Caroline, together with their three eldest daughters, and Caroline returned for the second performance too. None of the royal family ever went to see *The Beggar's Opera*.

Despite the rumours (well founded, in fact) that both Faustina and Senesino had had enough of opera in London, the star singers were still working at full stretch. There was a revival of *Radamisto*, in which Senesino and Boschi repeated their roles from 1720, but Faustina and Cuzzoni had to learn and perform theirs for the first time. And they were all also learning *Tolomeo*, another new opera put together quite quickly by Handel and Haym. Yet again, it stubbornly adhered to required formulae. It showcased two marvellous women, Seleuce (Cuzzoni) and Elisa (Faustina), who generally behave admirably. There was brotherly love, disguise, forgiveness and reconciliation, and, overall, a nice mix of the political and the pastoral. And there was the inevitable denouement in a prison, where Senesino had his finest moment. Another fragmented aria, 'Stille amare', in the remarkable key of B flat minor, petered out musically as a sleeping draught took its hold (recalling Bajazet's suicide scene in *Tamerlano*). But a dogged adherence to familiar devices now seemed, in the context of everything else, somehow desperate. All the arias in *Tolomeo*, good though they are, were short. There was no exuberant invention; Handel almost seemed to be filling in a form. Neither Handel nor Haym was a fool, and the writing on the wall was becoming abundantly legible. Haym's dedication of the libretto to the Academy director, William Kent, Earl of Albemarle, was an undisguised cry for help, for he begged his patron to 'rally support for operas, now almost failing in England', and to 'support an innocent amusement which was so well received . . . a few years ago'. Even the text of the final chorus in *Tolomeo*, 'Applauda ogn'un il nostro fato', smacks too of the despondency in the Academy's creative team. There were only six performances.

Throughout the month of May, the Academy's directors had held a series of meetings. On 31st May, the *Daily Courant* reported an adjournment while they tried to recover debts, considered the problems of paying everyone ('Performers, Tradesmen and others'), and even speculated on what to do with the sets and costumes 'if the Operas cannot be continued'.[18] Then Faustina fell ill and *Tolomeo* closed abruptly. The money had run out, and the directors seemed to have had enough. No further plans were announced for any future season. As Mainwaring later recalled, 'Thus the Academy, after it had continued in the most flourishing of states for upwards of nine years, was at once dissolved'.[19]

It was not just the directors of the Academy who had had enough: the singers too saw no reason to continue working in an atmosphere of such acrimony, financial anxiety and gathering unpopularity. The three superstars went home to Italy. Senesino, who had sung in every one of the thirty-two operas presented by the Academy since his debut in 1720, including therefore the thirteen by Handel, took his well-earned and substantial rewards back to Siena. Now he set about refurbishing his fine palazzo, not just with his English fees (he had an inscription mounted above the front door, proclaiming that 'the folly of the English had laid the foundations for it'), but in an English style. His eight years in London, and especially in the ambience of his patron Lord Burlington, had made a considerable impression on his personal tastes. At a time when Englishmen were returning from their grand tours with Italian art and trophies, Senesino reversed the tide. He imported to Siena English furniture, glass, locks, kitchen equipment, linen, even servants. The grounds of his palazzo were influenced by those of Lord Burlington's Chiswick House, built at precisely this time. Lord Burlington's gardens were being landscaped by William Keppel, and these designs too were imitated in Siena. After the manner of his patron, Senesino bought good paintings; he owned works by Holbein, Breughel and other members of the sixteenth- and seventeenth-century Flemish school. And he collected contemporary portraits – of himself, of his colleagues

and of his friends: upon his walls he boasted the company of Cuzzoni, Rolli, Bononcini, Ariosti. (There was no portrait of Handel,
nor of Faustina, in his collection.) Senesino liked to serve English
tea to his visitors, completing the illusion of an English stately
home. Although he planned now to stay in Italy, he enjoyed playing the role of the English aristocrat.

Cuzzoni too took her family back to Italy. For the next five
years she sang, for consistently high fees, in Venice, Bologna, Naples, Florence, Genoa and Turin – and also in Vienna, where, it
was mischievously rumoured, she entered into a new rivalry with
another singer.[20] Still in her early thirties, she was confident in
her vocal technique and interpretative gifts, and felt, correctly,
that there was still mileage in them. She would be back in London within a few years.

Faustina, on the other hand, would never return. Unlike Senesino and Cuzzoni, she had only been part of the Academy for
three seasons, and she had neither engineered nor enjoyed the
confrontations with her rival. Like Cuzzoni, she continued to
sing for a while in Italy, and in 1730 she married the young
and extremely promising opera composer Johann Adolf Hasse.
They were both subsequently engaged by the Dresden court, and
Faustina sang in her husband's many operas there until 1751.
After her retirement, she continued to travel with Hasse, and
would no doubt have met the young Mozart – first in Vienna, in
1767, when Mozart was eleven, and again in Milan, in 1771, when
the seventy-two-year-old Hasse's *Ruggiero* was completely outshone by the fifteen-year-old Mozart's *Ascanio in Alba*. But this
did not unduly trouble the generous Hasse; the two composers
enjoyed one another's company. One can only speculate as to how
much the teenager was aware that the elderly wife of his colleague
had had such an illustrious past, and with whom.

The departure of Handel's entire company of singers did not depress him in the least; rather it actually seems to have invigorated him. Freed now from his customary annual task of preparing operas for the following season, he poured his energies into the buying and selling of stock, playing the markets with liberated glee and, certainly, a practised hand. He continued his association with the royal family, being confirmed as 'Musick-Master' to the Princesses Anne, Amelia and Caroline (at a slightly lower retainer than that of Mr Anthony L'Abbé, their dancing master, who received £240 annually, as opposed to Handel's £200). He oversaw into print several of his compositions, and arrangements of them for amateur enthusiasts. And while the Haymarket theatre remained operatically dark in the autumn of 1728, he nevertheless continued to plan, with Heidegger, for a completely new start there, once the hullabaloo had died down.

Sure enough, early in 1729, the now-skeletal Royal Academy of Music was summoned to a general court, 'in order to consider Proposals that will then be offered for carrying on Operas; as also for disposing of the Effects belonging to the said Academy'.[21] Only twenty people turned up to this meeting, but one of them was Viscount Percival, who recorded in his diary that, having decided to prosecute the subscribers who had still not paid what they owed, the Academy agreed to 'permit Hydeger and Hendle to carry on operas without disturbances for five years and to lend them for that time our scenes, machines, clothes, instruments, furniture etc. It all past off in a great hurry.'[22] So Handel and Heidegger had their fresh start.

Immediately they set about recruiting a new company of singers, and there was one name that, above all others, was attracting attention in Italy. This was the twenty-five-year-old castrato sensation Carlo Broschi, known as Farinelli. Heidegger had indeed already travelled to Italy in the hope of securing his services; Rolli somewhat uncharitably reported this in a letter to Senesino, whose prime position in the castrato limelight was clearly about to be usurped. With cruel glee, Rolli informed him that 'news has recently arrived from Venice . . . that all throng to the theatre where Farinello is singing, and that the theatre where you and Faustina are is nearly empty'.[23] Heidegger however had failed to reel in the big fish, so Handel insisted that he himself should now go to Italy with his own shopping list of singers, and Farinelli's name would be firmly at the top of it. He consulted the King, whose continued patronage of opera would be essential; and, although George II still hoped to see the return of Cuzzoni (but not Faustina), Handel persuaded him 'that there was need of a change . . . in order to have the opportunity of composing new works for new performers.'[24] Accordingly, as the *Daily Post* reported on 27th January 1729, 'Yesterday Morning Mr. Handell, the famous Composer of Italian Musick, took his Leave of their Majesties, he being to set out this Day for Italy, with a Commission from the Royal Academy of Musick.'[25]

Handel's trip to Italy began in Venice, where most of the top singers were performing, including Farinelli, Senesino, Faustina and Cuzzoni. Fired no doubt by Rolli's malevolent provocations, Senesino made life difficult for Handel, as Rolli himself delightedly learned and dutifully passed back: 'The news that reached Riva concerning Handel's arrival in Venice was that you gave him a cold reception and that he was complaining and protesting about it'.[26] Perhaps because of this, Farinelli refused even to meet Handel, claiming that he had no intention anyway of going to England, because of the climate ('for fear our Air should hurt his Voice', as the English Resident in Venice, Colonel Burges, explained[27]). So Handel moved on to Bologna, Rome and Naples, exploring other possibilities, meeting and assessing singers, and hiring his new team as he went. In Rome, his old stamping ground, he enjoyed renewing acquaintance with former friends and patrons, including Cardinal Ottoboni. But in a strong statement of loyalty to his current monarch and patron, he refused an invitation from Cardinal Colonna, for the Cardinal's house guest was none other than James Stuart, still agitating for the British throne.

By the end of June 1729 Handel was back in London, and on 2nd July, in what seems like an extremely careful press release, the contents of his shopping basket were announced in the *Daily Journal*:

Mr. Handel, who is just returned from Italy, has contracted with the following Persons to perform in the Italian Opera's, vz.

Signor Bernachi, who is esteem'd the best Singer in Italy.

Signora Merighi, a Woman of a very fine Presence, an excellent Actress, and a very good Singer – A Counter Tenor [contralto].

Signora Strada, who hath a very fine Treble Voice, a Person of Singular Merit.

Signor Annibal Pio Fabri, a most excellent Tenor, and a fine Voice.

His Wife, who performs a Man's Part exceeding well.

Signora Bartoldi, who has a very fine Treble Voice; she is also a very genteel Actress, both in Men and Womens Parts.

A Bass Voice from Hamburgh, there being none worth engaging in Italy.[28]

If Londoners had been expecting Farinelli, they would have felt disappointment as they read this list. But there were singers of interest. The castrato, Antonio Maria Bernacchi, was the replacement for the great Senesino. For him this was a return to London, for he had been there in the 1716–17 season and had sung in revivals of *Rinaldo* and *Amadigi*. At forty-four, he was the same age as Handel (and indeed Senesino), and therefore somewhat older than the rest of his colleagues, all of whom were new to London. Antonia Merighi, Annibale Pio Fabri and Johann Riemschneider were all in their thirties, and would last only one or two seasons; Fabri's contralto wife, Anna Bombaciari, never sang for Handel at all. But the soprano, Anna Maria Strada del Pò, in her late twenties, and the nineteen-year-old contralto, Francesca Bertolli, were both to stay in London for many years, being coached as singers and moulded as performers by Handel himself, and involved therefore in many of his new works. Significantly, Strada was the only soprano. All these singers were due to arrive in London in the autumn, and meanwhile Handel vigorously returned to his summer routine of planning operas for the following season. Now that he knew his singers, he knew too how and what to write for them.

But there was one more big change to assimilate, for on 31st July Nicola Haym died at the age of fifty-one. After so many years of collaboration, both in creation as librettist and then in performance as continuo cellist, Handel will have felt keenly the loss of this man, literally, at his side. Haym's all-round achievements, including his antiquarian enthusiasms, were extraordinary, as apparently was his nature. His obituary listed not just his 'Genious for Musick' and 'indefatigable Industry', but also his 'uncommon Modesty, Candour, Affability and all amiable Virtues of Life'.[29] Handel had lost a true friend.

By October, the new company of singers was settled in London, and on 10th October Handel took them to Kensington Palace to introduce them to the King and Queen and their family. They all sang, Handel himself accompanied them at the harpsichord and, according to the press, 'their Performances were much approved'.[30] Inevitably, Rolli was uncharitable. He wrote to Riva on 6th November: 'If everyone were as well satisfied with the company as is the Royal Family, we should have to admit that there never had been such an Opera since Adam and Eve sang Milton's hymns in the Garden of Eden. They say that Signora Stradina has all the rapid execution of Faustina and all the sweetness of Cuzzona, and so on with all the others. We shall see how it turns out. The proof of the pudding is in the eating, as the English proverb says.'[31]

But he did grudgingly admit that Strada had better intonation than Faustina, that Merighi sang intelligently and that Bernacchi was 'quite exceptional', with most of which Mrs Pendarves, writing to her sister later that month, agreed. Having attended a late opera rehearsal, she wrote that Strada was a fine singer, but as yet something of an embarrassment as an actress ('her voice is without exception fine, her manner perfection, but her person very bad, and she makes frightful mouths'); Bernacchi, despite being 'as big as a Spanish friar', was an extremely accomplished singer; Merighi 'sings easily and agreeably'; and the young Bertolli was a poor performer, but a stunning girl ('she has neither voice, ear nor manner to recommend her; but she is a perfect beauty, quite a Cleopatra').[32] Spoken or unspoken, uneasy comparisons were inevitably being made with the troublesome but highly gifted team of departed singers, as the newcomers must only too keenly have been aware.

8

NEW ENDINGS

'Toss'd from thought to thought I rove'
[Alexander Balus]

The new company's first opera was to be *Lotario*. Handel completed it in mid-November, and it opened just three weeks later, on 2nd December, so his new singers had minimal preparation time. Like their predecessors, they would have to get used to this eleventh-hour delivery of material and the consequent scramble to absorb, memorize and rehearse whole roles. In the absence now of Haym, it was Rossi, Handel's old partner from *Rinaldo* and *Il Pastor fido*, who was given the task of adapting a libretto, *Adelaide*, by Salvi, to current specifications. The storyline, of divided realms and amorous rivalries, was comfortingly familiar. An honourable castrato hero, a selfless and vulnerable soprano heroine, a complex tenor king (as in Bajazet) and an ardent, amorous prince (as in Andronico) were all recognizable types; and there was still a prison scene (those old sets had to be utilized), albeit earlier than usual in the opera, in the second act. A scheming queen was a throwback to the sorceresses of Handel's earliest London operas. On the face of it, Handel must have thought the libretto a safe bet as the vehicle with which to introduce his new singers to their London audiences.

Strada was not (yet) Cuzzoni, so although as the sympathetic Adelaide she was given the same type and variety of music as her predecessor, it was all subtly different. Her big aria closing the first act, for instance, 'Scherza in mar la navicella', busy with marine metaphor and swirling coloratura, is actually quite restrained compared to the vocal acrobatics that came so easily to Cuzzoni or Faustina. Adelaide's sad little prison soliloquy in the second act, 'Menti eterne', would for the earlier regime probably have been a continuo aria in the mould of 'Falsa imagine' – a discipline of fragile vulnerability, which conversely requires the greatest confidence and security in a performer. But just as there was no Cuzzoni, there was no Haym either to co-navigate such an aria. So here Handel wove an angular and tormented violin line around a straightforward vocal part. Similarly, Adelaide's second soliloquy, the flashy 'D'una torbida sorgente', was shared with a solo violin, and in the final duet the focus was divided between Strada and Bernacchi. So Handel, ever the professional craftsman, wrote sensitively for his new soprano, with the aim of showing her off but not overtaxing her.

If Strada was no Cuzzoni, Bernacchi, in the title role, was certainly no Senesino. Handel was careful to give him arias which, whether amorous or warlike, were all engaging and exhibited the voice well; but they were not as dazzlingly difficult as those of his precursor. Fabri, on the other hand, was Handel's first tenor since Francesco Borosini, for whom he had created the great roles of Bajazet, in *Tamerlano*, and Grimoaldo, in *Rodelinda*, and he now relished the opportunity to write for another. All the music for his tyrannical character, Berengario, is slightly unhinged, from the jagged introduction to the opera's first aria, the reflective 'Grave è'l fasto di regnar', to his own crazed vocal patterns – rolling triplets in 'Regno e grandezza', dashing semiquavers in 'D'instabile fortuna' – in his faster arias. There is similar manic energy in the music for the mezzo-soprano, Merighi, whose role, Matilda, was a ruthless and power-crazed woman, bearing a strong resemblance to Lady Macbeth. Whether oilily manipulating her son in 'Vanne a colei ch'adori', taunting her rival, Adelaide, with a powerful image of a caged bird as she condemns her to prison in 'Orgogliosetto và l'augeletto', exuding sarcasm in 'Amo lo sguardo' or reflecting on changing stability in 'Quel superbo', the whole role is arresting, and exercises Merighi's wide range, agile technique and dramatic intensity. And it culminates in a brief but magnificent accompanied recitative, Handel's great hallmark, in which Matilda evokes the Furies. (Small wonder that Merighi, who was in fact paid more than Strada, demanded top billing, according to Lord Hervey. But Handel and Heidegger continued to respect convention, and put Strada's name first.) For the beautiful but inexperienced nineteen-year-old Bertolli, Handel wrote blandly undemanding music, as he did for his German bass, Riemschneider – clearly, no real replacement for Boschi. Numerically, there are fewer arias for the new singers than Handel had written for his previous company. Where for instance in *Alessandro*, the first opera for the 'rival queens', Senesino had ten arias or ensembles and Cuzzoni and Faustina each had nine, here, Bernacchi and Strada both have six, and Merighi five. Consequently Handel filled the operatic space with instrumental padding. There are more purely orchestral numbers than in earlier operas: the overture is long, with four movements, and there are introductory sinfonias too to the second and third acts, as well as a battle sinfonia with trumpets. Handel was clearly trying very hard to win back his audience after a gap of two years.

But in the event, *Lotario* did not please. According to Rolli, 'the great public failed to appear', and the new singers were disappointing: 'Not all beans are for market, especially beans so badly cooked as this basketful'. He concluded that 'everyone considers it a very bad opera'.[1] Colman's 'Opera Register' recorded, 'Opera's began again with an entire new company of singers – La Signora Strada del Pio was ye Cheife & best', although he judged 'the rest little esteem'd an Eunuch called Bernacchi'.[2] Even faithful Mrs Pendarves could not bring herself to enthuse. On the day of the final performance, she wrote bitterly to her sister:

> The opera [*Lotario*] is too good for the vile taste of the town: it is condemned never more to appear on the stage after this night. I long to hear its dying song, poor dear swan. We are to have some old opera revived, which I am sorry for, it will put people upon making comparisons between these singers and those that performed before, which will be a disadvantage among the ill-judging multitude. The present opera is disliked because it is too much studied, and they love nothing but minuets and ballads, in short the *Beggar's Opera* and *Hurlothrumbo* are only worthy of applause.[3]

Lotario had, quite frankly, flopped.

The 'old opera revived' was none other than *Giulio Cesare*. So Handel's new singers, in addition to performing *Lotario* and readying themselves for the next new arrival (*Partenope*), had to learn the longest and most celebrated opera ever presented in London. And, as Mrs Pendarves had so perspicaciously noted, they were to follow directly in the footsteps of the mighty ones who had gone before. Inheriting therefore the mantles of Senesino and Cuzzoni, Bernacchi and Strada were Giulio Cesare and Cleopatra. Surprisingly, young Bertolli was given the villain, Tolomeo, rather than Sesto, who was sung, as in the 1725 revival, by a tenor – here, Fabri. Merighi and Riemschneider were Cornelia and Achilla. Handel pruned and revised as necessary, and *Giulio Cesare* ran for nine performances from 17th January. And, as soon as that monumental opera was up and running, the cast were handed *Partenope*, which Handel finished on 6th February, and which, again, opened less than three weeks later, on 24th February.

Partenope is in a completely different mould to *Lotario*, or indeed any of the operas from the Academy's last gasps. It is a comedy, with genuinely bizarre situations and hilarious lines, almost as if Handel is taking on board Mrs Pendarves' observation that *Lotario* was too serious and scholarly ('studied'). The libretto, by Stampiglia, was written for Naples in 1699, an altogether different era operatically, and by 1730 it had already been set many times. Handel had probably seen the setting by Caldara in Venice, in 1708. *Partenope* had been considered by the Academy directors as a possibility in 1726, for there were two prominent roles for women. But, perhaps on the humourless advice of Owen Swiney ('It is the very worst book . . . that I ever read in my whole life'[4]), they rejected it. Handel however liked it, and now that he did not have to submit to the collective wishes of a committee, he set about making his own version.

The story is of Partenope, Queen of Naples (Strada), and three suitors; and of Rosmira, Princess of Cyprus, who, like Shakespeare's Viola, is disguised as a man, 'Eurimene', and pretending also to be a suitor for Partenope's hand. In fact, she loves one of the others. When, after many vicissitudes, 'Eurimene' is challenged to a duel, it is suggested that the fight be bare chested ('*a petto nudo*'), whereupon inevitably Rosmira is exposed as a woman. Nevertheless the young lovers are paired off in a happy ending.

Handel relished the cross-dressing confusion and inherent comedic opportunity from the older period. By now he knew his new singers better. The writing for Strada as Partenope, for instance, is subtly different from that in *Lotario*: the arias lie a little higher, including even a top C, and the coloratura is more spirited and altogether less cautious. Not unlike the role of Cleopatra, which Strada was performing at exactly the same time, Partenope is both seductive and powerful, and her music conveys all her characteristics. 'Qual farfalletta' has eyelash-fluttery coloratura and an alluring bass line; the vocal line in 'Sei mia gioia' is suggestively curvaceous and interrupted by provocative rests; while arias like 'L'amor ed il destin' or 'Spera e godi' are forthright and strong. So there is a wide range of colour and gesture here, and the title role is a joyous challenge for any singing actress. Mrs Pendarves may initially have frowned on Strada's stage technique, but by her third collaboration with Handel the singer was clearly making huge strides.

There is quality too in the writing for other singers, which again charts the development (or not) of individual performers. The enigmatic Merighi, as Rosmira/Eurimene, has well-contrasted arias, including a gentle siciliano, 'Se non ti sai spiegar', a fiery revenge aria, 'Furie son dell'alma mia', and a magnificent (if dramatically somewhat irrelevant) hunting aria, in prime position at the end of the first act, 'Io seguo sol fiero', complete with boisterous horns and oboes. Mindful perhaps of the billing problem that had so irked Merighi, Handel made sure she had show-stopping material at a prestigious place in the opera.

Only the music for Bernacchi still seems unremarkable, with restrained coloratura and careful, even predictable vocal writing. His one really gorgeous aria is 'Ma quai note di mesti lamenti', sung as he falls asleep in the final act. But even here the vocal line is not especially interesting; the aria is distinguished by its ravishing accompaniment of two flutes and a continuo theorbo (actually specified by Handel, which was rare), with a pizzicato bass line. The awful truth, which Handel understood all too well, was that Bernacchi was no good. So however much Handel's rapport with his female singers was growing, that with his leading man seems not to have progressed at all.

The real joy of *Partenope* is its pacing, through its ensembles and its vibrant recitative exchanges. Fired again by his libretto, with its completely different field of references from those to which he had most recently conformed, Handel was allowed to do what he instinctively did best: to tell a story. The drama seems constantly to be thrusting forward in a manner not seen since the glorious operas of 1724. There are ensembles – a trio and a quartet – so the state of mind of more than one person at a time is revealed. There are arias without the da capo convention, the device which inevitably puts the narrative impulse temporarily on hold, and some of these are extremely short, like the affecting nine-bar cavatina for Merighi, 'Arsace, oh dio'. So, there is much delight to be found in an opera which so skilfully combines comedy and dejection, joy and loss, animosity and reconciliation. After the tetchy and anxious years of the Academy's sad demise, Handel was once again having fun.

Sadly, the Haymarket audiences did not fully share Handel's enjoyment: *Partenope* ran for only seven performances. Doubly popular, with fourteen, was the pasticcio that followed it, *Ormisda*. Handel had little if anything to do with this, and it is likely that the singers themselves suggested arias that they knew, upon which an evening's entertainment could be constructed. But, however popular this patchwork compilation was, flimsily wrapped in its off-the-shelf story, the operatic cognoscenti were dismayed. Mrs Pendarves attended *Ormisda*'s final rehearsal, and wrote disconsolately to her sister: 'Operas are dying, to my great mortification. Yesterday I was at the rehearsal of a new one; it is composed of several songs out of Italian operas; but it is very heavy [compared] to Mr Handel's.'[5]

At the end of the season, Handel revived *Tolomeo*, but it was much curtailed from its original version. The new company was by now exhausted, and Bernacchi was simply not up to the challenges of music written for Senesino. As the season staggered to its close, Rolli was triumphantly malicious. Inventing a marvellous portmanteau word combining the names of Heidegger and Handel, he wrote to Riva on 12th June: 'I shall barely answer you on the matter of that *Coppia Eidegrendeliana* and their worthless operas. Because in truth they succeed no better than they deserve. The musicians will be paid, and that is all that can be done. I perceive besides that either there will be no operas in the new season or there will be the same Company, which is most certainly going from bad to worse.'[6]

In truth, the *Coppia Eidegrendeliana*'s first season in total control of operatic matters in the Haymarket had not been such a disaster. They had presented forty-six performances of five different productions, and they had introduced new talent to the London stage, some of which would continue to be integral to musical activity in the capital for many seasons. Far from ceasing operations altogether, as Rolli had hinted, Handel and Heidegger had four more years to run in their contract. But clearly something had to change. Bernacchi and Riemschneider would have to go, and maybe young Bertolli too.

Handel began to look for replacements even as his first season ended. On 30th June he wrote both to Swiney in Venice and to the British Envoy in Florence, Francis Colman (no relation of the man who had invented the 'Opera Register'). Ideally, he was looking for a male soprano and a female contralto, 'equally good at male and female parts'. (The bass, to replace Riemschneider, was less urgent, and not yet mentioned.) Handel named several singers of whom he had heard good report, proposed a sum of up to 1,100 guineas for two, and stipulated that, once hired, the two recruits should be in London by September. Still nervous of singers' egos and prospective rivalries, he begged his correspondents to make 'no specific mention . . . of *prima*, *seconda* or *terza donna*, since that embarrasses us in the choice of opera and . . . is a source of great inconvenience'.[7] Swiney and Colman put their heads together. Nobody now held out any hope for Farinelli, but there were two other possibilities for the Bernacchi replacement. One was Giovanni Maria Bernardino Carestini, a young singer of the same generation as Farinelli, and with similar wide experience in the opera houses of Italy. But Carestini was now engaged in Milan and therefore unavailable. So Swiney and Colman rather radically proposed an alternative solution: to try and entice Senesino back to London; apart from Farinelli, there was simply nobody in his class. Senesino himself was interested in the idea, but drove a hard bargain. Eventually, Handel swallowed a fair measure of pride and reluctance, abandoned his desire to replace Bertolli with another contralto, threw all his financial resources into Senesino's basket, and rehired the star for the exorbitant sum of 1,400 guineas.

London was delighted, and so was the King, who renewed his royal bounty of £1,000 to the opera. In early October, Senesino arrived (in his own time, therefore – not in September as Handel had requested), demanding an immediate advance of a hundred guineas, which Handel, businesslike as ever, duly paid. To open the new season, he revived *Scipione*, which back in 1725 had had thirteen triumphant performances. Senesino repeated his Lucejo, Strada was given the Cuzzoni role of Berenice, and Handel re-wrote the other roles for the rest of his company. As the 'Opera Register' recorded: 'Nov. 3 Tuesday Opera's began with Scipio Senesino being return'd charm'd much: the rest as last year – Scipio 4 times to Saturday *ye 14 Nov*: the King, Queen &c there each night.'[8]

A quick revival of *Partenope* followed, for seven performances. Here at least Strada, Merighi, Fabri and Bertolli could resume familiar material, while it was Senesino who learnt a new role; and Handel paid him the compliment of writing him a new aria, 'Seguaci di Cupido', in the final act. And in the meantime Handel was preparing his first new opera of the season, in which, of course, the title role would be assumed by Senesino.

Having enjoyed his initial encounter with the work of Metastasio in *Siroe*, Handel turned again to the exciting young poet. Metastasio's *Alessandro nell'Indie* was brand new; it had been premiered earlier that very year, in a setting by Vinci in Rome, and, like many other composers, Handel quickly seized on it. The story is of the benevolent Alexander the Great, his conquest of India and his magnanimous treatment of those he imprisoned. With five suicide attempts (by three different people), two battles and much disguise and deception, this is an apparently complex work, but in the theatre its narrative of devotion, jealousy, human frailty and, ultimately, clemency is abundantly clear. It is not surprising that, by the end of the eighteenth century, it had had more than sixty settings. Handel fashioned it to his own requirements, beginning with the actual title. He had already written an opera called *Alessandro*, so he adjusted the importance of the central characters, giving the focus to Alessandro's prisoner, Poro, and naming the opera accordingly. Senesino would therefore have his title role.

Handel was energized by the return of Senesino, by the better balance therefore between his main singers, and by the very quality of Metastasio's libretto. *Poro* is an extraordinary work, in which once again barriers are torn down and new sophistication is achieved. Senesino and Strada do most of the work; Strada's growth in confidence and execution had clearly continued, to the extent that she was as much an equal partner for Senesino as Cuzzoni had been before her. And again Handel knew exactly how to write for them both. Senesino's arias are reassuringly brilliant, and show the return of truly fiery and thrilling coloratura ('Vedrai con tuo periglio') and glorious line. His real musicianship is reflected in 'Senza procelle', an aria of dramatic irrelevance but musical enchantment, accompanied by flutes and horns in addition to lilting strings. Situated in the middle of the second act, and therefore at the very heart of the opera, this aria seems a 'Welcome back' offering to Senesino. The writing for Strada, too, similarly emphasises her particular strengths. Most of her music is slow and sustained, showing her penchant for reflective pathos, though 'Se troppo crede al ciglio' in the second act is extremely busy, with some fearsome coloratura at the top of her register, where Handel obviously trusted her to be secure. One aria, 'Se il ciel mi divide', is shared with a solo violin, so Pietro Castrucci, leading the orchestra, was still receiving his rewards too.

But the chief glories of the music for both Senesino and Strada are in the three duets that they share. All are significant, and all arresting. The first, which ends Act I, is the most astonishing, for it is built on two arias that the singers have already sung. Earlier in the act they exchanged vows of fidelity, he beginning with the tenderly ardent 'Se mai più sarò geloso' and she answering with the equally passionate and affecting 'Se mai turbo il tuo riposo'. By the end of the act, through a series of misunderstandings, each has become convinced that the other is faithless, and they bitterly quote back at each other their earlier oaths (and arias) in an edgy number of true dramatic sophistication. Early in the second act, the lovers are reconciled and have an all-too-brief duet (just twenty-four bars, no da capo), 'Caro/cara amico amplesso', with intimately entwined vocal lines and pianissimo string accompaniment over a gently moving bass line, in the seductive key of F sharp minor. This is an adaptation of a duet from Handel's own *Aci, Galatea e Polifemo*, of 1708, and a true testament therefore to his easy recall of his entire output, as he dug out of it exactly the right music for the right moment. And at the end of the opera, after everyone has acknowledged Alessandro's magnanimity and greatness, Strada welcomes Senesino to her arms in 'Caro, viene al mio seno'. Senesino responds, and they then come together as their music combines in duet, which in turn leads straight into the final chorus. It is one of the most well-crafted and therefore musically satisfying endings of all Handel's operas.

Beyond his two main singers, Handel did not ignore Merighi and Fabri, nor even Bertolli, though her aria count was now reduced to two. (The bass who had replaced Riemschneider was an inexpensive Italian called Giovanni Giuseppe Commano, but he was given no arias at all.) Fabri, in the important role of Alessandro, has four extremely varied arias, all well characterized, and good showpieces (for instance, 'Serbati a grandi imprese', with impressive coloratura) as well as being dramatically crucial. Merighi's five arias likewise exploit every aspect of her burgeoning vocal and dramatic gifts; and one of them, 'Son confusa pastorella', a beguiling and ingenuous andante, with a flute in addition to its string accompaniment, became extremely popular with amateur singers and flautists. As was Handel's continued instinctive preference, his recitative exchanges have real dramatic bite, and his deployment of arias without the da capo convention ensures that the storytelling is constantly active.

The excitement of a new opera for the returning hero, Senesino, certainly rekindled London's interest. As the *Daily Courant* reported on 17th February, 'Last Night their Majesties, together with the Prince of Wales, attended by the Earl of Grantham, the Lords Herbert and Harvey, &c, went to the Theatre in the Haymarket, to see acted the Opera of Porus.'[9]

As *Poro* continued a long and happy run (it had sixteen performances), a naughty rumour began to circulate that Cuzzoni would now follow Senesino back to London. On 8th March, the *Daily Advertiser* announced, 'We are credibly inform'd, that the celebrated Signiora Cuzzoni, with another famous Voice from Italy, are daily expected here, in order to perform in a new Opera which will soon be acted, and 'tis to be the last this Season.'[10]

Whether an excitable supposition, or even a malicious device designed to unsettle Handel's increasingly confident soprano, Strada, this was merely a rumour which never resurfaced. Handel marched on. He shrewdly chose and adapted two earlier operas with which to complete the season, and both of them had splendid roles for Senesino. First came *Rinaldo*, now twenty years old. Senesino would naturally assume Nicolini's title role, and Strada could take Girardeau's Almirena. But thereafter Handel had to make considerable alterations. The important role of Armida, which had been sung in 1711 by the vibrant soprano Pilotti-Schiavonetti, was adapted (and somewhat reduced) for the equally colourful contralto Merighi. Similarly, the bass role of Argante was diminished and reworked for the mezzo-soprano, Bertolli; the mezzo role of Goffredo now became a tenor role for Fabri; and Eustazio was completely cut. (The dismal bass, Commano, was fobbed off with the tiny role of the *mago*.) Considerably shorter therefore than its first version, *Rinaldo* was almost unrecognizable now, but it received 'New Scenes and Cloaths' and served its purpose, for it ran for six performances in April. Four days after it closed, the same singers were back yet again with a revival of *Rodelinda*, with Senesino repeating his great role of Bertarido. As Rodelinda herself, Strada inherited another Cuzzoni role, and presumably scotched once and for all the whisper that Cuzzoni might herself have come to sing it. After its opening on 4th May, *Rodelinda* had seven more successful performances, of which the last, on 29th May, was the forty-fifth that the company had delivered since *Scipione* premiered on 3rd November the previous year.

It had been another huge season. In less than seven months, six productions (five operas and a pasticcio) had been consecutively learned, rehearsed and performed, with absolutely no respite between them. To be sure, Senesino was being most extravagantly paid, and his colleagues did not fare badly either. But it is impossible to begrudge them their rewards, considering the relentless intensity with which they were being made to work in these Haymarket seasons. Handel and Heidegger drove their troops, especially Senesino and Strada, furiously.

∽

In the middle of that 1730–1 season, on 27th December, Handel's mother, Dorotea, died in Halle. She was two months short of her eightieth birthday. Since moving to London, Handel had only visited her three times, in 1716, 1719 and 1729, but he had kept sporadically in touch with her welfare through his brother-in-law, Michael Dietrich Michaelson, whom he regarded as his 'beloved brother'. Michaelson had indeed become like a son to Dorotea, even after the death of Handel's sister in 1718, and his two marriages since. It was Michaelson who organized the funeral, which Handel, locked in his Haymarket season, could not even think of attending. The oration was written and delivered by one Johann Georg Francke, and Michaelson sent Handel a copy of it, with a full account of the proceedings. Handel's reply, written on 23rd February, is the most personal and emotional letter he ever wrote. Contrary to his usual practice of corresponding in French, he reverted here to his mother tongue (which seems to have become a little rusty), and he was not ashamed to share his grief: '*Ich kan nicht umhin allhier meine Thränen fliessen zu lassen*' ('Here I cannot hold back my tears'). He acknowledged his debt to Michaelson: 'The manifold obligations which I owe to my highly respected brother for the continual loyalty and care with which at all times he assisted my dear, blessed mother, I will not declare with words alone but reserve to myself the opportunity of showing my true gratitude.'[11]

Handel undertook to repay all the funeral expenses, and to have Francke's oration printed. This full, if somewhat pious, account of Frau Händl's quiet life concludes with magnificent reference to her son, and to his current connection with the English throne. Despite some vague inaccuracy, this is truly indicative of the pride felt in Halle for the standing and achievements of its native composer: 'Georg Friedrich, born 23rd February, in the year 1685, who stands in especial grace, by reason of his exceptional knowledge of music, as Director of Music to the reigning Majesty in England and Elector of Hanover, George II, as also to

193

the late King of Great Britain, His Majesty George I, of glorious memory.'[12]

Handel was still corresponding with Michaelson and dealing with the inevitable aftermath of his mother's death as his 1730–1 season ended, and he and Heidegger were hatching their plans for the following one. Whatever his private feelings, his almost manic dedication to hard work always came first. Once again, there would have to be some changes in the company. For a start, the unsatisfactory bass, Commano, should go. He would be replaced by Antonio Montagnana, who was brought from Venice, and probably therefore at the instigation of Swiney. Handel was by no means dissatisfied with either Merighi or Fabri, but, after their two busy London seasons, they both elected to return to Italy. They were replaced by a Florentine tenor, Giovanni Battista Pinacci, and his contralto wife, Anna Bagnolesi. Handel's six-singer cohort was complete.

The new season opened with no fewer than three revivals: *Tamerlano* (three performances), *Poro* (four) and *Admeto* (six). As always, these productions followed each other in the quickest succession, with barely three or four days between the closure of one and the opening of the next.

The first new opera, to open in January, gave Handel some uncharacteristic indecision. He had been working on a libretto based on Racine's play, *Bérénice*. Its title was still in French, *Titus l'Empereur*, although the opera would naturally have been sung in Italian. But Handel abandoned it, as ever saving its existing components for later recycling, and, for the third time, turned instead to Metastasio for his new libretto. This was *Ezio*, premiered in Rome three years earlier, in a setting by Pietro Auletta. Another story with a heroic and noble title role for Senesino, it involves the Roman Emperor Valentiniano (Bagnolesi), his general, Ezio

(Senesino), a hostile patrician, Massimo (Pinacci), his daughter, Fulvia (Strada), Valentiniano's sister, Onoria (Bertolli), and the prefect, Varo (Montagnana). Alongside some complex amorous entanglements there is an assassination plot, some false accusation and incarceration (giving Senesino yet another soliloquy in a prison), and eventually the customary clemency and life-sparing.

Like its predecessor *Poro*, *Ezio* has splendid and ever-inventive music, some of it, including the overture, salvaged from the *Titus* draft. Again Senesino and Strada share musical prominence, each of them having seven arias, generally with the now-familiar traits for them both; singers and audiences alike would have their expectations. The demands on Senesino's coloratura seem perhaps a little reduced. Only one of his arias, 'Se la mia vita dono è d'Augusto', is truly busy, and then not for long, compared to the dazzling pyrotechnics of his earlier roles. But lyrical intensity and the sheer beauty of his artistry are shown in every other aria, from his opening 'Pena a serbarmi, o cara', which seems to begin as a continuo aria, but into which pianissimo string accompaniment is alluringly added, to his prison aria at the end of the second act, an affecting siciliano in Handel's favoured key of pathos, F sharp minor. Strada likewise has the tenderest music, beginning with 'Caro padre', together with lilting flutes, and including also an accompanied recitative and lament, very much in the Cuzzoni tradition, in the final act. But the music for the new singers is strong too, and most notably that for the bass, Montagnana. Although his role is small, he has four tremendous arias, especially the military 'Già risonar d'intorno al campidoglio', with blazing trumpets in dialogue with oboes, and matching vocal energy. It is as if Handel is expressing his delight in at last finding a true replacement for Boschi. And, at the end of the opera, he experiments with a finale borrowed from the French vaudeville, in which the four main characters each sing a verse before they join together for the concluding chorus.

But, despite all this invention, and the combination of refreshing novelty with what Handel knew went down well, *Ezio* was another baffling failure. The royal family showed their support as always, attending no fewer than four consecutive performances, but the public stayed away. (Colman's 'Opera Register' reported bleakly that the opera 'did not draw much Company'.[13]) After only five performances, *Ezio* was withdrawn and quickly replaced by four of *Giulio Cesare* – familiar territory at least for Senesino and Strada. But even this crowd-pleaser did not have a smooth run. At one performance part of the scenery collapsed, and, according to *Fog's Weekly Journal*, Senesino was 'so frightened that he trembled, lost his Voice, and fell a-crying'.[14] Since he had just sung the line '*Cesare non seppe mai che sia timore*' ('Caesar does not know fear'), he was much mocked in the press. Even a year later, when *Fog's Journal* was making a general point about political leaders, it referred to Senesino's ignominious behaviour: 'Every Tyrant or Tyrannical Minister is just such a *Cesar* as *Senesino*.'[15]

On 15th February the company opened its final production, Handel's new *Sosarme*, which he had finished composing just two weeks earlier, on 4th February. Even allowing for the customary intensity of production turnover, the manic sequence in that single month of composition and substitution, rehearsal and performance smacks of desperation. Handel slashed the text almost in half, cutting most of the recitative – indicating not so much his haste, but his awareness that his audiences were becoming indifferent now to anything that was not an aria. Borrowing as always from his own stockpile of material to reinforce the new arias, Handel quickly threw together the first two acts of *Sosarme*. But then politics intervened. Somebody must have suggested to him that it would be unwise to portray a King of Portugal, one of Britain's oldest allies, in an unflattering light (suffering violent rages and being easily duped). He went back over his score and changed the names of all the locations and all the characters. Portugal became Sardis, a remote area of ancient Persia; Ferdinand of Castile became Sosarme, an invented name. So the preparations were fraught, and the dramatic narrative was compromised. And yet Handel nevertheless produced a score of exceptional music.

In the title role, Senesino hardly appeared in the first half of *Sosarme*, a consequence perhaps of his workload, as he had spearheaded *Ezio* and *Giulio Cesare* in quick succession. But when he did fully enter the narrative, he and his rising co-star, Strada, sang one of Handel's most exquisite duets of misfortune and longing, 'Per le porte del tormento'. Similarly at the end of the opera, when all had been resolved, they sang together again for 'Tu caro sei', an altogether much lighter duet, but over which Handel had taken supreme compositional care. It is effectively an antiphonal piece, with Strada supported by violins and half the continuo team (one harpsichord, one cello), and Senesino by violas and the other half. Handel's meticulous dynamic markings here are also indicative of the constantly professional and practical musician that he was, always concerned with balance and projection, whatever the time pressures and constraints. Among a whole clutch of fine arias, two have violin obbligatos for Handel's faithful concertmaster, Castrucci.

Sosarme was a success with the unpredictable public, and Colman reported that it was 'for many Nights much crowded to some peoples admiration'.[16] So, at least Handel approached the end of his season in a more positive frame of mind. There were revivals too of *Flavio* and Ariosti's *Coriolano*, both with title roles originally sung by Senesino and therefore continuing vehicles for him. Significantly, this was the first time that Handel had made use of any opera by one of his former Academy colleagues since his new company had risen from the ashes of the old one. But, whether Handel liked it or not, Senesino was now steering artistic decision, dictating the terms of his appearances and agreeing to perform only in operas of his own choosing. For the following season, he proposed Bononcini's *Griselda*, also from a decade earlier, and Handel had to agree to its revival too.

As well as demonstrating the power of Senesino's persuasion, there are other surprises in these revivals of both *Coriolano* and *Griselda*. While Ariosti had died in 1729, Bononcini was still very much alive, but in 1732 suddenly in disgrace. He had apparently plagiarized a madrigal by Antonio Lotti, 'In una siepe ombrosa', and passed it off as his own composition, back in 1728. Letters were exchanged with Lotti in Venice; and, although the Italian was extraordinarily generous in implying that his madrigal had actually been improved, Bononcini never recovered from the public shame of his deceit. Fellow musicians refused to work with him; he quarrelled with his patroness, the Duchess of Marlborough, and eventually fled from London in October 1732, never to return. Handel will have felt some sympathy with Bononcini (Tweedle-dum to his Tweedle-dee) for these dramas, although there may too have been an element of Schadenfreude, which was certainly one of his pleasures. But Bononcini's disgrace did not stop Handel from presenting *Griselda*, for it was essential that Senesino was kept happy. More to the point, at the time, Handel was experiencing some intriguing distractions.

On 23rd February 1732, Handel was invited by his old friend and colleague, Bernard Gates, to celebrate his forty-seventh birthday at the Crown and Anchor Tavern in the Strand. Gates was a musician steeped in the cathedral tradition: he had been a boy chorister at the Chapel Royal, and, later, as a fine bass singer, one of its Gentlemen, often also serving Westminster Abbey. He had sung in all Handel's church music since Queen Anne's 'Birthday Ode' in 1713. Now, he was Master of the Children at the Chapel Royal, and as such a formidable educator and choir trainer. He was also a leading figure in a private music club called the Academy of Ancient Music, which since its foundation in 1726 (under the original title, the Academy of Vocal Music) had met regularly at the Crown and Anchor Tavern. The Academy of Ancient Music was formed of professional musicians interested in music from past eras, especially vocal polyphony from the previous century. The bulk of its members were from the choral establishments at St Paul's Cathedral, Westminster Abbey and the Chapel Royal, but foreigners were welcome too, and the Academy's first president, albeit in absentia, had been Agostino Steffani. Indeed, it was in the context of the Academy of Ancient Music that Bononcini had submitted Lotti's madrigal for performance, while claiming it to be his own. Other music clubs, such as the Philharmonic Society, also gathered in the Crown and Anchor, in which, as the historian Hawkins noted, there was 'a spacious room, in every respect proper for musical performances'.[17]

In February 1732, Gates had prepared for performance one of Handel's own scores, written during his time with the Duke of Chandos. *Esther*, with its Old Testament-based, Racine-derived libretto originally devised by Pope and Arbuthnot in 1718, had possibly been performed at Cannons in 1720. Somehow Gates had acquired a copy of the score and, in just over a week, he gave three performances of it at the Crown and Anchor (23rd February, 1st and 3rd March). The printed libretto describes their details:

Mr Bernard Gates, Master of the Children of the Chapel-Royal, together with a Number of Voices from the Choirs of St James's, and Westminster, join'd in the Chorus's, after the Manner of the Ancients, being placed between the Stage and the Orchestra; and the Instrumental Parts (two or three particular Instruments, necessary on this Occasion, excepted) were performed by the Members of the Philarmonick Society, consisting only of Gentlemen.[18]

Among the singers from those ecclesiastical choirs, whose names were printed in the libretto of the event, one stands out. The small role of the Priest of Israelites was sung by John Beard. This fifteen-year-old chorister would soon become a distinguished tenor soloist, and another of the singers whose vocal craft, and therefore whose career, would be carefully and skilfully developed by Handel. *Esther* was an ambitious choice of score for Gates to thrust upon his mainly young musicians. In addition to arias, accompanied recitatives and ariosos, there are seven choral numbers, two of which are especially long and complicated. The final chorus, 'The Lord our enemy has slain', is almost a standalone cantata (a multi-movement piece for choir and instruments) in its own right, for it has many contiguous sections contrasted in mood, texture and scoring, and incorporates within it a duet also for the characters Esther and Mordecai. The vocal writing is complex and demanding, indicative both of Handel's continuing interest (in 1720) in choral counterpoint and of Gates's confidence (in 1732) that his young charges could deliver it.

These three private performances of *Esther* were much liked. Viscount Percival reported in his diary, 'From dinner I went to the Music Club, where the King's Chapel boys acted the History of Hester, writ by Pope, and composed by Hendel. This oratoria or religious opera is exceeding fine, and the company were highly pleased, some of the parts being well performed.'[19]

Other musicians heard of this novel idea of performing a biblical story in English with full staging, and were intrigued. A rival group got together to mount *Esther* again in the Great Room of York Buildings in Villiers Street, on 17th April, making clear that this, unlike the Crown and Anchor performances, was open to the public ('Never Perform'd in Public before').[20] Handel seems to have been enraged by this appropriation of his own music, and he hastened to better it in every way, and at the King's Theatre, no less. In just two weeks, he altered the score considerably. Calling on his literary assistant at the King's Theatre, Samuel Humphreys, who had recently joined the company to help with English translations of the Italian operas for the printed word-books, he opened up the text. Accordingly, Handel then made substantial revisions to his score, adding and subtracting arias, and now choruses too, in his usual manner, rewriting much of the 1718 music, and adding many more instruments than had performed for Gates or in Villiers Street. After the overture, the first aria for Esther, 'Breathe soft, ye gales', immediately showed the new richness of his scoring, for it included two flutes, as well as oboes and bassoons, and specified a veritable battery of continuo instruments: harpsichord, theorbo, harp and organ. Later, he also added trumpets and timpani, especially for the mighty final chorus, 'The Lord our enemy has slain' – though, significantly, he also here shortened the choral passages. (Perhaps, after all, in those first performances under Gates, the young choristers had

201

not quite managed such complexity. Certainly, Viscount Percival had implied – 'some of the parts being well performed' – that there were areas of imperfection.)

Handel advertised his new *Esther* in the *Daily Journal* under the heading, 'By His Majesty's Command': 'At the King's Theatre in the Hay-market, on Tuesday the 2d Day of May, will be performed, *The Sacred Story* of ESTHER: an *Oratorio* in *English*. Formerly composed by Mr. *Handel*, and now revised by him, with several Additions, and to be performed by a great Number of the best Voices and Instruments.'[21]

His 'best Voices', unlike the exclusively cathedral singers for Gates, were indeed the stars of his opera company: Senesino (Assuerus), Strada (Esther), Montagnana (Haman), Bertolli (Mordecai) and, returning to Handel for the first time since singing Polissena in *Radamisto* in 1720, Ann Turner Robinson (Israelite Woman), the sole English singer now performing in her own language. But the cathedral choristers and Gentlemen were there too, for the choral numbers remained; and indeed Handel included two of his Coronation anthems, 'My heart is inditing' and 'Zadok the Priest', with their texts adjusted for the new story. And Handel made it clear in his press announcement that these performances, unlike those in the Strand or Villiers Street, were to be devoid of staging: 'N.B. There will be no Action upon the Stage, but the House will be fitted up in a decent Manner for the Audience. The Musick to be disposed after the Manner of the Coronation Service.'[22]

This firm statement of intent is deeply significant, both for the reasoning behind it and for its seismic consequences. Handel had attended Gates's February performances, in which the Chapel Royal Children had appeared in costume. Any kind of costumed staging, now, would have appeared to be a copycat imitation, and in any case the presence of a full choir on the stage complicated the space. So Handel struck out on his own. Drawing on, and indeed emphasizing, his royal credentials, Handel alluded to 'the Manner of the Coronation Service', implying solemnity, pomp, grandeur – and those contrapuntal choruses. And the royal family – who according to Burney had longed to see *Esther* but could never have attended a performance in a tavern – now supported Handel to the full. As the *Daily Courant* reported, they turned out in force for the opening night: 'Last Night their Majesties, his Royal Highness the Prince of Wales and the Three Eldest Princesses went to the Opera House in the Hay Market and saw a Performance called Esther, an Oratorio.'[23]

King George and Queen Caroline will have warmly recognized 'their' specific Coronation anthems in their new guise (which is indeed perhaps why Handel included them). And they came back three more times, for there were five subsequent performances, all of them well attended. The slightly puzzled Colman reported on this very different kind of performance in the King's Theatre: 'May 29 Hester Oratorio or sacred Drama, english all ye Opera singers in a sort Gallery no acting was performed six times & very full.'[24] Handel's gamble had more than paid off.

Encouraged, no doubt, by this somewhat surprising turn of events, Handel pulled off the shelf his other Cannons English composition, the mould-breaking *Acis and Galatea*. Again making substantial changes, expanding it from two acts to three, borrowing from his own cantatas and operas as well as from his old Neapolitan version of the same story, and being entirely comfortable with using two languages (English and Italian) side by side, he added some extra characters and cast his entire Haymarket company in all the roles. *Acis and Galatea* ran at the Haymarket theatre for four performances in June 1732. As with *Esther*, there was 'no Action upon the Stage', but there were beguiling pastoral representations, and there were choruses. The use of the English language, even if here not complete, touched a nerve with the audiences. So in just a few weeks, Handel had swiftly issued an instinctive counterpunch to his challengers and adversaries, and, fortified by both the needs and the support of the royal family, had – probably unwittingly – laid the foundations for a vast development in English music. It was entirely typical of him.

Public enthusiasm for Handel's Italian operas was maddeningly unpredictable, but by the summer of 1732 definitely on the wane. The old argument about the incomprehensibility of foreign singers performing foreign stories in a foreign language was never far below the surface. Ballad operas, after the manner of *The Beggar's Opera*, continued to be popular; and now, as a new season approached, a consortium of Englishmen, headed by Thomas Arne (father of the composer), Henry Carey and John Frederick Lampe, took over the Little Theatre in the Haymarket, provocatively just across the street from the King's Theatre, to present English operas there. Significantly, these were not ballad operas, but attempts to weld the English language onto Italian musical forms. Plots were chosen with care (Lampe's *Britannia*, for instance, struck many chords) and the singers had local appeal. Meanwhile on the other side of the Haymarket, Handel's greatest attraction, Senesino, was becoming increasingly dictatorial, and his demands caused Handel to rethink a little as he shuffled his pack of singers. After just one season, the tenor Giovanni Battista Pinacci and his contralto wife Anna Bagnolesi were returning to Italy, as was a minor castrato, Antonio Campioli. (Maybe they simply could not take the pace.) Since the departure of Faustina and Cuzzoni, Handel had had just one soprano in his company, Strada; but, in order to allow Senesino to revive his great title roles (*Alessandro* and *Tolomeo* were on his list of demands, both from the era of Faustina and Cuzzoni), another soprano would now be required. So Handel hired Celeste Gismondi from Naples, a gifted singer, certainly, if not in quite the same league as Faustina or Cuzzoni, or indeed Strada. Lord Hervey, a close friend of both Queen Caroline and Walpole, had heard her sing in Naples, and went in October 1732 to hear her again ('the new Opera-woman') at the house of Lady Pembroke, a passionate opera patron and supporter of individual singers – she had been Cuzzoni's benefactor too. Hervey pronounced that Gismondi was 'not as pretty as she was but sings better than she did',[25] the latter development perhaps the result of a combination of Handel's coaching and Lady Pembroke's patronage. In any event, Celeste Gismondi, or 'Celestina', as she became known, was immediately swept up in the whirl of operatic activity at the King's Theatre. She threw herself into the disastrous pasticcio which opened the season, *Catone in Utica*. Lord Hervey, who mistakenly believed it to have been written by Handel, loathed it, writing to his friend, Stephen Fox, on 4th November: 'I am just come from a long, dull, and consequently tiresome Opera of Handel's, whose genius seems quite exhausted.'[26] The revival of *Alessandro* later that month started well, but rapidly faded, struggling to reach six performances. In January, the revival of *Tolomeo* only had five.

Whether out of an awareness of a need for change, or mere creative whim, Handel now changed direction again. He returned to the type of magic opera, with supernatural characters and transformation scenes, in which he had so excelled two decades earlier (*Rinaldo*, *Teseo*). He took his story from Ariosto's *Orlando*

Furioso, via a libretto prepared by Capeci for Alessandro Scarlatti in 1711. But it was much altered for London in 1733, with the significant addition of a magician, Zoroastro, introduced both to guard the honour of Orlando and also to execute special effects. This was an important role for Montagnana, and further proof of his own performing strengths. But Senesino's title role, despite all the current tensions between composer and singer, was to be his greatest, and also one of his most demanding, for, during the course of the opera, Orlando undergoes a quite extraordinary psychological breakdown. And the music with which Handel charted this progressive madness was among the finest and most individual that he ever wrote.

In terms of sheer quantity of music, it is clear how Senesino was carrying this new opera. Strada and Gismondi each had nine arias (that old Faustina/Cuzzoni balance seemed still to resonate); Montagnana had seven and Bertolli six. But Senesino had fifteen, including the monumental, multipartite mad scene which concludes the second act, and the gestures of which continue well into the third act. And in terms of quality, Handel's level of imagination and invention, for every character and throughout the opera, is consistently stellar, recalling the creative energy of the golden period of a decade earlier (*Giulio Cesare*, *Tamerlano*, *Rodelinda*). There are intimate continuo arias (for example, Senesino's first, 'Stimulato della gloria'), blazing coloratura numbers (Montagnana's 'Sorge infausta') and alluring sicilianas (Gismondi's 'Se mi rivolgo al prato'). There are brief but special inclusions, entirely for musico–dramatic effect, of horns, flutes (not least in Strada's delicate pastoral aria, 'Verdi piante') and most especially of 'violette marine' – a type of viola d'amore invented by Handel's loyal orchestral leader, Pietro Castrucci, and played by him and his brother, Prospero. There is a trio at the end of the first act, in which a gently entwined love duet for Strada and Bertolli is offset by Gismondi's angular unhappiness, and a similar duet in the third act, where Handel ingeniously combines Strada's sorrow and Senesino's raging. On two occasions there are shared or interrupted arias: Strada's gentle 'Ritornata al suo bel viso' is taken over by Bertolli; and Senesino's still-deranged 'Unisca amor' of sweet pleading to Gismondi is repeatedly interspersed with her horrified protestations.

But all these glories pale beside the quite extraordinary mad scene for Senesino's Orlando. The scoring is deceptively simple, requiring only the basic strings and continuo instruments, and no added special effects at all. The strength of the scene is its utterly fragmented structure. No musical section lasts for more than a few bars, giving the sense therefore that nothing is sustainable or settled. There are brief passages written, for the first time in music history, in the irregular meter of 5/8. Here, this astonishing music is deployed as a literal interpretation of instability, for there is no audible order or regularity. What seems to begin as an energetic rage aria, 'Già latra Cerbero', subsides after only nineteen bars of manic repetition into a bewildered accompanied recitative, and then into a tender, weeping gavotte, 'Vaghe pupille, no non piangete, no', which has all the feeling of a da capo aria with a contrasted middle section. But this too is interrupted by continuing deranged thought, and angry cries of 'Ma sì pupille, piangete sì', before Montagnana's Zoroastro intercedes, and spirits Orlando away in his chariot. In the third act, before Orlando is at last relieved of his insanity, this episodic musical madness continues until, exhausted, he sinks into sleep in his aria, 'Già l'ebro mio ciglio', accompanied by the most rarefied sounds of those two 'violette marine'. *Orlando* may have been written at a time of administrative pressure and anxiety, but its consistent and innovative excellence reflects Handel's highest level of achievement, as posterity has shown.

Orlando opened on 27th January 1733, and Colman's 'Opera Register' pronounced it 'extraordinary fine and magnificent'.[27] The royal family, as ever, were intensely supportive to Handel and attended almost all its performances. But sadly there were not to be many of them, for after the sixth, on 20th February, Strada became ill and remained so for several weeks. Handel pulled together a hasty revival of *Floridante* (with another Senesino title role, naturally) to fill the performance slots, and then turned his attention to his final new offering for the season. Hoping to build on the success and popularity of *Esther*, he proposed not an opera, but another oratorio based on a religious subject, involving Gates's cohorts of Children and sundry Gentlemen from the ecclesiastical choirs, and with his own opera singers in the named roles. And, in pursuing these lines, Handel was no doubt encouraged by an important letter from an old friend.

Back in December 1732, as the performances of *Alessandro* were grinding to a halt, Aaron Hill had written to Handel, ostensibly to thank him for supplying opera tickets for him and his family ('my daughters are both such lovers of music that it is hard to say, which of them is most capable of being charm'd by the compositions of Mr *Handel*'). But the real purpose of Hill's letter was, in the renewed spirit of enthusiasm for operas in the vernacular, to beg Handel to stop writing these Italian operas based on poor librettos, and to build instead upon 'a foundation of good poetry; where the excellence of the *sound* should be no longer dishonour'd by the poorness of the *sense* it is chain'd to.' He continued, 'My meaning is, that you would be resolute enough to deliver us from our *Italian bondage*; and demonstrate that *English* is soft enough for Opera, when compos'd by poets who know how to distinguish the *sweetness* of our tongue from the *strength* of it, where the last is less necessary.' Hill had clearly run out of patience with the traffic of foreign singers in the Haymarket, believing that 'male and female voices may be found in this kingdom'. This superbly courteous and thoughtful letter concludes with a paragraph of generous humility: 'I am so much a stranger to the nature of your present engagements that, if what I have said should not happen to be so practicable as I conceive it, you will have the goodness to impute it only to the zeal with which I wish you at the head of a design as solid and unperishable as your musick and memory.'[28]

Handel's new oratorio was to be *Deborah*, which was dedicated to Queen Caroline. But Strada's illness and the rapid rehearsal of *Floridante* at the beginning of March will have taken time away from the preparation of *Deborah*, which opened just four days after *Floridante* closed. And it shows. *Esther* had been largely composed at leisure, in Cannons, and then confidently expanded with Coronation anthems and other borrowings; but here, starting from scratch, there is a sense that the work has been thrown together, with music from the Brockes Passion, from the Chandos and Coronation anthems (the two that had not been used in *Esther*), and from fragments of old cantatas. Based anyway on an indifferent libretto, devised solely now by Samuel Humphreys, *Deborah* lacks the overall coherence of *Esther* (and certainly that of *Orlando*). And if the solo music, still obediently but incomprehensibly sung by the Italians who so upset Aaron Hill, is by no means ever humdrum, nor is it anywhere near the inspirational level of that of *Orlando*.

What is good in *Deborah* is the choral material. The non-operatic singers from the ecclesiastical choirs returned to the King's Theatre, bringing their especial expertise, the execution of choral counterpoint, and were therefore part of the establishment of what would become the very backbone of the genre of oratorio. Contrapuntal writing was familiar territory for them; and they were familiar too with Handel's music, not just from its occasional inclusion in their regular services, but from special events, such as the annual festival for the Corporation of the Sons of Clergy, celebrated by the combined choirs of the Chapel Royal, St Paul's and Westminster, with a service in St Paul's Cathedral and then a dinner. Since 1731, Handel's music had dominated that service, which in 1733 took place just a few weeks before the performances of *Deborah*. So the new oratorio's double-choir writing, in up to eight parts, was not at all daunting for these accomplished Children and Gentlemen. And Handel would exploit their skills with his habitual combination of serendipity, canny awareness and visionary invention, and steer English music in an altogether new direction.

The royal family again supported Handel staunchly for *Deborah*, turning out in force for its opening and returning for later performances. Public reaction was mixed. Viscount Percival greatly liked it, pronouncing it 'very magnificent'.[29] Others were puzzled by it, again partly because of the Italians' pronunciation of the English text. Lady Irwin did not like it at all, finding it 'excessive noisy'.[30] But the chief reason for a disaffected reaction to *Deborah* was that, apparently encouraged by his eager pupil Princess Anne, Handel had doubled the ticket price. If the young Princess's cheerful solution to a funding crisis was startlingly naive, more startling still is the fact that Handel, normally so astute with his own financial matters, complied with her suggestion. The subscribers were furious and refused to accept the charges, forcing their way into the theatre for the second performance without paying the extra fee. As a public-relations exercise it was a disaster, and not helped by the fact that, three days earlier, Walpole had introduced into Parliament an Excise Bill taxing tobacco and alcohol. This was vehemently opposed and eventually defeated. But it handed a golden opportunity to the satirists, for the two acts of apparent greed were gleefully compared. An anonymous epigram, entitled, 'A Dialogue between two Projectors' (Walpole and Handel), appeared in the pamphlet *The Bee*, on 24th March:

> Quoth W—— to H——l shall we two agree
> And Join in a Scheme of *Excise*. H. *Caro sì*.
> *Of what Use is your Sheep if our Shepherd can't sheer him?*
> *At the* Hay-Market *I, you at* We——*er?* W. Hear him.
> *Call'd to Order the Seconds appear'd in their Place,*
> *One fam'd for his Morals, and one for his Face;*
> *In half they succeeded, in half they were crost;*
> *The* Tobacco *was sav'd, but poor* Deborah *lost.*[31]

❧

But this was merely the tip of an iceberg that had been forming steadily over several months. At the end of the previous season, another satirical pamphlet, *See and Seem Blind*, purporting to be a letter from 'Lord B——' (Burlington) to 'A—— H—— Esq' (Aaron Hill), had indicated total impatience with all Handel's activities:

> I left the *Italian* Opera, the House was so thin, and cross'd over the way to the English one, which was so full I was forc'd to croud upon the Stage . . . This alarme'd H——l, and out he brings an Oratorio, or Religious *Farce* . . . so away goes I to the *Oratorio*, where I saw indeed the finest Assembly of People I

ever beheld in my Life, but, to my great Surprize, found this Sacred *Drama* a mere Consort [concert], no Scenary, Dress or Action, so necessary to a *Drama*; but *H----l*, was plac'd in Pulpit, (I suppose they call that their Oratory), by him sate *Senesino, Strada, Bertolli*, and *Turner Robinson*, in their own Habits; before him stood sundry sweet Singers of this poor *Israel*, and *Strada* gave us a *Hallelujah* of Half an Hour long; *Senesino* and *Bertolli* made rare work with the *English* Tongue you would have sworn it had been *Welch*.[32]

By the beginning of 1733, the animosity towards Handel had built to such an extent that there was a plan to set up a rival opera company. The Earl of Delawarr recorded, in January, 'There is a Spirit got up against the Dominion of Mr. Handel, a subscription carry'd on, and Directors chosen, who have contracted with Senesino, and have sent for Cuzzoni, and Farinelli . . . Porpora is also sent for.'[33] The energy of this report is as shocking as is the stellar list of names it proposes to present in the new company. (Handel had completely failed to lure Farinelli to London.) Clearly Senesino, thoroughly disgruntled after all his years with Handel, was at the heart of the machinations, and he would have been keen to involve his old colleague, Cuzzoni, in any new venture. (It was her portrait that hung on the walls of his Siena palazzo; Faustina was neither on his wall, nor on his list.) The Earl's report continued, 'The General Court gave power to contract with any Singer Except Strada'. So Strada was considered to be too close to Handel, for she was his true and loyal protégée. The list of directors already chosen for this new company is as impressive as that of its prospective artistic personnel. Most of them were noblemen, and some were disgruntled former directors of the Academy. Politically they veered towards the opposition, indicating a general sense of rebellion against the status quo, be it governmental or operatic. And the most interesting name of them all was that of Frederick, Prince of Wales, who, despite his passionate enthusiasm for Handel's music, was more than ready to espouse any cause that obstructed those of his parents. Thus the stance of a seemingly innocuous enterprise, the establishment of an artistic endeavour, was in fact steeped in combative defiance – against Handel, against Walpole and against the monarch. Although in January 1733 the new company was, as yet, far from any operatic activity, the turn of the tide was abundantly clear.

By April, as *Deborah* approached the end of its run, the attacks on Handel had become very personal. The oppositionist newspaper *The Country Journal; or The Craftsman*, published another, apparently signed by Paolo Rolli ('P—LO R—LI'). It is highly unlikely that this slick society operator would have allowed his own malevolence to appear in print, reserving it for his private correspondence and, presumably, his conversation. But it was a wickedly astute attribution by whoever did write the article in the *Craftsman*:

The Rise and Progress of Mr. *H——l*'s Power and Fortune are too well known now for me to relate. Let it suffice to say that He was grown so insolent upon the sudden and undeserved Increase of both, that He thought nothing ought to oppose his imperious and extravagant Will. He had, for some Time, govern'd the *Opera*'s, and modell'd the *Orchestre*, without the least Controul. No Voices, no *Instruments* were admitted, but such as flatter'd his Ears, though they shock'd those of the Audience. *Wretched Scrapers* were put above the *best Hands* in the *Orchestre*. No Musick but *his own* was to be allowed, though every Body was weary of it; and he had the Impudence to assert, *that there was no Composer in* England *but Himself*. Even *Kings* and *Queens* were to be content with whatever low Characters he was pleased to assign them, as it was evident in the case of Signior *Montagnana*; who, though a *King*, is always oblig'd to act (except an angry, rumbling Song or two) the most insignificant Part of the whole Drama. This Excess and Abuse of Power soon disgusted the Town; his Government grew odious; and his *Opera*'s grew empty. However this Degree of Unpopularity and general Hatred, instead of humbling him, only made him more furious and more desperate.[34]

The article thus humiliatingly exaggerated Handel's commitment to the highest possible standards, and presented it as aggressive imperiousness. Even Handel's supporters acknowledged the stubbornness of his will (Mainwaring would variously refer to him as 'impatient' and 'inflexible', and to the 'violence of his passions'[35]), but here the hostility of description was utterly distorting. The *Craftsman* also seized on Handel's doubling of the ticket prices, claiming that, 'The Absurdity, Extravagancy, and Opposition of this *Scheme* disgusted the whole Town', and concluded that Handel himself was in 'a *deep Melancholy*, interrupted sometimes by *raving Fits* . . . It is much question'd whether he will recover'.[36] Handel was in general thick-skinned, but the thought that he might actually have read this vituperative diatribe is chilling.

As the season finally closed in June, so at last did the whole chapter of collaboration with Senesino. After creating no fewer than twenty-three operas together, both composer and singer had had enough, as the *Bee* reported: 'We are credibly informed, that one Day last Week Mr. *H—d—l*, Director-General of the Opera-House, sent a Message to Signior *Senesino*, the famous *Italian*

Singer, acquainting Him, that He had no farther Occasion for his Service: and that *Senesino* replied, the next Day, by a Letter, containing a full Resignation of all his Parts at the *Opera*, which He had performed for many Years with great Applause.'[37] So Senesino left, taking with him Montagnana, Bertolli and Gismondi. Only Strada, ever loyal, was left with Handel in the echoing rooms of the King's Theatre in the Haymarket.

9

DEFIANCE

'All danger disdaining'

[Deborah]

True to form, Handel refused to show any sign of distress at the battering that he had received in the 1732–3 season. Even as his Italians walked out on him, and there were rumours too that Cuzzoni would return to London to join Senesino and add yet more lustre to his starry line-up, Handel had his own immediate and very prestigious plans. He was about to visit the University of Oxford, where apparently he was to receive an honorary degree in July. On 23rd June, the *Bee* – often a hostile publication with regard to Handel's activities – could not fail to disguise a grudging respect and admiration:

Great Preparations are making for Mr. Handel's Journey to Oxford, in order to take his Degree in Musick; a Favour that University intends to compliment him with, at the ensuing Publick Act. The Theatre there is fitting up for the Performance of his Musical Entertainments, the first [of] which begins on Friday Fortnight the 6th July. We hear that the Oratorio's of

217

Esther and Deborah, and also a new one never performed before, called Athaliah, are to be represented two Nights each;
and the Serenata of Acis and Galatea as often. That Gentleman's Great *Te Deum*, *Jubilate*, and *Anthems*, are to be vocally
and instrumentally performed.[1]

In fact Handel was not about to receive any degree, but to supply music for the University's commemoration of the 'Oxford
Act', or Encaenia. This degree-giving ceremony of the utmost
formality was publicly celebrated with a week of surrounding
events, often including performances of music and drama. Handel's impressive pile of scores, one of them brand new, indicates
the density of musical activity in this Oxford week, and the seriousness with which he energetically prepared for it.

Not only did Handel take his music to Oxford, he took the musicians too. First, he gathered his entire orchestra from the King's
Theatre, referred to, somewhat startlingly, as 'a lowsy Crew . . .
of forreign fiddlers'[2] by one disaffected academic, Dr Thomas
Hearne. With greater difficulty, in view of the recent exodus, he
next assembled a team of singers. The faithful Strada would of
course stick by him. The other soprano would be a Mrs Wright,
who had sung for him only once before, as Orinda in the revival
of *Admeto* in 1728, but of whom little else (not even her first
name, let alone her age) is known. Handel had recently, in the
revival of *Floridante* in March, tried out a young German bass,
Gustavus Waltz, as a potential replacement for Montagnana.
Waltz had been in London for just over a year, performing English operas at the Little Haymarket Theatre with Arne and
Lampe, but, in crossing the street to take part in *Floridante*, he
began a long association with Handel, cemented perhaps in this
visit now to Oxford. Beyond these familiar voices, Handel really

had to improvise, and the names of the tenors appearing in his Oxford cast lists, Messrs Rocchetti and Salway, are both shrouded in obscurity. But Handel's biggest problem was that there was absolutely no substitute for Senesino. He was compelled to call into service an Oxford countertenor, Walter Powell, who was actually something of a local star. The 'celebrated Mr Powell', as the *Bee* called him, sang in the choirs of three of the four choral foundations, Magdalen, St John's, Christ Church and New College. And indeed it was with these combined choirs, schooled like their London equivalents in the daily execution of vocal counterpoint, that Handel would collaborate, as they formed the backbone of everything he was to offer in his busy Oxford week. One of the boys from these choirs, a 'Master Goodwill', would also be allotted an important solo role in the new oratorio, *Athalia*.

Handel's Oxford schedule seems to have been even more frantic than his customary London one. Between 5th and 12th July, he planned two performances each of *Esther*, *Deborah* and the new *Athalia* in Wren's magnificent Sheldonian Theatre; one of *Acis and Galatea* in Christ Church; and, for two services in the University Church of St Mary's, his 'Utrecht' Te Deum and Jubilate, and two of his Coronation anthems. Rehearsing all this music with unfamiliar forces could have been fraught with anxiety, but as always Handel seems to have taken it in his stride, even when the speeches in the Sheldonian ceremonies overran, and all the musical performances had to be moved around. (*Acis and Galatea* was actually performed in Christ Church at nine o'clock in the morning, and the second performance of *Deborah* was cancelled altogether.) There was perhaps inevitably some mealy-mouthed academic resistance to such Handelian saturation. Dr Hearne continued to fill his diary with complaints, some of them even referring to the amounts of money that Handel had accrued

– perhaps news of that disastrous doubling of the London ticket price for one of these very oratorios, *Deborah*, had registered beyond the capital. And someone objected to the use of the Sheldonian for musical performance rather than for its designated ceremonial purpose: '. . . truly, 'twas his Opinion, that the Theater was erected for other-guise Purposes, than to be prostituted to a Company of squeeking, bawling, out-landish Singsters'.[3] But the public – not just Oxonians, but visitors from far and wide, who filled the guest houses in the city and in several villages beyond it – continually offered 'utmost Applause'.[4] Handel returned to London with his weary forces, a full purse and a satisfied sense of artistic reward.

The new work, *Athalia*, was very much in the mould of Handel's oratorios for the King's Theatre. His colleague, Samuel Humphreys, had turned again to Racine for his libretto. An Old Testament story of the deposition of a tyrannical despot could have been a dodgy subject for Hanoverian London, but for the strongly Jacobite people of Oxford it was perhaps a canny one. The title role of Athalia, who has murdered many claimants to her husband's kingdom in order to rule herself, is not in fact the main protagonist. The High Priest Joad and his wife, Josabeth, who save and restore to the throne its rightful heir, the boy Joas, are the focus both musically and dramatically, and they were sung in Oxford by the local favourite, Walter Powell, and Strada. Their many arias and dramatic recitatives, plus a duet between them, quite outshine the music for Athalia herself, as sung by Mrs Wright, for whom, perhaps, the role was a step too far. As with *Esther* and *Deborah*, the choruses are all excellent, so the combined Oxford choirs must have been well up to the standard of those in London. And the rousing concluding chorus celebrating the return of Joas – 'Around let acclamations sing: Hail royal youth! Long live the King!' – echoed the real coronation of still-recent memory, whose own anthems had also bejewelled that glittery Oxford week.

∾

Once back in London, in the summer of 1733, Handel stayed where he was. He had been invited by his brother-in-law Michael Dietrich Michaelson to Halle, where there were still, after three years, many outstanding administrative issues relating to his late mother's estate. But he wrote to Michaelson, thanking him profusely for all that he had done, issuing some gentle instructions about further transactions, and explaining that, 'however much I long to pay a visit to the people of your place, nevertheless the imminent and inevitable matters of business, which indeed quite overwhelm me, do not allow me such a pleasure'.[5] And he did have pressing 'matters of business', for he had to assemble a new season and build a new company from scratch. There was also, as it happened, a royal wedding in prospect; his favourite Hanoverian pupil and staunch supporter, Princess Anne, was betrothed to Prince William IV of Orange.

Handel began first to rebuild his company. Strada of course was still with him, and young Gustavus Waltz had clearly passed his Oxford test and was rehired for the whole of the new season. Beyond them, Handel had to delve once more into untried talent, hiring for smaller roles an Italian castrato, Carlo Scalzi, and two sisters, Caterina and Rosa Negri, respectively contralto and mezzo-soprano. But, for his second soprano, he alighted on a very familiar singer indeed. Margherita Durastanti, who had first sung for Handel in *Agrippina*, in Venice, back in 1709, nearly a quarter of a century earlier, and then sung a clutch of roles for the Academy between 1720 and 1724, had retreated from the limelight. In an act that was surely somewhat risky – Durastanti was approaching her fifties – Handel now rehired her for 1733–4. Her once-soprano high tessitura had clearly lost its top register, for the roles that she would sing in the next year were markedly lower. But she was a known quantity to Handel, who appreciated her experience, her musicianship and her loyalty, and was prepared to wager that the public too would be happy to see her back in the Haymarket.

There was still one enormous gap in Handel's roster for the 1733–4 season: who could replace Senesino? He was now heading the opposition, and relishing his position as its chief focus and chief motivator. It was essential therefore to replace him with someone of similar ability and charisma. Luckily Handel's mental database of singers, like his database of arias as he moved his material around, was impressively efficient. Back in 1729, he had tried to hire the castrato Giovanni Maria Bernardino Carestini, a generation younger than Senesino and therefore an approximate contemporary of Farinelli. At that time, Carestini had not been available, but now he accepted Handel's renewed invitation, bringing to London a voice with both brilliant technique and beauty of line, and a decade of experience throughout Italy. According to Charles Burney, Carestini was 'tall, beautiful and majestic', a marvellous actor and a most accomplished singer, with 'the most perfect style'.[6] Handel's roster was complete.

But, just a mile away from the Haymarket, the opposing armies too were gathering. Cleverly locating themselves in a building which had already attracted enormous popular support through its presentation of *The Beggar's Opera* in 1728, Senesino, with his financial backers and artistic colleagues, hired the Lincoln's Inn Theatre in Portugal Street. Originally a tennis court in the

Restoration period, it had been converted into a theatre in 1714, and since 1723 had served mainly for elaborate pantomime, staged by its owner-manager, and indeed performer, John Rich. The success of *The Beggar's Opera* gave Rich huge resources with which now to build a brand-new theatre in Covent Garden (approximately midway between Lincoln's Inn Fields and the Haymarket), so Lincoln's Inn Fields was available as a venue. Senesino's company seized it. Lined up now in Portugal Street with Senesino were his fellow Handelian deserters, Bertolli, Montagnana and Gismondi; Cuzzoni and Farinelli were due imminently; Rolli, no less, had been reeled in as Italian secretary, the post he had held at the Academy; and, in a clever move, the distinguished Italian composer Nicola Antonio Porpora had also been enticed to London as the new company's Musical Director. Porpora was almost exactly the same age as Handel, and had a similar amount of experience therefore as a composer of Italian opera, thus far mainly in his native Naples, Rome and Venice. He had a formidable reputation too as a singing teacher, and his pupils included the great Farinelli himself. With the intention quite simply of outshining Handel in all artistic matters, Senesino's company (it has come to be known as the Opera of the Nobility, on account of its patrician directors, but at the time it was most often known simply as Senesino's Opera) had sourced and hired the biggest names in Europe.

Another significant element in the operatic battle lines forming in central London was the disposition of the royal family. George II and Queen Caroline continued their loyal support of their old friend, Handel, as did the devoted Princess Anne and to a lesser extent her younger sisters. But Prince Frederick was the visible figurehead of Senesino's company. According to Lord Hervey's memoirs, there was much more to this than met the eye. The

Prince of Wales, always at loggerheads anyway with his father, was now furious that his sister Anne was about to be married. He took it as a personal slight that a liaison for his younger sister should have been arranged before his own. Lord Hervey, having poured scorn on the Prince's logic ('As if her being married prevented his being so'), concluded, 'the Prince, in the beginning of his enmity to his sister, set himself at the head of the other opera to irritate her, whose pride and passions were as strong as her brother's (though his understanding was so much weaker), and could brook contradiction, where she dared to resent it, as little as her father.'[7] Lord Hervey, a close friend and confidant of the Queen, was always inclined to portray the Prince of Wales in a bad light, and in fact Frederick did in due course return to support Handel too, pledging him money, turning up to his performances, and later, in the 1740s, even giving him rehearsal space in his London residence, Carlton House. But at this point his espousal of a rival cause could not go unnoticed in London society. As Hervey continued:

> The King and Queen were as much in earnest upon this sub-
> ject as their son and daughter, though they had the prudence to
> disguise it, or to endeavour to disguise it, a little more. They
> were both Handelians, and sat freezing constantly at his empty
> Haymarket Opera, whilst the Prince with all the chief of the
> nobility went as constantly to that of Lincoln's Inn Fields . . .
> An anti-Handelist was looked upon as an anti-courtier, and
> voting against the Court in Parliament was hardly a less remis-
> sible or more venial sin than speaking against Handel or going
> to the Lincoln's Inn Fields Opera.[8]

Handel entered into this new competition with his usual acuity. He was determined to get a head start on Senesino, and also to parade his own superior royal connections. The rivals would not open their season until after Christmas, so Handel planned to be not one but two steps ahead of them. The 30th October was the King's birthday, and it was customary for the royal family to attend a ball in St James's Palace. But on this occasion all of them – including the Prince of Wales – came to the Haymarket for the opening of Handel's season: a pasticcio entitled *Semiramide riconosciuta*, for which Handel wrote new recitatives linking a collection of arias. The royal family, and the rest of the audience, were no doubt keen to assess the new singers. According to Lady Bristol, 'the first [performance] was full to hear the new man, who I can find out to be an extream good singer; the rest are all scrubbs except old Durastanti, that sings as well as she ever did.'[9]

Having thus celebrated the King's birthday in the Haymarket, Handel planned for his first full opera to open around the celebrations for Princess Anne's wedding, two weeks later, on 12th November. He was of course to be involved in that ceremony anyway, providing the anthem 'This is the day' (which he arranged mainly from music in *Athalia*, not yet heard in London). Choosing carefully, he selected a revival of *Ottone* for the day after the wedding, with Carestini now – provocatively perhaps – taking over Senesino's old title role, Strada in Cuzzoni's role of Teofane, and, significantly, Durastanti repeating the part of Gismonda, which she had created in the premiere of the opera. Waltz was in Boschi's place as Emireno, and Caterina Negri was Matilda – the role that had so troubled the emotionally fragile Anastasia Robinson, in 1723.

At this point, Handel was upstaged. Princess Anne's future husband was Prince William IV of Orange. The Dutch were a key ally of Britain against France, and although Orange power had waned since the seventeenth century, this union was judged to be politically expedient. Sanctioning its advantages, however, did not require the King actually to like his future son-in-law. When young William, a diminutive hunchback, arrived in London at the beginning of November, he was greeted with minimal ceremony ('the equipage the King sent to fetch him was only one miserable leading coach with only a pair of horses and a pair of footmen', reported Lord Hervey) and almost total indifference ('scarce common civility') from George II, who believed 'the Prince of Orange was a nothing until he had married his daughter'.[10] Queen Caroline was dismayed by reports of poor William's ugliness, and her younger daughters too joined in the general expressions of horror. Only Princess Anne herself sailed with serene insouciance through these family anxieties, not even being present with her mother and sisters when Lord Hervey described to the royal family his first meeting with the Dutch Prince. She apparently preferred the company of Handel and his singers: 'she was in her own apartment at her harpsichord with some of the Opera people, and . . . she had been as easy all that afternoon as [the Queen] had ever seen her in all her life'.[11] The visiting Prince was lodged, not in any of the royal palaces, but in Somerset House, the former residence of Catherine of Braganza, Queen of Charles II. The building had been empty since 1705, and, situated as it is beside the Thames, it was cold and damp. The sickly William became seriously ill, and collapsed in a thanksgiving service in the Dutch church on the day before his wedding. At the last possible moment, all plans were put on hold. The invalid was eventually allowed to be brought to St James's Palace, and later to Kensington Palace, but as soon as possible he was sent to Bath to recuperate fully. Through all these surprises and solutions Princess Anne maintained her equanimity: 'on his arrival in England, on the day for the marriage being set, on its being put off, on his illness, on his recovery, on his being in danger, on his being out of it, the countenance of the Princess Royal to the nicest examiners appeared exactly the same; which surprised everybody so much the more as she was known to be of a temper to which nothing was really indifferent, whatever it appeared.'[12]

Despite the postponement of the wedding, Handel's *Ottone* opened as planned on the following day, 3rd November, and the King and Queen, together with the Prince of Wales (though not Princess Anne), duly attended. Handel slipped in another pasticcio opera, *Cajo Fabrizio*, before Christmas, giving every indication that his company was as vibrant and as active as ever. But all London was agog with the prospect of the clash with Senesino's company. Abbé Prévost, author of *Manon Lescaut*, who was then living in England, edited a weekly digest of London news for French distribution, *Le Pour et Contre*. That autumn, his summary of the imminent opera feud, on a scale equalling that which had allegedly occurred between Cuzzoni and Faustina in 1726, was both succinct and telling:

Winter is coming on. You already know how there was an un-reconcilable rupture between Senesino and Handel, and how the former produced a schism in the company and hired a separate theatre for himself and his partisans. His enemies sent for the best voices in Italy; they pride themselves on keeping going despite his machinations and those of his clique. So far the English nobility has been divided; victory will remain in the balance a long time if they have enough determination not to change their minds. But it is expected that the first few performances will put an end to the quarrel, since the better of the two theatres cannot fail to attract very soon the support of them all.[13]

On Christmas Eve, the Prince of Wales hosted a 'Rehearsal of a new Opera' in Carlton House in Pall Mall, attended by 'a great Concourse of the Nobility and Quality of both Sexes'.[14] This was a preview of Senesino's opening production, Porpora's *Arianna in Naxos*, and again the Prince of Wales was signalling his loyalties. Even the subject matter was defiant: it was known that Handel's next opera was to be *Arianna in Creta*, due at the end of January. Choosing almost identical subject matter with which to go head-to-head with Handel cannot have been a coincidence, and it is tempting to infer that Rolli was the prime mover in all this. Better than anyone, he would have known of Handel's plans, and had both the malice and the wherewithal to thwart them. Porpora's *Arianna* duly opened on 29th December, to a great turnout and very favourable response. Notwithstanding this success, Handel (having slipped in a third pasticcio, almost as if he were still test-driving his new company) then countered with his own *Arianna in Creta* on 26th January. For several weeks, the two operas ran against each other, with Porpora's having by far the greater audiences, if contemporary reports are to be believed. Handel's *Arianna* – by no means his most distinguished new offering – had seventeen determined performances as it chased after its rival's tally of twenty-four. London's theatregoers were additionally offered yet a third version of the Ariadne legend at Rich's new theatre in Covent Garden, this time in the form of a danced pantomime, *Bacchus and Ariadne*. On one absurd night, 20th April, all three were performed against each other, at the same time.

With his customary agility, and his genius for building on the strengths of his individual performers, Handel carefully adjusted his *Arianna*. Carestini will have felt the pressure of being measured against Senesino, and perhaps had some requests of his own.

One of his virtuoso arias, 'Qui ti sfido, o mostro infame' – full of heroic bravura coloratura as Theseus prepares to fight the Minotaur – was a little uncomfortably high for him, so Handel transposed it down a semitone, from E major to E flat. Nevertheless, the passagework is still impressively challenging, and a foretaste of some of the even greater coloratura arias that Handel would write for Carestini in the future. At a later stage in the rehearsal period, Handel also added a lyrical aria for his primo uomo, 'Sdegnata con me', as if both he and the singer wished to demonstrate to the opposition that Carestini too had Senesino's ability to be tender as well as fiery. Another late addition was a duet in the third act for Carestini and Strada, 'Mira adesso', which again suggests a tactical reinforcement as the two *Arianna* operas ran against each other. It was certainly Carestini who gained most of the attention. Strada's music, compared to some of her recent roles, was relatively unremarkable. In his writing for his second tier of singers, Handel again indicated his professionalism and craftsmanship. Durastanti's best aria, 'Qual leon', shows her ageing voice off well by surrounding it with oboes, bassoons and horns; but, after rehearsals had begun, Handel was obliged to shorten it, suggesting that Durastanti no longer had vocal stamina. Most of the music for the newcomer, Caterina Negri, doubles the voice with flutes or violins, her inexperience evidently requiring some sort of helping hand. In the small role of Minos, and certainly in his first truly operatic role, Gustavus Waltz, for the moment, was given just one routine aria. Perhaps Lady Bristol's caustic dismissal of some of these newcomers as 'scrubbs' was not so far off the mark.

While the operatic Battle of the Ariadnes continued to be played out, both sides were planning their next moves. Again, Handel's trump card was his superior royal connection. That postponed wedding between Princess Anne and Prince William of Orange had at last been rescheduled for 14th March, and Handel planned to celebrate it in the King's Theatre in spectacular style. He was also to be involved in the ceremony itself. Originally Maurice Greene was announced as providing the music, but he had been somewhat humiliatingly displaced by Handel, presumably at the insistence of the bride. Handel's anthem, 'This is the day', had been ready since the autumn – and indeed had been rehearsed then in the presence of the royal family. There was a joyful confidence in him, therefore, as he put together a wedding serenata, *Parnasso in Festa*, visiting the well-travelled operatic territory of the marriage feast of the sea nymph, Thetis, and the Argonaut, Peleus, on Mount Parnassus, home of the gods and Muses. Carestini was cast as Apollo, and the second castrato, Scalzi, as his son, Orpheus; the Muses, Calliope, Clio and Euterpe, were sung respectively by Durastanti, Strada and Rosa Negri, while Caterina Negri played the huntress, Clori, and Waltz the god of war, Mars. Handel reworked much of *Athalia* into this cheerful piece, but added new music too, and it was presented four times in the Haymarket, probably unstaged but magnificently costumed and lit. The first of those four performances, on the eve of the wedding itself, was attended by the entire royal family, including the bridegroom, the recuperated Prince of Orange. The *Bee*, in the spirit of euphoria which tends to surround royal weddings, reported, 'Last Night Mr Handell's new Serenata, in Honour of the Princess Royal's Nuptials with the Prince of Orange, was perform'd . . . and was received with the greatest Applause; the Piece containing the most exquisite Harmony ever furnish'd from the Stage, and the Disposition of the Performers being contriv'd in a very grand and magnificent Manner.'[15]

On the following day, the focus shifted to the wedding ceremony itself, in the French chapel at St James's Palace – a rarely
used building, but a larger one than the Chapel Royal, no doubt
selected to accommodate numerous guests. It was lavishly lit, for
the ceremony took place at ten o'clock at night. Handel's anthem,
performed at its heart, again shows his extraordinary ability to
produce wholly appropriate music for royal occasions that are
both ceremonial and intimate. Just as he had for the 1727 coronation of the bride's parents, Handel chose his texts carefully. The
outer movements of 'This is the day' have words from Psalms 118
and 45, but the inner movements use very appropriate verses
from Ecclesiasticus and Proverbs: 'Blessed is the man', 'A good
wife is a good portion', 'Strength and honour are her clothing'
and 'The children rise up'. Some of the texts had been para-
phrased by Princess Anne herself, indicating again the closeness
and trust she enjoyed with Handel. Both *Parnasso in Festa* and the
wedding itself were glorious events in the London calendar that
spring. This was the first royal wedding in London for almost a
century; the last one had been in 1641, when the ten-year-old
daughter of Charles I had married the second Prince William of
Orange (and in due course had then given birth to the third, who
became King of England with his wife, Mary). Londoners were
thrilled to observe such elaborate nuptials, and took this fourth
Prince of Orange to their hearts. For all his physical challenges,
William was popular and welcome throughout the capital. And
Handel's close involvement with all the musical events was a sat-
isfying indicator of his social superiority in his face-off with
Senesino, down the road in Lincoln's Inn Fields.

But, while Handel flaunted his royal connections, Senesino
produced a trump card of his own – Cuzzoni. The diva returned
to London towards the end of the long run of Porpora's *Arianna*

and immediately took over the title role. As Senesino renewed his highly popular double act with Cuzzoni, the elaborate programme of his continuing season seems at every stage to have been provocatively chosen. There was a revival of Bononcini's *Astarto*, in which he and Cuzzoni had sung together very successfully in the early seasons of the Royal Academy of Music. (Memories of the old Tweedle-dum/Tweedle-dee taunt can only have delighted Senesino's supporters.) And there was an insolent advance into Handelian territory, in the form of an oratorio, as Senesino then got Porpora to write *Davide e Bersebea*, and scheduled its opening on the night before the Haymarket's *Parnasso in Festa*. But if Handel was in any way unsettled by his former colleagues now lining up as enemies against him, he did not show it, for he was ready to counter Senesino's every move. He revived his own *Deborah* for four performances, *Sosarme* for three, and then, for no fewer than sixteen nights, which extended way beyond the closure of Senesino's season, his old *Pastor fido*, from 1712, much revised. There was stamina on both sides.

In April, Handel's close friend and neighbour, Mrs Pendarves, hosted a musical soirée at her Brook Street home. Handel and his singers were the chief attraction, and, as Mrs Pendarves told her sister in a letter, 'Lord Shaftesbury begged of Mr Percival to bring him, and being a profess'd friend of Mr Handel (who was here also) was admitted'.[16] The party was a huge success. Mrs Pendarves continued, 'I never was so well entertained at an opera! Mr Handel was in the best humour in the world, and played lessons and accompanied Strada and all the ladies that sang from seven o'the clock till eleven. I gave them tea and coffee, and about half an hour after nine had a salver brought in of chocolate, mulled white wine and biscuits. Everybody was easy and seemed pleased.'[17]

But the stark truth of the 1733–4 season was that both Handel and Senesino had lost huge sums of money. After glittery opening nights, both houses had played to dwindling audiences. Mrs Pendarves was distraught: 'Tis vexatious to have such music neglected',[18] she wrote to her sister, as she prepared to attend a performance of Handel's *Sosarme* on 30th April. Over on the other team, Rolli acknowledged, 'We have not prospered this year because of two opera houses and because of our carelessness'. But he was confident that 'next year we will be masters of the field, and all will be well'.[19] The chessboard on which this operatic game was being played was about to take on a very different shape.

Handel had always known that his five-year contract with Heidegger at the King's Theatre in the Haymarket would expire after the 1733–4 season. But so of course had the Senesino/Rolli team, who had embarked on some skilful negotiation. In July 1734, Handel learned that Heidegger had in fact let his theatre to Senesino's company, no less; it was partly to this move that Rolli had referred in his letter about being 'masters of the field'. Perhaps, like the mutinous singers, Heidegger too had had enough of Handel's 'imperious and extravagant Will', as the *Country Journal* had put it in the previous year, and was happy to be rid of him. But there was another factor which was implicit in Rolli's crowing confidence, and the businessman in Heidegger will have sniffed the commercial potential. Senesino had succeeded where Handel had failed, and, with vast sums of money, had lured the great Farinelli to London. If the European sensation was now to be presented to avid London audiences, Heidegger was determined to be the man to do it. So Handel and his company were decidedly second best; his contract was not renewed, and he was now operatically homeless.

There was therefore real humiliation for Handel in that summer, and malicious rumours circulated. Prévost's *Le Pour et Contre*, for example, reported, 'Mr. Handel, director of one of the two London operas, had undertaken to keep his theatre going in face of the opposition of all the English nobility. He flattered himself – unjustifiably – that his reputation would always bring him a sufficient audience; but deprived of this support he has incurred so much ruinous expense and [written] so many beautiful operas that were a total loss, that he finds himself obliged to leave London and return to his native land.'[20] But in fact Handel – stubborn, determined, tactically aware – was never downcast for long, and the only travelling he did that summer was to Tunbridge Wells, for its health-giving waters. He looked upon the closure of the Haymarket door not as a disaster, but as an opportunity to open another one. He had watched the recent building of the new theatre in Covent Garden by John Rich, and admired its capacity (it seated 1,400), its excellent acoustic and its technical set-up, allowing for elaborate scenic effects. It even employed a small chorus, as well as the dance troupe headed by Marie Sallé, whom Handel had known since she and her brother had danced, as children, in a 1717 revival of *Rinaldo* in the Haymarket. She had now been with Rich at Covent Garden for three seasons, contributing, among many other things, to the pile of London Ariadnes. Above all, perhaps, Handel will have respected the acumen of Rich himself, who had hit such a jackpot with *The Beggar's Opera*. Within days of his apparent eviction from the King's Theatre, Handel was 'engaged with Mr Rich to carry on the Operas at Covent Garden',[21] as he wrote to a friend, Sir William

Knatchbull, on 27th August. By then, he had already started writing his next new opera, *Ariodante*, confident that he had a theatre in which to present it.

As he began his association with Rich, Handel made some adjustments to his company. For all his loyalty to the elderly Durastanti, she had not been of the greatest use to him, and she was not rehired for Covent Garden. (She in fact disappeared from all view at the end of that 1733–4 season, after a truly distinguished career of almost sixty roles in more than thirty years; and there is even a distressing suggestion that, like so many of her profession, she lived out the latter part of her life in financial straits.) Carlo Scalzi was similarly released and never resurfaced. In their places, Handel took a step in a quite different direction, and hired two young English singers – his first for opera since the delicate Anastasia Robinson, some ten years earlier. These were the soprano Cecilia Young, eldest of three sisters with strong musical connections, and the even younger – still a teenager – tenor John Beard, whose voice had only recently broken, necessitating his departure from the choir of the Chapel Royal. His burgeoning talent was astutely recognized by Handel, who would himself develop it, with thrilling results, over the next two decades.

Handel worked carefully to keep the King on side and ensure that the royal bounty of £1,000, which George II had continued to give annually to Handel and Heidegger at the Haymarket, should now follow him on his move to Covent Garden. (After 1734 the royal bounty would revert to the Haymarket Theatre). An entry in the Treasury minute book on 23rd October 1734 confirms, 'Mr. Chancellor [Sir Robert Walpole] says the King intends that the 1,000*l.* for the undertakers of the Opera shall be paid to Mr. Hendell and not to the Academy of Music, as the last 1,000*l.* was.'[22] Less than two weeks later, the *London Daily Post* reported that Handel had given His Majesty a preview of his new opera: 'We are informed, that when Mr. Handel waited on their Majesties with his New Opera of *Ariodante*, his Majesty express'd great Satisfaction with the Composition, and was graciously pleased to Subscribe 1,000*l.* towards carrying on the Operas this Season at Covent-Garden.'[23] But Handel was not yet ready to launch *Ariodante* on the public, with his inexperienced singers. He would have to break them in gently. This meant that, for the time being, the glories of Senesino's collection of stars would steal all possible thunder.

Handel's season opened tamely on 9th November, with a revival of the *Il Pastor fido* that had ended his previous season. In order to show off his novelty, he added a prologue ('*Terpsicore*') in which Madame Sallé, as the Muse of dance, performed various states of emotion while Carestini and Strada sang Apollo and Erato. He continued to brandish this new attraction with further dance suites at the end of each act. After just five performances of *Il Pastor fido*, Handel then revived *Arianna in Creta* for another five, and threw together a pasticcio, *Oreste*, for three more. But even though the King and Queen loyally attended everything, it was a decidedly muted start to Handel's new life at Covent Garden, and by Christmas he had presented only thirteen performances of three relatively undistinguished works.

Opera of the Nobility, meanwhile, had had a glorious autumn. Senesino pre-empted Handel's first night at Covent Garden by opening fully two weeks ahead of him, on 29th October; he had clearly learned that it was better to strike first. His opening production in the Haymarket was the event of the year: he presented Farinelli's London debut in Hasse's *Artaserse*, with a supporting cast of Cuzzoni, Montagnana, Bertolli and, of course, himself. Farinelli's singing astounded even his new colleagues. Rolli wrote to Riva on 9th November: 'Farinelli was a revelation to me, for I realized that till then I had heard only a small part of what human song can achieve, whereas now I conceive I have heard all there is to hear.'[24] Prévost, later that season in *Le Pour et Contre*, agreed: 'Signor Farinelli, who came to England with the highest expectations, has the satisfaction of seeing them all fulfilled by generosity and favour as extraordinary as his own talents. The others were loved: this man is idolized, adored; it is a consuming passion. Indeed, it is impossible to sing better.'[25] London was indeed in thrall, and *Artaserse* ran for twenty-eight performances. The composer, Hasse, was invited to London to witness his opera's great success. According to Handel's biographer, Mainwaring, the modest Hasse assumed that *Artaserse* was having to be performed because Handel was dead, and on learning the truth 'refused to come, from a persuasion, that where his countryman was (for they were both Saxons by birth) no other person of the same profession was likely to make any figure. He could not believe that in a nation which had always been famous for sense and discernment, the credit of such an artist as Handel could ever be impaired.'[26] Hasse's refusal of Senesino's invitation may also have been influenced by the opinion of his wife, Faustina Bordoni, who can have retained little affection for either Senesino or indeed Cuzzoni. But Senesino could not have wished for a more sensational opening to his season. And he had not yet finished with scoring points against Handel. With outrageous impertinence, he then mounted a production of Handel's own *Ottone*, with himself in the title role he had created, Cuzzoni similarly in her original role of Teofane, and, rather surprisingly, Farinelli in the supporting role of Adelberto. This had five performances, taking Senesino's tally by Christmas to thirty-three, as opposed to Handel's paltry thirteen.

And yet, as the Christmas season gave way to the new year, operatic fortunes also seemed to shift. Senesino's company, having spent much of its energies and finances on two spectacular shows in two months, now drifted rather lamely towards the end of the season with presentations of considerably lesser impact. Two operas by Porpora were bookends to a revival of his oratorio *Davide e Bersebea*, and there was also an opera, *Issifile*, by Cuzzoni's husband, Sandoni. The librettos were prepared for Porpora by Rolli, who, having enjoyed his sense of triumph at ousting Handel from the Haymarket, now seemed to be losing patience with his new operatic colleagues: 'I am so disgusted by it all that I do not care to talk about it, let alone write about it,'[27] he grumbled to Riva in November. Some of Senesino's company, so suffused with the success of their performances at the King's Theatre, were happily making guest appearances at music clubs based in the city's taverns, a move which curiously backfired on them, for it revived the age-old prejudice about overpaid foreign singers. An article in the *Prompter*, in December 1734, complained, 'Are not our English Singers shut out, with our Mother-Tongue? So engrossing are Italians, and so prejudic'd the English against their own Country, that our Singers are excluded from our very Concerts; Bertolli singing at the Castle, and Senesino at the Swan, to both their Shames be it spoken; who, not content with monstrous Salaries at the Opera's, stoop so low as to be hired to sing at Clubs! Thereby eating some English Singers bread.'[28] But Handel, with his burgeoning enthusiasm for oratorios sung in English, and his keen interest, too, in the young English singers he was now employing and training, was as always ahead of the game, as he cleverly exploited some sort of need in London's theatre-going public.

And so, on 8th January 1735, Handel finally unveiled his newest opera, *Ariodante*, of which in embryonic form he had already given the King a foretaste back in the summer. Now knowing the attributes, both strengths and weaknesses, of his new singers, and enjoying John Rich's small chorus and troupe of dancers, he made his adjustments: dances and some brief choral numbers were added, and the role originally intended for the departed castrato, Scalzi, was rewritten as a tenor for the young John Beard. His libretto was another (like *Lotario* and *Sosarme*) by Antonio Salvi – in this case, originally prepared from Ariosto's *Orlando Furioso*, for Perti, in 1708. Unlike most of Handel's operas, the story of *Ariodante* did not necessarily encapsulate the customary high-flown ideals (duty, loyalty, honour) of opera seria, but was a straightforward domestic plot of basic human conduct, motivated by sexual jealousy. There was no subplot; all the action was concentrated in one unfolding set of circumstances. The story was colourful and visually impressive, as Handel relished Rich's brand-new stage machinery, and it culminated in the pageantry of a tournament in the third act. Much of the action took place in the open air, either during the day or at night (there is a sublime sinfonia depicting the rising of the moon at the beginning of the second act), and, significantly, there was no prison scene. The relationships between all the characters, whether lover to lover, brother to brother, father to daughter, were sophisticated and credible. And the music that Handel supplied was exceptional.

Clearly, Carestini had by now found his confidence and his stride. His title role here is one of Handel's richest, and the sheer variety of intense emotion that the upright young Ariodante experiences (joy, despair at betrayal, political responsibility) all have superlative musical representations. Two of his arias have, rightly, become among the best known in all Handel's output. 'Scherza infida', in the second act, is a slow expression of

Ariodante's misery at the apparent faithlessness of his betrothed (Ginevra), revealed in long vocal lines of agony over a sympathetically searing bassoon and pulsating strings. Carestini's lyrical gifts, and his ability too to shape musical phrases, were truly extraordinary. And so too was his vocal technique in fast music. In the final resolution, when the metaphorical as well as the real sun shines after a night of bleak darkness, Ariodante's joy and relief explode in 'Dopo notte', of dazzling (and very difficult) coloratura, fully matching anything that Handel had ever written for Senesino. Carestini had reached his peak at just the right time.

Strada, as Ginevra, was similarly given a huge range of music and emotion, from playful joy in the first act, through tension and disaster in the second (an almost deranged 'Cor mio'), into a selfless dignity with which she faces execution in the third. Both as an actor and a singer, Strada had developed immeasurably since her Adelaide in *Lotario*, just five years earlier. She and Carestini were Handel's known quantities, whose reliable abilities he could display with confidence. But the music he wrote for his younger singers demonstrates equal trust. Gustavus Waltz was in truth far too young (often the fate of baritones) for Ginevra's father, the King of Scotland. But this role was by no means a mere vehicle for bass-clef aural variety; rather, it was an important character, making difficult and sensitive decisions. The King's three contrasted arias – a stirring fanfare, an affecting siciliano and especially an anguished farewell to the daughter he has condemned to die ('Al sen ti stringo') – make this a very adult and rounded role indeed. Caterina Negri, singing the trouser role of the villain, Polinesso, was given straightforward but not undemanding arias. And the young English couple, Cecilia Young and John Beard, were extremely promising, as the technical difficulty and emotional demand of the music for both of them attests; Handel would not have produced music that defeated, or even showed in a poor light, these very young newcomers. With the finest singers in Europe parading their wares around the corner in the Haymarket, here Handel was boldly displaying his own company's very different gifts to their best possible advantage; and they were impressive indeed.

Ariodante had eleven performances, implying a favourable response from audiences. Sadly, this seems not actually to have been the case; a letter in the *Old Whig*, published in March, revealed that Handel had 'this Winter sometimes performed to an almost empty Pitt'.[29] There was another opera up Handel's sleeve, but before embarking on it he tried a different tactic in an effort to prise audiences away from the Haymarket. For fourteen performances in the period of Lent, he mounted all three of his oratorios, *Esther*, *Deborah* and *Athalia*, and, for extra value, threw in organ concertos, which he himself would play in the intervals at every performance. But, although this was eventually to prove a prescient and thoughtful move on Handel's part, the correspondent in the *Old Whig* continued, 'even this has been far from bringing him crowded audiences; though there were no other publick Entertainments on those Evenings'. The Opera of the Nobility, while also losing money at an alarming rate, still had the upper hand.

Handel's final offering that season was his latest new opera, *Alcina*, written while *Ariodante* was being performed, and therefore reflecting Handel's observations on the quality and development of his singers. The levels of brilliance and invention are even more intense in *Alcina* than in *Ariodante*, partly because of his growing confidence in his new team, partly because the spirit of competition fired him to achieve exceptional results, and partly because he was returning in subject matter to the magic plots in which he had so excelled two decades earlier.

The story was derived from Ariosto's *Orlando furioso*. The sorceress Alcina, who has a history of discarding her many lovers and transforming them into trees, streams, rocks and even animals, has captured and seduced a young knight, Ruggiero. Ruggiero's fiancée, Bradamante, in disguise as a soldier, 'Ricciardo', comes to rescue him with the help of her tutor, Melisso, who also has convenient magic powers. They fend off the attentions of Alcina's sister, Morgana, who, after the manner of Shakespeare's Olivia, has fallen for 'Ricciardo'. Bradamante and Ruggiero are reunited, and Ruggiero destroys Alcina's magic 'power of Inchantment', restoring her captives to life.

Strada and Carestini, as Alcina and Ruggiero, fitted their roles perfectly, and developed their performing chemistry that had been so intensified during the run of *Ariodante*. Both of them were given a further batch of distinguished arias, whether searingly lyrical as in Alcina's 'Mi restano le lagrime', brilliantly virtuosic, for example Ruggiero's 'Stà nell'Iracana' with blazing horns and blistering energy in the strings, or deceptively simple, as in Ruggiero's glorious 'Verdi prati'. According to Burney, Carestini at first refused to sing 'Verdi prati' (shades of Cuzzoni and 'Falsa imagine' in *Ottone*), but Handel was forcefully insistent – there are implications of a furious argument – and when the aria became instantly popular with the public, it was Carestini who reaped its popular reward, just as Cuzzoni had before him. Caterina Negri was recompensed for having played the villain in *Ariodante*, and was given the sympathetic Bradamante, also with fierce coloratura ('Vorrei vendicarmi', for instance) among her many varied arias. Clearly, Gustavus Waltz was continuing to grow as an actor, having only one aria but considerable dramatic responsibility as Melisso.

And the young English singers, Cecilia Young as Morgana and John Beard as Alcina's general, had graceful and elegant music; Morgana's 'Tornami a vagheggiar' is one of the truly show-stopping arias in the whole of the opera. Even the treble, Walter Savage, as a young boy looking for his father (who has been turned into a lion by the sorceress), had three fine arias of not inconsid-erable technical difficulty; he must have been an astonishingly gifted teenager.

With all these top-quality arias sung by artists in peak condi-tion, some spectacular scenic effects using Rich's modern machinery, and Marie Sallé's dance movements, *Alcina* should have been the hit of the season, outshining even Opera of the Nobility's *Artaserse*. And indeed it had no fewer than eighteen ambitious performances, which gave Handel 'some sum in his favour, and a little recovered his losses',[30] even if the audiences did thin out towards the end of the run. His aficionados were thrilled. The devoted Mrs Pendarves enjoyed the extraordinary privilege of occasionally attending Handel's rehearsals in Brook Street, and as she basked in the presence of his musical genius, the precision of his demands and the warmth of his encourage-ment, she sharpened her own critical faculties. After coming to a rehearsal on 11th April, she wrote ecstatically to her mother: 'Yesterday morning my sister and I went with Mrs Donellan to Mr Handel's house to hear the first rehearsal of the new opera Alcina. I think it is the best he has ever made, but I have thought so of so many, that I will not say positively 'tis the finest, but 'tis so fine I have not words to describe it. Strada has a whole scene of charming recitative – there are a thousand beauties.'[31] And Mrs Pendarves concluded, gloriously, 'While Mr. Handel was playing his part, I could not help thinking him a necromancer in the midst of his own enchantments.'

243

The royal family came to *Alcina*'s opening night on 16th April, and dropped in again to subsequent performances. But inevitably there were detractors. Marie Sallé attracted prurient criticism, not for her dancing, but for her costume. Prévost, a passionate supporter of his countrywoman, leapt to her defence, but conceded that the 'male attire' in which she chose to dance the role of Cupid 'suits her very ill and was apparently the cause of her disgrace'.[32] Prévost also revealed how Handel's long run of *Alcina* still suffered in terms of audiences: '[Handel] is admired, but from a distance, for he is often alone; a spell draws the crowd to Farinelli's'. Handel and his singers may have been performing one of his most glorious operas, but he had still been utterly outclassed by the opposition.

It is ironic that what has been recognized by subsequent generations as one of the most distinguished of all Handel's opera seasons should at the time have left the composer jaded and weary. In an age when music was essentially transient – apart from the scheduling of revivals to fill out seasons and the filleting of operas for reuse in other works – Handel probably had little concept of the heights he had scaled with *Ariodante* and *Alcina*. And if he was dispirited, so too were others. Carestini had had enough: quite apart from the exhaustion of nine hefty roles in two seasons, the constant comparison with Farinelli and, to a lesser extent, Senesino was never going to conclude in his favour. Within a week of *Alcina*'s closing, Carestini returned to Italy. Marie Sallé too had slunk back to Paris, and suddenly Handel's company was markedly depleted.

Handel took himself off to Tunbridge Wells for some more

pampering, politely refusing another suggestion from his old friend Mattheson, who had been asking for it for sixteen years, that he write some sort of autobiographical article to be included in his *Ehren-Pforte*. (J. S. Bach also declined Mattheson's invitation.) In making his excuses, Handel played his royal card: 'To put together events of any period of my life . . . is impossible for me, since my continual application to the service of the Court and the Nobility keeps me from other business.'[33] And he was right. Beside his obligations to the royal family, he really did have to decide how to proceed now, with declining finances and personnel, in the face of the well-heeled and well-starred opponents in the Haymarket. One of the most loyal subscribers to his publications was a man who would soon assume an extremely important role in Handel's life: Charles Jennens, the son of a Leicestershire landowner. It was to this relative stranger that Handel confided, 'There is no certainty of any Scheme for next Season';[34] and indeed when he returned to London at the beginning of the autumn, the announcement in the *General Evening Post* on 16th October confirmed a significant change: 'We hear that Mr. Handell will perform Oratorios, and have Concerts of Musick, this Winter, at Covent-Garden Theatre.'[35] Handel had been forced to shelve his opera plans and search for new singers. Whoever was to replace Carestini, and be counted too against the mighty Farinelli, would have to be of the highest possible standard; and Handel was prepared to wait.

Opera of the Nobility saw the gap, and jumped in. They revived Porpora's *Polifemo* at the end of October, and then premiered Veracini's *Adriano in Siria*, which had a long run of seventeen performances. But it does seem that they too began to suffer the same audience fatigue that Handel had experienced. If Handel's music was not pulling in the crowds, that of Porpora and Veracini was also beginning to pall. Lord Hervey went to a performance of

Adriano in Siria, and hated it: 'I am this moment returned from the King with yawning four hours at the longest and dullest Opera that ever the enobled ignorance of our present musical Governors ever afflicted on the ignorance of an English audience',[36] he wrote to Mrs Charlotte Digby. He went on to complain that Farinelli and Cuzzoni had the 'two worst roles', while Senesino had the 'least bad' one, but, startlingly, had 'lost all his voice'. Handel indeed enjoyed some measure of Schadenfreude here, for, as Lord Hervey also reported, he came to a performance and 'sat in great eminence and great pride in the middle of the pit, and seemed in silent triumph'. But, as Lord Hervey makes clear, the stars themselves were suffering from overwork and exhaustion, and the one who finally cracked was none other than Senesino himself. Early in 1736 he called it a day and returned to Italy for ever, vocally bankrupt perhaps, but in all other respects extremely well rewarded, as he continued to furnish his Siena palazzo with his rich pickings from London.

After Senesino's departure, the Opera of the Nobility company seemed to stumble. One opera ran for only three performances, and another did not survive beyond its opening night. There was suddenly a sense of panic. The directors were squabbling, and some of them walked out; others defected to Handel's side and were vilified by their fellows. Rumours began to circulate that Hasse and his wife, Faustina, were to be invited back, but again Hasse did not want to be in competition with Handel, and Faustina would surely have resisted any repeat of her tempestuous collaboration with Cuzzoni. The quiet feelings of satisfaction that Handel had enjoyed when he attended Veracini's flawed *Adriano in Siria* will have redoubled now at the cracks and fissures in the countenance of the Opera of the Nobility company. He himself, astute and cunning as always, was heading with his young singers in quite another direction.

Handel's own new composition, premiered at Covent Garden on 19th February 1736, was *Alexander's Feast*, based on Dryden's mighty ode and sung therefore in English. The poem describes how Alexander the Great, most severe of rulers, was moved and charmed by the 'Power of Musick', as delivered to him by his court bard, Timotheus. The text was shaped into recitatives, arias and choruses by a newcomer to Handel's orbit, Newburgh Hamilton, an Irish playwright currently serving as steward to the Earl of Strafford. Hamilton's preface stated that his aim was to seize 'this favourable Opportunity' of uniting Dryden and Handel, the clear implication being that, although rare in a musical collaboration, a great poet and a great composer share equal footing. Certainly Dryden's verses have immense power, whether boisterous ('Bacchus' blessings are a treasure, / Drinking is the soldier's pleasure'), celebratory ('The many rend the skies with loud applause / So Love was crown'd, but Music won the cause') or heartbreaking ('On the bare earth expos'd he lies / With not a friend to close his eyes'). And Handel, ever sensitive to the essence of mood and ever inventive to its expression, produced a score of equally wide range and emotional power.

Alexander's Feast was in two parts, not the three that opera audiences would have expected, and there were only three soloists. Strada and Beard, Handel's oldest star and his newest, had the lion's share, with the tenor employed mainly as narrator in recitative, and the soprano bringing all her dramatic gifts to interpret amorous and tender arias. A new (to Handel) bass, Mr Erard, of whom tantalizingly little is known, had just two arias, one Bacchic and one military, but perhaps little impact; while he was singing, one of the audience scribbled in his word-book, 'O for Seneseno'. The excellent choruses are varied in texture and colour, and the basic orchestration of strings, oboes and bassoons is supplemented at appropriate moments with a solo cello (for amorous music), horns (for Bacchus), trumpets and timpani (for war) and flutes (to herald the arrival of 'divine Cecilia'). In order to stretch this shorter work into a full evening's entertainment, Handel inserted not just a new organ concerto, but a concerto grosso and a harp concerto too. And as if that were not enough, and Strada did not already have enough to sing (twelve numbers), he also added a relevant Italian cantata, 'Cecilia, volgi un sguardo'. It was almost as if he were taunting his now-rudderless opponents with the full battery of his own talents.

The big event in that spring of 1736 was the marriage, at last, of Frederick, Prince of Wales. As Lord Hervey reminded readers of his memoirs, 'It had been so long talked of without anything being done to forward it, that everybody began to think it was not designed.'[37] But, in the previous summer, the King had returned to Hanover, where he had interviewed the sixteen-year-old Princess Augusta of Saxe-Gotha, whom he pronounced to be a suitable bride for his troublesome son. Coincidentally, he also found himself a new mistress (he had recently tired of Lady Henrietta Howard), and in the pleasurable company of Amalie von Wallmoden, he had delayed his return to London by several months. Wallmoden was due to give birth to a son in the following spring, and this may well have decided the timing of Frederick's wedding, for the King was 'very impatient to return to the arms of Mme Wallmoden',[38] as Hervey put it, in the summer of 1736. Augusta was therefore summoned to London in April. She arrived, seasick and lonely ('knew not a mortal here'),[39] just two days before her wedding. She spoke no English, nor even French; her mother had blithely assumed that, after two decades of Hanoverian rule, everyone in England now spoke German, and had advised her that there was therefore no need of any other language. The King paid no more ceremonial attention to Augusta's arrival than he had to that of Prince William of Orange, and the young princess's immediate circle was limited to the united front of her intimidating future sisters-in-law.

The royal wedding took place in the Chapel Royal on 27th April. It was on an impressive scale, but not quite as grand as that for Princess Anne, two years earlier. Preparations had been rushed; the actual event had rather been sprung ('sooner than expected'[40]) on the Surveyors of His Majesty's Works. As soon as the celebrations of Easter Sunday were over, a large recruitment of construction workers laboured through the night to transform the Chapel. Handel's new wedding anthem, 'Sing unto God', had to be rehearsed not in the Chapel, but at the house of the Master of the Boys, Bernard Gates – and perhaps also not well enough, for Lord Egmont recorded in his diary that it had been 'wretchedly sung'[41] at the ceremony itself. But Handel provided a stirring anthem of appropriate texts, with choral movements enveloping arias and even an accompanied recitative; and he had supplemented the ecclesiastical choirs with some of his Covent Garden performers, including one completely familiar with the genre, the ex-chorister John Beard.

Handel's chief contribution to the wedding festivities was to be his opera *Atalanta*, with a glorious final scene depicting the gods blessing the marriage of Atalanta and Meleagro. Opera of the Nobility was similarly cooking up a celebratory serenata by Porpora: *La festa d'Imeneo*. Determined as always to outshine the opposition, Handel intended that his opera would be literally spectacular, bringing in 'great Numbers of Artificers' to decorate the stage, and even planning fireworks for the final scene. But there was still the problem of vocal fireworks. He had at last sourced two castratos to replace Carestini and be measured against Farinelli. One of them, Domenico Annibali, was not yet available, but the other, the twenty-two-year-old Gioacchino Conti, was, and on the 13th April, the *London Daily Post* had heralded his arrival: 'We hear, that Signior Conti, who is esteemed the best Singer in Italy, being sent for by Mr. Handell, is expected here in a few days.'[42] But neither Conti nor indeed the completion of *Atalanta* was quite on time for the wedding celebrations, so Handel mounted two quick performances of *Ariodante*, cutting all the ballet music now that Marie Sallé had gone, and throwing Conti straight into the title role. Conti could not possibly learn the score in two days, so he performed whatever showy pieces he had in his own repertoire. Curiously unsatisfactory though this production must therefore have been, Conti was nevertheless a success. The *London Daily Post* reported: 'Signior Gioacchino Conti Ghizziello made his first Appearance, and met with an uncommon Reception; and in Justice both as to Voice and Judgment, he may be truly esteem'd one of the best Performers in this Kingdom.'[43]

Atalanta was finally performed at Covent Garden on 12th May. Strada, Conti, Caterina Negri and Beard, in the main roles, were joined by two basses in very small roles: the young Waltz and a newcomer, Henry Reinhold, who had just arrived from Germany to study with Handel. Handel's music is altogether striking, especially that for his new castrato (the aria 'Non saria poco' shows that Conti had an extraordinary range, extending to a top C, and 'Tu solcasti' is formidably agile), and another searing lament,

'Lassa! ch'io t'ho perduta', for Strada. On the opening night, Handel himself was warmly received: 'at the appearance of that great prince of harmony in the orchestra, there was so universal a clap from the audience that many were surprized',[44] as Benjamin Victor wrote to the violinist, Matthew Dubourg (who, having married Bernard Gates's daughter in 1727, was now Master and Composer of State Music in Ireland). The fireworks inevitably attracted most of the attention and excited the audiences, which, even so, did not include the Prince and Princess of Wales, who rather pointedly went to see a play instead. But the rest of the royal family, probably just as pointedly, attended the premiere, as the *London Daily Post* reported on the following day: 'There were present their Majesties, the Duke [of Cumberland], and the four Princesses, accompanied with a very special Audience, and the whole was received with unusual Acclamations.'[45] Notwithstanding the absence of the bridal pair at the actual performance, a celebratory publication of *Atalanta* was issued. Handel's publisher, John Walsh the younger, whose father had died just two months earlier (like the Smiths, the Walsh family was loyal to Handel across the generations), seized on the royal wedding as an opportunity to start printing a new series of Handel's operas, and the commercial take-up of 143 subscribers was, given the circumstances, not unimpressive.

But there were few other commercial encouragements. Again, both Handel's company in Covent Garden and the Nobility company in the Haymarket had been struggling financially. Public enthusiasm for opera seemed ever on the wane. Even Farinelli, after only one season, was now 'exhibited here to empty benches',[46] as Benjamin Victor confirmed in his letter. He continued, 'As to the Operas, they must tumble, for the King's presence could hardly hold them up, and even that prop is denied them, for

251

his majesty will not admit his royal ears to be tickled this season.' But he concluded with a telling reflection on current musical taste, which was veering away from opera towards purely orchestral concerts and chamber music: 'As to music, it flourishes in this place more than ever, in subscription concerts and private parties, which must prejudice all operas and public entertainments.'

Handel had certainly dropped a level of creative energy since his second annus mirabilis of 1734–5. Nevertheless, after a restorative visit to the country at the beginning of the summer break in 1736, he returned to London and began to plan his new season. He chose two librettos and adjusted his roster of singers only slightly. His new castrato from Italy, Domenico Annibali, was due in the autumn. Cecilia Young was beginning a professional and indeed a personal relationship with Thomas Arne, whom she would soon marry, and she temporarily left Handel's orbit. But, rather deftly, Handel persuaded Francesca Bertolli to defect from Opera of the Nobility and return to his fold. Otherwise he did not feel any need to reconstruct his team; inspirationally led by the now stalwart Strada, the young cohort of the Negris, Beard, Waltz and Reinhold were all developing nicely. The Nobility company, meanwhile, was having to make drastic changes. They had already lost Senesino; now Cuzzoni decided that she too had had enough. With Bertolli changing sides, Farinelli was left somewhat isolated, and the Nobility directors scrabbled around to find him suitable partners. They lured back from Italy the contralto Antonia Merighi, who had sung for Handel at the Haymarket between 1729 and 1731. With her came two sopranos, Margherita Chimenti (known as 'La Droghierina') and Elisabeth

Duparc ('La Francesina'); neither of them was remotely in the same league as the departed Cuzzoni, let alone Farinelli. But even greater than the loss of singers for Opera of the Nobility was the loss too of Porpora as Music Director. Without a composer of his stature, experience and invention binding the company and matching Handel with his musical gifts and integrity, they would have to throw together a season of piecemeal ingredients. Handel will have been aware of all these desperate manoeuvres and might have allowed himself a smile of quiet satisfaction.

During the summer between the seasons, Handel maintained his relationship with the royal family. The King had left for Hanover and 'the arms of Mme Wallmoden' immediately after the Prince of Wales's wedding, and would stay there longer than he had on any of his previous visits – six months. His prolonged absence was ridiculed. Hervey quoted an ingenious notice posted on a gate at St James's Palace: 'Lost or strayed out of this house, a man who has left a wife and six children on the parish; whoever will give any tidings of him to the churchwarden of St James's Parish, so as he may be got again, shall receive four shillings and sixpence reward. NB. – This reward will not be increased, nobody judging him to deserve a Crown [five shillings].'[47] Queen Caroline settled herself resignedly in Kensington Palace, and the Prince of Wales, with his new wife (who was rapidly learning English), assumed a more visible and very popular presence in London. His sister Anne, firmly instructed by her father to remain in Holland as the Princess of Orange, and confined there in any case with her first pregnancy, evidently felt the loss of her former teacher and friend, Handel. So she sent for Strada for musical companionship over the summer: if she could not hear Handel's music in London, then Handel's music should come to her in the form of one of his star interpreters. Meanwhile

253

Handel's position as teacher to the next two Princesses, Amelia and Caroline, both now in their early twenties, was renewed.

Annibali duly arrived and was immediately taken by Handel to sing at Kensington Palace for the Queen and the two eldest Princesses, 'who express'd the highest Satisfaction at his Performance',[48] as the *Old Whig* reported. Strada returned from Holland. And while the King remained in Hanover, the Prince and Princess of Wales were only too keen to assume royal superiority, and announced that they would like to come to Handel's opening at Covent Garden. This took Handel by surprise. He had barely completed either of his two new operas, let alone had time to rehearse one of them with his regrouping company. But he was not about to turn down the Prince's support after its two-year absence, so he hastily mounted a revival of *Alcina*, as the *London Daily Post* announced on 1st November: 'Their Royal Highnesses the Prince and Princess of Wales intend to honour Mr. Handel with their Presence on Saturday next at the opera of *Alcina*, which is the Reason for performing Operas earlier in the Season than intended.'[49] Strada, Caterina Negri, Beard, Waltz and the boy, William Savage, all returned to their roles of 1735. Annibali, who had only just arrived in London, was not yet involved, but Conti was well placed to sing Ruggiero, and Rosa Negri replaced Cecilia Young as Morgana. This being the Prince of Wales's first visit to Handel's company at Covent Garden, and his first at any opera at all since his marriage, crowds flocked to the occasion. The *London Daily Post* was effusive: 'The Box in which their Royal Highnesses sat, was of white Satin, beautifully Ornamented with Festons of Flowers in their proper Colours, and in Front was a flaming Heart, between two Hymeneal Torches, whose different Flames terminated in one Point, and were surmounted with a

Label, on which were wrote, in letters of Gold, these words, MUTUUS ARDOR.'[50]

Despite the mighty presence of Farinelli, Opera of the Nobility's season was somewhat tame in comparison with Handel's splendid opening. A scattergun collection of operas and pasticcios did not ignite the fires of audience excitement. The admittedly partisan Mrs Pendarves described their presentations as 'dull Italian operas, such as you would almost fall asleep at'.[51] Confident therefore of the quality of his own operas as compared with those of the Nobility, Handel nevertheless felt it necessary to match their quantity, and the Covent Garden schedule was ferocious. *Alcina* was followed by revivals of *Atalanta* (just two performances, the first on the birthday of the Princess of Wales) and *Poro*. But the four performances of *Poro* were beset by ill health. There was a flu epidemic in London that December, and, as the *London Daily Post* reported, 'Yesterday Signora Strada was taken violently ill of a Fever and Sore Throat, so that the Opera of *Porus* could not be performed as was intended'.[52] A further performance, 'commanded' by the (at last) returned King, with Queen Caroline, also had to be cancelled, as the royal couple heard that day the sad news of Princess Anne's miscarriage in Holland. It was anyway, like so many of Handel's swift revivals, very different from its original manifestation, for Annibali in the title role sang his own arias. Handel was concentrating on preparing no fewer than three new operas, *Arminio*, *Giustino* and *Berenice*, which would start in the repertory after Christmas. He had already played the overtures of two of them to his good friend, Mrs Pendarves: 'Mr Handel has two new operas ready – Erminius and Justino. He was here two or three mornings ago and played to me both the overtures, which are charming.'[53] That unexpected return of support from the Prince of Wales possibly had an effect, too, on the order in which Handel would present his new works. He had originally started work on *Giustino* in the summer; but once there was the likelihood of the Prince's presence, he put it aside to concentrate instead on *Arminio*, the story of a German prince (Hermann). Only when that was complete did he go back to *Giustino* and then address *Berenice*.

The ferocity of the schedule continued in the new year of 1737. There were six performances of *Arminio*, four of a *Partenope* revival, six of *Giustino* and two of *Il Parnasso in Festa*. Then, for the Lenten season, with performances on Wednesday and Friday evenings, came three of *Alexander's Feast*, four of *Il Trionfo del Tempo* (a reworking of very early Italian work) and two of *Esther*. Between 12th January and 7th April, therefore, there were twenty-eight performances of seven different works, two of them brand new to all participants. After Easter would come the next new opera, *Berenice*, and a pasticcio, *Didone*.

Inevitably, the pace of all this took its toll. Handel's new operas had their royal openings, but none was of the consistently high quality of recent seasons, although distinguished music can be found in all three. It was almost as if Handel was simply following his own (highly successful) formulae, with little sense of novelty or true flair. What does stand out, however, is the quality of the writing for the oboe. Giuseppe Sammartini (brother of the composer Giovanni Battista) was reputedly the best oboist in Europe, and had been in London since 1729, recently playing for Opera of the Nobility in the Haymarket. Handel poached him from his rivals along with Bertolli, and rewarded him with some of his finest oboe writing. But this was not enough to keep audiences flocking to Covent Garden. Lord Shaftesbury admired *Arminio*, but gloomily noted, 'I fear 'twill not be acted very long. The Town dont much admire it.'[54] A Mr Pennington wrote to an acquaintance in Bath, during the run of *Giustino*, 'Mr. Handel has not due honour done him, and I am excessively angry about it'.[55] Just as the Lenten season was about to launch on its own frantic course, Handel too became uncharacteristically morose, even suggesting to Mrs Pendarves' sister, Ann Granville, that he was about to give it all up, as she explained, 'Music is certainly a pleasure that may be reckoned intellectual, and we shall *never again* have it in the perfection it is this year, because Mr. Handel will *not compose any more*!'[56] Nevertheless, Handel did find the energy to mount his oratorios, again playing organ concertos between the acts, and often, indeed, repeating those immediately by public demand. But just after Easter, as he was preparing to perform his latest pasticcio, *Didone*, and at the same time rehearsing *Berenice*, he finally succumbed to the pressures and strains. On 13th April 1737, Handel suffered a stroke. He was fifty-two years old.

10

~~~~~~

RECOVERY AND REINVENTION

'Strange reverse of human fate'

[Alexander Balus]

Following Handel's stroke, details of his indisposition remained, and remain, unclear, for there were conflicting accounts both in the press and in private correspondence. At first it was noted, in the *London Daily Post* on 30th April, that Handel 'has been some time indisposed with the rheumatism',[1] though two weeks later the *London Evening Post* alarmingly reported, 'The ingenious Mr. Handell is very much indispos'd, and it's thought with a Paraletick Disorder, he having at present no Use of his Right Hand, which, if he don't regain, the Publick will be depriv'd of his fine Compositions.'[2] A rumoured swift recovery was perhaps an exaggeration. Two of Handel's friends, Lord Shaftesbury and his cousin James Harris, were concerned; and later Lord Shaftesbury recalled that Handel suffered 'Great fatigue and disappointment,' which 'affected him so much, that he was this Spring (1737) struck with the Palsy, which took entirely away, the use of four fingers of his right hand; and totally disabled him from Playing'.[3] Although at the time Lord Shaftesbury had told his cousin that within two weeks of his seizure Handel had been 'on horseback twice', it seems there was some sort of relapse. Lord Shaftesbury's 1760 memoir continued, even more distressingly, 'when the heats of the Summer 1737 came on, the Disorder seemed at times to affect his Understanding'. Mainwaring, in his memoir, confirmed that there had been some considerable measure of melancholy, if not irrationality: 'how greatly his senses were disordered at intervals, for a long time, appeared from an hundred instances, which are better forgotten than recorded.'[4]

But however rough the course of Handel's convalescence, he was sufficiently lucid to recognize that – financially, if not artistically – opera at Covent Garden was simply no longer viable. Even as he began his recovery, he entered into negotiations with Heidegger. The Nobility directors had had an equally crippling season; their single remaining star, Farinelli, cancelled his final performances, claiming illness, and then promptly accepted an invitation to sing for King Philip V of Spain, in Madrid. He broke his Nobility contract, and would stay in Spain for the next two decades. So if opera was to survive at all in London, Opera of the Nobility really needed Handel, and Handel needed them. A coalition was reached, ensuring that opera could continue with all the forces united in the Haymarket. Handel was contracted simply to supply two operas for the upcoming season; and the new joint company sought – and found, in one Gaetano Cafarelli – a replacement for Farinelli. (Meanwhile, at Covent Garden, John Rich showed no sign of dismay at Handel's departure. Astutely reading the runes yet again, he spotted a burlesque by Carey and Lampe, *The Dragon of Wantley*, which had been performing rather flatly at the Little Haymarket Theatre, and brought it over to Covent Garden, where it ran for sixty-nine performances, outnumbering even the success of *The Beggar's*

Opera. Among the many indeed who enjoyed this comedy was Handel himself. Rich had no regrets.)

With some sort of future thus settled, Handel felt he could follow the advice of his doctors and go to the German spa town of Aix-la-Chapelle to take the cure in its famous steam baths. According to Mainwaring, he went reluctantly ('it was with the utmost difficulty that he was prevailed on to do what was proper'[5]), and, once there, defiantly broke all the rules: 'he sat near three times as long as hath ever been the practice. Whoever knows any thing of the nature of those baths, will, from this instance, form some idea of his surprising constitution. His sweats were profuse beyond what can well be imagined. His cure, from the manner as well as from the quickness, with which it was wrought, passed with the Nuns for a miracle.'[6] When he was not taking the cure, he busied himself playing the organ in the cathedral ('in a manner so much beyond any they had ever been used to').[7] He stayed in Aix-la-Chapelle for six weeks and returned to London at the end of October, in time for the opening of Heidegger's season in the Haymarket on the 29th, and for the King's birthday on the 30th. His arrival was enthusiastically anticipated, as the *London Daily Post* signalled on 28th October: 'Mr. Handel, the Composer of Italian Music, is hourly expected from Aix-la-Chapelle.'[8]

But it was a very different operatic scene, as the two broken branches of hitherto rival companies were now spliced together. In the company that Heidegger had assembled in the Haymarket, only two of the singers were familiar to Handel, and that was because it was he who had originally brought them to London; Antonia Merighi and Antonio Montagnana had both sung under him for the Academy, until their desertion to the Nobility company in 1733. The new castrato, Caffarelli, together with two sopranos, Elisabeth Duparc ('La Francesina') and Margherita

Chimenti ('La Droghierina'), a mezzo-soprano, Maria Antonia Marchesini ('La Lucchesina'), and a bass, Antonio Lottini, were all new to him, and he had had no part in their hiring. Most significant was the absence of his own favourite soprano, Anna Strada. She was still in London, but was reputedly forbidden by her husband to enter into a new contract until some outstanding financial claims had been settled. Furthermore, Handel's rising star, the tenor John Beard, had been lured to the theatre in Drury Lane by its manager Charles Fleetwood, there to perform ballad operas. Neither Strada nor Beard would have any part in the ensuing season in the Haymarket.

Heidegger launched his uneasy company with a pasticcio, *Arsace*, on 29th October. The King and Queen attended, again demonstrating their renewed support for any operatic venture that involved Handel. But within three weeks everything had changed dramatically. On 9th November, Queen Caroline, inspecting her new library in St James's Palace, was taken ill. The usual desperate round of bleeding and induced vomiting ensued, with no result or improvement. In fact she was suffering from a ruptured hernia, which had originated during the birth of her last child, Princess Louisa, back in 1724, and which she had endured ever since in stoic silence, with no treatment or medical attention whatsoever. So humiliated and embarrassed did she feel about her complaint that nobody, not her ladies of the bedchamber, let alone her husband, was ever allowed to see her naked; and her condition had been deteriorating, painfully and disfiguringly (she had become very stout), over the years. Now she finally let her doctors examine her, and they decided that surgery was the only remedy. After an unimaginable week of botched procedures repeated almost daily, and increasing agony borne without opiates, Queen Caroline died on 20th November, aged fifty-four.

Her Majesty's final days – fraught too with family tensions and subterfuges – were lengthily and minutely described in his memoirs by Lord Hervey, who witnessed, as closely as any non-family member, the relentless decline of the woman he regarded not merely as the King's consort but as a true friend. The King was distraught and barely left his wife's room throughout the week, sometimes even sleeping there on the floor. When Caroline calmly instructed her husband to take a new wife after her departure, George famously replied, '*Non, j'aurai des maitresses*'. The Princesses Caroline, Amelia, Mary and Louise, together with their brother the Duke of Cumberland, were regular visitors to their mother's bedside, but the Prince of Wales was strictly excluded, despite repeated messages and requests. Relations between Frederick and his mother had never been close, and were often troublesome, but they had deteriorated dramatically in the summer of 1737, when the Prince had taken his wife – who was already in labour – away from Hampton Court Palace in the middle of the night, in order to ensure that his first child (a daughter, also named Augusta) was born away from his parents' control. In September, Frederick and his wife, already pregnant again, had then been evicted by the King and Queen from St James's Palace, and they had taken up residence in Carlton House, in Pall Mall. As Caroline weakened, there was absolutely no reconciliation between her and her son. Rather, the animosity on the Queen's part intensified, as Lord Hervey recalled: 'The Queen often in her illness spoke of him, and always with detestation . . . and as the King and Princess Caroline both told me, the Queen would sometimes when she talked of dying cry: "At least I shall have one comfort in having my eyes eternally closed – I shall never see that monster again." She certainly hated him more and expressed that hate in stronger terms if possible in her illness than ever she had done in health.'[9]

After the Queen's death, the King showed both in private and in public what Hervey described as a 'tenderness of which the world thought him utterly incapable',[10] and his subjects warmed to him. George II planned and oversaw all the arrangements for Caroline's funeral, which eventually took place in Westminster Abbey on 17th December. In the event, he would not actually attend it; he made his private farewells as her body lay in state at the House of Lords, and he appointed Princess Amelia as chief mourner: it was she who would lead a long procession of court officials through the Abbey. Much building work was undertaken: in addition to elaborate reconstruction in the Henry VII Chapel where Caroline would be buried, a structure was erected in the west end of the Abbey to accommodate an extra organ and the large number of musicians who were to perform at the service. These were the combined choirs of Westminster, the Chapel Royal, St Paul's and Windsor, together with '100 instrumentalists from His Majesty's band, & from the Opera',[11] according to the *Grub Street Journal*. Naturally, it was to Handel that George II turned to provide special music for the occasion.

Handel had known Queen Caroline for twenty-seven years. The relationship he had established, back in Hanover in 1710, with this intelligent, tolerant and supremely cultivated woman, had remained of the greatest importance to him. Both as Princess of Wales and then as Queen, she had supported all his artistic ventures in London; he had produced music for every important occasion relating to the royal family, including her own Coronation anthem, 'My heart is inditing'. She had welcomed Handel and his singers to countless private occasions in the royal palaces, for previews of his operas or simply for musical entertainment. Their shared German heritage, and the way they had both adapted to British life and culture, must have remained a special bond between them. Like Lord Hervey, Handel considered Her Majesty a true friend, and the long anthem he wrote for her funeral was a clear expression of profound personal sorrow.

'The ways of Zion do mourn' is based on a selection of scriptural verses, probably put together by a Sub-Dean of the Chapel Royal, George Carleton. There are twelve choral movements, preceded by a brief and slow-moving sinfonia, and Handel wrote the work to be performed as a continuous unfolding thread. It must have been his choice to repeat one especial verse, 'How are the mighty fall'n: She that was Great among the nations and Princess of the Provinces', at two later stages after its initial appearance but with a slightly different musical slant, making these textual reiterations therefore the structural pillars of the whole work. With spare orchestration of strings, oboes, bassoons and organ continuo, there is absolutely no sense of bombast or even celebration: the sombre mood persists through each ensuing movement, whatever contrasts there are of musical style and content. One aspect which clearly makes reference to their shared German ancestry is Handel's deployment of German chorales, for which he had had little use since he left his homeland in his youth. Those recent hours in the organ loft in Aix-la-Chapelle during his convalescence may well have exposed him again to this foundation of Lutheran church music, and renewed his respect for the material which was at the very heart of the music of his great compatriot, Bach. The opening choral movement, therefore, 'The ways of Zion do mourn', is based on 'Herr Jesu Christ, du höchstes Gut', and as such breathes reverence and solemnity, as well as mourning. In the essential stillness of this movement, Handel again brilliantly exploits the architecture of the Abbey, allowing slow-moving and spare textures to resonate fully beneath its vaulted ceiling. During a comparatively active movement, 'She delivered the poor that cried', Handel breaks his own musical gesture to introduce the words, 'Kindness, meekness and comfort were in her tongue', which he sets simply and warmly before retrieving the nature of what had gone before. This, perhaps, is the most personal passage of text for him, and he allows himself to acknowledge it. He creates the intimacy of grief at 'Their bodies are buried in peace', again with straightforward and hushed word-setting, but, in the context of a funeral service, he evokes an appropriate grandiosity too, for 'The people will tell of their wisdom'. The cumulative effect of the twelve contiguous movements over forty-five minutes is powerful and cathartic.

Handel wrote 'The ways of Zion do mourn' (his first composition since *Il Trionfo del Tempo*, back in March) in about a week at the beginning of December 1737, finishing it on the 12th. Two days later, it was rehearsed privately in the Queen's Chapel (built for Henrietta Maria, the French wife of Charles I) at St James's Palace, with the King and other members of the royal family quietly listening in an adjacent room. Princess Amelia wrote to her sister Anne in Holland, 'We had Handel's Anthem last Wednesday in the French Chapel, that the King might hear it in Carolin's Bedchamber, and it's the finest cruel touching thing that ever was heard.'[12] Two days later it was rehearsed again, twice, but now in public at the Banqueting House in Whitehall; and then finally it was performed in the Abbey service on the following evening. The Duke of Chandos, who was in the ceremonial procession, wrote to his nephew: 'The Solemnity of the Queen's Funeral was very decent, and performed in more order than any thing I have seen of the like kind. [. . .] It began about quarter before 7, and was over a little after ten; the Anthem took up three quarter of an hour of the time, of which the composition was exceeding fine, and adapted very properly to the melancholly occasion of it.'[13]

∽

At the beginning of 1738, after six weeks of public mourning, life began to return to normal. As in 1727, when the warring operatic factions attendant upon Faustina and Cuzzoni had collapsed during the period of mourning for George I, so now the shared national grief for a genuinely loved member of the royal family had a calming effect. The sobriety of feelings for the late Queen, together with the remnants of a shocked sympathy for Handel's stroke, meant that any aggressive sniping at his projects seemed to melt away. A young entrepreneur, Jonathan Tyers, who had recently taken over New Spring Gardens, south of the Thames, and was turning them into the celebrated pleasure space known as Vauxhall Gardens, commissioned a statue of Handel from the equally young (they were both thirty-five) French sculptor, Louis-Francois Roubiliac. Erecting a statue to a living person was virtually unprecedented. And Handel repaid charitable thoughts with charitable deeds of his own. In the first instance, he was moved by the specific case of the oboist John Christian Kytch, who had played in Handel's orchestras since 1708, but had recently been overshadowed and ousted by Sammartini, and had then died in poverty. Some of Kytch's colleagues had come upon his two bereaved sons wandering in the Haymarket in a condition of extreme destitution, and had prevailed upon Handel to help them put together a charitable institution to support musicians and their dependants. So Handel was instrumental in setting up the Fund for Decay'd Musicians, which has continued in existence (if with different nomenclature) ever since. A less charitable indication of the resumption of normal life, however, was the continuing fractious impasse in relations between the King and the Prince of Wales. Early in 1738, Frederick asked Handel to give regular concerts for him in Carlton House, and Handel agreed to do so. But the King forbade Handel to have anything to do with his son, and Handel's loyalties of course rested with the monarch.

Heidegger's opera season in the Haymarket limped back into activity at the beginning of January. Over the next few months, he presented four operas (two by Handel, *Faramondo* and *Serse*) and a pasticcio, but the total performance count for the whole season was only thirty-nine. Even allowing for the fact that the theatres had been closed for the mourning period, this was a meagre tally when seen in comparison with, for example, the extraordinary season of 1723–4, which had presented sixty-two performances, or, indeed, with Rich's current sixty-nine performances of *The Dragon of Wantley* at Covent Garden. Towards the end of March a one-off concert, billed simply as 'An Oratorio', made up of excerpts from Handel's Chandos and Coronation anthems and from *Deborah*, was performed at the Haymarket. There was no new music, but, in another indication of returning sympathy, it was impressively presented (Burney recalled that there were approximately 500 people on stage) as a benefit concert for Handel, and extremely well attended. Handel made good money from this exceptional event; contemporary reports vary as to the precise amount (Burney calculated £800, Lord Egmont £1,000 and Mainwaring £1,500), but it was certainly not inconsiderable and would have cheered Handel enormously. So too would the attention being paid to his statue. And his final opera that season, *Serse*, while hardly a commercial success with just five performances, did reveal a blithe lifting of spirits. Now that Handel was no longer ultimately responsible for the company's financial stability, being merely a well-paid employee, his creativity seemed to have found a new freedom.

The libretto of *Serse* was originally written by Minato, for Cavalli, in Venice in 1655, an era of altogether different theatrical expectation. Although it was much reworked by Stampiglia, for Bononcini in 1694, it retained its characteristic Venetian amalgam of serious characters in complicated amorous arrangements, disguise, and a comic servant adding plot tangles as well as changes of mood. There was much in the story that was familiar to Handel's audiences, but what was not at all familiar was the rather puzzling opening to the opera, where (true to historical report) Serse (Xerxes, King of Persia) sings what seems to be a tender love song to a tree. 'Ombra mai fù', nevertheless, was an instant success in purely musical terms, and, translated into many other media, became known across the centuries as 'Handel's Largo' (even though Handel had given it the instruction 'Larghetto'). Following this unorthodox start to the opera, Handel cheerfully broke many more conventions: all the arias and recitatives are shorter than usual, and many of them reject the strict da capo formula. After its first performances in the Haymarket in 1738, *Serse* was not seen again until the twentieth century, when it finally achieved the acclaim and attention it deserved; and it has since become Handel's most performed opera all over the world.

Handel may no longer have had responsibility for the Haymarket company, but Heidegger did, and the realities were uncomfortable. On 24th May, he appealed for subscribers for the 1738–9 season, stating that he needed 200 of them to make the season viable at all, and that furthermore he would need to have them by the time his current season ended on 5th June. But when the deadline came he had collected only 133 – which would in fact have been enough to plan a new season, if Heidegger had not still been trying to pay debts accumulated from the past (some singers were simply not willing to enter into new agreements) – and, at the end of July, Heidegger conceded defeat. In the *London Daily Post*, he announced, 'Whereas the Opera's for the coming Season at the King's Theatre in the Hay-Market, cannot be carried on as was intended, by Reason of the Subscription not being full, and that I could not agree with the Singers th' I offer'd One Thousand Guineas to One of them: I therefore think myself oblig'd to declare, that I give up the Undertaking for next Year.'[14] With the greatest sadness and reluctance, Heidegger closed the company.

That same summer, Strada returned to Holland and to her friend and patron, the music-loving Princess Anne. Strada had been at Handel's side since 1729, creating, in the nine years to 1738, twenty new roles, and taking on the revivals of eleven others. She was the sole artist who had remained loyal to Handel when the rest of the Academy company had deserted him for Opera of the Nobility in 1733, and she had become a loved member of his inner circle of friends, performing with him on many private occasions, whether for Queen Caroline in Kensington Palace or for Mrs Pendarves in Brook Street. But she did not return to London after her Dutch summer, or ever again. She had not actually appeared in public for over a year, and she too must have been aware that an era was closing. She sang once more – with Senesino, in Naples, in 1739 – but, after that, she retired to her home town of Bergamo.

On many levels Handel must have been sad to lose Strada, mainly for her loyalty and friendship but also because she was, in effect, one of his success stories. She had arrived in London in

1729 with a fine voice and a sweet temperament, but little idea of style or presentation. By the time she left, with virtually all Handel's great soprano roles under her belt (Cleopatra, Partenope, Rodelinda, Asteria, Almirena, Galatea, Esther, Angelica, Deborah, Josabeth, Arianna, Ginevra, Alcina) and blessed with the matchless experience of delivering them under the guidance of Handel himself, she was a truly exceptional artist, capable of the greatest technical execution and emotional depth. According to Burney, Handel claimed the credit for this transformation of his loyal friend: 'Handel . . . used to say that by the care he took in composing for her, and his instructions, from a coarse singer with a fine voice, he rendered her equal at least to the finest performer in London'.[15] And he was no doubt right.

In the summer of 1738, with opera now moribund, Handel went in another direction and followed up on his three oratorios. Since the almost accidental arrival of *Esther* in his opera schedules in 1732, he had repeatedly revived it for performances during Lent, and added in the same vein *Deborah* and then *Athalia*. Despite the lack of any staging, costuming or theatrical lighting, all three of these oratorios had proved popular with the public, not least for their being sung in English – that old chestnut – but also for their magnificent use of the essentially English ecclesiastical choirs, with their especial expertise. *Alexander's Feast*, of 1736, had continued the English-language, choir-based narrative, but with a non-biblical text, told in a third-person narrative. Now, sitting on Handel's desk was another first-person oratorio, sent to him some time earlier by one of his subscribers. With time on his hands, and an (as ever) astute instinct for the current direction of the wind, Handel addressed himself to his new oratorio. This was *Saul*, an undeniable masterpiece that marked not just another of Handel's giant steps in standard and invention, it initiated too an epic collaboration with a man whose name would ever after be linked with his own: Charles Jennens.

Jennens was a Leicestershire art collector, bibliophile and passionate music lover, whose vast wealth came from the family business of the manufacture of iron. Prosperous, well educated and academically gifted, he might have been expected to assume some public office. But Jennens, albeit a Protestant, was also a supporter of the deposed Jacobites, and had refused to swear allegiance to the Hanoverians. His status, therefore, as a 'Nonjuror', which certainly defined his whole life, denied him any official position, so, until he inherited his father's estate and set about rebuilding Gopsall House, he occupied himself with assembling a magnificent collection of books and paintings. Since 1725, when *Rodelinda* had launched the publication of Handel's operas, Jennens had been one of his subscribers; so enthusiastic was he for Handel's music that, if a work was not available in print, he would employ Handel's own copyists to make scores for his collection. At what point the two men actually met is not clear, but a distinct possibility is the summer of 1733 in Oxford, when Jennens' cousin, Lord Guernsey, was graduating from the university. Attending the graduation, Jennens could therefore have heard some if not all of Handel's many performances in that Encaenia week, including the new *Athalia*. Some time after that he was in correspondence with Handel, for on 28th July 1735 Handel confirmed that 'The Opera of Alcina is a writing out and shall be sent according to your Direktion'. But the main point of his letter was to acknowledge receipt of a libretto: 'I received your very agreeable Letter with the inclosed Oratorio. I am just going to Tunbridge, yet what I could read of it in haste, gave me a great deal of Satisfaction. I shall have more leisure time there to read it with all the Attention it deserves.'[16] This was probably the text of *Saul*; and it was to this that Handel now, three summers later, turned his full attention.

Accelerations in creative energy and invention are often unfathomable and elusive, shrouded in mystery. Perhaps it was Handel's release from the pressures of administration; perhaps it was his return to health and thence to public affection; perhaps it was his awareness of the mood in London after the death of the Queen. Whatever the reason, Handel now moved into another gear. He had always worked hard in the summer months between seasons, but rarely so fixatedly or with results of such staggering quality as he now did, in 1738. *Saul* became something of an obsession for him. He wrote feverishly, discarding and rewriting more than he did with any other composition, and he sought, even invented, thrilling new sounds by bringing in instruments as yet unheard in such a context. Jennens, somewhat loftily proprietorial about his first attempt at any such endeavour, was both impressed and perplexed by Handel's fervour. On 19th September 1738, he wrote to Lord Guernsey, stating that 'Mr. Handel's head is full of more maggots than ever', and enumerating these as 'a very queer instrument which he calls carillon', a chamber organ from which Handel was now intending to direct his performances, and also his proposal for an 'Hallelujah' chorus at the end of the oratorio ('but this Hallelujah, Grand as it is, comes in very nonsensically, having no manner of relation to what goes before').[17] On this last issue, Handel and Jennens clearly had conversation, for, in the eventual score of *Saul*, the 'Hallelujah' chorus appears not at the conclusion, but towards the beginning of the work, which opens with a massive celebratory cantata. So

Jennens' involvement with the creative process was more than merely supplying Handel with a set of words; and, much as he enjoyed displaying a patronizing superiority ('I could tell you more of his maggots: but it grows late and I must defer the rest until I write next, by which time, I doubt not, more new ones will breed in his Brain'), the excitement of what they were hatching together is barely concealed.

Saul pushed the bar in many directions. It is one of Handel's longest works and has his largest collection of performers. Its concept, both in narrative and in emotional range, is vast, covering the replacement of one dynasty (Saul's) with another (David's), much activity, including battles and murder attempts, and the issues of true friendship, irrational jealousy, loyalty, duty and of course love. The rage ignited in Saul at the fanatical praise heaped upon David, a mere shepherd, after his slaying of the Philistine Goliath, drives the main action. Saul's son, Jonathan, is torn between loyalty to his father, who instructs him to kill David, and devotion to David, his best of friends. Saul's daughters, Michal, who loves David, and Merab, who does not, are involved; and there is a supernatural scene too, in which Saul consults the Witch of Endor, who raises the spirit of Samuel. In the briefest of battles (represented by a sixteen-bar sinfonia), both Saul and Jonathan are killed, and Israel, through the now-famous 'Dead March' and chorus, 'Mourn, Israel', is plunged into searing lamentation. David duly inherits the kingdom, and the final chorus, 'Gird on thy sword', is one of determination and courage rather than the triumphalist 'Hallelujah' that Handel had originally envisaged. (Jennens was right to persuade Handel of the substitution and rearrangement.) The extended mourning sequence at the end of Part III balances the lengthy celebratory music at the beginning of Part I, giving *Saul* a mighty symmetry.

274

From the very overture to *Saul*, Handel's new energy is apparent. It has no fewer than four movements – three of them based on an unpublished trio sonata, plus an additional minuet – which effectively, as early as 1738, anticipate the pre-classical symphony. These four movements are a vibrant allegro, a larghetto with concerto grosso features (solos for oboe and violin) and a carefully explicit continuo section of '*organo, cembalo e teorba*', and then another allegro in the manner of Handel's organ concertos, as he exuberantly shows off his newly acquired instrument and his own dazzling technique. Normally such a movement would have come in the interval between two acts, but here it has become part of the fabric of the piece itself. A quieter minuet concludes this remarkable overture of unprecedented length and variety; it is almost as if Handel is laying out his many technical weapons. And then comes what is effectively a huge cantata in praise both of the Almighty and of David's famed conquest of Goliath. Trumpets and timpani would have been customary for this sort of opening, but in addition there were new sounds here too: three trombones – a real novelty in concert orchestras – adding profound ballast to the texture, and special military battle drums – the very ones that had been used by the Duke of Marlborough at the Battle of Malplaquet, in 1709. These sounded an octave below standard orchestral timpani, and Handel needed them mainly for the sombre colours of his 'Dead March' in Part III. But, having once secured them – hired them, indeed, from the Tower of London – he used them again in the 'Hallelujah' chorus at the end of the opening celebratory sequence. A few moments later, his special carillon set of bells gives wholly individual colour to the sequence in which David is welcomed home, first by the women, and then by the whole community. Thus, within the first half-hour of the oratorio, a whole new concept of structure and sound has been laid before the audience, and Handel's vigorous passion is palpable.

The storytelling is achieved with all Handel's customary flair, and as always the characterization revealed in individual arias is sophisticated and subtle. The difference in nature between the two sisters, Michal and Merab, is extremely clear, as is the tenderness of affection between David and Jonathan, and the dangerous irrationality of Saul's fury. His violent actions are dramatically represented: the hurling of his murderous javelin is described in swift descending scales in the strings, startlingly unrelated to what has gone before. And there are many other examples of musical and dramatic dexterity: the intertwining of arias for Saul and Jonathan, for instance, as they argue over Saul's determination to kill David, giving the impression of genuine conversation. The music for the Witch of Endor is rhythmically disconcerting: 'Infernal spirits' is written with a 3/4 time signature, but the eight-bar introduction implies a quite other pulse of 2/4, and (not unlike the celebrated 5/8 music in the mad scene of *Orlando*) the sense of musical security becomes other-worldly. Similarly, the appearance then of the spirit of Samuel is accompanied just by the murky sinews of two bassoons and continuo – an experimental sound that Handel had not used before, but would again. The sonorities of the celebrated 'Dead March' are completely ingenious, achieved by the unlikely combination of strings, flutes, those newly recruited trombones and the Duke of Marlborough's drums. The solemnity of recent events, especially the funeral of Queen Caroline, surely still resonates in 'Mourn Israel', with its slowly controlled counterpoint and fragmented cries of desolation. And the very final chorus of determination and propriety, 'Gird on thy sword', succeeds in being uplifting, but not complacent. Jennens may have found it necessary to argue with Handel about this ending, but he must have been completely thrilled at hearing his words translated into music of such stirring quality. *Saul* is unquestionably one of Handel's greatest masterpieces, and indeed one of the greatest masterpieces of the eighteenth century; for all their creative sparring in this initial collaboration, the partnership between Handel and Jennens had got off to a blistering start.

Saul opened at the King's Theatre in the Haymarket on 16th January, before a 'numerous and splendid Audience'[18] headed by the King, the Duke of Cumberland and the Princesses (but not the Prince of Wales). This was the King's first appearance at a musical event since the Queen's death. *Saul*'s complex title role – the first for a bass – was taken by Gustavus Waltz. A newly married John Beard was Jonathan, and Merab and Michal were sung by Cecilia Young and Elisabeth Duparc ('La Francesina'). The role of David was given to the relatively obscure 'Mr Russell', who was possibly the same Mr Russell, actor and puppeteer, who a few years later got himself hopelessly into debt and was thrown into Newgate prison, where, according to Tobias Smollett, 'his disappointment got the better of his reason, and he remain'd in al the ecstasy of despair'. He ended his days in Bedlam, 'still happily bereft of his understanding'.[19] It is to be hoped that this fragile performer had at least the dramatic heft for the pivotal role of David. In the absence of any opera at the King's Theatre, this January performance, and three more in the following weeks, was the Haymarket's main offering that winter. A fifth performance on 17th April occurred during Lent, by which time Handel's second new oratorio, *Israel in Egypt*, was also in the schedules. As this second consecutive masterpiece showed, Handel's burst of creative energy was by no means sapped after *Saul*. Within three days of completing one, he was already launched into the next. And the rich seam continued.

There was as yet no pattern for Handel in the writing of oratorio. *Esther*, *Deborah* and *Athalia*, from the beginning of the 1730s, had seemed to establish the concept of sacred drama based on a biblical story and told in a first-person narrative. But between *Athalia* and *Saul* there had been a five-year gap. Handel's other large-scale non-theatrical work thus far had been *Alexander's Feast*, which was based on the work of a considerable poet, and there would be more forays into English literature before biblical dramas became re-established as a regular source for the oratorios. At the same time that Handel had been setting his *Saul*, Jennens had been compiling some biblical texts, initially for a long anthem of thanksgiving to God for the safe delivery of the Israelites through the Red Sea. It was this setting of texts from Exodus, chapter 15, entitled 'Moses' Song', that Handel addressed within days of completing *Saul*. Having finished that, he then prepared a text for what was effectively a prequel to 'Moses' Song'. 'Exodus' describes the ten plagues sent by God, which felled Egypt and allowed Moses and Aaron to liberate the Israelites from Egyptian bondage. These texts were assembled from wider sources (several parts of Exodus, together with Psalms 78, 105 and 106), and it is tempting to speculate that Jennens, who had certainly been around Handel in the previous month as they worked together on *Saul*, had had a hand in this complex and sophisticated assembly, especially as this section could be seen as a political metaphor for the deliverance of the Jacobites, so firmly professed by the Nonjuror, Jennens. And then there was a decision to join these two narrative sections together and precede them with yet another, entitled, 'The Lamentation of the Israelites for the death of Joseph'; and, for this, Handel simply adapted (only by the alteration of a few lines of text) the anthem, 'The ways of Zion do mourn', which he had written for Queen Caroline's funeral. So the mighty choral masterpiece which thus became *Israel in Egypt* was, in effect, written backwards, almost implying that even Handel himself was taken by surprise as the work dictated its own unconventional structure.

Unorthodox or not in its creative process, the writing, and especially the choral writing, in *Israel in Egypt* is astounding. There are extraordinarily few solo movements, an indication that the original conception was for an extended anthem rather than an oratorio; and, given the order in which he wrote new material in Parts III and II, it seems that Handel gathered considerable dramatic and descriptive momentum as he continued. So confident was he now in his choral singers that much of the writing is for double choir, and involves complex counterpoint. But there are many other gestures too, utilizing the richness of eight-part harmony through great choral recitatives, and incorporating (in 'He is my God', for example) internal florid ornamentation reminiscent of the spatially separate choirs of sixteenth-century Venetian composers. It certainly does seem that an ecclesiastical acoustic was in Handel's ear as he wrote these movements. But the descriptions of what actually happened before and during the Israelites' safe passage through the parted Red Sea, both in choruses ('the horse and his rider hath he thrown into the sea' – with the wonderful introduction of trumpets and timpani into the texture at this point) and in solo arias or duets ('his chosen captains also are drowned'), define the very nature of 'Moses' Song' as much as the paeans of praise and thanksgiving. Perhaps it was this process of producing a retrospective survey of these events, and the richness therefore of their dramatic situations, that actually propelled Handel to go back and, in 'Exodus', describe the dramas of the ten plagues and the parting of the Red Sea as they happened.

'Exodus' contains some of the most exuberant, vivid and ingenious choral music ever written. Apart from a tenor narrator (Beard) in brief recitatives, and some solo writing for an alto (the rapidly developing William Savage, gradually moving away, as his voice broke, from his boy roles – Joas, Oberto – to more adult participation), it is the choir which describes with almost cinematic precision the arrival and consequent impact of the ten plagues. Here, it seems, a cathedral context has been supplanted by a theatrical one, and Handel clearly relished the opportunities to describe and enhance horrific situations. Sometimes two or more of the ten plagues were combined. The alto aria, 'The land brought forth frogs', for instance, also includes pestilence, 'blotches and blains'; and, in possibly the most hilarious passage of the whole work, the chorus 'He spake the word' describes flies, lice and locusts with onomatopoeic buzzing and swirling in the orchestra. Other movements are devoted to single plagues, as in 'He gave them hailstones for rain' (wonderfully introduced by a gathering storm of intermittent raindrops), or 'He sent a thick darkness', with its slow-moving, freezing-fog-like harmony and straightforward word-setting. His instructions for 'He smote the first-born of Egypt' are '*A tempo giusto e staccato*', implying the hammer-stroke violence of the murder of children. And then, at the beginning of the section in which the Israelites are saved, 'But as for His people', these dramatic gestures change completely, and the music smiles with the greatest tenderness. The climactic parting of the Red Sea is told in huge eight-part chords of contrasted dynamic and accompaniment; 'He led them through the deep' is appropriately busy with scurrying counterpoint; and the destruction of the drowned enemy is represented in cascades of falling triplets in the orchestra. 'Exodus' concludes with another vast hymn of relief, praise and gratitude. Handel must have had superlative performers to have written such exhilarating, varied and demanding virtuosity for choral singers, and *Israel in Egypt* is a great tribute to them.

For the orchestra in *Israel in Egypt*, Handel retained his trombones from *Saul*, using them adroitly for ballast and support; and he brought in two flutes for a single number, 'But as for His people', the chorus in which the colour and mood is changed completely after the descriptive excitements of the plagues. The softening of the texture with the flutes here is a masterstroke. His very underused soloists sang just four arias, three duets, two introductions to choruses (the first of 'Exodus', the last of 'Moses' Song') and Beard's few recitatives. Elisabeth Duparc was joined on the soprano line by one of the boy choristers ('Master Robinson' – perhaps the son of the organist, John Robinson, and his wife, Ann Turner Robinson, who had occasionally sung for Handel in the past); and the two basses were Waltz and Reinhold for one mighty duet ('The Lord is a man of war'). Duparc, Waltz and Beard will have been relieved to have such a minimal workload immediately after the demands of *Saul*.

Israel in Egypt opened at the King's Theatre on 4th April, but had only three performances. The second one, a week after the first, was already 'shortned and Intermix'd with songs'[20] (as the *London Daily Post* observed): a recitative and three arias for Duparc were substituted for some of the choruses, implying perhaps that the public had not been happy with the original choral saturation. The Prince and Princess of Wales attended the third and, as it happened, final performance. For an advertised fourth performance on 19th April, *Israel in Egypt* was replaced by *Saul*, and after that Handel barely revived it in his lifetime. Like *Serse*,

Israel in Egypt required the passage of considerable time before it received the attention and praise it deserved; but since the nineteenth century it has rightly become and remained one of Handel's most popular and revered works.

Between *Saul* and *Israel in Egypt*, Handel had also revived *Alexander's Feast* for three performances; the last of these was a charitable occasion for the benefit of his new Fund for the Support of Decay'd Musicians and their Families. According to the *London Daily Post*, the audience was 'numerous and polite', and, more to the point, extremely generous, as indeed was Handel, who 'gave the House and his Performance, upon this Occasion, Gratis'; Heidegger too personally 'made a Present of Twenty Pounds to defray other incident Expenses'.[21] Handel's charitable initiative had clearly hit a nerve with his audiences. He closed his season with two performances of a pasticcio, *Giove in Argo*, for his regular singers Duparc, Beard and Reinhold, together with a recent arrival in London, the mezzo-soprano, Costanza Posterla, and her soprano daughter. Much of the music was borrowed from nine of his own works, and, in telling the racy story of Jove's infatuation for Callisto, there was strong dramatic potential. But this too, like *Israel in Egypt*, met little favour with the public. There was a real sense that the audience had had enough.

∾

In the summer of 1739, the King's Theatre in the Haymarket underwent a refit, from which it emerged 'made up of little boxes, like the playhouses abroad',[22] as Mrs Pendarves reported to Lady Throckmorten. The King, still desperately missing Caroline, despite his plural '*maitresses*', remained on icy terms with the Prince of Wales, and effectively banished him from any of the royal palaces. Frederick moved his wife and two small children, Princess Augusta and the one-year-old Prince George, who would eventually succeed his grandfather as George III, to the countryside at Cliveden, establishing himself there with his pleasures and his courtiers. Politically there was mounting tension in relationships with Spain. In an attempt to increase commercial and military domination in the Atlantic, Britain made capital out of an eight-year-old incident (which may not even have happened) in which a naval captain's ear had apparently been severed by a Spanish coastguard, and declared war – the War of Jenkins' Ear – against Spain. Walpole, himself also recently widowed and in failing health, grew increasingly despondent and offered his resignation, but the King would not hear of it. Although there were to be passing victories in the autumn, war was once more draining the nation's purse and young personnel. The Commander-in-Chief in the Mediterranean was Admiral Nicholas Haddock. 'Plays we have none', wrote Richard West to Horace Walpole in December 1739, 'or damned ones . . . No Opera, no nothing. All for war and Admiral Haddock.'[23]

Handel, as always aloof from the political fray though never unaware of it, played a waiting game. Once more there was a tentative move to start up a new opera company. Lord Middlesex, a close friend of the Prince of Wales, had just returned from his European travels with his (mediocre) soprano wife, Lucia Panichi, for whom he was endeavouring to secure a platform, and he began to collect supporters and money. But Handel bided his time. With no immediate prospect of, or demand for, any of his own operas, his customary routine was again disrupted, and he turned his attention instead to the composition of instrumental music, including his ingenious Opus 6 Concerti Grossi, which would be useful for inclusion in his oratorio performances.

Alexander's Feast, unlike *Israel in Egypt*, had been a success, and, in that summer of 1739, Handel took up Dryden again, alighting on his eight-stanza poem from 1687, 'A Song for St Cecilia's Day'. Handel, a foreigner with a somewhat eccentric command of the English language, nevertheless recognized the quality of great poetry. The ode celebrates the power of music, which creates an ordered world out of chaos, 'when Nature underneath a heap of jarring Atoms lay, / And could not raise her head', through the harmony of the spheres, 'through all the compass of the notes it ran, / The diapason closing full in man'. Different emotions are conquered by the deployment of different musical instruments: a 'corded lyre' for passion (though, in fact, Handel gave this to a solo cello), trumpets for war, a 'soft complaining flute' for hopeless lovers, and 'sharp violins' for jealousy and desperation. Finally, St Cecilia herself plays the organ to outshine them all; and the concluding chorus represents the Day of Judgement: 'The dead shall live, the living die, / And music shall untune the sky.' Handel responded to the poetic glories with musical vigour and subtlety. The tender solos for cello, flute and trumpet reflect the quality of his individual players and the confidence he had in them (the cello solo at the end of 'What passion cannot Music raise' is marked '*ad libitum*', a sure indication that Handel trusted his cellist to take the interpretative reins himself). His orchestral depiction of chaos, with strange melodies and taut harmonic progressions, truly anticipates that of Haydn in his *Creation*, some sixty years later. All the vocal writing, whether arias or the supporting and framing choruses, is utterly distinguished.

Handel's *Ode for St Cecilia's Day* was first performed, while the King's Theatre was undergoing its refurbishment, in Lincoln's Inn Fields, on St Cecilia's Day, 22nd November 1739. With it, in a major celebration of Dryden's poetry with Handel's music, was *Alexander's Feast*. This concentration on English texts led Handel to his next encounter with poetry of the highest order. With the help of Jennens, he had turned to Milton. They certainly had time to prepare their texts, for not only were the theatres frequently closed ('war and Admiral Haddock' still restricting leisure pursuits), but, even when they were open, there was such a severe winter in January and February 1740 that many performances had to be postponed or even cancelled. Theatre managers found it difficult simply to keep the buildings warm enough. A double bill of *Acis and Galatea* and the *Ode for St Cecilia's Day* was scheduled for 7th February, but 'in consideration of the weather continuing so cold' was 'put off for a few nights',[24] according to the *London Daily Post*. It was eventually rescheduled for a week later, 14th February, with the announcement stressing that 'Particular Care has been taken to have the House survey'd and secur'd against the Cold, by having Curtains plac'd before every Door, and constant Fires will be kept in the House 'till the time of Performance'.[25] But, in the event, this too was postponed, now because two 'chief Singers' had been taken ill. By the time *Acis and Galatea* was at last performed, on 27th February, it was not with the *Ode for St Cecilia's Day*, but with the new, Milton-based oratorio, on which Handel and Jennens had been working: *L'Allegro, il Penseroso ed il Moderato*.

James Harris, a Salisbury-based author and music lover, and one of Handel's close circle of friends, first suggested Milton's poem as a vehicle for musical setting. He was taken not just by the majesty of the language, but by its conversational, and therefore quasi-dramatic potential as a dialogue between two opposing points of view. L'Allegro (the Cheerful Man) espouses a life of jollity and mirth, embracing both pastoral delights and energetic city pleasures, while Il Penseroso (the Pensive Man) prefers calm and quiet, cloistered contemplation and, essentially, solitude. Many of Handel's friends were involved in the conceptual stages of *L'Allegro*. Harris made the first draft of a two-part libretto, and sent it via his cousin, Lord Shaftesbury, to Jennens, who refined it before showing it to Handel. Handel himself had his own views and suggestions, and it was he who proposed adding a third part, perhaps Milton's 'At a Solemn Music'. Jennens then had the better idea still of writing a conciliatory middle path, *Il Moderato*, between the two opposites, and he did so in a style which commendably referenced Milton's poems. (Handel would find occasion to use Milton's 'Solemn Music' text on a later occasion.) There would be contrasts, too, in the musical personification of the opponents. Il Penseroso would be sung by Elisabeth Duparc, who had effectively become Handel's replacement for Strada and shared many of her tender and expressive qualities. L'Allegro was to be sung mainly by a boy soprano (billed simply as 'The Boy', but perhaps the gifted Master Robinson again), representing an uncomplicated innocence. But his music was supported by arias too for a tenor (Beard, of course, who would also deliver some brief recitatives, in the way he had in *Israel in Egypt*), a bass (Reinhold) and, especially for the busiest and sometimes most comic effects, the chorus. For the third part, Il Moderato, a different voice was introduced, and this would be the young William Savage, whose vocal graduation from treble in 1735 (*Athalia*, *Alcina*), to alto in 1738 (*Israel in Egypt*), was now in 1740 remarkably secure as a well-trained baritone. But the penultimate number of the whole piece – and its true conclusion, therefore – would be a duet of shared reconciliation of the two formerly opposed voices, Duparc and Beard.

Every single musical number in *L'Allegro* is of the greatest

17. Princess Anne,
Handel's pupil and
passionate supporter.

18. Prince Frederick
enjoyed making music
with his sisters.

19. The first opera house in the Haymarket, which burned down in 1789.

20. Mrs Mary Delany (née Granville, later Mrs Pendarves): one of Handel's closest friends.

21. Anna Maria Strada del Pò, the loyal soprano who, trained by Handel, sang thirty-one of his roles in just nine years.

22. The tenor John Beard, likewise trained by Handel, who sang for him for over twenty years.

23. Charles Jennens, librettist of *Messiah*, *Saul* and *Belshazzar*, and Handel's greatest collaborator.

24. From Handel's autograph draft score of *Messiah*.

25. Susanna Cibber, whose searing intensity as a performer captivated Handel.

26. Kitty Clive, an enchanting addition to Handel's company in the 1740s.

27. London in 1745.

28. Servandoni's 'Fireworks Machine', built in Green Park in 1748,
and the backdrop to Handel's 'Music for the Royal Fireworks'.

29. Dr Charles Burney, who oversaw the massive Handel memorial events in 1784.

30. Handel's funerary monument by Roubiliac, in Westminster Abbey.

31. Thomas Hudson's magnificent 1756 portrait of Handel.

distinction. Given the difficulty in projecting with clarity some of Milton's more complex lines (there are fewer that are harder to bring off than, 'Come thou goddess, fair and free, / In heav'n y-clept Euphrosyne'), the young boy chorister who took the lion's share of L'Allegro's music must have been as remarkable a musician and communicator as his predecessor and now senior colleague, William Savage. It was Beard, though, followed by the chorus, who was given, 'Haste thee nymph, and bring with thee / Jest and youthful jollity', with its hilarious musical characterization of, 'Laughter holding both his sides'. There is a genuine sense of high-spirited camaraderie in this music, reminiscent perhaps of those evenings in the taverns adjacent to St Paul's Cathedral, when Handel would unwind at the end of the day with these very Gentlemen from the choir. This specifically urban energy is present too in 'Populous cities please me then / And the busy hum of men', set for Reinhold and the chorus with bustling brilliance, and reflecting Handel's great love for the city of London, its parliamentary process ('where throngs of knights and barons bold / In weeds of peace high triumphs hold') and its social scene. Handel's own theatrical milieu appears with great affection in the jaunty, 'I'll to the well-trod stage anon', also for Beard. But even *L'Allegro* has its quietude. At the end of a day of dancing and merriment (and Handel's carillon from *Saul*, brought back for 'Or let the merry bells ring round'), the exhausted revellers retire for a peaceful night ('Thus past the day to bed they creep / By whispering winds soon lull'd asleep') in one of Handel's most ravishing passages of release and repose. But L'Allegro's final utterance, 'These delights if thou canst give, / Mirth, with thee I choose to live', is again bursting with the energetic joy of the optimistic showman, creating wave after wave of exuberance.

If the music for the Cheerful Man represents one clear side of

Handel's own gregarious and generous personality, that for his Pensive opposite strikes a chord of equal authenticity. The contemplative life is so staggeringly well observed and realized that it is tempting to detect the true identity of Handel the loner, too. The work opens with three bars of dark and smoky mystery, played on the same bassoons and lower strings that Handel had used to conjure up the spirit of Samuel in *Saul*. Here it is Melancholy who is summoned, 'of Cerberus and blackest midnight born, / In Stygian cave forlorn'. In due course, there are truly arresting portrayals of a 'pensive nun', of 'gorgeous Tragedy', of the 'Sweet bird that shun'st the noise of folly' (another extraordinary duet for soprano and birdlike flute, similar to one in the recent *Ode for St Cecilia's Day*). Handel is not afraid to slow the tempo almost to stasis in 'Oft on a plat of rising ground / I hear the far-off curfew sound', with a chilly virtual silence punctuated by regular, remote pizzicato bass strings (the 'far-off curfew'); but, at the end of this aria, he brings in the warmth of slowly moving upper strings for 'where glowing embers through the room / Teach light to counterfeit a gloom'. There is magical stillness again in 'Hide me from day's garish eye', and a symbolic reduction of texture for the continuo aria, 'May at last my weary age / Find out the peaceful hermitage'. Il Penseroso's last utterance, 'These pleasures, Melancholy, give / And I with thee will choose to live', is, in fact, an affirmative and brilliant choral fugue, positive, intellectual, radiant, profound, and utterly content.

The masterstroke of the final, non-Miltonic section, *Il Moderato*, after three placatory arias for William Savage and one more each for Duparc and Beard, is the great duet, 'As steals the morn', for their now reconciled voices. Jennens devised this text by paraphrasing part of a speech by Prospero in Act V, Scene 1 of *The Tempest*. Thus

> And as the morning steals upon the night
> Melting the darkness, so their rising senses
> Begin to chase the ignorant fumes that mantle
> Their clear reason

becomes

> As steals the morn upon the night
> And melts the shades away,
> So truth does Fancy's charm dissolve
> And rising reason puts to flight
> The fumes that did the mind involve,
> Restoring intellectual day.

Fortified now by Shakespeare as well as by Milton and his own literary friends, Handel produced one of his most exquisite duets, with a gently walking bass line, softly undulating upper strings, and solo lines for oboe and bassoon which then intertwine with the two vocal soloists. This resolution is the true end of the intellectual argument between L'Allegro and Il Penseroso: the final chorus of all, 'Thy pleasures, Moderation, give, / In them alone we truly live', is a straightforward, almost chorale-like syllabic setting. No further imaginative armament is required.

L'Allegro opened at Lincoln's Inn Fields on 27th February 1740, together with *Acis and Galatea*; and, for good measure, Handel threw in two of his twelve new concerti grossi (imminently due in publication). One of these would have acted as an overture, for Handel wrote no new one here. He also played one of his organ concertos. It was still bitterly cold, so the public was again reassured that 'Particular Care is taken to have the House secur'd against the Cold, constant Fires being order'd to be kept in the House 'till the Time of Performance'.[26] Four further performances followed, together with, in the Lenten weeks, one each of *Saul*, *Esther* and *Israel in Egypt*. This last was still the least well received, and Handel shelved it for several years. In amongst these three oratorios, there was also a charity performance of *Acis and Galatea*, again for Handel's Fund for the Support of Decay'd Musicians, on 28th March. As the quantitatively short season ended, the Twelve Grand Concertos in Seven Parts (later known as Opus 6) were published on 21st April, with an interesting and impressive list of subscribers. The royal family were well represented; though neither the King nor the Prince of Wales signed up, the Duke of Cumberland and all his sisters did, including the absent Princess Anne in Holland. Handel's friends, Jennens, Bernard Granville (brother of Mrs Pendarves), William Knatchbull, James Harris and his cousin, Lord Shaftesbury, all appear; and it seems that His Lordship had persuaded his mother and wife to subscribe as well. There are those with a professional interest in owning this set of concertos, including John Rich at Covent Garden, John Robinson, organist at Westminster Abbey, and Jonathan Tyers, manager of Vauxhall Gardens. And then there are the amateur music societies, including several for the London taverns which hosted them (the Crown and Anchor, the Globe Tavern, the Castle in Paternoster Row), and, further afield, the Academy of Musick in Dublin, music societies in Oxford, Canterbury and Salisbury, and, most delightfully, the 'Ladies Concert in Lincoln'. Handel's popularity was spreading through the land.

Handel travelled to Europe in the summer of 1740, and returned refreshed and energetic. But if he had reflected coolly on the season just ended, one stark truth would have stared him in the face. All his performances, and indeed publications, had been in the English language. There had been no new Italian opera, nor even any revival of an old one. This was unprecedented. Still reluctant, however, to admit final defeat in a medium that he loved and in which he felt supremely comfortable, Handel cast around one final time for some new Italian singers, and prepared two more operas. One of them, *Imeneo*, had been on his desk for some time. He had begun it in September 1738, while he was also working on *Saul*, and scheduled it for the end of the 1738–9 season, after Costanza Posterla and her daughter had arrived in London. But such was the failure of their performances in *Giove in Argo*, especially that of the daughter, that they had almost immediately fled straight back to Italy, and Handel had had to shelve *Imeneo*. Now determined to get it performed, he made some changes to it, and hired a castrato, Giovanni Battista Andreoni, to complete a cast otherwise made up of his new regulars, Duparc, Savage, Reinhold and a Miss Edwards. The King 'and all the St. James's royall family' (so, not the Prince of Wales) attended the opening on 22nd November, along with 'a very good house',[27] according to James Harris's brother. Determined not to miss this new opera, the Prince of Wales then ordered another performance that he could attend, but had to wait until 13th December, as Duparc was indisposed. But these were the only two performances that *Imeneo* received, and even Handel's most loyal supporters had their doubts about it: Jennens bluntly told Harris that it was 'the worst of all Handel's compositions'.[28] And indeed, although there is unmistakeable quality in individual numbers, *Imeneo* does not begin to match the recent *Saul* or *L'Allegro*. And the same is true of his second opera that season, *Deidamia*, which had just three performances in February 1741. He added a new Italian soprano to his roster, Maria Monza, who here joined Duparc, Andreoni, Savage, Reinhold and the elusive Miss Edwards. Monza was clearly no second-rate singer, for her music demonstrates a wide range and some technical dexterity. But, unlike her great predecessors Cuzzoni and Strada, she could not inspire Handel to write his greatest music for her, and she does seem to have lacked stature and stage presence. (Mrs Pendarves wrote disparagingly to her sister, 'Her voice is between Cuzzoni's and Strada's – strong, but not harsh, her person *miserably bad*, being very low, and *excessively* crooked.'[29]) In short, *Deidamia*, like its season partner, *Imeneo*, seems lukewarm in creative energy and in audience reaction. Its only dubious distinction is that it was the last of Handel's Italian operas.

The season fizzled out, and over the course of the ensuing summer Handel at last threw in that operatic towel. The enthusiastic Lord Middlesex's company had persuaded Heidegger to come and join them, and obtained a licence to perform at the King's Theatre for four years. Handel was happy to leave them to it. His uncharacteristic lack of competitive spirit inevitably drew rumour and gossip, that he was again contemplating going abroad, possibly never to return. And in fact Handel was about to leave London, but not for Europe. He had received an irresistible invitation from the Lord Lieutenant of Ireland to visit Dublin, where his music was extremely popular. He was also, again through his friends Jennens and Lord Shaftesbury, continuing to work on English-language texts. Lord Shaftesbury had followed Handel's success with *L'Allegro* by pointing him in the direction of Milton's great drama, *Samson Agonistes*. And, back in 1739, Jennens had presented Handel with a second compilation of biblical texts, which he hoped he could turn into another oratorio. So energized was Handel by this project that he actually completed his first draft of it in just three weeks.

While Handel thus worked on two large English-language librettos in the early autumn of 1741, a scintilla of operatic life returned without him to central London. Lord Middlesex assembled his company in the Haymarket and mounted a production of a pasticcio by Galuppi, *Alessandro in Persia*, which opened the season, as usual, on 31st October, the day after the King's birthday. Handel actually attended the performance and – with the same Schadenfreude that he had experienced back in 1735, when 'in silent triumph' he had been to one of Opera of the Nobility's faltering performances – delighted in its mediocrity. Four days later, he began his travels to Ireland, and the memory of what he had seen and heard in the Haymarket 'made me very merry all along my journey', as he gleefully reported to Jennens.[30]

Handel took a great deal of music with him to Ireland. Within his bags were his now sure-fire successes, *Acis and Galatea*, the *Ode for St Cecilia's Day*, *L'Allegro*, *Esther*, *Alexander's Feast* and *Saul*. For good measure, he threw in *Imeneo*, still feeling, perhaps, that there was unfinished business there. And he also brought with him one of the two new compositions on which he had recently been working: *Messiah*.

11

'Hallelujah'

As he trundled away from London in such high spirits, of both expectation and relief, can Handel have had any possible notion of what his latest score would become? *Messiah* was a bold and new departure, a profoundly dramatic but essentially contemplative Christian reflection centred on the Lenten story of crucifixion and resurrection in Part II, but incorporating, too, the Christmas story in Part I and concluding, in Part III, with a consideration of redemption. It was told not in the first person but, like *Alexander's Feast* or *Israel in Egypt*, in the third person, through very familiar biblical texts brilliantly assembled by Jennens. *Messiah* would enter the public world quite modestly, in a city which, for all its eighteenth-century prominence, was not one of major international importance. After its enthusiastic reception in Dublin, Handel would nevertheless be anxious about presenting it in London; Jennens, curiously, would never feel that Handel had got it right ('he has made a fine Entertainment of it, though not near so good as he might and ought to have done',[1] he later concluded, astonishingly), and Handel would continue to tweak its details for many years, worrying even about its very title as he faced criticism for presenting an 'Act of Religion' in a theatre rather than a church. That *Messiah* would become a veritable cornerstone of European and therefore world culture, resonating spectacularly through the centuries and across the globe, changing the whole nature of music-making and to an extent also that of concert-going, as well as uplifting countless millions of performers and listeners, would – even for the confident, resilient and optimistic Handel – have been utterly unimaginable.

Dublin, to which Handel now travelled with his priceless cargo, was the largest provincial city in the British Isles, and was governed by a Lord Lieutenant, currently William Cavendish, the Duke of Devonshire. Like Ireland as a whole, the city was fraught with tensions between Protestants and Catholics, but by the beginning of the eighteenth century the Protestants had established their superiority, largely through several generations of them having been educated at Dublin's Trinity College, founded under Elizabeth I in 1592; and harsh penal laws had been imposed on the Catholic majority. As in London, the eighteenth century saw considerable expansion of Dublin: medieval streets were being demolished and replaced by wider boulevards and squares, giving the city an elegance that imitated that of London or Paris; but a huge slum population remained too.

The eighteenth century also saw the expansion of musical activity in Dublin, cultivated especially by the sophisticated ruling class and therefore reflecting English and European taste rather than that of Ireland's own population. There were concerts, operas and plays, in theatres in Smock Alley or Aungier Street, and in concert halls in Crow Street or – newly opened, just before Handel's arrival – Fishamble Street. As in London, music flourished under the auspices of charitable institutions: the Mercers' Hospital, the Charitable Music Society for the Relief of Imprisoned Debtors, and the Charitable Infirmary were all presenting concerts. And, drawn by this healthy musical activity, an increasing number of European musicians were finding their way to Dublin, some of whom would settle there permanently. Among the first of these was the violinist and composer Francesco Geminiani, and his ex-pupil, Matthew Dubourg. Both of these men were well known to Handel, and it is highly likely that they themselves had been instrumental in securing his invitation to spend some time in Dublin. Other friends with Anglo-Irish connections also encouraged Handel to undertake a long journey to a strange city in winter (an altogether different experience from travelling in the summer, as Handel generally did). These included Lord Egmont and his brother, Percival, and Mrs Pendarves, who had already lived in Dublin in the 1730s, and would again soon, after she married her second husband, the Irish Anglican cleric, Patrick Delany, in 1743. And so, having travelled through Chester and Holyhead, Handel arrived in Dublin on 18th November 1741, and took lodgings in Abbey Street. He would stay there for ten months.

The plan was for Handel to mount a subscription series of six concerts in Neale's Music Hall, the brand-new venue on Fishamble Street. His three certain successes, *L'Allegro*, *Acis and Galatea* and *Esther*, would each be presented twice. As with his Oxford engagement, he would be working for the most part with local musicians. For instrumentalists, he was happy to let his old colleague Matthew Dubourg recruit the best players, but he himself was more directly involved in selecting the singers. He brought with him from London a soprano, Christina Maria Avoglio, although she had not yet worked for him. Perhaps this Irish engagement was some sort of trial for her, away from the prying attentions of the London audiences. He had also summoned from London a husband-and-wife team, a Mr Maclaine, who played the organ, and his soprano wife. So, Handel already had two sopranos who were known to him, but as yet untested by him. By coincidence, an actress who was also something of an expressive and affecting singer, for she came from a musical family, was similarly travelling to Dublin. Susanna Cibber, the twenty-seven-year-old sister of the composer Thomas Arne, arrived just after Handel did, in early December, to perform with John Rich in a company run by James Quin at the theatre in Aungier Street. Mrs Cibber had fled from London three years earlier in a cloud of disgrace, having been appallingly treated during her marriage to Theophilus Cibber, son of the celebrated actor and dramatist, Colley Cibber. Her separation from her husband had been very public, very dramatic (her brothers had rescued her from the clutches of her enraged husband) and deeply shaming, and Mrs Cibber would suffer from anxious bouts of ill health for the rest of her life. But she was a warm and charismatic performer, and Handel was very taken with her and with the intelligence she brought to the roles she performed. She was soon included in his plans.

For the choir, Handel turned to the choral establishments at the two Cathedrals in Dublin, St Patrick's and Christ Church, whose singers' release had already been granted. Their commitment to Handel's music was established just three days after his arrival, on 21st November, when his Te Deum, Jubilate and 'two new anthems' were performed as part of a charity service for the Mercers' Hospital, in St Andrew's Church. (On the same occasion, at the specific request of the Mercer Governors, Handel himself played the organ.) But then Handel set about working with the sixteen boys and sixteen men who made up the choirs. And here he would have been especially forensic in his scrutiny, for he required soloists from their ranks for all his performances. He already knew, and rated well, one of the tenors, James Baileys, who had been in London in 1737 and had sung at the funeral of Queen Caroline. But he must have been impressed by the overall standard of the choirs, for he duly entrusted many solo opportunities to different individuals over the next weeks, training and coaching those chosen and, if necessary, adapting his music to their individual abilities. Similarly, he rehearsed the choirs as a group, and again felt confident that, with his directorial expertise, they could deliver his often complex music to the standard he required.

After thus assembling and then rehearsing his performers, Handel opened his subscription series on 23rd December 1741 with *L'Allegro*. The new concert hall was packed out, and the audience effusive with their applause. According to the *Dublin Journal* of the following week, 'The Performance was superior to any Thing of the Kind in this Kingdom before; and our Nobility and Gentry to show their Taste for all Kinds of Genius, expressed their great Satisfaction, and have already given all imaginable Encouragement to this grand Musick.'[2] Handel was delighted, and wrote an uncharacteristically long account of his triumph to Jennens, tactfully paying special attention to the success of Part III of *L'Allegro* (with Jennens' words), but barely concealing his own excitement:

> I am emboldned, Sir, by the generous Concern You please to take in relation to my affairs, to give You an Account of the Success I have met here. The Nobility did me the Honour to

make amongst themselves a Subscription for 6 Nights, which did fill a room of 600 Persons, so that I needed not sell one single Ticket at the Door, and without Vanity the Performance was received with a general Approbation . . . I opened with the Allegro, Penseroso, & Moderato and I assure you that the Words of the Moderato are vastly admired.[3]

Handel loved the audience ('so many Bishops, Deans, Heads of the Colledge, the most eminent People of the Law as the Chancellor, Auditor General &c'), and he loved the new concert hall and its acoustic ('the Musick sounds delightfully in this charming Room'). And, as if all that were not enough, the joy that Handel was experiencing in Dublin was, as he confided to Jennens, increased again by gloomy reports of failed operatic performances in London, whose 'ill success . . . furnished great Diversion and laughter'. Handel was having the time of his life.

Immediately, everyone realized that Handel's series would be a sensation, and that six concerts would not be nearly enough. So a second series of six was being planned even as the first had barely begun. Handel recognized that he would have to stay longer than he had intended, and told Jennens that the Duke of Devonshire had applied to the King for a longer period of absence. (He was however confident that this would be 'easily' achieved.) So by Christmas 1741, Handel's spirits had been boosted by the high standards he could achieve with the Dublin musicians, and by the overwhelming warmth of the city's audiences. And as his first series continued in the new year with a further *Allegro*, two performances of *Acis and Galatea* (with the *Ode for St Cecilia's Day* thrown in) and two of *Esther*, there were anxious pleas in the press for crowd control and traffic management: 'Gentlemen and Ladies are desired to order their Coaches and Chairs to come down

Fishamble-street, which will prevent a great deal of Inconvenience that happened the Night before; and as there is a good convenient Room hired as an Addition to a former Place for the Footmen, it is hoped that the Ladies will order them to attend there till called for.'[4] The only slightly alarming snag in the proceedings was delivered by Jonathan Swift, now Dean of St Patrick's Cathedral, who, manifesting signs of the dementia which would all too speedily cause his decline and death, furiously denied that he had ever given permission for his singers to 'assist at a club of fiddlers in Fishamble Street',[5] and instructed his Sub-Dean and Chapter to prevent their further involvement. This somewhat unhinged instruction seems to have been quietly ignored, for there was absolutely no let-up in the pace at which the choirs, under Handel's direction, continued to work.

The first series ended on 10th February. Just a week later, the second was launched with *Alexander's Feast*, and there were plans for another *Alexander's Feast*, another *Esther*, another *Allegro*, and two performances of *Imèneo*, presented without action as a 'serenata', and retitled *Hymen*. The Dublin musicians kept fully abreast of this intense rate of musical turnover, and continued to deliver superlative performances to packed audiences, week after week. There was an unplanned hiatus in mid-March when Susanna Cibber succumbed to a 'sudden illness',[6] but in general the second set of six concerts was as great a success as the first, and the public were still baying for more.

So, at last, Handel turned to *Messiah*. Displaying, not for the first or indeed the last time, that essential humility and generosity that belied the bluster of his outgoing, confident personality, Handel chose to present this monumental narration and reflection, the very foundation of all Christian faith, in Passion week, and, despite its surrounding clamour, for no personal gain. This new work would be performed for the benefit of the three local charitable societies, as the announcement in the *Dublin Journal*, on 27th March 1742, proclaimed: 'For Relief of the Prisoners in the several Gaols, and for the support of Mercer's Hospital in Stephen's Street, and of the Charitable Infirmary in the Inns Quay, on Monday the 12th of April, will be performed at the Musick Hall in Fishamble Street, Mr. *Handel's new Grand Oratorio, call'd the Messiah*, in which the Gentlemen of the Choirs of both Cathedrals will assist, with some Concertoes on the Organ, by Mr. Handell.'[7] Again, even while his second subscription series was in full flow (*Hymen* and *Esther* were still being rehearsed and performed), Handel set to work to fit his new score to his current performers. Making the necessary adjustments – transpositions, additions, subtractions – to accommodate individual abilities, he allotted solos to a number of the Gentlemen from the choirs: the altos, William Lambe and Joseph Ward, the tenor, James Baileys, and the basses, John Mason and John Hill. And he certainly included Signora Avoglio, the elusive Mrs Maclaine, and Mrs Cibber, making modifications for them too. Late in the preparation stages, on 9th April, there was a rehearsal to which the public ('the most crowded and polite Assembly'[8]) were admitted, after which the buzz about this new work was thrilling. On the following morning, the *Dublin News-letter* declared that, 'Mr Handel's new sacred Oratorio . . . in the opinion of the best Judges, far surpasses anything of that Nature, which has been performed in this or in any other Kingdom.'[9] Great crowds were anticipated as usual for the first performance on 13th April, to the extent that the ladies were now urged to 'come without Hoops, as it will greatly increase the Charity, by making the Room for more Company'. Similarly, 'the Gentlemen are desired to come without their Swords'.[10]

And so *Messiah* received its first performance. If the rehearsal had generated excitement, it was nothing compared to the breathless eulogies which followed this premiere. The *Dublin Journal*, *Dublin News-letter* and *Dublin Gazette* all carried, in more or less identical form, the following report:

> Words are wanting to express the exquisite Delight it afforded to the admiring crouded Audience. The Sublime, the Grand and the Tender, adapted to the most elevated, majestick and moving Words, conspired to transport and charm the ravished Heart and Ear. It is but Justice to Mr. Handel, that the World should know, he generously gave the Money arising from this Grand Performance, to be equally shared by the Society for relieving Prisoners, the Charitable Infirmary, and Mercer's Hospital, for which they will ever gratefully remember his Name; and that the Gentlemen of the two Choirs, Mr. Dubourg, Mrs. Avolio, and Mrs. Cibber, who all performed their Parts to Admiration, acted also on the same disinterested Principle, satisfied with the deserving Applause of the Publick, and the conscious Pleasure of promoting such useful, and extensive Charity.[11]

According to legend, Susanna Cibber received an especial tribute. After she had sung 'He was despised', the longest aria in the whole work, combining sorrow, desolation, guilt and even rage, the Reverend Dr Delany, Chancellor of St Patrick's (and soon to be the husband of Handel's friend, Mary Pendarves), leapt to his feet, crying, 'Woman, for this be all thy sins forgiven thee!' If Susanna's reputation as a fallen woman had followed her from London to Dublin, she had certainly received the most public absolution, and in the most august of circumstances. It is to be hoped that this brought her comfort rather than embarrassment.

'Sublime, Grand and Tender' does indeed encapsulate both the range and the manner of the achievement of *Messiah*. Handel was apparently quite undaunted by the vastness of Jennens' concept – telling the whole story of Christ's birth and death, together with parallel and subsequent commentaries. Not unlike Bach's two mighty Passion settings, here both the narrative and the reflective are maintained at the same time with absolutely no loss of momentum, even when events are frozen. Inevitably, Handel's theatrical skills shine in the sections of most activity. In Part I, for instance, sleepy shepherds are startled and bedazzled by the appearance of, first, one angel announcing the birth of Christ, and then a 'multitude' of them, setting the heavens ablaze with their praises (and here, in 'Glory to God', with their aural surprise of the first appearance of trumpets – still at this point off stage). Through this scene, the progression from a tranquil 'Pifa', or pastoral interlude, through human panic to heavenly celebration is typically masterly. Less overtly dramatic, but similarly effective, is the searing sequence of crucifixion events in Part II, with Mrs Cibber's lament, 'He was despised', taunting cries from ugly crowds ('He trusted in God: let Him deliver him'), and Christ's heavy sorrow ('Thy rebuke hath broken his heart'). Sandwiched among all this are three contiguous but highly contrasted choruses ('Surely He hath borne our griefs', 'And with His stripes we are healed' and 'All we like sheep have gone astray') in which the Christian awareness that we are all responsible for the outrage of the crucifixion concludes with 'And the Lord hath laid on Him the iniquity of us all', delivered in the appalled, hushed tones of individuals' guilt. Only at 'Lift up your heads' is the mood turned around, and gathering energies finally burst forth once more with the most celebrated chorus ever written, 'Hallelujah', fortified brilliantly by the reappearance of the trumpets (now very much on stage). Part III is the most personal and most contemplative, beginning as it does with 'I know that my Redeemer liveth'. Here, the affirmative rising fourth of the opening phrase is an inversion of the falling fourth in Part I's opening, 'Comfort ye', and in the same key (E major). Whether conscious or unconscious, these fourths and their symmetry in the overall structure offer compelling insight into Handel's own faith. The serenity of 'Redeemer' leads to more affirmation and celebration, including a typically atmospheric accompanied recitative for 'Behold, I tell you a mystery' and the bracing authority of a now solo trumpet in 'The trumpet shall sound'. And Handel's great masterpiece ends with a major sequence for the choirs: a thoughtful, steady choral recitative for 'Worthy is the lamb', an energetic celebration for 'Blessing and honour, glory and power be unto Him', and the finest choral 'Amen' ever written – tranquil and reverential at its beginning, and building through ingenious controlled counterpoint to a thrilling climax. Whether performed by 250 singers or just eight, this 'Amen' never fails to make an impact, and triumphantly to express the conclusion of the world's most serious and important story. As Jennens concluded in his preface to the published word-book of *Messiah* (the quotation is from 1 Timothy 3:16): 'And without Controversy, great is the Mystery of Godliness: God was manifested in the Flesh, justified by the Spirit, seen of Angels, preached among the Gentiles, believed on in the World, received up in Glory. In whom are hid all the Treasures of Wisdom and Knowledge.'

After the triumph of *Messiah* and the celebration of Easter, Handel rested a little. He and his hard-working Dublin team had been operating at a cracking pace for three months – a pace which was familiar to him, but probably overwhelming to his colleagues. But the Irish public were still unwilling to accept that Handel's engagement with them was over, and pressed him for yet more. So, Handel produced *Saul*, no less, which he performed just once, on 25th May. With scant extant information about this performance, it is impossible to do more than speculate as to who sang what, though it is tempting to surmise that Susanna Cibber sang David, and Handel's two sopranos, Avoglio and Maclaine, sang Michal and Merab. One of those Dublin basses will have had the time of his life, and the challenge of his life, preparing and then performing the title role under Handel's direction. While none of these solo Gentlemen ever moved away from an ecclesiastical base, remaining instead in relative obscurity, their contribution to Handel's success in Dublin cannot be ignored. Handel had found performers equal to the hefty demands of his music, and none of them had disappointed him. After *Messiah*, his confidence in them to deliver *Saul*, one of his longest and most exacting oratorios, speaks volumes.

Again 'At the particular Desire of the Nobility and Gentry', Handel's final promotion in Dublin was a repeat performance, equally well received, of *Messiah*, on 3rd June. He would also have been present for, if not participant in, benefit concerts for Signora Avoglio and Mrs Cibber. The second of these, for Avoglio, was actually deferred for a week as another influx of visitors from London had seized Dublin's excitement. First came the great actor David Garrick, along with Margaret ('Peg') Woffington. They took the theatre in Smock Alley, and there performed the invigorating repertory of Farquhar's comedy, *The Constant Couple*, and then *Hamlet*, which Handel is said to have attended. After them came Susanna Cibber's brother, 'the Ingenious'

Thomas Arne, and his wife, 'the celebrated Singer' Cecilia (née Young), who, six years earlier, had sung Dalinda (in *Ariodante*), Athalia and Morgana (in *Alcina*) for Handel.[12] During this family reunion, there was a benefit concert for Cecilia on 21st June, in which Cecilia and Susanna sang together the most enchanting programme of arias and duets by Handel. Planned for the theatre in Aungier Street, this concert was actually moved to the concert hall in Fishamble Street, presumably for its greater capacity and better acoustic, and then repeated there a week later. Not only were these events delightful outings for the two sisters–in–law, but in a sense also a tribute to Handel, who must have relished having one of his favourite singers from the past sharing a platform with his latest discovery. And the music they sang included, as well as highlights from the Dublin repertoire, *Esther*, *Saul*, *Imeneo* and *L'Allegro*, arias and duets too from *Faramondo* and *Sosarme* (the infinitely alluring duet, 'Per le porte del tormento'). The implication is surely that Handel had a part in the selection, preparation and even performance of this programme, and it is hard to imagine a more charming musical occasion.

Before Handel left Dublin, he had one sombre farewell to take: he went to see Jonathan Swift. By now the great man was distressingly deranged. According to the memoirs of Laetitia Pilkington, wife of one of Swift's curates, this visit occasioned 'the last sensible Words [Swift] uttered'. As she described the scene, 'The Servant was a considerable Time, e'er he could make the Dean understand him; which, when he did, he cry'd "Oh! A *German*, and a Genius! A Prodigy! Admit him." The Servant did so, just to let Mr *Handel* behold the Ruins of the greatest Wit that ever lived along the Tide of Time, where all at length are lost.'[13]

Handel finally left Dublin on 13th August. He had adored his time there, both artistically and socially, and he had made a lot of money. He had every intention of returning. On his way back to London, he tried to call on Jennens, in Gopsall, but, finding Jennens away, wrote him a letter instead, and his euphoria is touchingly apparent:

> It was indeed Your humble Servant which intended You a visit in my way from Ireland to London, for I certainly could have given You a better account by word of mouth, as by writing, how well your Messiah was received in that Country . . . As for my Success in General in that generous and polite Nation, I reserve the account of it till I have the Honour to see you in London.[14]

It was a well-content Handel who finally returned to Brook Street.

∾

Politically, much had changed during Handel's absence. In February 1742 the Prime Minister, Robert Walpole, had resigned, and there had been a cautious rapprochement between the King and the Prince of Wales.

The sequence of events which led to these determined decisions had begun back in October 1740, with the death of the Emperor Charles VI and the consequent War of the Austrian Succession. Before his death, the Emperor had persuaded many European powers, including Britain, France, Hanover, Prussia and Spain, to abide by the Pragmatic Sanction. This would guarantee that his daughter, Maria Theresa, would succeed him to the imperial title, although as a woman she should, by Salic law, be debarred from it. Upon his death, however, this agreement seemed to evaporate, and alternative imperial candidates were promoted. Suddenly, European countries and their animosities towards each other were being realigned. Frederick II of Prussia invaded Silesia, part of Maria Theresa's territory, and proposed that she yield it to him in return for his support against any other invaders. France allied itself to Prussia, but Britain supported Maria Theresa, sending her £300,000 and 12,000 troops. War seemed inevitable, and George II, instinctively of a military bent, was eager to be involved. He visited Hanover, to Walpole's great concern, and there secured a promise from France to let Hanover remain neutral if he supported their own candidate for imperial succession, Charles Albert of Bavaria. The British people were furious that the King had apparently given priority to his Hanoverian rather than his British interests, and blamed Walpole. Continuing parliamentary bickering about the Prince of Wales's allowance also contributed to Walpole's discomfiture, and he decided he had had enough. Walpole had been beside the King throughout his reign, and George II was desolated to lose him. He granted him a pension of £4,000 per annum, and elevated him to the peerage, as the Earl of Orford.

The man who was now to be closest to the King was his Secretary of State for the Northern Department, Lord John Carteret, who had previously been a popular Lord Lieutenant of Ireland, and who also owned some territories in America. He had a good grasp of foreign affairs, and was impressive in debate. But he had taken the side of the Prince of Wales in the very public feud with his parents, and therefore, while Queen Caroline had been alive, he had not been close to the seat of power. Now, having gained the confidence of the King, Carteret was anxious to effect a reconciliation between George II and his son. A reunion was engineered, and a tentative rapprochement reached. The King and Prince of

Wales made a triumphant tour together through London's cheering crowds, and the Prince of Wales's allowance was duly increased, to his considerable satisfaction. If this royal truce was indeed only temporary, it must have seemed momentous to Handel as he returned to the capital after his Irish triumphs, and he will have welcomed being at ease once more with both generations of the royal family. Less comforting to him would have been the constant threat of Britain being drawn into war.

But if there was turmoil in the wider political scene, so there was in Handel's immediate milieu, the London opera scene. In spite of a continuing annual royal bounty of £1,000, still paid somewhat mystifyingly to the 'Royal Academy of Musick', though on this occasion pocketed by the passionate Lord Middlesex and his team, Italian opera in London was limping to a close. In May 1742, while Handel had been winding up his Dublin residency with his triumphant *Saul*, the Middlesex company had presented Pergolesi's *Meraspe* at the King's Theatre in the Haymarket. It had just three performances, and at that attended by Horace Walpole, on 25th May, 'there were but three-and-forty people' in the audience.[15] Furthermore, over in Drury Lane, John Beard and his young soprano/actress colleague, Kitty Clive, were offering farcical imitations of the Haymarket singers: 'There is a simple farce at Drury Lane, called "Miss Lucy in Town", in which Mrs. Clive mimics the Muscovita admirably, and Beard, Amorevoli tolerably.'[16] Although Handel may have been approached to contribute to, if not rescue completely, any further operatic endeavour in the Haymarket, he would have none of it. In his letter to Jennens on his return to London, he was at pains to make this abundantly

310

clear: 'The report that the Direction of the Opera next winter is committed to my Care, is groundless. The gentlemen who have undertaken to middle with Harmony can not agree, and are quite in a Confusion.'[17] (Handel will have been proud of his pun on Lord Middlesex's name.) His letter continued, 'Whether I do some thing in the Oratorio way (as several of my friends desire) I can not determine as yet. Certain it is that this time 12 month I shall continue my Oratorio's in Ireland, where they are going to make a large Subscription allready for that Purpose.'

But, at the beginning of 1743, with the Lenten season approaching, Handel decided to return after all to oratorio. His *Samson*, on which he had been working since before his Irish sojourn, and a piece very much in the mould of *Saul*, was ready for exposure, and so too of course was *Messiah*, though Handel was, rightly as it happened, entertaining misgivings about presenting it in a theatre. He entered again into negotiations with John Rich at Covent Garden, and, for the first time since his stroke in 1737, went into business with him to present oratorios there on Wednesdays and Fridays during Lent. These would be the new *Samson*, the ever-reliable *L'Allegro* (but with the *Ode for St Cecilia's Day* in place of Jennens' third part, *Il Moderato*) and *Messiah*, with a blandly evasive billing as a 'New Sacred Oratorio'. One of these would be a sensational success – not, surprisingly, *Messiah*, but *Samson*.

Milton's *Samson Agonistes* was written in the form of a drama, though not one ever intended for the stage. This part of the story of the great Israelite hero, Samson, was taken from Judges:16. Samson has been betrayed by Dalilah, captured by the Philistines, had his hair, the source of his great strength, cut off and his eyes torn out. His father, Manoa, the apparently penitent Dalilah and the Philistine giant, Harapha, respectively try to buy his freedom, care for him and provoke him. After initial self-pity and resignation, Samson gradually retrieves enough strength to fulfil his prophesied heroic deed, and he brings down the temple of Dagon; but, in the process of doing so, he dies.

While Lord Shaftesbury had initially pointed Handel once more in the direction of Milton for his new oratorio, the man who adapted *Samson Agonistes* into a libretto was Newburgh Hamilton, who had prepared Dryden's 'Alexander's Feast' for him. In his preface, dedicated to the newly rehabilitated Prince of Wales, Hamilton stated that he was especially convinced of its suitability because of Handel's track record with other biblical oratorios: 'Mr. *Handel* had so happily introduc'd here *Oratorios*, a musical Drama, whose Subject must be Scriptural, and in which the Solemnity of Church-Musick is agreeably united with the most pleasing Airs of the Stage.'[18] He divided his story into three parts, and added another character – Micah, a 'friend to Samson' – with text arranged from other parts of *Samson Agonistes*.

Now that the performance of *Samson* was imminent, Handel revised it, not least because he wanted to include in his cast his two recent Dublin singers. The role of Micah was considerably expanded, for this was to be sung by Susanna Cibber, and its very length, culminating in the great lament, 'Ye sons of Israel', indicates the warm regard in which Handel now held her, and especially for her power to communicate sorrow. Signora Avoglio, too, would be employed variously as a Philistine or Israelite Woman. Handel's similar grateful enthusiasm for her caused him to add, after the original ending mourning the death of Samson, a short scene of celebration; this both made use of Milton's poem, 'At a Solemn Musick', which he had once considered as a possible text for the third part of *L'Allegro*, and also gave Avoglio the now universally popular and dazzling aria, 'Let the bright seraphim', before the final chorus, 'Let their celestial chorus all unite'.

Handel's thus rewarding his two Dublin colleagues with great music was not merely an expression of staunch loyalty. As he wrote for the strengths of each of them, it also made extremely good business sense. These women would sell the piece.

Beyond Avoglio and Cibber, the rest of Handel's large cast for *Samson* is also interesting. The title role was written for the tenor John Beard, who was still in his mid-twenties but whose own loyalty to Handel, and ever-gathering distinction in his music under Handel's tutelage, was already nearly a decade old. Samson would be Beard's nineteenth role for Handel, and, even after Lurcanio (*Ariodante*), Oronte (*Alcina*) and Jonathan (*Saul*), it would be his greatest challenge yet, both physically and emotionally. The casting of Dalilah is similarly fascinating. Handel gave this to Kitty Clive, better known at the time as a comic actress at Drury Lane. But she had already worked for him: two years earlier, in 1740, she had stepped in for an indisposed Duparc during Handel's run of *L'Allegro*, and tackled at short notice the high-lying music for Il Penseroso, including the challenging duet with flute, 'Sweet bird'. Clearly, she had acquitted herself to everyone's greatest satisfaction, for she had then had her portrait painted with a copy of 'Sweet bird' in her hand, and Handel had now written a dramatically important role for her here in *Samson*. The rest of the cast included the two basses that Handel's regular audiences would have expected to see and hear, William Savage as Samson's father, Manoa, and Henry Reinhold as the Philistine, Harapha; the elusive Miss Edwards (who had previously sung in Handel's last two operas, *Imeneo* and *Deidamia*); and another young tenor, who had just appeared at the edge of Handel's radar, but would gradually gain greater focus there, Thomas Lowe. And an added bonus to Handel, as *Samson* approached, was that the violinist, Dubourg, was over from Dublin, and could therefore lead his orchestra.

Told as a Miltonic rather than a biblical story, *Samson* is dramatic, exquisitely crafted, and uplifting on many levels. Its strong message of salvation through suffering was wholly appropriate to its Lenten timing, and largely carried through the metaphor of darkness being transformed into light. After the opening Philistine celebration – another ebullient scene with impressive choruses and rousing, trumpet-clad accompaniment – comes a descent into the world of the blinded Samson. His signature aria, 'Total eclipse', agonizingly describing his condition and his desolation, leads to a chorus, 'O first-created beam'. Here, at the line, 'Let there be light', there is a burst of choral and instrumental exuberance that truly anticipates Haydn's treatment of the same line in his *Creation*, over half a century later. And these contrasts persist throughout *Samson*, nowhere more poignantly than at its end. But the whole of the third part is also where Handel's sure-footed musico–dramatic instincts are most ingenious. As the climax (the destruction of the temple) approaches, the individual musical numbers get ever shorter, thus continually focusing dramatic tension. A recitative between Manoa and Micah is interrupted by the crash of falling walls, represented in fast orchestral scales (not dissimilar to those depicting Saul throwing his javelin), which, with chromatic figures over a bass pedal, summon a sense of real chaos. The fleeing Philistines are heard 'at a distance' in great panic ('We sink, we die!'), and gradually the turmoil subsides into a pianissimo ending, as the silence of traumatic aftermath descends. After Micah's great lament, 'Ye sons of Israel', the chorus takes up the volume again with praise of Samson, and there is another 'Dead March', very like that in *Saul* and similarly scored with contrasting flutes, trombones and the special drums. A final requiem tableau, 'Glorious hero', ties up many ends, despite its relative (fifty-four-bar) brevity; and all tension is gloriously released in 'Let the bright seraphim', with its related chorus. The very last line of the oratorio, and a measure of the distance travelled since Samson's initial 'Total eclipse', is 'an endless blaze of light'.

Towards the end of 1742, with his revised *Samson* now ready, Handel played parts of it to his friends. On 23rd December, Lord Shaftesbury wrote to James Harris that he had been a lucky recipient of such a preview, and with prescient judgement declared, 'I think I may dare venture to affirm at one hearing only, that it surpasses any of his greatest performances . . . The whole is inexpressibly great and pathetic.'[19] He was right. *Samson* opened at Covent Garden on 18th February and received an unprecedented number of performances for an oratorio: there were eight altogether, before the end of March. Such was the impact and instant popularity of *Samson* that Handel would revive it in nine subsequent seasons; and it would travel too beyond London, immediately finding performers and audiences in Oxford, Dublin, Gloucester (at the Three Choirs Festival), Salisbury, Bath and Bristol. *Samson* has remained continually popular from its premiere to the present day, uniquely. The strength of its subject matter and the veracity of its telling are both approachable and appealing, as generations of audiences can attest.

But inevitably *Samson* had its detractors. Horace Walpole, son of the retired Prime Minister, and a staunch aficionado of Italian opera and Italian singers, was particularly damning, disapproving of Handel's casting of actresses whom he claimed could not sing. On 24th February, he wrote waspishly to his friend, Horace Mann: 'Handel has set up an Oratorio against the Operas, and succeeds. He has hired all the goddesses from farces and the singers from *Roast Beef* from between the acts at both theatres, with a man with one note in his voice, and a girl without ever an one; and so they sing, and make brave hallelujahs; and the good company

315

encore the recitative, if it happens to have any cadence like what they call a tune.'[20] A week later, he was still grumpy: 'The Oratorios thrive abundantly – for my part, they give me an idea of heaven, where everybody is to sing whether they have voices or not.'[21] But a private letter, published in the *Dublin Journal* on 8th March, was thrilled to report the success of *Samson* to Irish supporters. Proprietorial not just about 'our friend Mr. Handell', but about Dubourg too, the euphoria that had surrounded all Handel's Dublin performances is here delightfully transferred to the new work: 'That Gentleman is more esteemed now than ever. The new Oratorio (called SAMSON) which he composed since he left Ireland, has been performed four times to more crouded Audiences than ever were seen; more People being turned away for Want of Room each Night than hath been at the Italian Opera. Mr. Dubourg (lately arrived from Dublin) performed at the last, and played a Solo between the Acts, and met with universal and uncommon Applause from the Royal Family and the whole Audience.'[22] Between the last two performances of *Samson*, Handel cleverly reinforced his Milton connection by reviving *L'Allegro*. With Beard and Reinhold from the original cast, and Avoglio and Cibber from the Dublin performances, this would have been relatively straightforward to mount and rehearse. For now, all Handel's main energies, nervous and physical, were directed towards presenting *Messiah* in London.

12

WINDING DOWN

'Great in wisdom, great in glory'
[Judas Maccabaeus]

Messiah's passage to its London premiere was more troubled than Handel could possibly have imagined. Surprisingly, one of the problems was Jennens, who believed that the speed – just three weeks – with which Handel had written *Messiah* was a sign, not of ecstatic energy, but of careless negligence. In January 1743, Jennens wrote to his friend Edward Holdsworth: 'His Messiah has disappointed me; being set in great haste, tho' he said he would be a year about it, & make it the best of all his Compositions. I shall put no more Sacred Words into his hands, to be thus abus'd.'[1] Relations between the two men seem to have been greatly strained at this point, as Jennens urged Handel to make improvements and Handel refused to do so, partly because he was occupied with getting *Samson* rehearsed and performed, partly through knowing that *Messiah* worked perfectly well as it was, and partly – in all likelihood – from his own stubbornness. Words were exchanged. Jennens, continuing to report this sorry saga to Holdsworth, wrote, 'As to the Messiah, 'tis stil in his

317

power by retouching the weak parts to make it fit for a public performance; & I have said a great deal to him on the Subject: but he is so lazy and obstinate, that I much doubt the effect.' Jennens continued, 'What adds to my chagrin is, that if he makes his Oratorio ever so perfect, there is a clamour about Town, said to arise from the B[isho]ps, against performing it.'[2]

And, sure enough, on the very same day (19th November) that the anodyne announcement appeared in the *Daily Advertiser* for the forthcoming 'new Sacred Oratorio', a strong letter was published in the *Universal Spectator*. Signed by 'Philalethes' (an oft-adopted pseudonym, literally meaning 'lover of truth'), the writer claimed to be a true supporter of Handel and his presentations ('being one of the *few* who never deserted him'). But, he argued, a theatre was no place for such religious subjects. 'An *Oratorio*', he wrote, 'either is an *Act of Religion*, or it is not; if it is one I ask if the *Playhouse* is a fit *Temple* to perform it, or a Company of *Players* fit *Ministers* of *God's Word*, for in that Case such they are made.'[3]

Nevertheless, plans went ahead. Handel's cast included his two women from the Dublin performances, Avoglio and Cibber, and he supplemented them with Kitty Clive, who sang the pastoral section of Part I, with its shepherds and angels. For his male singers, those in his current cohort were a step up from the gifted lay clerks of Dublin. John Beard and Thomas Lowe would share the tenor music, and Henry Reinhold, now an artist similarly well moulded by Handel, was the bass. Handel planned to give four performances, beginning on 23rd March. Jennens was of course there, and now that he had actually heard Handel's music, his fury was marginally but by no means completely mollified. On the following morning, he wrote, 'Messiah was perform'd last night, & will be again to morrow, notwithstanding the clamour rais'd against it, which has only occasion'd it's being advertis'd without its Name; a Farce, which gives me as much offence as anything relating to the performance can give the Bs. and other squeamish People. 'Tis after all, in the main, a fine Composition, notwithstanding some weak parts, which he was too idle and too obstinate to retouch, tho' I us'd great importunity to perswade him to it.'⁴ But Jennens' lukewarm response reflected the initial public reaction. Seventeen years later, Lord Shaftesbury looked back at the year 1743 and recalled that, after the 'uncommon Applause' that had greeted *Samson*, 'The Messiah . . . was indifferently relish'd'.⁵ After just three performances, Handel decided to cancel the fourth, and put on instead his blockbuster success, *Samson*. *Messiah* would have to wait for a few years before it retrieved, and then triumphantly maintained, the thrilled reception it had received in Dublin.

One enormous question about that initial, aborted run of *Messiah* concerns the presence or absence of the King. Normally, all movements of the royal family were meticulously monitored, logged and reported, but there is absolutely no record of George II having attended any of the three performances, let alone of his having been so moved during the 'Hallelujah' chorus that he rose to his feet, requiring the rest of the audience to follow suit. This myth has become indelibly imprinted in the consciousness of all music lovers everywhere; audiences continue to stand up in the opening bars of the 'Hallelujah' chorus, and remain thus until its end. Other theories have been formulated as to the start of such a 'tradition': that it was not unusual anyway for audiences to stand at certain parts of a performance – for example, during the 'Dead March' in *Saul*; or that the King (if he was there) was anxious to stretch his legs, moved perhaps less by the power of Handel's rousing music than by pressures on his royal bladder. Whatever the root of the custom, it is actually a charming one, even without any historical justification. An audience rising as one to its feet is somehow a gesture of unity, not just of its own members, but between audience and performers too. And there is no more appropriate or literally uplifting music in which to make this gesture that Handel's rousing, trumpet-bejewelled 'Hallelujah'.

The strain in his now disappointing relationship with Jennens, coupled perhaps with end–of–season exhaustion, caused Handel to become ill again in the late spring of 1743. On 29th April, Jennens wrote to Holdsworth that, 'Handel has a return of his Paralytick Disorder, which affects his Head and Speech. He talks of spending a year abroad, so that we are to expect no Musick next year';[6] and this was clearly no exaggeration, for, on 4th May, Horace Walpole wrote to Horace Mann, 'Handel has had a palsy and can't-compose'.[7] In due course Handel himself blamed Jennens, confiding this to Lord Guernsey, who of course passed it back to Jennens. Writing again to Holdsworth, Jennens was almost boastful: 'I don't yet despair of making him retouch the Messiah, at least he shall suffer for his negligence; nay I am imform'd that he has suffer'd, for he told Lord Guernsey, that a letter I wrote him about it contributed to the bringing of the last illness upon him.'[8] An unfortunate froideur had descended on the relationship between Handel and his most important literary collaborator. And perhaps Handel, as he recovered from his illness, did intend to take life a little easier over the summer of 1743, for he had no foreign travel. But he did continue to compose, and seemingly at his customary pace. By the time autumn approached, he had planned and drafted two new oratorios for the 1744 season. And he had also – in secret, apparently – written a new setting of the Te Deum.

Following the retirement of Walpole and the rise of Carteret in political influence on the King, George II had been persuaded to end Hanover's neutrality in the War of the Austrian Succession, and to send an army of British, Hanoverian and Hessian troops to create a diversion on Maria Theresa's behalf. This army assembled in the Low Countries in the summer of 1743, and, without Walpole, who would surely have counselled against it, George II was determined now to have some active part in the inevitable skirmishes with France. He and his younger son, the Duke of Cumberland, aged twenty-two, travelled with Carteret, first to Hanover and then to the assembled armies, where he took command. He was fifty-nine, and had not seen active service for thirty-five years, since Marlborough's Battle of Oudenarde in 1705. But he was exhilarated by the prospect of engagement again, and then by the reality of it, for at Dettingen on 19th June, his armies drove back the advancing French forces in a remarkable victory. Although George II wore a Hanoverian rather than a British uniform, representing primarily therefore his German subjects, he had cause to be greatly involved with, and then proud of, the British contingent. According to a Mr Kendal, serving in Lord Ashburton's troop, George II was almost Shakespearean in the rallying of his men: 'Then the King flourished his sword and said: "Now, boys, for the honour of England, fire, and behave bravely and the French will soon run."'[9] The Duke of Cumberland received a leg wound, which actually pleased the King enormously once he had established that his son was out of danger. Visiting him during his treatment, he congratulated him on his bravery, telling him that, if he recovered well, 'I shall not be sorry for your wound'.[10] George II's elation at the whole Dettingen experience would have been even greater had he realized that he had just made history, for he was the last British monarch to lead his armies on the battlefield.

After the campaigns were over, the King and his son remained in Hanover for some months, partly to bask in his renewed popularity there following his triumph, but also to oversee the marriage arrangements for his youngest daughter, Princess Louisa, who was betrothed to Prince Frederick of Denmark. London meanwhile, also now impressed by the military exploits of the monarch, had long since hatched plans for the celebration of them, and inevitably these involved Handel. Within weeks of the actual victory in Dettingen, on 28th July, Handel's copyist and right-hand man, John Smith, had written to Lord Shaftesbury: 'He is now upon a Grand Te Deum and Jubilate, to be performed at the King's return from Germany (but He keeps this a great secret and I would not speak of it to any Body but to your Lordship) and by the Paper he had from me I can guess that it must almost be finished.'[11] Handel presumed that the Te Deum, like the one he had composed for the Peace of Utrecht in 1713, would be performed in St Paul's Cathedral, and he wrote this new one accordingly, scoring it for three rousing trumpets with timpani, as well as the customary oboes, bassoons and strings, and using short phrases with huge textural contrasts, brilliantly anticipating therefore the substantial echo in the cathedral's acoustic. By the time the King and his son actually returned to London, the new Te Deum had had several public rehearsals: two in the Chapel Royal at St James's Palace, attended by the Princesses, and two more in the chapel of the Banqueting House in Whitehall. Handel's friend Mrs Delany attended one of the rehearsals in Whitehall, and as always she was full of warm praise and enthusiasm: 'It is excessively fine, I was in rapture and so was our friend D.D. [Dean Delany, to whom she was now married] as

you may imagine; everybody says it is the finest of his compositions; I am not well enough acquainted with it to pronounce that
of it, but it is heavenly.'[12]

London, like Hanover, gave the King a warm welcome when at
last he and his son returned, in mid-November. Plans for performing the new Te Deum had slightly cooled after such a delay,
which was made even longer, as the first Sunday after George II's
return was the anniversary of Queen Caroline's death, and he
would not countenance any celebration on a day of such personal
solemnity. Handel's 'Dettingen' Te Deum was therefore finally
performed on 27th November 1743, not in St Paul's, but in the
Chapel Royal, where its large and loud forces must have been
overwhelming. But brass fanfares and rousing trumpet solos
would have gratified the King, as he relished his role of military
hero and his consequent new popularity.

Over in the King's Theatre in the Haymarket, Lord Middlesex
had still not quite accepted operatic defeat. With a rather desperate impertinence, and probably the malicious hand of Rolli too,
Middlesex took Handel's old opera, *Alessandro*, got Rolli to tweak
it, and then presented it as *Rossane*. Handel had written *Alessandro* for the first public encounter between Cuzzoni and Faustina
back in 1726, and those with long operatic memories would
therefore recall the fine music he had supplied for the two divas,
and also for Senesino in the title role, but perhaps too a limited
dramatic flow, as he doggedly maintained parity of exposure for
his celebrities. Although Handel's name was certainly on the billing, now in 1743 he had no part in this *Rossane*, and there is no
record of him having attended a performance of it. The loyal Mrs

Delany wrote to her sister, 'it vexed me to hear some favourite songs mangled.'[13] Horace Walpole too was deeply critical of the singers: 'The Rosa Mancini, who is second woman . . . is now old. In the room of Amorevoli, they have got a dreadful bass.'[14] Clearly these singers were no Cuzzoni, Faustina or Senesino. But, whether or not Handel was furious at Middlesex's presumption, he might also, on another level, have felt a little smug. For in his own plans for the coming season, one of his two new oratorios, *Semele*, was very far from being a scriptural essay. Once more, Handel was moving goalposts.

The story of *Semele* was originally taken from Ovid's *Metamorphoses*, by Congreve, no less, who worked it into a libretto, probably for John Eccles, in 1707, though this *Semele* had never been performed. Now, after nearly four decades, it was reworked for Handel, very possibly by Newburgh Hamilton, whose recent experiences with other scions of English literature (Dryden, Milton) could have led him to this one. The story tells of Semele, daughter of King Cadmus of Thebes. She is betrothed to Athamas, who is in turn loved by Semele's sister, Ino. Jupiter desires Semele, disrupts her wedding and, in the form of an eagle, abducts her. The furious Juno disguises herself as Ino and persuades Semele to ask Jupiter to make love to her in his divine form, as the Thunderer, which he does; Semele is consumed by the fire of his lightning, and dies. Apollo consoles Cadmus with the (dubious) news that Bacchus will arise from her ashes. What place Handel thought this story had in a season of oratorio is difficult to imagine. But the composer of *Saul*, *Samson* and *Messiah* was, even in Lent, refusing to be chained to a particular fence, and at the same time probably aiming a satisfied dart at the Middlesex company in the Haymarket. *Semele* was clearly not a purveyor of a religious message, but a comic opera, and in English. It was an ingeniously audacious sleight of hand.

Handel cast *Semele* well. Elisabeth Duparc ('La Francesina'), who had sung for him before his visit to Ireland, was back in London; with her sparkling technical agility and appealing personality, she was ideal for Semele herself. John Beard was given Jupiter, a role combining the greatest lyricism with real comedic skills (which Beard had so often displayed in Drury Lane), and which could not be further from that of the tragic hero, Samson. Beard would also double as the deus ex machina Apollo at the end. Similarly, Henry Reinhold sang both King Cadmus and Somnus, the god of sleep. Ino and Juno were, for obvious reasons, performed by the same singer, in this case Esther Young. She was new to Handel, but he would certainly have known her work, for she was the sister of Cecilia Young, and though of a lesser profile, she had been appearing in London's lighter theatrical fare for some time. She must have relished the challenge of playing one character disguised as another. The only true newcomer to Handel was a male alto, Daniel Sullivan, who sang Athamas.

Quite apart from exploiting dramatic and comic situation, Handel continued his rich seam of musical invention in *Semele*. A wide range of arias covers every possible mood, from outrageously perky vanity (Semele's 'Myself I shall adore') or fiery determination ('No, no, I'll take no less'), to desolate fragility ('O sleep, why dost thou leave me?') and of course to ravishing seduction (Jupiter's 'Where'er you walk'). There is dramatic accompanied recitative, mainly for furious Juno, and there are ensembles: three duets and even a quartet, in which three people (Semele, Athamas and Cadmus) attempt to cheer up a fourth (Ino). And then, almost startlingly in this quasi–operatic context, there are choruses, liberally sprinkled throughout the action and very much reflecting all the styles of choral writing that Handel deployed in his (real) oratorios. In a sense, all Handel's operatic and oratorio skills – structural, textural, narrative, dramatic and emotional – were on display here. There was humour, there was sexual energy, there was pathos. Handel was enjoying the best of all possible worlds.

Unfortunately, the public did not share Handel's enthusiasm. When *Semele* opened on 10th February at Covent Garden, the audience was clearly bewildered by it, finding it either shocking or lightweight, and completely out of place in a season devoted to Lenten doctrine. (And yet how ironic it seems that, just a few months earlier, Handel had been castigated for mounting *Messiah* in a theatre, and now he was being chided for offering a secular work in the same building.) As Mrs Delany wrote on 21st February, 'Semele has a strong party against it, viz. The fine ladies, petit maitres, and *ignoramus's*.'[15] Among other detractors were her own new husband, Dean Patrick Delany, who did not think it 'proper' to go and see it, and Jennens, who dismissed it as a 'baudy' opera. The Prince of Wales had wanted Handel to write an opera for Middlesex, so was also inclined not to support *Semele*: as Mrs Delany told her sister, 'Mr Handel and the Prince had quarrelled, which I am sorry for. Handel says the *Prince* is quite out of *his* good graces!'[16] Mrs Delany herself, loyal as ever to Handel, loved *Semele*. 'It is a delightful piece of music, quite new and different from anything he has done,' she wrote, after hearing an early rehearsal in Brook Street. Later, she was more detailed in her critical assessment: 'There is a four-part song that is delightfully pretty; Francesina is extremely improved, her notes are more distinct, and there is something in her running-divisions that is quite surprising. She was much applauded';[17] and, after her third hearing, she wrote, 'Semele is charming; the more I hear it the better I like it, and as I am a subscriber I shall not fail one night.'[18] But there was only one more performance, on 21st February, and on 25th February Handel put on *Samson* instead, in an attempt to win back his audiences and their goodwill. This performance too had its problems, for it was probably thrown together quite hurriedly while Handel was, at the same time, preparing his other new oratorio, *Joseph and his Brethren*. Even Mrs Delany was lukewarm in her praise: 'I was last night to hear Samson. Francesina sings most of Mrs. Cibber's part and some of Mrs. Clive's: upon the whole it went off very well, but not better than last year.'[19] So, the cheerfulness with which Handel had no doubt composed *Semele* will have evaporated completely in the face of its hostile reception. After 1744, he never revived *Semele* again. Like *Orlando*, or *Israel in Egypt*, it would win its passionate supporters only in later eras.

By this time Handel was possibly having misgivings about *Joseph and his Brethren*, even though he knew it was more appropriate as Lenten fare than *Semele*. The narrative, as supplied by his librettist, the Reverend James Miller, was a mess: it is very unclear what is actually happening. Mrs Delany confided to her sister alarming reports of Handel's concern: 'Joseph, I believe, will be next Friday, but Handel is mightily out of humour about it, for Sullivan, who is to sing Joseph, is a *block* with a very fine voice, and Beard has *no voice at all*.'[20] *Joseph* did fulfil one important purpose, which was the steadying of the whole oratorio enterprise after two heavily criticized promotions. And Handel, ever astute to the cause of his problems, knew that he needed the basis of a good libretto rather than a chaotic text. Nobody had ever been as invigorating a collaborator as Jennens. Their conversations about the structure of *Saul*, for instance, and indeed the whole masterly compilation of scriptural texts for *Messiah*, had greatly impressed Handel. He was not good at giving in to his adversaries, but now was certainly the time to rebuild his relationship with Jennens.

∾

On 9th June 1744, Handel wrote an extremely careful letter to Jennens, beginning with civil concerns about his well-being: 'Dear Sir, It gave me great Pleasure to hear Your safe arrival in the Country, and that Your Health was much improved. I hope it is by this time firmly established, and I wish You with all my Heart the Continuation of it, and all the Prosperity.'[21] He then outlined, with very impressive and businesslike clarity, the arrangements he had made for the following season, emphasizing the quality of the singers, and the lengths to which he was going to secure the precious services of Susanna Cibber:

I have taken the Opera House in the Haymarketh, engaged as Singers, Sig.ra Francesina, Miss Robinson, Beard, Reinhold, Mr Gates with his Boyes's and several of the best Chorus Singers from the Choirs, and I have some hopes that Mrs Cibber will sing for me. She sent me word from Bath (where she is now) that she would perform for me next winter with great pleasure if it did not interfere with her playing, but I think I can obtain Mr Riches's permission (with whom she is engaged to play in Covent Garden House) since so obligingly he gave Leave to Mr Beard and Mr Reinhold.

And, finally, he got to the point: he was ready to receive the first act of a new oratorio text, evidently previously discussed, but not yet forthcoming: 'Now should I be extreamly glad to receive the first Act, or what is ready of the new Oratorio with which you intend to favour me'. And certainly Jennens was more disposed to work with Handel again. On 7th May, he had written to Holdsworth, 'I must take him as I find him, and make the best use I can of him'.[22] Sure enough, over the course of the summer, Jennens delivered, one act at a time, their next magnificent collaboration, *Belshazzar*. Handel was genuinely energized by it: 'Your most excellent Oratorio has given me great Delight in setting it to Musick and still engages me warmly. It is indeed a Noble Piece, very grand and uncommon',[23] he wrote, as he begged Jennens for the last act. He was even politely conceding that he might address again the alterations that Jennens wanted in *Messiah*: 'Be pleased to point out these passages in the Messiah which You think require altering,' he wrote in July.[24] And by October, when he had received the whole text of *Belshazzar*, and therefore had the full measure of the work, he was able to enter into detailed discussions with Jennens. His relationship with Jennens was restored.

This vigorous correspondence with Jennens over the summer of 1744 indicates that Handel was far from retreating from the limelight. Whatever his setbacks, musical, administrative or medical, there was still a need in him to be composing and performing to the highest possible standards. As the Middlesex company had for the moment ceased to present opera in the Haymarket (His Lordship had just made a good match and was about to marry a rich heiress), Handel himself, as he had told Jennens, hired the King's Theatre for a full season of oratorios there, not just in Lent but through the winter as well. He was continuing his practice of writing two large works at the same time: in addition to *Belshazzar*, he was also working on another secular music drama, *Hercules*. (He had evidently not been completely derailed by the furore surrounding *Semele*.) Both these would be introduced during the course of the next season, together with revivals of *Deborah*, *Samson*, *Saul*, *Joseph*, and – defiantly – *Semele*.

As he had also informed Jennens, Handel took his usual care in assembling the singers he needed. His 1744–5 company would consist of Duparc, Cibber, Beard and Reinhold, and a newcomer to the roster, though not to his acquaintance, a Miss Robinson. This mezzo-soprano was another member of the gifted family of the organist John Robinson and his wife, Ann Turner Robinson (who had sadly died in 1741). Their son, young 'Master Robinson', had sung as a treble in *Israel in Egypt* and *L'Allegro*, and now a third member of the family was about to sing under Handel's direction. Though little is known of this Miss Robinson, she was obviously an immensely accomplished singer, and actress too, for Handel wrote her one of his greatest mezzo-soprano roles. She was to be no also-ran in the Haymarket that winter.

Handel's brave new season opened on 3rd November 1744 with a revival of *Deborah*. With the exception of Duparc in the title role (originally sung by Strada), the singers were now all British, and Handel may well have felt that they were an improvement on his Italians. Senesino's role of Barak was given to Miss Robinson – a sure indication of her gifts, however much there was rewriting. A month later Handel briefly revived *Semele*, and then in January came the first of his new works, *Hercules* – billed on this occasion still as a 'new Musical Drama'. Another literary polymath, the Reverend Thomas Broughton, editor of Dryden, translator of Voltaire, had prepared the libretto for Handel, and he built it skilfully from a wide variety of sources, including Sophocles and Ovid. Hercules returns home to his wife, Dejanira, and son, Hyllus, after years away, bringing with him the captive Princess Iole. Dejanira believes Hercules to be infatuated with his prisoner, and sends him a poisoned robe, which kills him. She herself is driven mad with guilt. Hercules is received on Mount Olympus, where a priest declares that Iole should marry Hyllus. There are parallels in this decidedly non-religious story to *Semele* in its secularity, to *Saul* in that jealousy is one of its driving emotions, and even to *Orlando*, for the most powerful and remarkable music comes in Dejanira's mad scene.

Handel's cast, whose very assembly for the whole season had been defined by suitability for these roles, was impressive. The title role was, as in *Saul*, for a bass, but no longer for Gustavus Waltz, whose solo days – so vital in the previous decade – seemed to be over; his musical activities now included duties as an organist at the German Lutheran Church in the Savoy. (According to Burney, Handel, in conversation with Susanna Cibber, once criticized Gluck for knowing 'no more of contrapunto as mein cook Waltz',[25] the intriguing if completely unverified implication being that Waltz had now joined Handel's domestic household.) Now Henry Reinhold, who had shaped up so well in his eight years' tutelage with Handel, was to be the first-choice bass, and he got his first title role. Miss Robinson would play his wife, Dejanira. Both would receive superb arias, and remarkable individual scenas as well. Duparc and Beard were cast as the younger couple, Iole and Hyllus. The originally small and dramatically insignificant role of the herald, Lichas, was given to Susanna Cibber, and once Handel had established from John Rich that she could be available (as he had explained in his June letter to Jennens), he expanded the part considerably, giving her drop-in aria appearances, including the measured and masterly 'He who for Atlas propp'd the Sky'. The several interjections of the chorus are again consistently excellent in quality, both contributing to scenes and commenting upon them. 'Jealousy! Infernal pest', reacting to Dejanira's mounting suspicion of her husband's fidelity, is one of

Handel's most extraordinarily powerful mulitpartite choruses. It has jagged rhythms and dissonant harmonies on its initial word, and contrasting sections of stern injunction or airy contrapuntal word-setting ('Trifles light as floating air / Strongest proofs to thee appear'). Coming as it does midway through the second part, this extended musical essay on 'Jealousy' puts it, and therefore its message, at the heart of the whole oratorio.

But the most extraordinary music comes in the final part, and it is completely operatic in its dramatic impact. First, Hercules has an extensive and excruciating death, as the poisoned cloak Dejanira has sent him unstoppably works its evil. His agonies are conveyed in fiery coloratura accompanied by wild strings. But his energies fade, and so does that of his music, in accompanied recitative punctuated by helpless cries from his son. Hercules' final utterance, a request that his body be borne to the top of Mount Oeta so that his funeral pyre may transport him quickly to the gods and a 'scene of glorious death', is accompanied by now hushed and static string chords, as a fearful quiet descends. And then, after Hyllus's brave 'Let not fame the tidings spread', comes Dejanira's mad scene. Racked by guilt for what her mistaken jealousy has effected, she crashes through an incoherent series of wild fragments of thought. She calls on the Furies to punish her, summoning them into her deranged imagination. She collapses into a slow-moving plea, 'Hide me from their hated sight', repetitive and circular, for she is locked into her predicament; and then she springs again to terrified and energetic life as her imagined Furies close in on her and destroy her. Following these two individual scenas, the resolution of the story could have seemed bland. But the supreme quality continues through the duet for Iole and Hyllus and a fine closing chorus. After the shortcomings of the unfortunate *Joseph*, *Hercules* breathes quality on every page.

With absolutely miserable luck, this new work was beset by problems at its opening on 5th January. Susanna Cibber, for whom the whole work had been so lovingly expanded, became ill and could not sing, causing an extraordinary last-minute reshuffle. Her arias were either cut or given to other characters. Her dramatically more important recitative was sung, virtually at sight, by none other than the rejected bass, Gustavus Waltz. Whether Handel summoned him from his kitchen or from an organ loft, the fact that he trusted him thus to rescue *Hercules* is a sure indication of Waltz's quick musicality. But, according to Jennens, the theatre was barely half full, and although Cibber was sufficiently recovered to appear at the second performance four nights later, the audience was no bigger. There were even suggestions that rival events in private households were being set up in opposition to Handel, in order deliberately to drain his audiences. What was certainly true was that the Italian opera faction had not gone away. Handel might have taken up residency at the King's Theatre in the Haymarket, but at the Little Theatre, opposite, a pasticcio opera, *L'Incostanza Delusa*, was about to open and do well, with newer Italian singers and under the vigorous direction of Geminiani. Handel was dismayed, and not a little disgruntled. On 17th January 1745, he published a letter in the *Daily Advertiser*, lamenting with an uncomfortable combination of self-righteousness and irascibility that he had given the public what it claimed to want, namely dramas in English, but that the public had stayed away:

Sir. Having for a Series of Years received the greatest Obligations from the Nobility and Gentry of this Nation, I have always retained a deep Impression of their Goodness. As I perceived, that joining good Sense and significant Words to Musick, was the best Method of recommending this to an English Audience; I have directed my Studies that way, and endeavour'd to shew, that the English Language, which is so expressive of the sublimest Sentiments is the best adapted of any to the full and solemn kind of Musick. I have the Mortification now to find, that my Labours to please are become ineffectual, when my Expenses are considerably greater.[26]

Handel therefore proposed to cancel the rest of his season, and pay back his subscribers. Reaction was instantaneous. The *Daily Advertiser*, on the following day, carried a letter signed merely by 'Subscribers': 'Sir, Upon Reading Mr. Handel's Letter in your Paper this Morning I was sensibly touch'd with that great Master's Misfortunes, failing in his Endeavours to entertain the Publick; whose Neglect in not attending his admirable Performances can no otherwise be made up with Justice to the Character of the Nation, and the Merit of the Man, than by the Subscribers generously declining to withdraw the remainder of their Subscriptions.'[27] Following this interesting example of the press acting as a forum for commercial negotiation, Handel had no choice but to continue his season.

And so he ploughed on. For the Lenten season, he revived *Samson* (but without Cibber in her role of Micah, for her fragile vocal health still caused her frequent indispositions), *Saul* and *Joseph*, and the final offering was his second new piece, the fruit of his invigorating collaboration with Jennens: *Belshazzar*. Jennens' libretto is so liberally endowed with stage directions that it almost seems as if he had designed it for an actual production at the King's Theatre, though he can have had no doubt that Handel would present it without action or costume. But, in that the audiences would have had the stage directions as well as the text printed in their word-books, both he and Handel were – rightly or wrongly – trusting their public to use their imagination in following the course of this most dramatic of stories.

Belshazzar is the King of Babylon, which is being besieged by the Medes and Persians, led by Cyrus. Cyrus plans, ingeniously, to divert the River Euphrates and then enter the city through its dry bed while the Babylonians celebrate the feast of Sesach. Belshazzar insists on holding this festival, despite pleas from his mother Nitocris and the prophet Daniel who has foreseen the fall of Babylon. At the licentious banquet, Belshazzar challenges the god of Judah to show his hand, and miraculous writing appears on a wall, which Daniel interprets as a sign that Belshazzar's days are numbered and that his kingdom must be taken by the Medes and Persians. Cyrus duly enters Babylon and defeats Belshazzar, but declares an end to all hostilities, vowing to rebuild the city in Jerusalem.

This superbly dramatic story, so brilliantly assembled from wide sources by Jennens, combines many of Handel's preferred ingredients. There is an essential conflict, here between Belshazzar and Cyrus. There are highly dramatic incidents (the writing on the wall; a battle) and quiet soliloquies. And there are opportunities for every emotion, from riotous abandon to private despair. Every character is vividly drawn. Belshazzar's mother, Nitocris, to be sung by Duparc, has an extraordinary pride of place, with monologues of profound thought at the beginning of the first and third parts, and many instances of impassioned pleading with her son. Her opening scene, in which she reflects upon the 'Vain fluctuating state of human empire', is the political equivalent to Shakespeare's 'Seven ages of Man' speech for Jacques, in *As You Like It* (which Jennens, as a Shakespeare scholar, would have known intimately). Nitocris defines five stages in the development of an empire in the guise of a human being: that of a small and weak infant; its gradual growth and strength; its arrival at maturity, in which it 'grasps all within its reach'; then its growing old, at which point others take advantage; and finally its infirmity. To each of these five stages, Handel adds vividly descriptive and illustrative music, all in a scena accompanied by strings which mirror and enhance the vocal line and its message. Nitocris's third-act monologue vacillates between hope and fear, and is similarly fragile, angular and distraught. By contrast, Beshazzar himself is a blustery party-lover, whose only saving grace is that he goes to meet his adversary with courage; all of his role is energetic and colourful, exploiting the youth, dramatic vitality and vocal flexibility of his interpreter, John Beard.

The pivotal role of Cyrus, written for Miss Robinson, is quieter and more measured than the crazed Dejanira that she had just sung; Cyrus's dignity and humanity show calmer facets of the singer's clearly considerable gifts. The prophet Daniel was written for Susanna Cibber, and all her arias reflect her especial qualities of low, sustained lyricism and a radiant serenity, which, in Daniel's pleas to Belshazzar, contrast vividly with Nitocris's intensity. The Assyrian nobleman Gobrias, who joins Cyrus in the assault of Babylon, was written for Reinhold, who, after his own labours of *Hercules*, had less to do here. There are two duets, in which Handel's operatic skills naturally shine. One, between Nitocris and Belshazzar, is laid out as a conversation, in which she foresees destruction and he is interested only in delight. Set with completely gentle gestures, Handel nonetheless conveys the passion and urgency of both arguments. The duet between Nitocris and the victorious Cyrus, in Part III, shows the opposite sides literally coming together, in the spirit of her humility, his generosity and finally their unity. And as always the choruses are superb throughout, whether representing Jews, Persians or Babylonians, whether conveying drunken merriment, religious fervour or heroic battle cries, or, most especially, when describing the appearance of the writing on the wall and the King's reaction to it. There are illustrative instrumental interludes; one, a scurrying sinfonia for the quest and then arrival of the so-called Wise Men (who fail to interpret the writing on the wall), which in its clarion calls in octave leaps imitates the sounding of a postilion's coach horn, and justifies its hilarious tempo indication of 'Allegro postillions'. And of course there is a rousing martial symphony, complete with trumpets and drums, to depict the battle between Belshazzar and Cyrus. The momentum in this exceptional score never ceases, and the audience is swept along by dramatic incident and individual, personal comment. It is not difficult, here in *Belshazzar*, to feel the influence of Shakespeare on Jennens, who knew his plays so well, and whose own text inspired Handel to similar heights. As with their *Saul*, Jennens and Handel had created another of the truly great works of the eighteenth century.

But, yet again, Handel was thwarted by unforeseeable disaster just as *Belshazzar* was about to open. Poor Mrs Cibber was once more unable to sing through recurring illness (this would be the last time that Handel ever composed specifically for her), and, for such a crucial role as Daniel, it was impossible to find a late replacement. The only solution – and it was a truly drastic one – was to redistribute virtually all the roles among the singers who had been rehearsing the piece and were therefore familiar with it. Only Duparc, as Nitocris, stayed where she was. Miss Robinson, cast as Cyrus, now took Daniel as well as some of her own part; the rest of Cyrus went to the bass, Reinhold (with some reworking of the vocal line), whose own role of Gobrias had to be sung by (the tenor) Beard, in addition to performing Belshazzar himself. As before, when Gustavus Waltz had jumped in at the last minute to rescue *Hercules*, the alert and sophisticated musicianship of every member of Handel's company, as they swapped and relearned one another's roles, is impressive. But the first performance cannot have been totally confident or secure, and for members of the audience – such as there were – it was no doubt baffling. One person who appreciated *Belshazzar* was an Elizabeth Carter, who described it in a letter to Catherine Talbot. But she could not deny that the audience was thin, and the performance, unsurprisingly, 'bad': 'Handel, once so crowded, plays to empty walls in that opera house, where there used to be a constant audience . . . Unfashionable that I am, I was I own highly delighted the other night at his last oratorio. 'Tis called Belshazzar, the story of the taking of Babylon by Cyrus; and the music, in spite of all that very bad performers could do to spoil it, equal to any thing I ever heard.'[28]

Handel, now seeming almost as physically vulnerable as Mrs Cibber, was himself ill again by the end of this season. The crises and pressures were too much, and he abandoned all thought of continuing to mount oratorio in the Haymarket. *Belshazzar* was the last of his works performed in the King's Theatre, where, astonishingly, he had presented twenty-seven other premieres since his *Rinaldo*, in 1711. For him, this was truly the end of an era.

Meanwhile, the Young Pretender, 'Bonnie' Prince Charles Stuart, decided once more to take up his Jacobite cause, and sailed from France towards Britain in June 1745. He landed in the Hebrides and began a long march south, with increasing numbers of supporters joining him in a poorly disciplined and poorly armed – but wholly enthusiastic – group. A genuine fear grew throughout the country. The King was in Hanover, and he returned immediately to London, not over-dismayed by the prospect of conflict, but actually rather relishing it. The Prince of Wales offered his services to his father, who refused them on the reasonable grounds that Frederick had never done any soldiering in his life, and sensibly summoned instead his other son, the properly military Duke of Cumberland, who had recently (still aged only twenty-three) been appointed Captain General of the British Land Forces. By 4th December the Jacobites had got as far south as Derby, and panic increased in the capital. But in fact Charles Stuart was now losing morale as his men were peeling away again, so he retreated to Scotland, there to await reinforcements. He was encouraged by the news that Louis XV of France, together with King Charles Emmanuel of Sardinia, might support his proposal that George II should rule England, but that the Stuarts, under his own rule, should take back Scotland. The Duke of Cumberland was briefly recalled to London to meet the threat now of a French invasion, but was sent straight back to take over the Scottish command after Charles Stuart had won a minor victory in Falkirk, in January. In April, he gathered his troops to advance on Inverness, just as the Jacobites headed south. The two armies met on Culloden Moor on 16th April, and the resulting bloody massacre of the exhausted and diminished Jacobite army by Cumberland's thoroughly superior tactics, both then and on subsequent days, earned him the title (initially designed as a compliment) 'Butcher' Cumberland. Charles Stuart, disguised as a maid to Flora Macdonald, escaped to the islands and finally back to France. The Jacobite threat was again quietened.

The '45 rebellion had a considerable effect on London and its cultural activity. Once again, there was no opera at all in the autumn of 1745 (though there were plays), but patriotism abounded in the composition and performance of stirring songs. Handel wrote two, 'From scourging rebellion' and, for the Gentlemen Volunteers of the City of London, 'Stand round, my brave boys'. There were many renditions of old and new versions of 'God Save the King'. Handel's setting, from his Coronation anthem 'Zadok the Priest', was as popular as ever, but in due course it was rather surpassed by Thomas Arne's arrangement of an old galliard, to which the words 'God save great George, our King' had been added. This version was initially performed at Drury Lane on 28th September 1745, by Arne's sister, Susanna Cibber, together with Beard and Reinhold. A year later, it was published in the *Gentlemen's Magazine*, and soon afterwards adopted officially as the national anthem. And so it has remained.

The patriotic fervour engendered by all these events was still apparent when Handel took up the writing of oratorio again. For him, the ceasing of activity in the autumn of 1745 had been welcome; he was still recovering from his bout of illness, which had been rather obsessing him. The Reverend William Harris had written to his sister-in-law at the end of August: 'I met Handel a few days since in the street . . . He talks much of his precarious state of health, yet he looks well enough.'[29] On 24th October, Lord Shaftesbury wrote to James Harris: 'Poor Handel looks something better. I hope he will entirely recover in due time, though he has been a good deal disordered in his head.'[30] But by January Handel was able to make plans, which were announced in the *General Advertiser* on the 31st: 'Mr *Handel* proposes to exhibit some Musical Entertainments on Wednesdays and Fridays the ensuing Lent, with Intent to make good to the Subscribers (that favoured him last Season) the Number of Performances he was not then able to complete in order thereto he is preparing a New Occasional Oratorio, which is design'd to be perform'd at the Theatre-Royal in Covent Garden.'[31] This *Occasional Oratorio*, so called because it had no specific narrative but was constructed to mark an occasion, was an expression of support for the monarchy and country, and a piece of propaganda rather than of celebration. It was hastily compiled from several of Handel's works, including *Samson*, *Athalia*, *Israel in Egypt* and 'Zadok the Priest'. William Harris attended a rehearsal of it on 7th February and explained to his sister-in-law, 'The words of his Oratorio are scriptural, but taken from various parts, and are expressive of the rebels' flight and our pursuit of them. Had not the Duke carried his point triumphantly, this Oratorio could not have been brought on.'[32] The *Occasional Oratorio* was performed at Covent Garden on 14th February, with Duparc, Beard and Reinhold as soloists. Free admission was granted, as promised, to subscribers from the previous season. There were five more performances through February and March, but at all of them the audiences were sparse. The only significant development for Handel was that, at later performances, Duparc was replaced by a mezzo-soprano new to him, Caterina Galli, who had initially come to London to sing for the Middlesex company. She would now assume increasing importance in Handel's team.

Meanwhile, another intriguing foreigner had arrived at the King's Theatre. Lord Middlesex, having enjoyed the services of Galuppi in 1741, and Lampugnani in 1743, now lured across the

English Channel the young (twenty-nine-year-old) Gluck. In similar recognition of patriotic fervour, Middlesex got Gluck to write *La Caduta dei giganti*, which was performed in the Haymarket in January 1746, and dedicated to the Duke of Cumberland. In due course, Gluck and Handel met, and the older resident was extremely civil to the younger visitor, arranging for them to give a concert together in aid of his Decay'd Musicians charity, the programme consisting partly of highlights of *La Caduta dei giganti*, together with excerpts from Handel's *Alessandro*, *Alexander's Feast* and *Samson*. The singers were all from Middlesex's company, and included the soprano Giulia Frasi, who would also soon join Handel's side. While harmony apparently reigned on this evening of generosity and decorum, Handel was subsequently dismissive of Gluck's very different compositional style, and made his claim that Waltz, his cook, knew more of 'contrapunto' than the interloper. Gluck, however, had been dazzled by his encounter with the legendary genius at the heart of London's music. Years later, in 1788, the Irish tenor, Michael Kelly, sang the role of Pylade in Gluck's great opera, *Iphigénie en Tauride*, and had 'the greatest gratification of being instructed in the part by the composer himself'. As Kelly continued, in his richly engaging *Reminiscences*:

One morning, after I had been singing with him, he said, 'Follow me up stairs, Sir, and I will introduce you to one, whom, all my life, I have made my study, and endeavoured to imitate.' I followed him into his bed-room, and, opposite to the head of the bed, saw a full-length picture of Handel, in a rich frame. 'There, Sir,' said he, 'is the portrait of the inspired master of our art; when I open my eyes in the morning, I look upon him with reverential awe, and acknowledge him as such, and the highest praise is due to your country for having distinguished and cherished his gigantic genius.'[33]

After his brutal victory in Culloden, in April 1746, the Duke of Cumberland returned to London once more as a 'conquering hero'. The next three oratorios by Handel would all have heroic or military subjects and be seen as joyful salutes to the Duke and his exploits. The first of these was *Judas Maccabaeus*, whose story of charismatic leadership, as Judas repeatedly guided his Jewish armies to victory over their Syrian oppressors and restored the temple of Jerusalem, was a perfect fit for young Cumberland, to whom the work was dedicated. But this was not merely a rabble-rousing battle cry: it was concerned with courage, liberty and the restoration of peace. The libretto was prepared for Handel by a new collaborator, the priest Thomas Morell, who much later (and possibly therefore unreliably) claimed to have been approached by Handel himself, together with the Prince of Wales: 'I should never have thought of such an undertaking . . . had not Mr Handell applied to me, when at Kew, in 1746, and added to his request the honour of a recommendation from Prince Frederic.'[34] Despite humble beginnings, Morell had received a good education (Eton, Cambridge, Oxford), and had taken his MA at Oxford in 1733 when Handel had been performing so conspicuously at its Encaenia. He had later been patronized and encouraged by Queen Caroline, who had appreciated his scholarship, so his royal credentials were impeccable. In 1745 (not 1746, as he remembered), when Cumberland was beginning his pursuit of the Jacobite rebels, Morell put together the libretto of *Judas Maccabaeus*, mainly from the two Books of Maccabees in the Apocrypha. After

Culloden, Handel saw the expediency of celebrating both the victory and the peace, and wrote *Judas Maccabaeus* over the summer, planning it to be the main focus of his 1747 season. Judas himself would be another good title role for Beard, and Reinhold would sing the bass role of Simon. Handel's new discovery, the mezzo-soprano Caterina Galli, was to sing the quantitatively important role of the Israelite Man, while a soprano of whom all too little is known, Elisabetta de Gambarini, would sing the equally important Israelite Woman.

Although *Judas Maccabaeus* is actually one of Handel's shorter oratorios (his own score gives it a timing of 105 minutes), it is densely packed with action and resolution, and with his customary excellent contrasts of pace, mood and texture. As in *Israel in Egypt*, the energy is with the chorus, who are effectively centre stage from the outset, with their mourning for the fall of Jerusalem (an indication that *Judas Maccabaeus*'s structure was established before Cumberland had yet secured any sort of victory). The chorus are also involved in many arias or duets. 'Sion now her head shall raise / Tune your harps to songs of praise', for instance, begins as an extensive duet before the chorus continue with ecstatic waves of descending and ascending scales. After a major setback for Judas and his troops, 'O wretched Israel' begins as a desolate soliloquy for the Israelite Woman, and, as if crowding sympathetically around her, the chorus collectively assume her music and her mood. Handel continues this technique in more active music too. Judas's 'Sound an alarm', already heroic and rousing, is thrillingly taken up by the chorus and orchestra, including (for the first time) three trumpets and timpani. Although there is a moment here of silence and doubt ('If to fall'), energy and determination build again into martial rallying cries. And the duet for the Israelite Woman and Man, 'O never bow we down', leads to the great choral affirmation, 'We never will bow down', and a mighty resolution, 'We worship God and God alone'. This involvement of the chorus at every stage of the narrative makes the victory celebration, as *Judas Maccabaeus* has become, a truly collective experience, articulating the sentiments of the troops (the people) as well as those of the leaders.

What distinguishes *Judas Maccabaeus* most of all, however, is the music celebrating peace, and, poignantly, Judas's own greatness in his sensitive reflections on its implications. The prayer sung by a Priest at the beginning of Part III, 'Father of Heaven', quietly celebrates the recapture of the temple and the initiation of the 'feast of lights', over a serenely moving bass line with supportive string accompaniment. After the return of Judas and a chorus of gratitude, 'Sing unto God', Judas, in recitative, takes stock. 'But pause awhile,' he says, 'due obsequies prepare to those who bravely fell in war'. (Such pensive solemnity in the middle of a victory celebration was perhaps not typical of the 'Butcher' to whom *Judas Maccabaeus* was dedicated.) The penultimate musical number is certainly one of the great highlights, the duet, 'O lovely peace', for the Israelite Woman and Man, featuring flutes and a lilting pastoral joy. The two voices intertwine with 'Let fleecy flocks the hills adorn / And valleys smile with wavy corn', with which Handel makes affectionate and imitative play. By the time Handel had completed *Judas Maccabaeus*, news had arrived of Prince Charles Stuart's final capitulation. The pastoral idyll presented here was a truly welcome outcome after decades of Jacobite threat.

The aftermath of that threat did, however, continue to resonate long after Bonnie Prince Charlie had disappeared to France, for there were exposures, trials and executions of Jacobite intriguers. And one of these even affected Handel's performance schedule in his Lenten season of 1747. On 16th March Simon Fraser, Baron

Lovat, a high-profile Jacobite sympathizer, went on trial for high treason. London's attentions were thoroughly engaged, as Lord Shaftesbury wrote to James Harris: 'The trial interrupts our harmonious system extremely. To-morrow Handel has advertised "Joseph", though I hope he will not perform, for nothing can be expected whilst the trial lasts.'[35] Lord Shaftesbury was similarly worried about the new *Judas Maccabaeus*: 'The week after, we flatter ourselves that "Judas" will both give delight to the lovers of harmony and profits to the foundation whence it flows. However, I am not certain that "Judas" will be performed next week.' Handel did indeed postpone *Joseph*, if only for two days, and *Judas Maccabaeus* indefinitely. Lovat's trial lasted a week, at the end of which he was found guilty and sentenced to death by hanging, drawing and quartering – though this was later commuted by the King to beheading. Only after the trial was over could Handel properly reschedule *Judas Maccabaeus*, to be performed on 1st April. (As it happened, its dedicatee, the Duke of Cumberland, was once more far away, serving in France.) It was repeated on five subsequent evenings in the next two weeks (though avoiding 9th April, when Lord Lovat was finally executed before a huge crowd). Its patriotic fervour ensured that *Judas Maccabaeus* was enormously popular, as it continued to be: it was revived more than fifty times in Handel's lifetime, and brought him great financial reward. In a sense, therefore, Cumberland's triumph had been Handel's triumph too, and another satisfying link to the royal family was sealed.

~

Just as the mezzo-soprano Caterina Galli had slipped into Handel's company as a replacement for Susanna Cibber (now working permanently as an actress with David Garrick in Drury Lane), so he made other changes to his roster of singers before the following season. The staunchly reliable Henry Reinhold was still with him. But, for whatever reason, after a fine period of service to him, Elisabeth Duparc now disappeared from Handel's lists, and was replaced, just for one year, by the soprano Domenica Casarini. Equally significant to the loss of Duparc was the temporary disappearance of John Beard, who was also employed by Garrick at Drury Lane where his workload, and the fare he delivered there, were altogether lighter than the hefty roles (Samson, Judas Maccabaeus) he had been performing for Handel. There have been many speculations as to the reasons for Beard's defection. Perhaps the vocal problems that had beset him in 1744 had returned; or perhaps he was greatly taken up with some protracted financial and legal problems pertaining to his wife, and had lightened his obligations accordingly. Whatever the cause, Handel found himself, for the moment, without one of the singers whose talents he had been nurturing now for over a decade, and the one for whom indeed he was probably planning another significant title role. But fortunately Thomas Lowe, who had been shadowing Beard both at Drury Lane and in Handel's enterprises since 1743, was available. Beard and Lowe, while exact contemporaries, were very different tenors, as Burney remembered in his 1789 *General History of Music*. Lowe seems to have had the finer voice, but Beard the greater musicianship and all-round intelligence: 'with the finest tenor voice I ever heard in my life, for want of diligence and cultivation, [Lowe] never could be safely trusted with any thing better than a ballad, which he constantly learned by his ear; whereas Mr. Beard, with an inferior voice, constantly possessed the favour of the public by his superior conduct, knowledge of music, and intelligence as an actor.'[36] But Lowe could now step into Beard's roles, beginning with a revival of *Judas Maccabaeus*, no less, with which Handel proposed to open his next season.

For his two new oratorios, Handel continued the military-hero theme he had launched with *Judas Maccabaeus*, and produced *Joshua* and *Alexander Balus*. The Duke of Cumberland was still engaged with the War of the Austrian Succession, which was not proceeding well for the allied armies. Things had moved on while Britain had been preoccupied with Charles Stuart. In 1745 Charles VII of Bavaria had died, giving Austria the opportunity to elect Maria Theresa's husband, Francis of Lorraine, as Emperor; and the British navy had been harassing French ships in the Atlantic. Some focus had shifted towards the American territories, and also those in India. In Britain, fear of the French and Spanish in the wider theatre of war was just as great as it had been of the Jacobites in the more localized one, and much responsibility, if only for the boosting of morale, lay on the young shoulders of the Duke of Cumberland. *Joshua*, another story concerning liberation and possession (here, of the promised land of Canaan), was a shot in the arm to the nation's pride, and Lowe's title role was another flattering quasi-portrait of Cumberland himself. Two highlights from Handel's score instantly assumed and retained popularity beyond their original context. Towards the end of the final part, Joshua is welcomed as a 'conquering hero'. Handel ingeniously built this welcome as a developing processional. It begins with just the boys in a 'Chorus of Youths', accompanied by the organ, singing, 'See the conquering hero comes'; this music is then taken by two adult women soloists, accompanied by two flutes and the organ, and finally the full chorus join in, together with the rest of the orchestra and a side drum too. It is as if the whole procession is heard approaching from a distance before bursting triumphantly on to the stage. So successful was this part of *Joshua* that Handel immediately incorporated it into *Judas Maccabaeus* too, where it has remained. And an aria that has achieved similar longevity outside its original habitat (the end of Part III) is 'O had I Jubal's lyre', whose fresh and vibrant coloratura also reveals much about Casarini's soprano. It requires the same technical agility as much of her predecessor Duparc's music, but the vocal range is altogether lower. It is to Handel's credit that this now-celebrated aria is still of dazzling brilliance, even without the flashiest high notes.

Joshua opened at Covent Garden on 9th March, and, like *Judas Maccabaeus*, it was greatly popular with audiences, both at the time and in subsequent years. Sadly, the third work in this Lenten season was not. Morell's second libretto for Handel was *Alexander Balus*, and was intended almost as a sequel to *Judas Maccabaeus*, since Judas's brother Jonathan is one of the main characters – and, like Judas himself in that season, was also sung by Lowe. In a story which maddeningly combines complexity and inactivity, both Morell and Handel seemed to struggle, with Handel even complaining about the invariable iambic rhythms that Morell delivered. (As Morell recalled, 'when Mr Handell first read it, he cried out "D—n your Iambics".'[37]) The chief interest of *Alexander Balus* is the namesake of one of Handel's great operatic characters, Cleopatra; one of her highlights is the aria, 'Hark, hark! He strikes the golden lyre', with another rich combination of accompanying instruments (flutes, harp, mandolin and pizzicato cellos) recalling the great invention that Handel deployed for Cleopatra in *Giulio Cesare*, a quarter of a century earlier. But such passing delights were not enough to please audiences in 1748. Compared to *Joshua* and *Judas Maccabaeus*, *Alexander Balus* was very much the dud of the season.

∼

On 24th April, the day after *Alexander Balus* opened at Covent Garden, a congress of warring nations assembled in Aix-la-Chapelle. After eight years of conflict in the War of the Austrian Succession, France was ready to negotiate for peace, and, with the exception of Silesia, whose seizure by Frederick II in 1740 had launched the whole international crisis, all the territories occupied in the ensuing years were restored to their previous owners. Bavaria, occupied by the Austrians, was returned to its own Elector, and Austria itself retrieved the Austrian Netherlands from the French. The Treaty of Aix-la-Chapelle was signed on 18th October 1748 by France, Britain and the Dutch Republic; later, two implementation treaties were also signed, in Nice, by Austria, Spain, Sardinia, Modena and Genoa. Although no country, least of all Britain, was particularly happy with this outcome, the fragile treaty did provide an opportunity for celebration – magnifying no doubt its implications and assigning some credit to George II. As early as June, long before the treaty was actually signed, an elaborate firework display was being planned for Green Park in London, and by October it was clear that this extravaganza would be accompanied by music on an equally vast scale. Although Handel was not, at this stage, yet named, there could be only one man whose music would ever match the brilliance and scope of a vast firework display. By the end of 1748, Handel was beginning to be involved in planning and discussion.

But, while all the peace celebrations were hatching over the summer, Handel was, as usual, writing two new oratorios and organizing his singers. The mysterious Domenica Casarini retreated into her obscurity, and Handel replaced her with Giulia Frasi, who had sung for the Middlesex company since 1742, but would now assume considerable importance for him. Galli, Lowe and Reinhold would all return for the next season, giving Handel a rare stability among his cohort. His two new oratorios, whose texts would be compiled for him by a Jewish author of ballad operas, Moses Mendes, were *Susanna* and *Solomon*. And here Handel once more hit his stride.

Susanna and *Solomon* were both a complete change of direction from the hero worship of the previous seasons. They were also very different from each other. *Susanna*, written mainly for Frasi (Susanna) and Galli (Joachim), was more operatic, including comedic elements, with Lowe and Reinhold as two prying Elders, and relatively little chorus involvement. *Solomon*, with a much greater choral element, recalled the structure and features of *Israel in Egypt*. Its three parts present different aspects of the great Solomon (his building the temple, and his domestic bliss; his wisdom, in the celebrated judgement between two women claiming the same baby; and his material wealth, as displayed to foreign visitors – in this case, the Queen of Sheba, with her famous 'Arrival' music). After all the attention paid to the Duke of Cumberland, *Solomon* could be seen as a tactfully flattering portrait of George II himself, showing him to be a wise and beneficent ruler during a climate of peace. The section to which Handel effortlessly applied his operatic skills was Part II, in which a second soprano, Sibilla Gronamann, stepped up to sing the Second Harlot, who is happy to have a child divided into two rather than lose a contest. Her one aria, 'Thy sentence, great King, is prudent and wise', is repetitive and appropriately lightweight, as befits the character, but demonstrates that Gronamann was a perfectly useful singer.

351

But the music for Frasi, as Solomon's queen, then the First Harlot and finally the Queen of Sheba, requires the pathos and lyrical control of a Cuzzoni or a Strada. Handel must have been delighted with her, and aware that she could now be a welcome fixture in his company. And Galli – here as Solomon – also had a wide range of challenges, both vocal and dramatic, which she evidently met, thus securing her future too.

Through all the glories of *Susanna* and especially *Solomon*, Handel continued to mine his richest seam of invention. The choral writing, often in double choruses, is as stupendous as it had been in *Israel in Egypt*, and his sparing but judicious use of trumpets and timpani is always a masterstroke. And yet, as so often with him, the most impressive moments are the quieter, pastoral ones. Part I of *Solomon*, for instance, which portrays the happy marriage of Solomon and his Queen, ends with the tenderest wish from the chorus: 'May no rash intruder disturb their soft hours', as 'nightingales lull them to sleep with their song'. Without in any way ever giving the impression of adopting a cliché, Handel sets this over an undulating bass line, over which the upper strings enact 'zephyrs, soft breathing' in gently paired semiquavers, and two flutes represent the calls of the nightingales. The chorus is magical, nowhere more so than at its conclusion: zephyrs and nightingales retreat, and the strings gently subside, lulled indeed into sleep. This was by no means the first time that Handel had written in this way (the end of Part I of *L'Allegro*, for instance, has a similar hushed descent into stasis), but again Handel's glorious, fresh control takes the breath away.

Susanna opened Handel's 1749 season on 10th February, and there was a very full audience. It had four performances in twelve days, finishing on 22nd February, and was immediately followed, on 24th February, by one of *Hercules*. (Handel cut completely the role of Lichas, which he had really only written for Cibber; Frasi, Galli and Lowe were natural fits for Iole, Dejanira and Hyllus, while Reinhold repeated his title role.) Then, just a week later on 3rd March, he revived *Samson* for four performances, ending on the 15th; and on the 17th, *Solomon* opened. As if this rehearsal and performance schedule was not already tight enough, on the 21st, between the second and third performances of *Solomon* on the 20th and 22nd, Handel, together with Frasi and Galli, performed in a concert in the Haymarket, for his Decay'd Musicians charity; and then, on the 24th, the day after the final *Solomon*, he and his entire team performed *Messiah* back in Covent Garden. Quite apart from the stamina required for such a brutal schedule – from singers, chorus, orchestral players, and not least from Handel himself – the logistics of it, in terms of learning and rehearsing so much music and having to make sure so many people were in the right place at the right time, are mind-boggling. As a result, though, Handel had regularly deposited large sums of money into his account, and it is to be hoped that his colleagues, too, had been magnificently rewarded.

The Green Park celebration of the Peace of Aix-la-Chapelle was being overseen by the Duke of Montagu, Master-General of the Ordnance, and his colleague, Charles Frederick, Comptroller of His Majesty's Laboratory at Woolwich. An area of the park had been chosen and marked off by November 1748, and the French–Italian scene designer, Giovanni Niccolo Servandoni, had been hired to build an elaborate pavilion in which to house a 'Fireworks Machine'. Servandoni had known Handel in the 1720s, when he had briefly worked as a scene painter in the

Haymarket. Since then his reputation as a designer had developed enormously, and in Paris he had also built structures for huge firework displays – for the birth of the Dauphin in 1729, and for the peace celebrations in 1739. In Green Park, Servandoni and his four Italian assistants designed and built 'The Temple of Peace', a huge wooden construction in the Palladian style, with a central arch and colonnades, a bas-relief of George II and sundry gods in statuary. As this temple grew before the eyes of London, there was speculation about the scale of the musical contribution too. On 14th January 1749, the *London Magazine* wrote, 'The band of musick that is to perform at the fire-works in the green-park, is to consist of 40 trumpets, 20 French horns, 16 hautboys, 16 bassoons, 8 pair of kettle-drums, 12 side-drums, a proper set of flutes and fifes; with 100 cannon to go off singly at intervals, with the musick.'[38] Certainly, Handel was being pressed to use vast forces, but, even with his fondness for the grand gesture, he found such a proposal preposterous; as always, he knew exactly what numbers he would need for the best possible sound in such a venue. The Duke of Montagu wrote to Charles Frederick at the end of March (just as Handel was emerging from his fearsome oratorio season):

I think Hendel now proposes to have but 12 trumpets and 12 French horns; at first there was to have been sixteen of each, and I remember I told the King so, who, at the time, objected to there being any musick; but, when I told him the quantity and nomber of martial musick there was to be, he was better satisfied, and said he hoped there would be no fidles. Now Hendel proposes to lessen the nomber of trumpets, &c. and to have violeens. I dont at all doubt but when the King hears it he will certainly be very much displeased.[39]

Alarmed by Handel's apparent insubordination, Montagu continued, 'If the thing war to be in such a manner as certainly to please the King, it ought to consist of no kind of instruments but martial instruments . . . I have very lately been told, from very good authority, that the King has, within this fortnight, expressed himself to this purpose.' By 9th April, it was clear that Handel had dug in his heels, and Montagu was seriously considering replacing him. And then there was another bone of contention between them. Montagu was entering into a fruitful business deal with Jonathan Tyers, manager of Vauxhall Gardens, who had offered to supply Green Park with lamps, lanterns and a crew of thirty, in exchange for a public rehearsal of Handel's music in his own park. Furthermore, the King himself supported such a deal. But Handel disapproved of the whole idea of a rehearsal in an ultimately irrelevant venue, and there was further argument. Montagu repeated his threat to replace Handel: 'Mr Hendel has hitherto refused to let it be at Foxhall, which his Majesty seemed to think he was in the wrong of; and I am shure I think him extreamly so, and extreamly indifferent whether we have his [music] or not, for it may very easily be supplied by an other'.[40] Handel had to back down on the Vauxhall rehearsal, which was duly advertised for 17th April. But then the Duke of Cumberland made his own difficulties. He wanted to attend the rehearsal, but 17th April was a 'drawing-room day', a court ritual which prevented him from doing anything else. The rehearsal was duly moved to the 21st. Handel did also heed the King's instruction for having no string players (though he added them later), but he persuaded Montagu (and the King) that a total of fifty-seven musicians (twenty-four oboes, twelve bassoons, nine trumpets, nine horns and three drummers) would be more than enough for his music, even when played out of doors and in possible competition with exploding fireworks.

The rehearsal in Vauxhall went well, as far as the music was concerned. But it was so popular that, according to a report in the *Gentlemen's Magazine*, 'above 12000 persons' turned up to witness it, leading to crowd trouble (some footmen behaved 'very sausily', and 'a scuffle happen'd, in which some gentlemen were wounded'[41]) and a traffic jam: London Bridge was so blocked that 'no carriage could pass for three hours'. The actual celebration, back in Green Park (with no bridges to cross) on 27th April, was similarly packed. Among the crowd was John Byrom, who back in 1725 had written the little 'Tweedle-dum and Tweedle-dee' poem about Handel and Bononcini. As he waited for it all to start, he sat beside a tree, looking at Servandoni's Temple of Peace (which he dubbed 'Squib Castle'), and wrote to his wife, describing the sights: 'The building erected on this occasion is indeed extremely neat and pretty and grand to look at, and a world of fireworks placed in an order that promises a most amazing scene when it is all to be in full display. His Majesty and other great folks have been walking to see the machinery before the Queen's Library; it is all railed about there, where the lords, ladies, commons, &c. are sat under scaffolding, and seem to be under confinement in comparison of us mobility, who enjoy the free air and walks here.'[42] Inevitably, the fireworks attracted more attention than Handel's music, not least because one of the side pavilions caught fire, causing Servandoni to lose his temper and threaten Charles Frederick with his sword. He was arrested, and only released from custody after the personal intervention of the Duke of Cumberland. For Servandoni, this was an ignominious end to a noble and spectacular project. But the royal family took it all in their stride, first watching the display from the Queen's Library in St James's

Palace, and then, when it was all over, walking back through the 'Machine' and handing royal purses to those who had operated it. While they did this, the music was played again, reminiscent perhaps of the manner in which Handel's 'Water Music' had been often repeated for George I, on that summer night on the River Thames in 1717.

Handel's 'Music for the Royal Fireworks', presented at the time as a 'Grand Overture of Warlike Instruments', however much it may have been literally outshone on its initial performance, was predictably brilliant. He handled his huge bodies of instruments with the dexterity of a chamber musician, dividing his twenty-four oboes into three judicious groups (of twelve, eight and four players), his twelve bassoons into two (of eight and four), and his nine horns and nine trumpets all into groups of three; and he alternated, combined and balanced them with apparently effortless skill. The largest and most impressive music is that simply called 'Ouverture', in two parts ('Adagio' and 'Allegro'). But there are also five dance movements, two of which, 'La Paix' and 'La Réjouissanace', bear titular witness to the occasion they were celebrating. Alert as always to the circumstances in which his music would be performed, out of doors and with little acoustical help, Handel nevertheless gave enormous variety of colour, texture and mood. No doubt aware that it would be challenging for wind and brass players to maintain lip control for such a long time, he made sure that each group got enough bars' rest to allow facial muscles to recover. But the addition of strings before his next performance of the 'Fireworks Music' gave considerably more opportunity for such respite, as the extremely practical Handel knew all too well.

Handel found a new platform for his 'Fireworks Music' almost immediately. He was beginning an association, which would continue for the rest of his life and far beyond it, with the Foundling Hospital. This major charitable institution had opened ten years earlier for the 'education and maintenance of exposed and deserted young children', founded by the philanthropist and former merchant sailor Thomas Coram, and greatly supported by leading members of London's community of artists, headed by William Hogarth. As many painters donated their pictures to the hospital, visitors would pay to come and see them (making the Foundling Hospital effectively London's first public art gallery), and their donations were crucial to the charity's funding and administration. This was exactly the sort of enterprise that appealed to the profoundly compassionate side of Handel's multifaceted nature, combining as it did help for the most vulnerable, with the promotion of artists. In May 1749 he offered to give a benefit concert specifically to help pay for the completion of the chapel, and then, at his own expense, install in it a specially built organ. The committee was thrilled, and immediately invited Handel to become one of the Hospital's Governors, though Handel politely turned this down, claiming he could serve the charity better as an outsider. A year later, he did in fact join the Foundling Hospital as a Governor, cementing his loyalty forever.

After two postponements, both caused by conflicting obligations for members of the royal family, who all wished to support the charity, Handel's Foundling Hospital concert took place on 27th May 1749. Bringing with him apparently 'above one Hundred Voices and Performers'[43] from his choirs and orchestras, Handel's programme consisted of the 'Fireworks Music' (with its newly added strings, but no doubt with greatly reduced winds), an 'Anthem on the Peace', which he had written for the Chapel

Royal service of thanksgiving for peace in the previous month, some extracts from *Solomon*, and a work composed especially for the occasion, the Foundling Hospital anthem, 'Blessed are they that considereth the poor and needy'. This was drawn together from other works, including Queen Caroline's funeral ode, *Susanna* and *Messiah*, whose 'Hallelujah' chorus concluded the proceedings. The Prince and Princess of Wales attended the concert, together with 'the young Princes and Princesses' (of whatever generation), and 'a prodigious Concourse of the Nobility and Gentry'.[44] With tickets priced at half a guinea, and over a thousand people in the audience, plus private donations including a magnificent one of £2,000 from the King, vast sums of money went towards the charity, and Handel resolved to repeat the event in a year's time, when his new organ would be installed in the chapel. (At the same time that he dealt with organ builders, he was also advising Jennens on a similar instrument for Gopsall, offering specific, knowledgeable and wise counsel.)

Over the summer months of 1749, Handel made his customary plans for the following season. But where he had traditionally written two new works each year, now he composed just one, *Theodora*, to a libretto by Morell. As to his cohort of singers, Frasi, Galli, Lowe and Reinhold had all served him well now as a group for two seasons, and were happily returning. But an exciting young Italian castrato had just appeared in London. Since the departure of both Farinelli and Senesino, castrato singers had somewhat retreated from the vocal limelight. Handel himself had increasingly given male roles that would have been designed for their voice type to female singers, especially in his oratorios; and the public had become perfectly acclimatized to this suspension of disbelief, and complicit therefore in the tradition which had developed. But the arrival of the twenty-one-year-old Gaetano

Guadagni stopped Handel in his tracks. With his unassailable ability to identify and nurture raw talent, he immediately started to include him in his plans. Others too crowded round the young Italian with advice and encouragement: Dr Burney helped him with the pronunciation of the English language, and later Garrick would oversee his stage technique. The man who, just over a decade later in 1762, would create the title role in Gluck's *Orfeo*, and thus achieve international and historical renown, was about to cut his dramatic teeth amongst London's finest practitioners and with the best possible mentors.

As the 1750 oratorio season approached, Handel seemed to be in excellent spirits. On 13th February, Lord Shaftesbury wrote to James Harris, 'I have seen Handel several times since I came hither, and I think I never saw him so cool and well. He is quite easy in his behaviour'.[45] This sense of well-being was partly due to affluence. Handel had made a great deal of money in the previous year, and was now buying pictures, including, if Lord Shaftesbury is to be believed, a Rembrandt. With just one new oratorio for Lent, he was perhaps more relaxed as he approached his rehearsal period, though his schedule for 1750 was just as fierce as that of the previous season. His twelve performances would begin with two of *Saul* (with those artillery drums specially hired, as usual) and four of *Judas Maccabaeus*, in the middle of which would be three of the new *Theodora*. The season would conclude with two performances of *Samson* and, again on the final day, *Messiah*. Handel's new recruit, Guadagni, would probably have sung David in *Saul*, certainly created the role of Didymus in *Theodora*, and also sang Micah in *Samson*, before sharing the mezzo-soprano music in *Messiah* with Galli. So excited was Handel by Guadagni's vocal prowess, he wrote new versions of 'But who may abide' and 'How beautiful are the feet' expressly for him.

The new *Theodora* marked another change of direction. Instead of conquering heroes and military exploits, *Theodora* is a story of Christian martyrdom – and as such is Handel's only oratorio other than *Messiah* which deals with a Christian subject. Morell based his libretto partly on Corneille's *Théodore, vierge et martyre*, of 1645, and partly on a novel by Robert Boyle, *The Martyrdom of Theodora and Didymus* (1687). Theodora (Frasi) is the head of a Christian community in Antioch, which is under Roman rule. The Governor, Valens (Reinhold), instructs the people to celebrate the Emperor's birthday with a festival to Jove, which Theodora refuses to do. She is sentenced to imprisonment and, far worse, to service as a prostitute. Didymus (Guadagni), a Roman whom she has converted to Christianity, rescues her by exchanging clothes with her and allowing her to escape. He is tried for treason and sentenced to death; but Theodora returns, and elects to die with him.

Handel's choice of this story at this stage of his life (he was sixty-five, and had had recurring health problems since 1737) is poignant. Many of his oratorios had ended with glorious deaths, but none at such a measured and thoughtful pace, or with such radiance. After years of war, both in reality and on the concert platform, the fundamental pacifism of this story ('The rapturous soul defies the sword', sings Didymus) seems central to Handel's own convictions, as does the strength of the Christian message. *Theodora* is mainly delivered in slow tempos; apart from the aggression of Valens and the crudity of the Roman armies, especially when foully anticipating the violation of prostitutes, arias are protracted and considered thoughts of immense intellectual power. Theodora's assistant Irene (Galli), who holds together the

Christian community after the arrest of their leader, becomes a pivotal figure in the spiritual narrative, constantly stressing the omnipresence of God's protection, even as circumstances look most bleak. Her first–act aria, in the face of mounting panic at the threat of death to the community, could even be a signature movement for Handel. The text, of infinite comfort and poetry, is not dissimilar to that of the duet at the end of *L'Allegro*, 'As steals the morn upon the night'. But where that arrival of daylight restored 'intellectual day', here the return of dawn constantly confirms the presence of Almighty protection:

> As with rosy steps the morn
> Advancing, drives the shades of night,
> So from virtuous toils well borne
> Raise thou our hopes of endless light.
> Triumphant Saviour! Lord of day,
> Thou art the life, the light, the way.

In *L'Allegro*'s duet, there was measured treading in the bass line and gentle activity above it. Here, Handel reverses the technique: the upper strings tread calmly above persuasive stirrings in the bass line, and Irene's comforting message is integrally entwined in the texture. Similarly, her Part III opening prayer, 'Lord, to thee each night and day / Strong in hope we sing and pray', is positive, reassuring and calm. This sense of conviction is sustained even through Theodora's darkest moment of isolation and fear in her prison cell – hauntingly conveyed in a brief (ten bar) and bleak 'Symphony' of slow string chords punctuated by single, lonely notes on a flute, which leads to her harrowing lament, 'With darkness deep as is my woe'. But the strength of her own beliefs turns her round:

But why art thou disquieted, my soul?
Hark! Heaven invites thee in sweet rapturous strains
To join the ever singing, ever loving choir
Of Saints and angels in the courts above.

Her aria, 'Oh that I on wings could fly', is truly joyous in its positive coloratura. And after Didymus has changed places (and clothes) with her, the concluding chorus of Part II interprets these events as a true symbol of the Resurrection, with the mighty 'He saw the lovely youth' in three sections of mounting pace, texture, activity and strength. In the final Part, after Theodora and Didymus have resolved to die together, even the Roman chorus become reflective in 'How strange their ends and yet how glorious', which slowly builds through measured counterpoint to its climax, 'Where Virtue its own Innocence denies / And for the vanquished the glad Victor dies', before contracting again to a serious and quiet solemnity. Before they are sacrificed, Theodora and Didymus sing a gentle duet, 'Streams of pleasure ever flowing', which ends with true radiance: 'Wake the song and tune the lyre / Of the blissful holy choir'. And the final chorus, 'O love divine', another unhurried movement of immense positivism and sinew, releases a true catharsis, unequalled in any other of Handel's greatest works.

Presenting oratorios of such consistent quality as *Saul*, *Judas Maccabaeus*, *Theodora*, *Samson* and *Messiah*, it is truly difficult to comprehend how Handel's 1750 season could have been a failure with audiences. But it was. And part of the cause, astonishingly, was seismological. On 8th February, between performances of *Saul* and *Judas Maccabaeus*, and then again on 8th March, London experienced earthquakes. The second was more serious than the first, causing structural damage from Richmond in the west, to

Whitechapel in the east, from Hatfield in the north, to Croydon in the south; and the top of a pier on the north side of Westminster Abbey fell down, together with the ironwork that fastened it. Londoners were terrified, particularly when a mad guardsman predicted a third quake on 5th April (between the two performances of *Samson*), and many well-to-do people left London and fled to the country. That third quake did not materialize, but the effect on Handel's takings was certainly shocking. According to Morell, 'The 2d night of *Theodora* was very thin indeed, tho' the Princess Amelia was there. I guessed it a losing night, so did not go to Mr Handell as usual'.[46] Some members of the public were brave: Mrs Elizabeth Montagu wrote to her sister, 'I was not under any apprehension about the earthquake, but went that night to the Oratorio . . . The Wednesday night the Oratorio was very empty, though it was the most favourite performance of Handel's.'[47] And an intrepid French visitor, Madame Anne-Marie Fiquet du Bocage, was enchanted: 'The Oratorio, or pious concert, pleases us highly. English words sung by Italian performers, and accompanied by a variety of instruments . . . The Italian opera, in three acts, gives us much less pleasure.'[48] Madame Fiquet's letter also affords the most vivid description: 'Handel is the soul of it: when he makes his appearance, two wax lights are carried before him, which are laid upon his organ. Amidst a loud clapping of hands he seats himself, and the whole band of music strikes up at exactly the same moment.'

By May, when Handel gave two performances of *Messiah* for the Foundling Hospital, the shocks and aftershocks had retreated and life had returned to normal. Londoners who had abandoned the capital in mortal fear were able once more to support this noble cause, and Dr William Stukeley recorded in his diary, on 1st May, 'An infinite croud of coaches at our end of the town to hear Handel's music at the opening of the Chapel of the Found-lings.'[49] And these post-earthquake performances of *Messiah* for the Foundling Hospital marked a crucial junction. When it had been performed in a London theatre, *Messiah* had met with dis-approval or indifference. Now, after a period of terror, it was performed in the chapel of a charitable foundation, and generated true enthusiasm. Mrs Delany, now in Dublin with her husband, heard a report of it from her brother, Bernard Granville, and wrote back in delight: 'I am glad the Foundling Hospital was so full, and carried on with such decency; I am sure it pleased our friend Handel, and I love to have him pleased.'[50]

After his sobering spring, however, even the normally irre-pressible Handel was perhaps finding it hard to be constantly pleased. His health continued to worry him, and his eyesight too was troublesome. His trusted colleague, Heidegger, had died in September 1749; in the summer of 1750 his great contemporary Johann Sebastian Bach, whom he had never met but with whom he shared enormous mutual respect, would also die. On 1st June, Handel made his will, a typically detailed and thorough docu-ment, remembering his family, his friends both German and English, and his servants. For the first time in decades, he wrote no new music at all that summer. Instead, he travelled once more to the continent, partly to visit his old friend and pupil, Princess Anne, at the Hague, but mainly to see his family. It was to be his last journey out of England.

13

THE FINAL ACT

'With honour let desert be crown'd'

[Judas Maccabaeus]

Somewhere between The Hague and Haarlem, the coach in which Handel was travelling overturned, and its illustrious passenger was 'terribly hurt'. The *General Advertiser* reported the news to London at the end of August, albeit reassuring readers that the accident had occurred 'some time since' and that Handel was 'now out of danger'.[1] Whether or not this was some sensationalist exaggeration is hard to determine. Handel certainly enjoyed the company of Princess Anne in The Hague that summer, playing for her on at least three occasions, and he presumably also travelled on to Halle, to visit his family. Even though he was by now quite preoccupied with his own health, he himself never referred to an accident or injury in any extant letter or document. At the end of the year, on 3rd December, Ann Dewes enquired of her brother, Bernard Granville, 'I hope you find Mr. Handel well'.[2] No other letter between any of the Granville siblings (Bernard Granville, Mrs Delany and Mrs Dewes – all passionate supporters and close friends of Handel) makes any reference to a misadventure in Holland. But even if this incident was overblown in the London press, it did perhaps mark the beginning of a slow decline in Handel's health and activities. From that summer on, the routines established over many years were gradually abandoned; after it, everything became more laborious.

Having composed no oratorio now for well over a year, and still with nothing new to present in his 1751 season, Handel at last began to write again in late January. Morell had for some time been preparing his next libretto for Handel: *Jephtha*, based on a story in Judges (10–12). Jephtha, an Israelite chieftain, vows that, if he is victorious over the Ammonites, he will sacrifice the first living being he meets on his return. It is his daughter who greets him; but in this version an Angel intervenes before Jephtha carries out the sacrifice, and declares that the daughter may survive, but in a virgin state for the rest of her natural life. Although this is a story of Old Testament brutality and the destruction of human happiness, its wider implications, as in *Theodora*, are much more profound; and again Handel infused his new work with an intense reflection on human suffering that cannot but be seen as personal. For his own suffering – specifically, his rapidly deteriorating eyesight – was all too real. He began to compose *Jephtha* on 21st January, and by 2nd February had completed Part I with his customary inventive speed. But he was forced to stop writing just ten days later. Having struggled to the end of a chorus with the unbearably poignant text, 'How dark O Lord are thy decrees, all hid from mortal sight', he wrote at the foot of the page (in German): 'Reached here on 13th Febr. 1751, unable to go on owing to weakening of sight in my left eye'; and he laid down his pen.

But with or without any new work, Handel's plans for his imminent oratorio season – the entire focus now of his annual creative activity – had to be finalized. So, with his same singers from the previous year – Frasi, Galli, Lowe and the young Guadagni – all returning, he put together revivals of *Belshazzar*, *Alexander's Feast*, *Esther* and *Judas Maccabaeus*, and, on 22nd February, opened the series with *Belshazzar*. Perhaps the very process of rehearsing and performing this mighty work energized him, for on the following day (his sixty-sixth birthday), he returned to his desk and to the unfinished *Jephtha*, writing at the top of the page, 'the 23rd of this month, feeling rather better, began again'. But this phase lasted for only four days. On the 27th, the day of the second performance of *Belshazzar*, he was again forced to abandon the project, this time for several months. He continued to direct his oratorio season, and managed to introduce something new for his audiences in *The Choice of Hercules*, which he performed with *Alexander's Feast*. This was in fact the music that he had written for an aborted project in the previous summer. There had been a plan to mount a play by Tobias Smollett, *Alceste*, at Covent Garden, with extremely elaborate scenery by Servandoni (who had therefore not entirely disgraced himself with his night in gaol following his Green Park firework debacle). Handel had been asked to supply extensive incidental music, and he had lined up suitable actor-singers (different from his oratorio team) and written specially for them. For unknown reasons the play had then been abandoned. So now Handel took up the *Alceste* music again, adapted it to new words (probably by Morell) as *The Choice of Hercules*, and recast it for his current singers, instead of those originally chosen for

Smollett's play. With four performances of this double bill, as well as *Esther* and *Judas Maccabaeus*, Handel could still offer a varied season to his loyal, if diminishing, audiences.

But even before he could conclude his twelve-concert series with a *Messiah* on Passion Sunday, the whole season suddenly had to be abandoned, for on 20th March there was truly shocking news. Frederick, Prince of Wales, had died at the age of forty-four. On the following day, the *London Advertiser* carried the customary sober injunction: 'Last Night an Order came to both Theatres to forbid their Performances on the Account of his Royal Highness the Prince of Wales's Death; and we hear all public Diversions will be discontinued during his Majesty's Pleasure.'[3]

There had been anxiety that winter, but for the health of the King rather than his son. The Prince of Wales had been pursuing his own activities with his habitual energy amidst continuing family tensions. In addition to retaining sour feelings for his father, he was increasingly jealous of his brother, the Duke of Cumberland – still harbouring resentment that Cumberland had had military opportunities, and therefore triumphs, which he himself had been denied – and even began to suspect that Cumberland was planning, like their predecessor, Richard III, to seize the throne himself on the death of their father. George II was now sixty-seven, and since the end of the War of the Austrian Succession had lost all interest in politics, domestic or foreign. Frederick was preparing for his own succession, assembling around him men who would be sympathetic to his needs and beliefs, and planning even to remove his brother from all military posts and repeal any innovations in military law that Cumberland had supported. In March 1751 the Prince of Wales caught a cold, in itself not life-threatening, but sufficiently severe for his medical advisers to recommend the drawing of his blood. He refused to stay at home to recuperate, but insisted on attending the final session of Parliament, where bills were being passed into law, and also his father's drawing-room ritual. He reassured his supporters in the House of Lords that he was ready to rule whenever his father died; but, on returning home on the evening of 20th March, he developed a catastrophic coughing fit, and himself died. Popular rumour blamed his death on a sporting injury from some years earlier (he had been hit on the head by a ball while playing Prisoner's Base), but it was more likely to have been the consequence of pleurisy and pneumonia. Whatever the cause, the nation was totally unprepared for Frederick's death, and even the King, after years of cruel animosity, was moved to tears in the ensuing days as he consoled Frederick's widow, Augusta, pregnant now with her ninth child.

The future George III was still only twelve years old and, as a minor, too young to rule should his grandfather also now die. So an uncomfortable Regency Bill was drawn up, making Augusta regent for the boy, but advised by a council headed by the Duke of Cumberland. (How Frederick would have hated that arrangement.) Frederick's funeral took place on a lavish scale, but without the presence of the King, who had not attended his wife's funeral either, and without any specially commissioned music. Neither Handel nor any other composer was called upon to mark the gravity of a major royal occasion.

∽

By mid-April, London life had returned to normal. In the week after Easter, Handel was able to perform *Messiah* at the Foundling Hospital on 18th April, and repeat it there four weeks later. Both performances attracted, as before, a 'very numerous and splendid Audience' and 'the greatest Applause'.[4] *Messiah* continued its rehabilitation, and was rapidly becoming the popular stalwart that it remains. Handel also gave the annual concert for his Decay'd Musicians charity on 16th April in the Haymarket, with performers including Frasi, Galli, Guadagni and Beard, together with a star from Handel's greatest days in that very King's Theatre. Francesca Cuzzoni was back in town.

The once exorbitantly paid Cuzzoni had last been seen in London in 1736, singing for Senesino's Opera of the Nobility. After that, her career had continued to prosper on the continent, and for the next three years she had earned equally large fees in the major opera houses of her native Italy. But her fortunes had then changed dramatically. Her marriage to Pier Giuseppe Sandoni had collapsed, and back in 1741 there had even been a rumour that she had murdered him. (Londoners had been thrilled to read press reports that 'the famous singer, Mrs C–z–ni is under sentence of death to be beheaded, for poisoning her husband.'[5]) The story was completely untrue, but after the break-up of the marriage Cuzzoni had fallen into serious debt through gambling and other irresponsibilities. She had appeared in opera houses in Holland and Germany, and was even briefly employed as a church singer in Stuttgart. But her debts had continued to grow, and – at over fifty years old and in financial straits – she decided to try and renew her career in London, the city that had witnessed her finest years. She had given one benefit concert in Hickford's Concert Room in Brewer Street, in May 1750, and in that year was also rumoured to have been bailed out of a debt for thirty pounds by none other than the Prince of Wales.

Handel was sensitive to distress in others, and now he had distressing circumstances of his own to acknowledge. He was going blind and his greatest successes were behind him; Cuzzoni was well past her prime and in desperate need of money. And so, although his previous working relationship with Cuzzoni had ended on a sour note, he now agreed to present her again in London. At his charity concert on 16th April 1751, while Frasi, Galli and Beard sang arias from the current successes *Samson*, *Judas Maccabaeus* and *Esther*, Cuzzoni performed arias from their past shared triumphs, including 'Falsa imagine', from *Ottone* (1722) – over which Handel had threatened to defenestrate her all those years ago – and, with Guadagni, a duet from *Giulio Cesare* (1723). So Handel enabled her to recall her two greatest roles, Teofane and Cleopatra; and, as she sang 'Più amabile beltà' with Guadagni, the great voice of opera's past (she was fifty-five) was, for a glorious flash of historical coincidence, paired with the great voice of opera's future (he was twenty-two). A month later, Cuzzoni gave another benefit concert in Brewer Street, and Guadagni, no doubt conscious that his partner was a legend, sang beside her again. But Cuzzoni's own press statement underlined the continuing precariousness of the singing profession:

I am so extremely sensible of the many Obligations I have already received from the Nobility and Gentry of this Kingdom (for which I sincerely return my most humble Thanks) that nothing but extreme Necessity, and a Desire of doing Justice, could induce me to trouble them again, but being unhappily involved in a few Debts, am extremely desirous of attempting every Thing in my Power to pay them, before I quit England; therefore take the Liberty, most humbly to intreat them, once more to repeat their well-known Generosity and Goodness, and to honour me with their Presence at this Benefit, which shall be the last I will ever trouble them with, and is made solely to pay my Creditors.[6]

Whether or not Cuzzoni's debts were paid, she left London shortly after this concert, and retired in her penury to Italy, where she tried to support herself by making buttons. She lived, in great poverty, until 1778.

Handel meanwhile had his own problems to address. In the summer of 1751 he visited both Bath and Cheltenham, spa towns where, as he had in Tunbridge Wells and indeed Aix-la-Chapelle, he took the waters in an attempt to rebuild his health. His galloping blindness was devastating. His eyes had allowed him to appreciate his fine art – he now owned over 140 paintings and prints, and loved to visit other collections and auctions – and to engage with people. But, beyond these pleasures, if he could not see he simply could not operate professionally, for he could not put notes on paper. His sight was to him as essential as was his hearing. He consulted specialists, the first of whom was Samuel Sharp at Guy's Hospital, who diagnosed a 'gutta serena', or loss of sight due to an inoperable disease of the optic nerve. Sharp could contribute little relief beyond suggesting that Handel employ someone else to play the organ in his concerts, and even proposed the blind composer, John Stanley, whose memory never failed. Handel had at least not lost his sense of humour, for he is reported to have 'burst into a loud laugh, and said "Mr Sharp, have you never read the Scriptures? Do you not remember, if the blind lead the blind, they fall into the ditch?"'[7] Nevertheless, Sharp's basic suggestion, that his patient take on some assistance, was a good one, and Handel turned to John Christopher Smith the younger, son of his great friend and principal music copyist who had effectively moved to England with him and for years been an essential cog in the wheel that was Handel's composition and performance machine. The younger Smith, after receiving composition and keyboard lessons from Handel and Pepusch, had also become part of the team of copyists in Brook Street before heading off to Europe in the 1740s. Now Handel summoned him back to London and asked him to help manage and direct his oratorio seasons. It was a good fit for both men. Handel knew he could trust Smith's abilities and loyalties, and Smith was completely familiar (for he had grown up in the middle of it all) with Handel's methods, his needs and certainly his foibles. For the rest of Handel's life, Smith would remain as essential to him, if in a somewhat different way, as his father had been.

In August 1751, Handel managed to return to his unfinished *Jephtha*, completing it at last at the end of the month. He added his own age, 'aetatis 66', to the final page, a recognition perhaps that he was finding the physical process of composition ever more impossible, and that *Jephtha* might even be his last major work. By November, Handel's friends were acknowledging the change in him among themselves. Mrs Delany wrote to her sister, Ann, on 16th November, 'Did you hear that poor Handel has lost the sight of one of his eyes? I am sure you (who so truly taste his merit) will lament it'.[8]

But one factor would have greatly cheered Handel as he anticipated his 1752 oratorio season, and that was the return to his fold of the tenor, John Beard. Since his defection to David Garrick in Drury Lane, in 1748, Beard had been unavailable to Handel for his own presentations, and Handel had relied for his tenor roles on the fine voice but limited communication skills of Thomas Lowe. In the previous year, just after the death of the Prince of Wales, Beard had joined Handel's team of soloists for *Messiah* at the Foundling Hospital, and had been so affected by the charity for which they were performing that he, like Handel, had refused to take a fee. This solicitous generosity had re-established a link between them. From then on, Beard joined Handel annually at the Foundling Hospital *Messiah*s, always performing for no fee; he, too, became one of the Hospital's Governors. And he made himself available to Handel for other projects. Like *Samson* and *Belshazzar*, the new oratorio, *Jephtha*, had a tenor title role, requiring a wide range of emotion as well as challenging vocal artistry. Though Beard was still a young man of thirty-five, Handel knew he would have just the right imagination and depth for it, and yet again he wrote the role to Beard's strengths.

The main focus of Handel's now customary twelve-concert series in 1752 was to be *Jephtha*, and it also included *Joshua*, *Samson* and *Judas Maccabaeus*. All these oratorios had rewarding tenor title roles for Beard. (And there would be two more performances of *Messiah*.) Frasi and Galli were again part of the company – in the new work, to sing Jephtha's daughter, Iphis, and wife, Storgè. A Mr Wass appears in the cast list as a bass soloist for the first time – though he could possibly have been the same Mr Wass who sang in the choir at the funeral of Queen Caroline, in 1737. He would take the role of Zebul, Jephtha's half-brother. Hamor, who loves Iphis, was perhaps originally conceived by Handel for Guadagni, but the young Italian castrato was touring other cities (Mrs Delany heard him in Dublin) and so was unavailable. This role was therefore taken by a Charlotte Brent. A boy treble stepped out from the choir to sing the small but crucial role of the Angel.

With the knowledge that Handel struggled physically to write this last great work, it is not difficult to read into *Jephtha* an unprecedented expression of personal engagement, even after the intense solemnity of *Theodora*. Handel's narrative sweep is as sound as ever, despite those often lengthy interruptions in the creative process. The biggest moment of drama, at the heart of the work, in Part II, is that of Iphis greeting her father and his appalled reaction; and it is superbly handled. Not unlike the cumulative structure of 'See the conquering hero comes', in *Joshua*, Iphis' 'Welcome as the cheerful light', with its blithe gavotte rhythm, is taken up by a chorus of boys, whose own innocent voices increase the ingenuous charm. As Jephtha realizes the horror of what his rash vow has achieved, he shouts at his daughter, 'Be gone, my child, / Thou hast undone thy father', and begs to be hidden from reality, in the tortuously jagged, 'Open thy marble jaws, O tomb, / And hide me, earth, in thy dark womb'. When he explains to his wife, his brother and Hamor that he must fulfil his vow and sacrifice his own daughter, Storgè reacts in the only way a mother could: 'First perish thou', she sings in forthright accompanied recitative, 'and perish all the world!' Her aria, 'Let other creatures die', is wildly agitated, only dissolving into still sorrow at her summary of her daughter's qualities ('so fair, so chaste, so good'). Hamor selflessly offers to die instead of Iphis, before Handel's masterstroke, a quartet in which Storgè, Hamor and Zebul plead with Jephtha to spare Iphis, and Jephtha can only resist them with his doggedly repeated resolution, 'Recorded stands my vow in heaven above'. Iphis, who now understands the consequence of the vow, with the bravest courage accepts it: 'For joys so vast, too little is the price of one poor life', she sings, in calm accompanied recitative; and in her gentle aria she insists that 'this vital breath with content I shall resign'. Such sweet magnanimity is too much for Jephtha, who, in a quite astonishing accompanied recitative, wrestles with their predicament, but breaks down in a personal grief that literally robs him of speech in mid-sentence ('Therefore, tomorrow's dawn – I can no more').

So the chorus conclude this remarkable second part, with the intense 'How dark, O Lord, are thy decrees', which broke Handel, too, as he wrestled with his own affliction and was forced to abandon his labours.

The suffering of Jephtha in his self-inflicted sorrow is matched by suffering for all the other characters: for Iphis and her appalling sentence, for Storgè's imminent loss of her child (a mother's greatest fear), for Hamor's loss of his love, and even for Zebul's sense of communal responsibility. All of these are expressed with a potency that again points to the relevance of Handel's own condition, and his helpless acceptance of it. The very first words of the oratorio, articulated by Zebul, are, 'It must be so', and, later, in Part II, these are repeated by Jephtha. The chorus's moralizing, at the conclusion of the second part, ends with a quotation from Alexander Pope's *Essay on Man*: 'Whatever is, is right'. Handel completed that chorus, and therefore the setting of those words, in the four days' temporary remission from his rapid loss of sight, in late February 1751. The fatalism of their bald setting and then their harsh repetition speaks volumes for his state of mind as, once more, his own light was being extinguished.

By the time Handel addressed Part III, in the summer of 1751, his acceptance of his situation was calmer. As with the radiance that he had found for the end of *Theodora*, here in *Jephtha* redemption is offered in the form of an Angel, the commuting therefore of Iphis' sentence, and apparently another comforting affirmation of his own religious belief. In the same spirit as Theodora's 'Angels ever bright and fair', or even 'I know that my redeemer liveth', here, at the beginning of Act III, Jephtha confronts his obligation to sacrifice his daughter, and begs the angels to take care of her: 'Waft her, angels, through the skies', he sings, in an utterly serene aria with the same measured tread (andante larghetto) as Irene's 'As with rosy steps' in *Theodora*. The Angel itself, as sung by a boy treble, brings innocent relief ('Happy Iphis shalt thou live'), and again it is the chorus who articulate more universal reflections on the profundity of divine intervention. The protracted composition process of *Jephtha* – so different from the manner in which Handel, even recently, would dash off a masterpiece in just three weeks – and the accompanying deterioration of Handel's own physical state, unquestionably reflect a struggle to face the imposition of a condition, and then the coming to terms with its consequences. In *Jephtha*, Handel was being truly autobiographical. But however much the mechanism for transcribing his musical thought onto paper may have been broken, his invention was as vital and inspired as ever.

After his 1752 Lenten season or oratorio, Handel gave his customary concerts for charity: for the Decay'd Musicians, featuring Frasi, Galli, Beard and Wass; for a new concern of his, the Lock Hospital for women in distress, founded in 1746; and then his two Foundling Hospital performances of *Messiah*, which continued to attract enormous support and therefore money. But his own spirits were low (Mainwaring wrote of his 'deepest despondency'[9] at this time); and then in August he catastrophically suffered what the *General Advertiser* described as another 'Paralytick Disorder in his Head, which has deprived him of sight'.[10] From now on, Handel was completely blind. He consulted a second specialist, Dr William Bromfield of the Lock Hospital, and surgeon to Princess Augusta of Wales, and on 3rd November he had a cataract operation, or was 'couch'd', according to the *General Advertiser*. At first there was optimism: 'it was thought there was all imaginable Hopes of Success by the Operation, which must give the greatest Pleasure to all Lovers of Musick';[11] and, when she heard the news in Dublin, Mrs Delany wrote to her sister, 'Poor Handel! How feelingly he must recollect the "*total eclipse*". I hear he has now been couched, and found some benefit from it.'[12] But all this optimism was in fact unfounded, and on 27th January it was dejectedly confirmed, 'Mr Handel has at length, unhappily, quite lost his sight. Upon his being couch'd some time since, he saw so well, that his friends flattered themselves his sight was restored for a continuance; but a few days have entirely put an end to their hope.'[13]

Handel now had to rely on others for absolutely everything, and although he continued with Smith the younger to plan his oratorio seasons and his charity concerts, and certainly to be involved in preparation and rehearsal (some of which still occurred in Brook Street, as well as Carlton House), he gradually released the reins of his performing activity. He carried on playing organ concertos between the acts of his oratorios, for there was clearly no decline in his technical dexterity. And if he could not remember precisely what he had once written, he would simply improvise with all his customary brilliance, as Smith's stepson and biographer, William Coxe, recalled: 'he had recourse to the inexhaustible stores of his rich and fertile imagination. He gave to the band, only such parts of his intended composition, as were to be filled up by their accompaniment; and he relied on his own powers of invention to produce, at the impulse of the moment, those captivating passages, which arrested attention, and enchanted his auditors.'[14] That pleasure for Handel's audiences was no doubt equalled in the thrill felt by his accompanying musicians, as the great man embarked on musical excursions into the unknown. But audiences were intensely moved too by the spectacle now of a once so robust dynamo of energy reduced to a pitiful state, as Coxe again described:

> during the first year of Handel's blindness, Samson was performed, and Beard sung, with great feeling,
>
> > Total eclipse – no sun, no moon,
> > All dark amid the blaze of noon.
>
> The recollection that Handel had set this air to music, with the view of the blind composer then sitting by the organ, affected the audience so forcibly, that many persons present were moved even to tears.[15]

Burney agreed: 'To see him, however, led to the organ, after this calamity, at upwards of seventy years of age, and then conducted towards the audience to make his accustomed obeisance, was a sight so truly afflicting and deplorable to persons of sensibility, as greatly diminished their pleasure in hearing him perform.'[16]

In the years following his final 'total eclipse', Handel's oratorio seasons continued at the King's Theatre. The repertoire varied subtly from year to year, but *Messiah* always concluded each series, and Handel's biggest sellers, *Samson*, *Judas Maccabaeus*, *Saul* and *Jephtha*, made the most regular appearances. But changes were rung. *Athalia* and *Deborah* reappeared, and so, bizarrely, in 1754, did an opera, *Admeto*, under the direction of Francesco Vanneschi, who had taken over the opera company in the Haymarket from Lord Middlesex in 1748. Apart from Frasi, who was also busily singing in all seven oratorios that season, *Admeto*'s cast was made up of Italian singers working for Vanneschi; but this single performance was received with indifference. In 1756, 1757 and

1758, Handel programmed *Israel in Egypt*, which had not done well on its initial outings in 1739, but for which Handel (rightly) retained the greatest affection; but, yet again, it proved unpopular, or, as Mrs Delany concluded, 'too solemn for common ears'.[17] The one work on whose preparation Handel, with Smith's considerable assistance, did spend time and trouble, was *The Triumph of Time and Truth*, for the 1757 season. This was in effect a translation, by Morell, of his Italian oratorio, *Il Trionfo del Tempo e della Verità* of 1737, revised with new recitatives (probably by Smith) and an added character, Deceit, who sides with Pleasure against Counsel and Time, in offering advice to Beauty. It had five performances in 1757, an unusual number when most other oratorios were receiving only one or two, or very rarely three. Back in 1707, in Rome, Handel's first oratorio had been *Il Trionfo del Tempo e del Disinganno*, which served as the basis for its 1737 revival in London. The fact that this *Triumph of Time and Truth* of 1757, half a century away from its original source, was also Handel's last oratorio, is poignantly symmetrical.

The intimations of mortality that Handel had first felt in 1750 as, before his final journey to Europe, he had drawn up his will, now crowded in on him increasingly through the 1750s. With a glance perhaps at his own afterlife, he allowed the portrait painter Thomas Hudson, who had already painted him once in 1748, to do so again. Hudson was not merely the most successful portraitist now in London, but also a good supporter of the Foundling Hospital, and he and Handel were therefore sympathetic to one another. Hudson's magnificent 1756 portrait was of a man of the greatest distinction, authority and sensitivity, whose eyes betrayed no suggestion of their new worthlessness. Had Handel been able to see the painting, he would surely have been delighted with it.

Handel also stepped up his communion with the Almighty. According to Coxe, he attended church regularly at St George's, Hanover Square, where 'his devout posture of humility, and earnestness of voice and gesture, avowing his faith, acknowledging his errors, and appealing to his Maker for mercy, were strongly impressive.'[18] But his infirmity otherwise drew him increasingly into his own private shell. As Burney recalled, 'in his latter years, except when he went to pay his duty to the royal family at St. James's, or Leicester-House, he seldom visited the great, or was visible, but at church, and the performance of his own Oratorios.'[19] He thought constantly about his will, and dictated three different codicils to it in 1756 and 1757, adding another executor, the London merchant and lawyer George Amyand, to his niece Johanna Friederike Flörcke, and adjusting its details when the intended beneficiaries (his cousin Christian August Roth, for instance, or his servant Peter LeBlond) died. In the summer months he sometimes travelled to England's spa towns to take the waters. On one visit to Tunbridge Wells, in 1755, he had a blazing row with Smith the elder, and they parted company most acrimoniously. In 1758, on another visit to Tunbridge Wells, apparently now with Morell, Handel met a quack oculist, John Taylor, who performed some 'operation' on him and then wrote a crowing article in the *London Chronicle*, 'On the Recovery of Sight of the Celebrated Mr. Handel, by the Chevalier Taylor'. Claiming to have cured not only Handel, but also, back in 1750, Bach, Taylor indulged his own weaknesses for self-publicity and self-delusion; Handel's sight was certainly not restored, any more than Bach's had been. Taylor's infuriating meddling can only have caused Handel extreme discomfort, and yet more dashed hope.

At the beginning of 1759, Handel must have been saddened by the death of Princess Anne of Orange – the third of the King's adult children to predecease him, for Princess Louisa had died at the age of twenty-six in 1751, just after her brother, Frederick. As Handel's pupil, friend and patron, Anne had been a true part of his London life, and although she had lived in Holland since 1734, she had continued to support him and his projects, buying manuscript copies of his music from Smith the elder, subscribing to his publications, and welcoming him and his singers to The Hague. Throughout Lent in 1759, Handel attended all his oratorio performances (*Solomon*, *Susanna*, *Samson*, *Judas Maccabaeus* and, of course, *Messiah*), and after the final *Messiah*, on the Friday before Palm Sunday, proposed then to travel to Bath the next day, to take the waters. But he was not well enough to undertake the journey. He retreated to Brook Street, and finally to his bed.

Throughout Easter Week, friends came and went. Selina, Countess of Huntington, wrote in her diary, 'I have had a most pleasing interview with Handel – an interview which I shall not soon forget. He is now old, and at the close of his long career; yet he is not dismayed at the prospect before him.'[20] One of the clergy from the Lock Hospital, the Reverend Martin Madan, was there, according to the Countess, 'often', and so of course, constantly, was Smith the younger, who finally succeeded in patching up whatever quarrel had caused such an appalling rift between Handel and his father in Tunbridge Wells:

before Handel's death, he desired Smith junior to receive the sacrament with him. Smith asked him how he could communicate when he was not at peace with all the world, and especially when he was at enmity with his former friend; who, though he might have offended him once, had been faithful and affectionate to him for thirty years. Handel was so much affected by this representation, that he was immediately reconciled . . . and left Smith senior two thousand four hundred pounds, having before given him one thousand pounds.[21]

According to James Smyth, a Bond Street perfumer and close friend, who should have travelled with Handel to Bath that week, other old friends too were similarly summoned and exonerated: 'I had the pleasure to reconcile him to his old friends: he saw them and forgave them, and let all their legacies stand!'[22] On Tuesday, 10th April, Handel added another, final, codicil to his will, expressing his desire to be buried in Westminster Abbey, assigning £600 to the building of his monument there, and making sure that all his servants would receive a year's wages after his death. It was apparently his hope to die, like his Maker, on Good Friday. As Smyth subsequently described in a moving letter to Bernard Granville, 'He took leave of all his friends on Friday morning, and desired to see nobody but the Doctor and Apothecary and myself. At seven o'clock in the evening he took leave of me, and told me we "should meet again"; as soon as I was gone he told his servant "*not* to let me come to him any more, for that he had *now done with the world*".' Handel died at eight o'clock on the following morning, Saturday, 14th April, 'as he had lived – a good *Christian*, with a true sense of his duty to God and man, and in perfect charity with all the world.'[23]

∽

Handel's funeral took place in Westminster Abbey on Friday, 20th April. The choirs from the Abbey, St Paul's and the Chapel

Royal, all of whom would have been singing regularly for Handel in his oratorio seasons, took part, and sang the Burial Service by Croft. Dr Zachary Pearce, Bishop of Rochester, was also Dean of Westminster and conducted the service. The *London Evening Post* reported, 'there were not fewer than 3000 Persons present on this Occasion',[24] and the *Universal Chronicle* agreed: 'from the respect due to so celebrated a man, the Bishop, Prebends, and the whole Choir attended . . . There was also a vast concourse of people of all ranks.'[25]

According to his carefully calibrated will, Handel remembered his family, his friends, his colleagues, his servants and his charities. He left his harpsichord and chamber organ to Smith the elder, and his larger organ to John Rich, who installed it in his Covent Garden theatre for use in continuing oratorio performances there. His three major librettists were all remembered: Jennens received paintings from his collection, Morell £200 and Hamilton £100. Matthew Dubourg, the violinist who had been such a staunch colleague in London and Dublin, also received £100. Bernard Granville, like Jennens, was left paintings, and other friends and neighbours received sums up to £500. A doctor friend from Guy's Hospital, John Belchier, and all his servants had legacies; and Handel's manservant, John DuBurk, was particularly generously rewarded, with £800 and 'all my wearing apparel'. The Foundling Hospital received a fair copy and a set of instrumental parts for the work which had already delivered it so much bounty, and with which it will be forever associated, *Messiah*.

∾

But Handel's real legacy, to the infinite benefit of posterity, is his quite remarkable compositional output: over seventy dramatic works (opera and oratorio), and impressive lists of sacred music, secular cantatas, instrumental music and keyboard music. Throughout this massive oeuvre, quality is consistent. Handel was always individual and repeatedly of startling, exhilarating innovation; and although he was sometimes routine, he was never mediocre. There was no question of him ever resting on his laurels, or submitting to defeat if things went against him. If one door closed, he would find another straight away and march confidently through it. And the manner, too, in which he delivered his immortal masterpieces speaks of a supreme professionalism. In his assessment of singers, his building of teams, his challenging the supremely gifted to even greater heights, to their glory as well as his own, his accommodating weaker components with sympathetic skill, he was constantly vigilant and inspirational. The preparation of all his musical material and the rehearsal of so much music – often at a pace, especially in his latter years, almost unimaginable – was staggeringly impressive. To be sure, he had around him the right people to keep his engines running. But there is no doubt that it was his own charismatic energy and fierce insistence on the highest possible standards that drove the whole machine.

In 1784, as London approached the centenary of Handel's birth, a mighty commemoration of his life and music was organized, largely at the encouragement of George III, who had eventually succeeded his grandfather in 1760, a year after Handel's death. Three major events were planned: a concert of sacred works in Westminster Abbey; another, mainly of secular music, in the Pantheon concert hall in Oxford Street; and a concluding performance of *Messiah* in the Abbey, on a scale hitherto unprecedented. Over 500 musicians took part. Dr Charles Burney, who was also involved in the whole planning and administration of the festival, lovingly recorded its details, and his own succinct and highly perceptive recollections of Handel and his music, in his *Account of the Musical Performances in Westminster-Abbey*, of 1785. Not only had Handel provided the reason for such vast events, but his own supreme organizational skills had brought about the whole mechanism which allowed them to happen. As Burney observed, 'Handel . . . though not a native of England, spent the greatest part of his life in the service of its inhabitants: improving our taste, delighting us in the church, the theatre, and the chamber; and introducing among us so many species of musical excellence, that, during more than half a century, while sentiment, not fashion, guided our applause, we neither wanted nor wished for any other standard.'[26]

Afterword

Mrs Delany to her sister, Mrs Dewes, 5th May 1759: 'I could not help feeling a damp on my spirits, when I heard that great master of music was no more, and I shall now be less able to bear any other music than I used to be.'[1]

Dr Charles Burney, *Sketch of the Life of Handel*, 1785: 'Handel's general look was somewhat heavy and sour; but when he did smile, it was his sire the sun, bursting out of a black cloud. There was a sudden flash of intelligence, wit, and good humour, beaming in his countenance, which I hardly ever saw in any other.'[2]

From the *Public Advertiser*, 17th April 1759:

AN ACROSTIC
He's gone, the Soul of Harmony is fled!
And warbling Angels hover round him dead.
Never, no, never since the Tide of Time,
Did Music know a Genius so sublime!
Each mighty Harmonist that's gone before,
Lessen'd to Mites when we his Works explore.[3]

389

Acknowledgements

This book was originally commissioned by the late Penelope Hoare, whose sad death in 2017 prevented her from seeing the final product into publication. As it took shape over many years, Penny was ever encouraging; and in the latter months of her life she continued to be wholly impressive in her rigorous evaluation of my manuscript. After her death, I was thrilled to come once again under the warm care of Georgina Morley at Macmillan: renewing a working relationship with her sharp and cheerful expertise has been the most natural and welcome of steps. She and her colleagues, especially Laura Carr and Penelope Price, have been exemplary in their vision and attention to detail. And throughout this whole process I have, as before, been constantly supported by my agent Margaret Hanbury, with her hallmark combination of kindness and strength.

Existing biographies of Handel, and examinations of his craft, are legion, and none is more brilliantly magisterial than that by Jonathan Keates. So it was with total trepidation, but nevertheless a conviction that it was the right thing to do, that I asked him if he might read this before publication. Later, at proof stage, two more Handelian luminaries, Ellen Harris and Ruth Smith, also read the book. The generosity of all three of them, and the thoroughness with which they discussed specific detail with me or pointed out errors and obfuscations, was overwhelming, and I am more grateful to them than I can ever express. This book is honoured to join a shelf beside theirs.

Across the world I have been welcomed into libraries at many universities and conservatories, and to all those who have there given me courteous and practical assistance I offer sincere thanks. Specific colleagues in the academic world, who have spoken or corresponded with me and carefully pointed me in right directions, include Colin Timms, John Greenacombe, Beth Glixon and John Ramster. And my brother-in-law, the antiquarian book dealer John Price, has brilliantly produced many thrilling eighteenth-century sources. To all these individuals I am deeply grateful.

Throughout my lifelong engagement with the music of Handel, in opera houses and on concert platforms, I have been blessed with outstanding colleagues (singers, musicians and directors), who have made immeasurable contributions to my understanding of and insights into this remarkable music. To all of these I profess my profound gratitude. It would be invidious to single out any individuals from such a distinguished pool of talent; but I would perhaps especially mention my former students and colleagues in the opera department of the Royal Academy of Music, without whom this book would no doubt have been finished eight years ago, and to whom I therefore dedicate it with affection and respect.

Bibliography

~~~~~

DOCUMENTARY SOURCES

Deutsch, Otto Erich, *Handel: A Documentary Biography* (London, 1955)
George Frideric Handel: Collected Documents, Volume I, 1609–1725, ed. D.
  Burrows, H. Coffey, J. Greenacombe and A. Hicks (Cambridge, 2013)
  (*HCD* I); Volume II, 1725–34, ed. D. Burrows and H. Coffey (2015)

DETAILED HANDELIANA

The Cambridge Handel Encyclopedia, ed. A. Landgraf and D. Vickers
  (Cambridge, 2009)
Catalogue, *Handel: A Celebration of His Life and Times 1685–1759*, ed. J.
  Simon (London, National Portrait Gallery, 1985)

GENERAL HANDELIANA

Burrows, Donald, *Handel, Messiah* (Cambridge, 1991)
Burrows, Donald (ed.), *The Cambridge Companion to Handel* (Cambridge,
  1997)
Burrows, Donald, *Handel and the English Chapel Royal* (Oxford, 2005)
Burrows, Donald, *Handel* (Oxford, 2012)
Burrows, Donald and Dunhill, Rosemary, *Music and Theatre in Handel's
  World: The Family Papers of James Harris 1732–1780* (Oxford, 2002)
Dean, Winton, *Handel's Dramatic Oratorios and Masques* (London, 1959)
Dean, Winton, *Handel and the Opera Seria* (Oxford, 1970)

Dean, Winton, *Handel's Operas 1726–1741* (London, 2006)

Dean, Winton and Knapp, John Merrill, *Handel's Operas 1704–1726* (Oxford, 1987)

Field, Ophelia, *The Kit-Cat Club, Friends who Imagined a Nation* (London, 2008)

Fiske, Roger, *English Theatre Music in the Eighteenth Century* (Oxford, 1973)

Fortune, Nigel (ed.), *Music and Theatre: Essays in Honour of Winton Dean* (Cambridge, 1987)

Gibson, Elizabeth, *The Royal Academy of Music (1719–28): The Institution and its Directors* (New York and London, 1989)

Greenacombe, John, 'Handel's House: A History of No.25 Brook Street, Mayfair' in *London Topographical Record* 25: 111–30 (1985)

Harris, Ellen (ed.), *The Librettos of Handel's Operas: A Collection of Seventy-One Librettos Documenting Handel's Operatic Career* (13 volumes, New York, 1989)

Harris, Ellen, *Handel as Orpheus, Voice and Desire in the Chamber Cantatas* (Harvard, 2001)

Harris, Ellen, *George Frideric Handel, A Life with Friends* (New York, 2014)

Heriot, Angus, *The Castrati in Opera* (London, 1956)

Hogwood, Christopher, *Handel* (London, 1984 and 2007)

Jenkins, Neil, *John Beard, Handel and Garrick's Favourite Tenor* (Bramber, 2012)

Keates, Jonathan, *Handel, The Man and his Music* (London, 1985 and 2008)

Larue, C. Steven, *Handel and His Singers: The Creation of the Royal Academy of Music, 1720–1728* (Oxford, 1995)

Lindgren, Lowell, 'Musicians and Librettists in the Correspondence of Gio. Giacomo Zamboni' in *RMA Research Chronicle* 36 (2003)

Luckett, Richard, *Handel's Messiah, A Celebration* (London, 1992)

Sadie, Stanley and Hicks, Anthony, *Handel Tercentenary Collection* (London, 1987)

Strohm, Reinhard, *Essays on Handel and Italian Opera* (Cambridge, 1985)

Smith, Ruth, *Handel's Oratorios and Eighteenth-Century Thought* (Cambridge, 1995)

Smith, Ruth, *Charles Jennens, The Man behind Handel's Messiah* (London, 2012)

Treasure, Geoffrey, *Who's Who in Early Hanoverian Britain* (London, 1992)

Young, Percy, *Handel* (London, 1948)

CONTEMPORARY WITNESSES

Burney, Charles, *A General History of Music* (four volumes, London, 1776–89), ed. Frank Mercer (two volumes, London, 1935)

Burney, Charles, *An Account of the Musical Performances in Westminster-Abbey, and the Pantheon . . . In Commemoration of Handel* (London, 1785)

Coxe, William, *Anecdotes of George Frederick Handel and John Christian Smith* (London, 1799)

Delany, Mary, *The Autobiography and Correspondence of Mary Granville, Mrs. Delany*, ed. Augusta, Lady Llanover (six volumes, London, 1861)

Defoe, Daniel, *A Tour Thro' the Whole Island of Great Britain* (three volumes, London, 1725)

Hawkins, John, *A General History of the Science and Practice of Music* (five volumes, London, 1776; republished in two volumes 1853)

Lord Hervey's Memoirs, ed. R. Sedgwick (London, 1963)

Mainwaring, John, *Memoirs of the Life of the Late George Frederic Handel* (London, 1760; republished 2007)

Roger North on Music, transcribed from his Essays of *c.*1695–1728, ed. J. Wilson (London, 1959)

de Saussure, Cesar, *A Foreign View of England in the Reigns of George I and George II* (London, 1902, reprinted 2010)

LONDON IN THE EIGHTEENTH CENTURY

Bucholz, Robert O. and Ward, Joseph P., *London, A Social and Cultural History, 1550–1750* (Cambridge, 2012)

Cockayne, Emily, *Hubbub: Filth, Noise and Stench in England 1660–1710* (London, 2007)

Hyde, Ralph (ed.), *The A–Z of Georgian London* (London, 1981)

Mackerness, E. D., *A Social History of English Music* (London, 1964)

White, Jerry, *London in the Eighteenth Century: A Great and Monstrous Thing* (London, 2012)

Worsley, Lucy, *Courtiers: The Secret History of Kensington Palace* (London, 2010)

THE THRONE

Gregg, Edward, *Queen Anne* (London, 1980)

Hatton, Ragnhild, *George I, Elector and King* (London, 1978)

van der Kiste, John, *King George II and Queen Caroline* (London, 1997)

Marlow, Joyce, *The Life and Times of George I* (London, 1973)

Plumb, J. H., *The First Four Georges* (London, 1956)

Somerset, Anne, *Queen Anne, The Politics of Passion* (London, 2012)

Thompson, Andrew, *George II* (Yale, 2011)

Notes

~~~~~~~~

CHAPTER 1

1   Mainwaring, *Memoirs*, p. 4
2   Ibid., p. 5
3   Ibid., p. 7
4   Ibid., p. 9
5   Ibid., p. 13
6   Quoted in full in *Handel Collected Documents* Volume I, pp. 25–6
7   Mainwaring, p. 18
8   Ibid., p. 26
9   Ibid., p. 28
10 Ibid., p. 41
11 Ibid., p. 50
12 *HCD* I, p. 182
13 Ibid., p. 183
14 Mainwaring, p. 71
15 Ibid., p. 72
16 Ibid., p. 73

CHAPTER 2

1   Daniel Defoe, *A Tour Through the Whole Island of Great Britain*, p. 133
2   Quoted in Anne Somerset, *Queen Anne*, p. 13
3   *Roger North on Music*, p. 307

4 Ibid.
5 Deutsch, pp. 32–3; *Handel Collected Documents* I, p. 200
6 Ibid.

CHAPTER 3

1 Deutsch, p. 33; *HCD* I, p. 201
2 Ibid.
3 Burney, *General History*, p. 661
4 *Handel Collected Documents* I, p. 196
5 Ibid., p. 198; Deutsch, p. 31
6 Mainwaring, *Memoirs*, p. 83
7 Deutsch, pp. 35–6; *HCD* I, pp. 204–6
8 Deutsch, pp. 36–7; *HCD* I, pp. 208–9
9 Quoted in catalogue *Handel: A Celebration of his Life and Times*, p. 77
10 Mainwaring, p. 84
11 Deutsch, p. 31
12 Mainwaring, p. 84
13 Deutsch, p. 42; *HCD* I, p. 217
14 Mainwaring, p. 85
15 Ibid.
16 Deutsch, p. 44; *HCD* I, p. 223
17 Deutsch, pp. 46–7; *HCD* I, pp. 234–5
18 Deutsch, p. 49
19 Mainwaring, pp. 85–6
20 Deutsch, p. 50; *HCD* I, p. 249
21 Deutsch, p. 52
22 Ibid.; *HCD* I, pp. 255–6
23 *HCD* I, p. 285
24 Mainwaring, p. 89
25 Hawkins, *General History*, p. 859
26 Coxe, *Anecdotes of Handel*, p. 16
27 Ibid.
28 Deutsch, p. 70
29 Quoted in Anne Somerset, *Queen Anne*, p. 505

30   Ibid., p. 510
31   Ibid., p. 531

CHAPTER 4

1   Quoted in Anne Somerset, *Queen Anne*, p. 532
2   Ibid., p. 531
3   Quoted in Joyce Marlow, *George I*, p. 69
4   Mainwaring, *Memoirs*, pp. 89–90
5   Deutsch, p. 66
6   Burney, *General History* II, p. 678
7   Deutsch, p. 67; *Handel Collected Documents* I, p. 314
8   Deutsch, p. 68; *HCD* I, p. 317
9   Ibid.
10   Coxe, *Anecdotes*, p. 37
11   Deutsch, p. 76; *HCD* I, pp. 379–80
12   Deutsch, p. 77; *HCD* I, p. 382
13   Ibid.
14   Deutsch, pp. 76–7; *HCD* I, p. 383
15   Defoe, *Journey*, p. 169
16   Ibid.
17   Mainwaring, p. 96
18   Deutsch, p. 78; *HCD* I, p. 387
19   Deutsch, p. 81; *HCD* I, pp. 394–5
20   Deutsch, pp. 84–5; *HCD* I, pp. 409–10
21   Mainwaring, pp. 96–7
22   Deutsch, p. 86; *HCD* I, p. 411
23   Deutsch, pp. 89–90; *HCD* I, pp. 429–30

CHAPTER 5

1   Quoted in *Cambridge Handel Encyclopedia*, p. 582
2   Deutsch, pp. 93–4; *Handel Collected Documents* I, pp. 433–4
3   Deutsch, p. 95; *HCD* I, p. 447
4   Deutsch, p. 94

5   Deutsch, p. 97; *HCD* I, p. 450
6   Deutsch, p. 97; *HCD* I, p. 454
7   Deutsch, p. 100; *HCD* I, p. 472
8   Deutsch, p. 101; *HCD* I, p. 473
9   Mainwaring, *Memoirs*, p. 99
10 Deutsch, p. 103; *HCD* I, p. 483
11 Mainwaring, *Memoirs*, p. 99
12 Burney, *General History* II, p. 702
13 Deutsch, p. 113; *HCD* I, p. 513
14 Deutsch, p. 115; *HCD* I, p. 515
15 Quoted in Joyce Marlow, *George I*, p. 163
16 Deutsch, p. 112; *HCD* I, p. 512
17 Deutsch, p. 118; *HCD* I, p. 522
18 Deutsch, p. 123; *HCD* I, p. 532
19 Deutsch, p. 128; *HCD* I, p. 548
20 Deutsch, p. 129; *HCD* I, p. 555
21 Deutsch, p. 111; *HCD* I, pp. 507–8
22 Deutsch, p. 136; *HCD* I, p. 600

CHAPTER 6

1   G. B. Mancini, *Pensieri e riflessione sopra il canto figurato*, 1774
2   Mainwaring, *Memoirs*, p. 110
3   Dean, *Operas* I, p. 435
4   Deutsch, p. 147
5   Ibid., p. 148
6   Ibid., p. 149
7   Ibid., p. 151
8   Ibid., p. 148
9   Ibid., p. 155; *Handel Collected Documents* I, p. 656
10 Quoted in *Handel: A Celebration of his Life and Times*, p. 176
11 Dean, *Operas* I, p. 318
12 Deutsch, p. 157
13 Ibid., p. 158
14 Ibid., p. 160
15 Ibid., p. 175

16   Dean, *Operas* I, p. 556
17   Burney, *General History*, p. 731
18   Dean, *Operas* I, p. 589
19   Deutsch, p. 180
20   Ibid., p. 182
21   Ibid., p. 185
22   Ibid.
23   Ibid., p. 184
24   Ibid., p. 185
25   Burney, *General History*, p. 734
26   Ibid., p. 746
27   Deutsch, p. 201
28   Ibid., p. 198
29   Ibid., p. 199
30   Dean, *Operas* II, p. 3
31   Deutsch, p. 207
32   Ibid., p. 210
33   Dean, *Operas* II, p. 5
34   Joyce Marlow, *The Life and Times of George I*, p. 209

CHAPTER 7

1   César de Saussure, *A Foreign View of England*, p. 75
2   Ibid., p. 76
3   Deutsch, p. 213
4   Ibid., p. 214
5   Ibid.
6   de Saussure, p. 81
7   John van der Kiste, *King George II and Queen Caroline*, p. 97
8   de Saussure, p. 85
9   Burrows, *Handel and the Chapel Royal*, p. 263
10   Ibid.
11   de Saussure, p. 87
12   Deutsch, p. 211
13   Ibid., p. 212
14   Ibid., p. 218

15 Ibid.
16 Ibid., p. 220
17 Hervey, *Memoirs*, p. 20
18 Deutsch, p. 226
19 Mainwaring, *Memoirs*, p. 109
20 Deutsch, p. 230
21 Ibid., p. 234
22 Ibid.
23 Ibid., p. 237
24 Ibid., p. 235
25 Ibid., p. 236
26 Ibid., p. 242
27 Gibson, *The Royal Academy of Music (1719–1728)*, pp. 380–2
28 Deutsch, p. 243
29 *Cambridge Handel Encyclopedia*, p. 320
30 Deutsch, p. 245
31 Ibid., p. 246
32 Ibid., p. 247

CHAPTER 8

1 Deutsch, pp. 249–50
2 Ibid., p. 250
3 Ibid.
4 *Cambridge Handel Encyclopedia*, p. 489
5 Deutsch, p. 254
6 Ibid.
7 Ibid., p. 257
8 Ibid., p. 262
9 Ibid., p. 270
10 Ibid., p. 272
11 Ibid., p. 269
12 Ibid., p. 263
13 Ibid., p. 282
14 Ibid., p. 305
15 Ibid.

16 Ibid., p. 286
17 Hawkins, *A General History of the Science and Practice of Music*, p. 805
18 Dean, *Oratorios*, p. 204
19 Deutsch, p. 286
20 Ibid., p. 288
21 Ibid.
22 Ibid., p. 289
23 Ibid., p. 290
24 Ibid., p. 292
25 Ibid., p. 296
26 Ibid.
27 Ibid., p. 304
28 Ibid., p. 299
29 Ibid., p. 309
30 Ibid., p. 310
31 Ibid., p. 309
32 Ibid., pp. 300–1
33 Ibid., pp. 303–4
34 Ibid., pp. 310–11
35 Mainwaring, pp. 111, 121
36 Deutsch, pp. 310–11
37 Ibid., p. 315

CHAPTER 9

1 Deutsch, p. 316
2 Ibid., p. 319
3 Ibid., p. 367
4 Ibid., p. 329
5 Ibid., p. 331
6 Burney, *General History*, p. 782
7 Hervey, *Memoirs*, p. 42
8 Ibid., pp. 42–3
9 Deutsch, p. 336
10 Hervey, pp. 32–3
11 Ibid., p. 33

12 Ibid., p. 34
13 Deutsch, p. 335
14 Ibid., p. 337
15 Ibid., p. 360
16 Ibid., p. 363
17 Ibid.
18 Ibid., p. 364
19 Letter to Antonio Cochi, 27 April 1734, quoted in Lindgren, *Zamboni*, p. 345
20 Deutsch, p. 368
21 Ibid., p. 369
22 Ibid., p. 370
23 Ibid., p. 372
24 Ibid., p. 374
25 Ibid., p. 390
26 Mainwaring, pp. 116–17
27 Deutsch, p. 374
28 Ibid., p. 377
29 Ibid., p. 384
30 Lord Shaftesbury *Remeniscences of Handel*, quoted in Dean *Operas* II, p. 327
31 Deutsch, p. 385
32 Ibid., p. 391
33 Ibid., p. 392
34 Ibid., p. 394
35 Ibid., p. 395
36 Ibid., pp. 395–6
37 Hervey, p. 115
38 Ibid.
39 Ibid.
40 Deutsch, p. 405
41 Ibid., p. 405
42 Ibid., p. 404
43 Ibid., p. 406
44 Ibid., p. 409
45 Ibid., p. 407
46 Ibid., p. 409

47 Hervey, p. 141
48 Deutsch, p. 416
49 Ibid., p. 416
50 Ibid., p. 417
51 Ibid., p. 418
52 Ibid., p. 419
53 Ibid., p. 418
54 Burrows and Dunhill, p. 23
55 Deutsch, p. 426
56 Ibid., p. 428

CHAPTER 10

1 Deutsch, p. 432
2 Ibid., p. 434
3 Burrows and Dunhill, pp. 26–7
4 Mainwaring, p. 121
5 Ibid., p. 12
6 Ibid.
7 Ibid., p. 123
8 Deutsch, p. 441
9 Hervey, pp. 240–1
10 Ibid., p. 264
11 Deutsch, p. 444
12 Quoted in Richard G. King, 'Handel's Travels', p. 384
13 Deutsch, p. 443
14 Ibid., p. 464
15 Burney, *General History*, p. 342
16 Deutsch, p. 394
17 Ibid., p. 465
18 Ibid., p. 473
19 Ibid., p. 634
20 Ibid., p. 479
21 Ibid., p. 478
22 Ibid., p. 490
23 Ibid., p. 492

24   Ibid., p. 494

25   Ibid., p. 495

26   Ibid., p. 496

27   Burrows and Dunhill, p. 108

28   Ibid, p. 110

29   Deutsch, p. 508

30   Ibid., p. 531

CHAPTER 11

1   Deutsch, p. 622

2   Ibid., p. 529

3   Ibid., p. 530

4   Ibid., p. 534

5   Ibid., p. 537

6   Ibid., p. 541

7   Ibid., p. 542

8   Ibid., p. 545

9   Ibid., p. 544

10   Ibid., p. 545

11   Ibid., p. 546

12   Ibid., p. 551

13   Laetitia Pilkington, *Memoirs . . . 1712–1750 written by herself*

14   Deutsch, p. 554

15   Ibid., p. 549

16   Ibid.

17   Ibid., p. 554

18   Ibid., p. 599

19   Burrows and Dunhill, *Music and Theatre in Handel's World*, p. 152

20   Deutsch, p. 560

21   Ibid., p. 561

22   Ibid., p. 562

CHAPTER 12

1   Quoted in Luckett, *Handel's Messiah*, p. 139
2   Ibid., p. 140
3   Deutsch, pp. 563–4
4   Quoted in Luckett, *Handel's Messiah*, p. 143
5   Ibid.
6   Quoted in Luckett, *Handel's Messiah*, p. 150
7   Deutsch, p. 569
8   Quoted in Luckett, *Handel's Messiah*, p. 151
9   *The Gentleman's Magazine,* quoted in J. D. Griffith Davies, *A King of Toils*, p. 200
10 Ibid.
11 Betty Matthews, *Unpublished Letters Concerning Handel*, pp. 265–6
12 Deutsch, p. 573
13 Ibid., p. 574
14 Ibid., pp. 573–4
15 Ibid., p. 584
16 Ibid., p. 582
17 Ibid.
18 Ibid., p. 584
19 Ibid., p. 585
20 Ibid.
21 Ibid., p. 590
22 Correspondence between Charles Jennens and Edward Holdsworth, Foundling Hospital Museum
23 Deutsch, pp. 594–5
24 Ibid., p. 592
25 Burney, *Sketch*, p. 33
26 Deutsch, p. 602
27 Ibid., p. 603
28 Ibid., p. 610
29 Ibid., p. 622
30 Ibid., p. 624
31 Ibid., p. 629
32 Ibid., pp. 629–30

33 Michael Kelly, *Reminiscences*, p. 129
34 Deutsch, p. 851
35 Ibid., p. 637
36 Burney, *General History*
37 Deutsch, p. 852
38 Quoted in *The Cambridge Handel Encyclopedia*, p. 429
39 Deutsch, p. 661
40 Ibid., p. 663
41 Ibid., p. 668
42 Ibid., p. 667
43 Ibid., pp. 671–2
44 Ibid., p. 672
45 Ibid., p. 680
46 Ibid., p. 852
47 Ibid., p. 683
48 Ibid., p. 686
49 Ibid., p. 688
50 Ibid., p. 693

CHAPTER 13

1 Deutsch, p. 693
2 Ibid., p. 695
3 Ibid., p. 705
4 Ibid., p. 709
5 Ibid., p. 521
6 Ibid., p. 709
7 Coxe, *Anecdotes*, p. 44
8 Mainwaring, p. 138
9 Deutsch, p. 713
10 Ibid., p. 726
11 Ibid., p. 727
12 Ibid.
13 Ibid., p. 731
14 Coxe, p. 25
15 Ibid.

NOTES

16 Burney, *Sketch*, pp. 29–30
17 Deutsch, p. 771
18 Coxe, p. 28
19 Burney, op. cit., p. 34
20 Deutsch, p. 813
21 Coxe, p. 48
22 Deutsch, p. 818
23 Ibid.
24 Ibid., p. 821
25 Ibid., pp. 821–2
26 Burney, *Account of the Musical Performances in Westminster-Abbey*, p. iii

AFTERWORD

1 Deutsch, p. 824
2 Burney, *Sketch*, p. 37
3 Deutsch, p. 818

Index